A Social History of the Welsh Clergy
circa 1662-1939

Roger Lee Brown

PART ONE
sections one to six
in THREE VOLUMES

The cover picture depicts St David's College, Lampeter, circa 1830

A Social History of the Welsh Clergy
circa 1662-1939

Roger Lee Brown

PART ONE
sections one to six

VOLUME ONE

Published by Roger Lee Brown, 2017
Cartref, 14 Berriew Road, Welshpool, SY21 7SS

© Roger Lee Brown

ISBN: 978-1-9998936-4-4

Volume Two ISBN: 978-1-9998936-5-1
Volume Three ISBN: 978-1-9998936-6-8

Book Design by Russell Holden
www.pixeltweakspublications.com

Pixel Tweaks Publications
SELF-PUBLISHING MADE SIMPLE

Printed by Ingram

All rights reserved without limiting the rights under copyright reserved above, no parts of this publication may be reproduced, stored in or introduced into a retrieval system, or transmitted in any form, or by any means (electronic, mechanical, photocopying, recording or otherwise) without the prior written permission of both the copyright owners and the publisher of this book.

CONTENTS
VOLUME ONE

Introduction i

Synopsis of volumes iv

Section One
The Route to Ordination 1
Endnotes 149

Section Two
The Inferior Clergy 185
Endnotes 319

INTRODUCTION

This study of the social history of the Welsh clergy is more an interim report or even a work in progress rather than a final assessment. Age and infirmity have forced me to publish it in this typescript format, and I have deliberately kept the text unjustified to emphasise this position. I had hoped to abridge it but this is not to be. It is produced in a extremely limited edition in the hope that this work may be useful as a source to draw upon, especially as many of the sources used, both manuscript and printed, are scarce and a few remain in private hands. The first six sections relating to the life of the clergy from ordination to death, are contained in this part, comprising three volumes, and the next eight sections dealing with their parochial work, in part two, are to be published in due course. As each section is complete in itself there is an unavoidable amount of duplication.

We need to remember that until 1920 the four dioceses of St Davids, Llandaff, Bangor and St Asaph, formed part of the Province of Canterbury. In that year they were formally disestablished and the Church in Wales was formed. The diocesan boundaries of the Church in Wales were not coterminous with the national boundary. Parts of the diocese of St Asaph embraced the Oswestry area of Shropshire, while some of its southern parishes, such as Montgomery, formed part of the diocese of Hereford. At disestablishment all but one of the border parishes, that is, those parishes which lay in both England and Wales, elected to remain in the Church of England.

It is the contention of this work that the social history of the Welsh clergy is distinct from that of the English clergy and worthy of its own treatment. Although there were great similarities, for both the English and the Welsh dioceses were governed by the same Canons and legislative enactments, there were also significant differences. The major difference is that of language, for the Welsh language was spoken in most parts of Wales save for the border areas, parts of Glamorgan, Monmouthshire and Pembrokeshire. The poverty of many parishes, especially in west Wales, linked to the poverty of its population, meant that those men who were ordained who had obtained a university education or came from gentry families generally looked elsewhere for preferment, while the need for Welsh-speaking clergy meant that men were ordained whose background and education became the despair of many of their bishops. Furthermore, the growth of Nonconformity in Wales, due mainly to the Church's difficulties in providing an adequate pastoral ministry to these poverty-stricken parishes, necessitated pluralism and single rather than double duty. This position, combined with the difficulties of ministering in two languages, had immense repercussions. The difficulties of church planting, as compared to Nonconformity, were immense, and the major effort of the Church to utilise the schoolroom as a means of winning back the youth led to anger that the Church was using its privileged position as a means of proselytising. Issues over the church rate, and later the tithe, at a time of agricultural hardship, combined with the mistaken concept of the Church being an Anglicising institution and anti-Welsh, led to the long drawn out disestablishment campaign.

The period of this study is roughly from 1662 as indicating the ending of the monopoly of the Established Church to the outbreak of Second World War in 1939, allowing the early years of disestablishment to be brought into the study, though on occasions we venture a little beyond that date.

This study embraces the whole arena of clerical life, from ordination to retirement and beyond, taking in parochial life in its widest aspects, as well as interaction with the wider church, church parties, Nonconformity, and Welsh nationalism. However, it excludes an administrative history of the Church or an account of its bishops and cathedral bodies.

It makes clear that there was no golden age for Church life: at most stages clergy were beset with their own issues and difficulties. The clerical lot was not an easy one for most clergy. However, it is difficult to generalise. The southern dioceses were poor, while St Asaph was reasonably wealthy, and within each diocese there were rich parishes, albeit few, and poor parishes. The poverty in the south necessitated the ordination of literate men, while in the north it was possible to obtain a reasonable number of university men. In addition in the south, pluralism was rife because of poverty, although it will be shown it was more often than not a technical pluralism, while in the north it was often occasioned by greed and nepotism. Episcopal patronage was substantial in the north but scarce in the south, bringing further distinctions to the picture. There was also a linguistic divide, especially in the diocese of Llandaff by the nineteenth century, though this spread to other dioceses as the English language became more common and impacted more on daily life. This again led to difficulties, as English speaking clerics were appointed to Welsh parishes, and employed Welsh curates to undertake the duty at a pittance, making them feel devalued and marginalised.

In the course of the forty years during which I have studied this topic, I have been greatly encouraged by many of my colleagues, both historians and clerics, who have provided me with resources and assistance. In particular I would wish to thank John Morgan-Guy, Densil Morgan, Robert Pope, Fred Cowley, Fred Holley, Bill Pritchard, Brian Ll. James, and Bill Gibson, in addition to many who have now died, including Professors Owen Chadwick and Glanmor Williams, T.J. Prichard and Crystal Davies. I am grateful to the editors of many journals who have published my papers, and to innumerable acts of kindness on the parts of the staff of Cambridge University Library, the Bodleian Library, the National Library of Wales, the British Library, Lambeth Palace Library, the university libraries at Swansea, Cardiff, Bangor and Lampeter, and of the Representative Body of the Church in Wales. My parishioners in Tongwynlais and Welshpool provided numerous resources, but above all I express my thanks to my wife, Phyllis, who has had to live with this study for most of our married life, and has accompanied me to many of the libraries noted and also helped in innumerable ways to facilitate its progress.

In a work of this extent there may well be differences of interpretation, and possibly one or two inaccuracies. Although I have used original material whenever possible, there is still a wealth of material in the Church in Wales records at the National Library of Wales that has not been utilised here, merely a sample, as is the case for the records of the Ecclesiastical Commission and Queen Anne's Bounty. Much of my material comes from secondary sources, utilising the work of those who have studied these records for particular purposes, but also including under this description the work of local historians. It will be noted that I have quoted extensively from the Montgomeryshire Collections, as this journal, founded in the 1860s, specialised for many years in publishing within its pages local histories. In addition, D.R. Thomas's scrapbooks containing press cuttings and ephemeral material relating to the diocese of St Asaph, which formed the basis of his monumental history of that diocese, have been used: (National Library of Wales: Church in Wales Records, SA/DR – its pagination is complex). Episcopal and archidiaconal charges, reports of diocesan conferences and societies, have also been fully utilised as well as the ecclesiastical and national press, especially the Church

Times, the Guardian, the Record and Yr Haul. Much of my own published work has also been incorporated, and I have mainly quoted these works in the endnotes, as noted in the Bibliography, rather than include the fuller references given there.

The rendering of Welsh place names is no easy task. Elwyn Davies' Gazetteer of Welsh Place Names is regarded as offering the culturally correct spelling, but is notoriously difficult to use, as the older spellings are not always recorded, and many of his suggestions are not in common use, especially in the English-speaking parts of Wales. Swansea is still regarded as Swansea rather than Abertawe, to give but one example. I have endeavoured to use the names in common use. Place names not recorded by Davies have been given according to the 1933 Handbook of the Church in Wales, though the Clergy List of 1849 has also been consulted for place names that have fallen out of use. Names recorded in eighteenth century documents have been transcribed into the more modern versions, but some have defied recognition, and in these cases these names have been placed in inverted commas, such as "Llacharn" or "Llanfawr" which is probably Llanfor.

The Bibliography, in volume three, contains a list of the most frequently used material, and the short titles of the books quoted in the endnotes. It also includes a list of abbreviations of material in general use in the footnotes. A explanation of ecclesiastical terms used in the text and a list of the bishops of the Welsh sees during the period under review are also included.

A SOCIAL HISTORY OF THE WELSH CLERGY
SECTIONS THREE TO SIX, in the following two volumes, comprise:

VOLUME TWO

Section Three: PATRONAGE
1	Introduction	355	467
2	The Restraints on Patronage	365	471
3	Crown and Lay Patronage	386	477
4	Lay Abuse of Patronage	400	481
5	Episcopal Patronage	422	488
6	In Pursuit of Patronage	439	494

Section Four: THE INCOME OF THE CLERGY
1	Introduction	501	659
2	Wealth and Poverty	524	664
3	The Glebe Land	547	669
4	The Tithe	559	672
5	The Tithe Disputed	582	677
6	Queen Anne's Bounty	602	683
7	The Ecclesiastical Commission	619	687
8	Diocesan and other Sources of Finance	643	691

VOLUME THREE

Section Five: THE DOMESTIC POSITION OF THE CLERGY
1	The Social Make-up	699	833
2	The Clerical Duty	705	835
3	The Idle, Neglectful and Unworthy	730	842
4	The Daily Round, the Common Task	755	849
5	External Lifestyle	771	854
6	The Parson's Family	787	857
7	Retirement and Dissolution	806	861

Section Six: THE PARSON'S HOUSE
1	The Parsonage House in Decay	869	977
2	Episcopal Concern and Consequences	884	980
3	The Applied Remedies	898	983
4	The great Rebuilding	918	986
5	Problems and Issues	936	988
6	The Curse of Dilapidations	955	990
7	A Conclusion	973	

APPENDICES
The Bishops of the Welsh Dioceses for the period 1660-1950	993
An explanation of the Ecclesiastical Terms used in the Text	995
Bibliography, including a list of abbreviations used	998
Index	1017

PART TWO will comprise the following:

Section Seven: THE WORSHIP OF THE CHURCH
1. The Pattern of Worship
2. The Holy Communion
3. The Language of the Service
4. The Music of the Service
5. The Occasional Offices

Section Eight: PROCLAMATION
1. The Sermon
2. Catechism and Confirmation
3. The Sunday School
4. Education and Day Schools
5. The State and Education from 1870 onwards

Section Nine: PASTORALIA
1. The Pastoral Care of Parishioners: Introduction
2. The Gradual Outworking of Pastoral Visitation
3. Nurturing Spiritual Life
4. Working within Society

Section Ten: MISSION
1. A Realisation for Mission
2. A Concern for Buildings
3. The Question of the Pew
4. Restoration and Rebuilding
5. Extending the Mission of the Church
6. Mission and Evangelism

Section Eleven: THE CLERGY, THE DIOCESE AND PARISH
1. Introduction
2. The Episcopal Office
3. Clergy and the Parish
4. The Clergy and the Laity

Section Twelve: THE LINGUISTIC ISSUE
1. Introduction
2. The Language of the Service
3. The Inferior Position of the Welsh
4. The Growing Pressure of Nationality

Section Thirteen: THEOLOGICAL ISSUES

Section Fourteen: NONCONFORMITY AND DISESTABLISHMENT
1. A Fear of Nonconformity
2. The Growing Antipathy between Church and Chapel
3. Disestablishment

SECTION ONE
THE ROUTE TO ORDINATION

CHAPTERS

		Text	Endnotes
1	Introduction	1	*149*
2	The Welsh Dilemma	21	*152*
3	The Education of the Future Clergy		
	1. From Grammar School to University	54	*161*
4	The Education of the Future Clergy		
	2. St David's College, Lampeter	81	*166*
5	The Education of the Future Clergy		
	3. The Theological Colleges and		
	Private Enterprise Establishments	97	*171*
6	The Final Hurdle	120	*177*

Table on Clerical Education and Footnotes   *overleaf*

TABLE: CLERICAL EDUCATION

in brackets where places or courses are not identified
and placed between two areas if the figures cannot be separated
the figures in italics relate to percentages
The references are placed on the page immediately after this table

	DIOCESE/ CHURCH	DATE	TOTAL	GRADS Oxbridge & others	LIT	Ox-BRIDGE	TCD	Durham & other univs.	Durham S.Th. AKC(Lond)
1	St Asaph[1]	1710	116	71(61%)					
2	St Davids[1]	1714	265	87(32%)					
3	Llandaff[1]	1726	115	72(63%)					
4	St Davids ord[2]	1750-1800	762	45	717				
5	*England & Wales, ord*[3]	*1833-43*		*80%+7%*	*10%*				
6	England & Wales ord[4]	1841	606	512+43	48				
7	England & Wales total[5]	1841	14500			*86%*		*7%*	
8	England & Wales total[5]	1861				*65%*		*9%*	
9	Bangor ord.d.[6]	1850	10			9			1
10	England & Wales ord.[4]	1862	489	298+45	146				
11	Wales ord.[7]	*1865*	49			*25%*			
12	Prov. Canterbury Exc. Wales[7]	*1865*	337			*78%*	*[6%]*		
13	St Asaph[8]	1863	257			152	19	1	6
14	Bangor[9]	1866	195			99	12	2	
15	Bangor, ord.d.[6]	1870	13			2	3		
16	Llandaff ord.[10]	1874	12			3			
17	Llandaff[11]	1875	344			149		11	3
18	St Davids, ord[12]	1875	12			2			
19	St Davids, appls.[13]	1874-5	50			7			
20	Llandaff, ord.d[14]	1888-91	77			29	2	4	7
21	Ch in Wales[15]	1888	1427			492	52	47	
22	St Davids, ord.d[17]	1886-9	39			12		1	
23	St Davids[18]	1889	506			149	11	7	9
24	Ch in Wales Incumbents[16]	1890	919			318	33	13	
25	Bangor, ord.d[6]	1890	11			4		1	
26	Llandaff, ord.d[19]	1894	25			6	[3]		
27	Ch in Wales[20]	1910	1597			474	9	[96]	
28	Llandaff[21]	1911							
29	Ch in Wales ord.[22]	1927-36	563			123		179	

ABBREVIATIONS: SDC - St David's College, Lampeter: SMC - St Michael's College, Llandaff: TCD - Trinity College, Dublin: ord - ordinations (specific): ord.d. - ordination of deacons: d - deacon: litt – literates: Ch in Wales – the disestablished Church in Wales.

SDC Grads	SDC other	St Bees	St Aidans	B'ham	Other	Grad. Theol.C	Pure Literates	SMC	No.
									1
									2
									3
									4
									5
									6
									7
							7%		
									8
							26%		
									9
									10
						[55%]	20%		11
									12
						13%	3%		
7	28	24	2				15		13
4	32	19	5	2	13		0		14
		7	1						15
4	1	1		2			1		16
21	26	9	1	10	5		109		17
1	3	1		1	2		2		18
	[24]					[12]	7		19
14	10	5	5			2	7		20
	[448]					[240]	133		21
11	13					[2]	0		22
123	102	27	10	12	9		46		23
125	148	73	24	29	[32]		124		24
3	2		1						25
2	9	[4]					1		26
	[663]					[355]			27
							58	[inc 29]	28
	[261]								29

REFERENCES for the TABLE on CLERICAL EDUCATION

01 Jenkins, *Literature, Religion and Society in Wales*, pp. 213-4. The graduates probably include those from TCD.

02 Parsons, *Religion in Victorian Britain*, I, 190. Approximately 6% were graduates. These figures are qualified by Price, *A History of St David's University College*, I. 5, who notes that excluded from the university list were 37 who left without a degree, so that the number of those who did not attend a university was 680. Price notes that between 1700-50 about one third were graduates.

03 Virgin, *The Church in an Age of Negligence*, p. 132.

04 Espin, *Our Want of Clergy*, pp. 21-2. He notes that between 1841-62 the number of graduates decreased by 26.75% and the number of literates increased by 193.25%. For figures for 1860, 1867 and 1874 see Bullock, *Training for the Ministry 1800-1874*, p. 100. Bullock notes that in 1874 of 655 men ordained 422 were Oxbridge, 39 Durham and Dublin, and 194 literates.

05 Parsons, *Religion in Victorian Britain:* I, 25. The figure of 26% as "other" includes Lampeter, St Bees and literates.

06 Pryce, *The Diocese of Bangor*, pp. 133-4, 140.

07 Haig, *Victorian Clergy*, p. 118.

08 *St Asaph Clerical Directory*, 1863. Graduates amounted to 67%, theological college men 27% (St Bees 9.3% and SDC 13.6%), literates 4.6%. Of these 15 three noted themselves as alumni of Ystrad Meurig. The details of three are not recorded.

09 *Bangor Diocesan Directory*, 1866. The 2 "other" universities were both foreign institutions, and 7 clerics gave no indication of their educational background.

10 *Llandaff Diocesan Calendar and Clergy List*, 1875, II, 122.

11 Taken from entries in the *Llandaff Diocesan Calendar and Clergy list*, 1875. The Oxbridge numbers include 4 who had not taken a degree, and 2 in the case of Dublin. There are 121 entries for the Welsh names of Davies, Evans, Jones, Morgan, Thomas and Williams, of whom 47, 38% were literates (cf. to the average of 31%), 22 had attended SDC, 22% (cf. 18%), 14 had attended a theological college, 11.5% (cf. 7.5%), and there were 38 graduates, 31% (cf. 45%). It seems possible that those who were Welsh might have been under some educational disadvantages. The figures quoted by Wilton D. Wills are at some variance with those given here. He suggests, in round numbers, that one third of the diocesan clergy in 1870 were literates and an equal number were from SDC: "The Clergy in Society in mid-Victorian South Wales, *JHSCW*, xxiv (1974) 39.

12 SD/MISC/B/80, for June and July 1875. Two, noted in "other", were trained for the Nonconformist ministry in Nonconformist colleges.

13 Knight, in Williams, *The Welsh Church*, p. 343. The list is of those who applied for ordination in the diocese of St Davids August 1874 to December 1875. Not all were ordained in the diocese and 7 were rejected.

14 Lewis, *Charge (Llandaff)*, 1891, p. 8.

15 *Report of the Church Congress, Manchester, 1888*, p. 91. The speaker noted that the number of clergy in 1856 was 1163 and in 1876 1279.

16 Clarke, *The Revenues of the Church of England in Wales*, pp. 16, 31, 47, 70. He notes that his numbers are not consistent because of vacancies in benefices. The number of beneficed literates varied considerable between the dioceses: Bangor had 13 (9% of total incumbents in that diocese), St Asaph 16 (8%), Llandaff 42 (19%), and St Davids 53 (15%). Of the 148 Lampeter non-graduate men Llandaff had 24 and St Davids 90.

17 Basil Jones, *Charge (St Davids)*, 1889, pp. 10-11.

18 *St David's Diocesan Directory and Calendar*, 1889. The figures for Oxbridge include 2 who had not graduated, and 20 of the non-graduates of SDC had the L.Div. diploma. Of the other theological colleges 2 were for Abergavenny and 4 for Lichfield. The literates formed 9% of the total, theological college trained 13.5%, all those from SDC 44%, and graduates other than SDC 33%.

19 Brown, *The Followers of Jeroboam*, p. 7.

20 *Report of the Royal Commission, 1911*, I.I, 43. Each diocese used a different classification system which makes it difficult to analyse their returns.

21 Taken from entries in the *Llandaff Diocesan Calendar*, 1911, pp.116-34. The figures relate to those who had attended theological colleges for post-graduate training. Those for SMC are also included in the main figure.

22 *Church in Wales: Report of the Revisory Sub-Committee on Training for the Ministry*, 1938, pp. 76-7. The numbers do not agree in all instances, possibly because men trained at two different colleges were counted at both. Included in the Oxbridge numbers are 35 who also attended SDC and 18 who graduated as well from the University of Wales, of whom 156 are noted in the graduate figures.

CHAPTER ONE: INTRODUCTION

It was not until the mid-Victorian period that the established Church realised that it needed to organise its procedures for ordination. Up to that time each bishop had drawn up his own procedure, albeit on lines suggested by some of the archbishops of Canterbury; the universities where most of the clergy were educated were a law to themselves; the theological colleges that had arisen were almost private venture colleges, and there was a total lack of any central administration or control by the Church. If a man wished to be ordained the procedure was that he wrote to a diocesan bishop indicating his intention to offer himself for examination at the next Embertide, having found a title or curacy in that bishop's diocese, and presented the requisite papers. He would then appear on the Wednesday or even Thursday before the Sunday ordination date and face an examination, conducted sometimes by the bishop himself or more often by his examining chaplains. If he passed he would probably be told on the Saturday before the ordination, and would accordingly present himself before the bishop at that service to be duly made a deacon. If he failed, or was "plucked", he would disappear, his hopes dashed. As William Latham Bevan of St Davids maintained at its 1882 diocesan conference, in many cases the bishop and his chaplains would not know about these men until they presented themselves for ordination, while few met their future bishop before that event.[1] Many bishops made it clear they would only ordain graduates, but in most of the Welsh dioceses and such dioceses as Carlisle and Chester, namely those areas where the livings were poor, bishops were prepared to consider men who had no university education but who had studied in a grammar school, with a clergyman, or by themselves, to prepare for the bishop's examination.

The mid-Victorian Church for reasons that will become clear later realised this procedure was haphazard, especially as it allowed little or no spiritual preparation or pastoral experience to be given before a man was sent out into a parish, sometimes to cope on his own as a curate for a non-resident incumbent. It was even recognised that such matters as vocation, moral fitness and spiritual aptness, had been forfeited for an examination based almost exclusively on academic subjects. In all probability it was

Dean Edwards of Bangor who wrote about his diocesan Clerical Education Fund, when it was formed in 1871, that it was the whole Church which needed to be involved in the calling and training of men for its ministry. This included the bishop and candidate, the colleges and universities, as well as the parish clergy, all of whom needed to work together towards that common aim.[2]

By the 1900s there were four clear routes to ordination within the Church in Wales, as outlined to the Royal Commission on the Church of England and other Religious Bodies in Wales. The preferred route was that of graduating from a University, preferably Oxford or Cambridge, sometimes followed by a year's residence at a theological college for pastoral and spiritual training, though that was not compulsory. The second was entry to St David's College, Lampeter, from an intermediate or public school, and there reading for a degree, with the option of undertaking a further year at a theological college, generally St Michael's College, Llandaff. Third, was entry to St David's College for men who would be described today as more mature, having previously worked as laymen, who would take a biennial course of study for the L.Th. diploma. The last route was for those who were trained at one of the theological colleges that catered for non-graduates and offered courses in theology, pastoralia and spirituality.[3]

This study is specifically about how the Church in Wales coped with the many difficulties of obtaining an adequate and fit supply of men for its ministry. It needs to be remembered that until the Disestablishment of the Church in 1920 it was in reality but four dioceses of the province of Canterbury. Nevertheless, because of the peculiar difficulties some of the dioceses faced, the Welsh Church had to find alternative ways and means of obtaining this manpower, even though these ways might have been seen as lowering the standard required by the more traditional English diocesans. We also need to accept that it is impossible to speak of the Church in Wales as a single entity. The dioceses were very different in their needs and requirements. The southern dioceses of St Davids and Llandaff were far poorer than the northern ones, St Asaph and Bangor. In part this was due to the medieval practice of appropriating livings, or parishes, to monastic houses, which appears to have been more common in the southern dioceses than the northern. The abbot would serve as rector and obtain the great tithes, and appoint a deputy or vicar who would subsist on the lesser tithes or on a small stipend in lieu. At the Reformation these livings were given to, or purchased by ecclesiastical corporations, colleges and individuals, with the requirement that a stipend be paid to the cleric who cared for the parish and who was termed a perpetual curate. Generally, the stipend remained the same as has been set originally, so that what had been a sufficient income in Tudor times was a totally inadequate one a century later. By the eighteenth century a living worth £200 per annum was regarded as a reasonable one, but in St Davids only 121 out of 407 livings fell into this category, Llandaff had 92 out of 192, whereas St Asaph had 92 out of 132 and Bangor 72 out of 123.[4] Conybeare, in an essay on the "Church in the Mountains", of 1851, considered that the number of those who held livings under this figure totalled about 800 in Wales and 200 in the north of England. Describing them as the "mountain" or "peasant" clergy he suggested that most were to be found in Wales; in particular in Cardiganshire, but also in Carmarthenshire, Breconshire, Radnorshire, north Pembrokeshire (all in the diocese of St Davids), Glamorgan (in the diocese of Llandaff), and south Merioneth and west Montgomeryshire (in the diocese of Bangor). These were the areas, he significantly added, where the Church had been despoiled of its assets.[5]

The dilemma faced by the Welsh bishops and their advisors was a difficult one. They were faced with finding men for inadequate livings at a time when the Church at large was dominated by what became known as "the gentry heresy", namely that the clergy should be socially on a par with the local gentry. That was not all. These parishes were almost exclusively Welsh-speaking, and Welsh-speaking men were required to serve them, but the number of Welsh-speaking gentry was extremely limited and few of those ordained from this class would be prepared to serve in what they would see as culturally backward areas. At the same time too there was another pressure facing these bishops. This was the growing concern that the clergy should be seen as forming a professional elite. We look at each in turn.

THE GENTRY CLERGY

It was Kitson Clark who noted that there was a distinct change in the status of clergy during the eighteenth century. At first, he suggested, few were rated higher than upper servants in a great house, but a century later they had assumed the status of gentry and had adopted a more civilised culture.[6] Anthony Russell made the same observation. The parson, from being almost indistinguishable from a yeoman farmer had become a member of the professional upper middle class.[7] The reason for this was an economic one. The income of the clergy derived mainly from tithes and the glebe attached to their living, and the increase in agricultural prosperity of that period, allied to the enclosure movement which also benefited the clergy as landowners, substantially increased their resources, and made "the Church" an attractive proposition for the younger sons of the gentry and those of the middle class, who appreciated the new status of gentry that the clerical occupation offered. A writer in the *Quarterly Review* of 1862 suggested that this social rank of the clergy drew into the ministry those who had money but not rank, and who presumably wished to make good that deficiency,[8] especially as livings could be bought for a son, either by the purchase of an advowson or of a next presentation. Although this was not general in Wales, and where it did apply it was mainly in the north, the leaders of Church and State in England and Wales accepted what became known as the gentry heresy, that is, that a clergyman was *ipso facto* a gentleman, and anything less was a source of regret and even apology. It could almost be argued that being a gentleman involved a university education. The novelist Anthony Trollope held this view. He argued that the parson was "almost necessarily" educated at Oxbridge and was a gentleman equal in rank to the squire. Literates, however capable, could never be equal to such a man, being "less attractive, less urbane, and less genial – in a word, less of a gentleman."[9] It was an ideal that persisted in the Church long after it had proved impossible to maintain,[10] and Dean Goulburn's comment of 1892 that while the clergy worked harder they had, as a class, sadly deteriorated in breeding, was one that had to be reluctantly accepted.[11]

It was argued that the lower orders, to use Archdeacon Hale's expression, did not want people of their own class as their ministers. They preferred a learned and thus a gentry ministry.[12] An unknown writer in the *Quarterly Review* of 1868 argued that any change in the social position of the clergy would be injurious and incalculable. The upper classes, he hinted, would no longer supply sons for ordination as the Church would no longer be a gentry profession, while the lower classes needed an English gentleman as their pastor, who had the natural sympathy and kindness of his class to offer them or, as others put it, to influence them.[13] Not all agreed. Surely, a few argued, God had not confined the ministry to one particular social class alone. This was a point emphasised by the 1908 Report on the Supply and Training of Candidates for Holy Orders. Cost, it argued, had confined the ministry to one rank of the social order, and those who had entered it without such a background were looked upon with disfavour.[14] Henry Mackenzie, speaking at the Cambridge Church

Congress of 1861, argued that the towns were populated by the middle and lower class, and the gentleman-cleric was seen by them as superior and condescending. They needed men drawn from their own ranks,[15] though others suggested that men ordained from this class were apt to be regarded rather critically even by their own people.[16] Although most of these quotations come, of necessity, from English sources, this last statement was partly true of Wales. J.E. Vincent, an acute observer, wrote that the old Anglesey parsons were mainly gentlemen, some were even squarsons. As the number of such men who spoke Welsh was diminishing, and the bishop of Bangor required his clergy to speak Welsh, he was forced to accept men from a lower stratum than he might desire. Such men, many of whom had started life as farm labourers or quarrymen, were resented by their congregations, who felt a sense of bitterness that men who now occupied a superior position were from the same background as themselves.[17] Whether this comment relating to one diocese was true of the whole of Wales is doubtful, for the clergy of the mountain areas, to use Conybeare's term, had always been from this class, and had never replaced the gentry clergy as was the case in Anglesey.

    This dilemma was ever present for the Victorian Church, especially for the Welsh dioceses. The Church needed faithful men in its ministry whatever their background, while society required their clergymen to be gentlemen as well. But we may note a comment of 1880 made by Bishop Ollivant of Llandaff in a sermon at the reopening of the chapel of St David's College, Lampeter, after its refurbishment. Noting that the links between the various classes in England which contributed to the welfare of the whole community were lacking in Wales, he argued that the Church needed a clerical body which even if it lacked high birth nevertheless had refinement and a sound education, so that it might be of influence amongst the upper as well as the lower classes.[18] It was an aspiration rather than a reality, as Ollivant well knew, though the bishops never relaxed their insistence on a classical education. The point was elaborated some years earlier by a paper delivered to a Church Conference at Bangor by Henry T. Edwards, then vicar of Caernarfon and later dean of Bangor. Noting that the many Welshmen were gifted with the natural powers of oratory, he wished to attract this kind of person into the ministry of the Church, rather than allow them to be captured by Nonconformity. But, he added, there was also the requirement that they should have "a hearty acquaintance with the definite scriptural and Catholic theology" of the Church, and that they should understand the sympathies of the masses, thus allowing them to be influential and popular. He was happy that they should come from the same classes that provided such men in the past, namely from the class of "the small tradesmen, small farmers and artisans", but they would need a training that "will render them more refined, more highly educated, than the Clergy of the last five or six generations."[19] Walter Morgan observed, however, that much of the training such men received was based on a classical curriculum that had been designed for the gentleman parson of a previous century; one that was totally unsuitable for a Welsh environment.[20]

A PROFESSIONAL CLASS?

Around the same time as the concept of a gentry clergy was being challenged, another concept gained predominance, namely that the clergy formed a professional class akin to such groups as lawyers and doctors, who had established themselves as a learned body of men who were gaining a near-monopoly in their specialisation. Although this is sometimes allied with the emphasis placed by the Oxford Movement on the sacerdotal nature of the ministry, requiring it to be a distinct and separate order,[21] it may well be that these are two distinct emphases, although united in the requirement for a particular form of specialised training. If the Tractarians emphasised a spiritual and theological preparation, evangelicals and others tended to concentrate on a pastoral and doctrinal training. Yet both Tractarians and Evangelicals encouraged their adherents, and through them the wider Church, to see the clergyman as one who had acquired specialised knowledge and skills, and who lived a distinctive lifestyle.

The reasons offered for this professionalism within the ministry are many and various. It might well have been a reaction to the loss of gentry status and a need to obtain some other form of identification that allowed both university men and non-graduates an equal status. It might be linked to a fear of being seen as amateurs in a growing world of specialisation. It was probably linked to the gradual marginalisation of religion that made the clergy seek a distinguishing role and one that could compete with the other professions, especially as the town parson was replacing the rural incumbent in importance and status. The developing pastoral role of the clergyman, as distinct from the more social role of his eighteenth century predecessor, involving such matters as running schools and Sunday schools, pastoral visiting, outreach and mission, liturgical and musical developments, preaching, caring for para-Church organisations, organising lay assistance, and the training of curates, required a specialised knowledge and resulted in the production of numerous manuals of pastoral theology. In addition, a dedicated church press produced newspapers and journals for clerical consumption. It also meant specialised training in colleges dedicated to these matters, a training tested by examination procedures, and an attempt to establish greater accountability with standards of conduct and ministry re-emphasised. This took place against a growing background of the clergy losing their role in society at large, especially towards the end of the nineteenth century. School boards, county and local councils, the opening up of the magistracy to the middle class, took away from the parson some of the authority he once possessed and narrowed his role, while others took his place in such simple domestic matters as providing poor relief, drawing up wills, offering advice and acting as mediators, though these roles were not entirely lost in rural areas. It meant that the clerical status needed to be defined in a more precise way. Arthur Burns suggests that this sense of professionalism was assisted by the revival of the office of rural-dean, thus conferring a career pattern open to more of the clergy as well as a further status and authority, with the resulting emergence of clergy chapters and meetings chaired by these men.[22] Not all were in favour of this development. Dean Vaughan expressed his concern that this professionalism might be accompanied by a sense of craft and mystery that made the Gospel mysteries the heirlooms of the clergy rather than of the Church.[23]

THE LACK OF SUITABLE MEN

Although the number of clergy in England and Wales increased between 1841 to 1911 from 14,613 to 24,968, when given as a percentage of the population the figures were far less encouraging. In 1841 there was one clergyman for every 1,098 of the population, in 1911, one per 1,451.[24] If the figures had been divided between the rural and urban-industrial populations it would have given even more anxiety as there were many industrial parishes with populations of 8,000 and more staffed by one incumbent and perhaps a curate. When John Griffith, vicar of Aberdare, complained to his bishop in 1856 about the shortage of curates, Ollivant informed him he should not be surprised. When Griffith entered the parish in 1846 he had but one curate, now he needed five.[25] Richard Lewis, bishop of Llandaff, told his clergy that the annual number of men made deacons in the first two years of his episcopate averaged eighteen as against eleven during the last two years of his predecessor, Ollivant.[26] Indeed, between 1883-1910 844 deacons had been ordained in or for that diocese,[27] but these numbers were still insufficient, though the point might be made that the resources of the Church were stretched already to provide for those who were currently ordained.

It was not always so. The eighteenth century Church was notorious for the number of its unemployed clergy. In 1828 Bishop Copleston of Llandaff, writing to his father, wrote that he had fifteen or sixteen candidates for ordination, more than he really wanted, adding "[t]he profession is certainly overstocked, scanty as it's endowments are here".[28] In that same year Bishop Jenkinson in his charge to the clergy of the diocese of St Davids made clear that as the clerical profession was "inconvenienced" by a superabundance rather than a deficiency of clergymen, he would not ordain on any "short term" title.[29]

The position was soon to change, and in 1877 Bishop Basil Jones of St Davids could argue that while he had many enquiries for ordination, the number of suitable bilingual candidates was inadequate, and this meant that the want of duly qualified persons pressed heavily on his diocese. Twenty-five years ago the diocese needed ten deacons per annum to make up numbers, but while forty had been made deacon in the past three and a half years this number was still insufficient to meet the need. Three years later in his 1880 Charge, the bishop was more confident. Much had been said about the insufficient supply of candidates for orders, he told his clergy, but his own experience did not justify such complaints. Yet we may note that the number of deacons he had ordained in the previous three years, 32, was less than those noted in his earlier charge.[30] As a result he declined to ordain literates, and because of the lack of titles in his own diocese he was forced to allow some men to seek titles in other dioceses, men he would have been glad to have kept, a concern also noted by Bishop Lewis of Llandaff in his primary visitation charge of 1885.[31]

This was a position which applied to the wider Church as well. Many of the Church Congresses, held from 1861 as an unofficial yet influential forum for the Church, the debates in Convocation and at diocesan conferences, frequently expressed concern about the supply and training of the clergy, always against a background of a deficiency in numbers.[32] The bishops in their Charges also noted their concerns. Bishop Edwards of St Asaph in his visitation charge of 1898 lamented that there was a dearth of candidates for Holy Orders, and those who came forward were predominantly "less qualified" men, and this was compounded by the language issue.[33]

The reasons for this lack of candidates were frequently recorded and debated. High on the list at every debate was the lack of gentry sons offering themselves for ordination, thus continuing the gentry heresy noted earlier.[34] Bishop Short of St Asaph, who retired in 1870, wrote that the "candidates for orders are rarely the sons of landed proprietors."[35] A hint was given by J.C. Vincent, the vicar of Carnarfon in 1869, that many gentry fathers would think it derogatory for their sons to be associated with fellow clergy who came from a much humbler background.[36] This was argued in relation to Wales as early as 1768 by John Jones, a fellow of Queen's College, Oxford. Gentry fathers would not educate their sons at university in order to receive a paltry curacy worth £20 per annum, especially as preferment was not by merit but by interest.[37] Conybeare made the same point in 1855 though by then he was speaking about livings worth £200 and under. The cost of education would be in the region of £1,500 and for the same sum a life annuity of £150 could be purchased.[38] The agricultural depression of the 1870s to the early 1900s made the position even more acute, as the value of many livings was substantially reduced.[39] When Stephen Jackson at the 1907 Llandaff Diocesan Conference expressed his sadness at the lack of the sons of the gentry coming forward as candidates, he was met with the retort from another speaker that what was needed were labourers not gentlemen farmers.[40] An industrial diocese needed a far different breed of men from what was required in former days.

As hinted above, it was a question of expense for many would-be candidates from Wales. At a time when parents expected their sons to be contributing to the family income by the age of sixteen, the cost of further education was almost out of the question. It was not a shortage of candidates, rather it was the lack of resources for their training.[41] The Bangor Diocesan Conference of 1910 heard S.L. Brown, warden of the Church Hostel, state that in the previous four months he had been in contact with 103 possible candidates or enquirers about ordination. Most needed financial assistance in order to be ordained. This even applied to the sons of the clergy.[42] Bishop Edwards of St Asaph in 1900, himself a clergy son, argued that the poverty of the clergy made it impossible for them to educate their sons for the Church. Yet they lived in surroundings conducive to turning their thoughts towards Holy Orders.[43]

Another issue was that the majority of candidates were required to be Welsh-speaking. English candidates, especially those who had had an Oxbridge education, tended to seek pastures in England, which offered not only better prospects but also avoided the necessity of obtaining a proficiency in a language that many assumed was dying out. Other reasons suggested were that the new standards for ministry and clerical character, or its vocational nature, made men nervous of entering it or feeling insufficient about its demands. In addition there were numerous new channels for men of education to obtain employment in education, banking, or the competitive fields of the civil service, army and navy, where ability rather than influence had become the dominant requirement. The thought of a long curacy and a poor incumbency, existing on £100 per annum, often meant that families discouraged their sons from considering the ministry of the Church as their career, and fathers felt concern that the cost of training was not supported by future income. Alan Haig noted how after 1870 those books which described career choices were more pessimistic about a career in the Church's ministry than those written before that time. The concentration on urban rather than rural ministry, and the loss of authority within the Church itself at its local level, were other factors that were mentioned. Higher criticism too, it was thought, had a bearing as men felt unease about the validity of Biblical authority, while the secularisation of education was also mentioned by Bishop Lewis of Llandaff as it meant that the Church's influence in schools had diminished and the classical education they once provided had been lost. Surprisingly, the only person who mentioned a lack of spiritual interest in the society of his day was W.H. Griffith-Thomas in a speech to the Swansea Church Congress of 1909.[44]

The disestablished Church faced the same issues, and though many of the reasons adduced for the lack of ordinands were similar, it was now argued that in addition the loss of private patronage had prevented the sons of gentry from coming forward, while the sons of the clergy were repelled from ordination because of the pettiness of parochial church councils.[45] One constant concern of the Church in Wales then and previously was the number of its younger clergy who left its fold and departed for the brighter hopes and greater advantages of England. This concern had been mentioned in the 1850s and continued thereafter, so that in 1948 Bishop Williamson of Swansea and Brecon estimated that about twenty of the younger clergy ordained in Wales went annually to England. He added that over the past two years that rate had trebled.[46] In addition men were no longer prepared to wait years for livings of their own, and those whose Welsh was insufficient realised that the livings available to them were limited in number, while the senior posts were almost unobtainable.

To meet the lack of these sons of gentry or those educated at the Universities various expedients were adopted or proposed. The first was the acceptance that candidates of a lower class, or at least those who could not afford a university education, would need to be ordained. Both Bishops Lewis of Llandaff and Basil Jones of St Davids, whose comments about the number of deacons who had been ordained in their dioceses are noted above, were also at pains to stress in almost the same sentence that there had been no lowering of standards even though many of those ordained had been trained at Lampeter or at a theological college as non-graduates.

It was thus accepted by the whole Church by the mid-nineteenth century that to meet the need for sufficient clergy, men would need to be ordained whose training lay elsewhere than at a university and who might well be in Trollope's phrase, "not gentlemen". These were the men whom Lord Grimthorpe alleged had risen from the ranks of primary school teachers, commercial clerks, small merchants, higher class artisans and the sons of farmers.[47] Conybeare in his essay on the Church in the Mountains noted that while the sons of the gentry or those financially well-endowed might decline to be ordained because of the lack of financial rewards or of a decent maintenance, added "[s]ecular motives are not excluded by small emoluments, but only brought to bear upon a lower class."[48] But that was a cynical view. Thomas Arnold in the 1830s considered that men from such a background could be extremely useful as ministers, considering that many of this class, unable to afford a university education but desiring to be ordained, had become Dissenting ministers and thus "necessarily hostile to the Established Church".[49]

Archdeacon Ffoulkes of Montgomery defended these men by claiming they led devoted lives and had many good qualities,[50] and, it might be argued, the colleges they attended offered a far better and practical training for the ministry than that received by Oxbridge graduates. The real concern might have been more a social than an academic one, namely that they lacked breeding and refinement and were ill at ease in polite society. However, Ffoulkes' bishop, Vowler Short of St Asaph, remarked that while it had been thought that this "class of peasant clergy" would give to the lower orders "a greater sense of unity with the Church than they at present possess", this had not been the case in Wales.[51] John Griffith of Aberdare had made this claim in the 1840s, arguing that the Nonconformist preacher, having come from the same social class as his congregation, was acquainted with all the feelings, habits and weak points of those people he wished to influence. This was not so with the Church, who ordained men straight from college who had no real knowledge of these matters and lacked those attributes that made a man into a pastor. Twenty-five years on he had changed his tune and he defended those whom he described as the lower grade of the Welsh clergy, who though inferior in almost every other respect, being rough, coarse, uneducated, even rude in their manner, yet fulfilled the necessities of the case far better than those men who had come from more genteel and educated backgrounds.[52] This need to accept men socially inferior to those whom the Church would have preferred to ordain will be more fully discussed in the Welsh context in another part of this section.

Many of the bishops in their visitation charges or speakers at diocesan conferences appealed to the clergy to seek out men who might be encouraged to offer themselves for ordination. By necessity this probably meant young men "of the right type", in John Owen's phrase, who, if offered financial help, would be able to complete secondary education and enter one of the older universities, Lampeter or a theological college for their training, and thus, in the words of Archdeacon John Evans of Carmarthen, "fill an office full of dignity and importance".[53] At times desperation replaced episcopal wisdom. Wynford Vaughan-Thomas recalls that his father, a well-known composer, met one of the Welsh bishops, who suggested that he might be ordained, as the Church, now disestablished, needed men of distinction in its clergy. He was assured that his time in a theological college would be enjoyably short, a pleasant rectory in the country would allow plenty of time for his composing, and if it was in the Towy Valley there would be the fishing. As his son added, his father was no fisherman and a rationalist.[54]

A third approach, although it was never implemented, was the creation of an order of sub-deacons or a permanent diaconate. Various suggestions were put forward and frequently debated, from setting apart men from the professions or merchant classes who could give assistance to their incumbent during their spare time whilst remaining in secular life, to establishing an order of men who would never obtain the necessary qualifications for Holy Orders but whose heart was in the right place and who could act as stipendiary assistants in a parish, though there were many variations in between. The difference between such men and the new order of lay readers was often vague and uncertain. The matter was debated and commended by many Church Congresses and diocesan conferences, by Convocation and mentioned by bishops in their Charges.[55] The first reference I can find in Wales is that of a conference of clergy called by the bishop of Bangor in 1869 to discuss laymen continuing their secular calling while also serving as Scripture or lay readers.[56] John Griffith of Aberdare had advocated such a policy in 1846, and it had been discussed as early as 1851 by a clergy synod at Exeter.[57]

When Archdeacon Edmondes proposed such an order to the Llandaff Diocesan Conference of 1890 it was heavily defeated,[58] even though it had been persuasively argued by Bishop Perry, the assistant bishop, from his diocesan experiences in Australia some years earlier,[59] while his colleague, Archdeacon Bruce, in a debate at the Cardiff Deanery Chapter in 1885, considered that an excellent layman might be spoiled by ordination and an ineffective clergyman produced instead.[60] Bishop Campbell of Bangor was equally concerned, for speaking to his diocesan conference in 1884 he argued that allowing men working in the secular field to be "ordained" would mean that the distinctive character of Holy Orders would be lost. Men of "inferior education" would be unable to pass the examination for priests' orders but having been ordained as deacons might assume that their service in the Church entitled them to enter the priesthood, or, even worse, being local men might attain to a popularity greater than their incumbents and thus become a challenge to their ministry. In addition, a part-time man might be used instead of a stipendiary curate.[61] The earl of Powis, speaking at the St Asaph Diocesan Conference of 1887, shared with his bishop the fear of such men engaging in secular work and given the title "reverend", because of the risk of lowering the ministry in public estimation. His lordship also felt that such men might find themselves so busy in their secular role than they might neglect their sacred duties. Archdeacon Ffoulkes said much the same.[62] It was for such reasons that this particular experiment was never implemented.

Another suggestion made, one commended by many speakers in these debates, such as Archdeacon Ffoulkes and Walsham How, later bishop of Wakefield, was of lowering the age of being made deacon from the canonical twenty-three years to twenty-one or twenty-two This they argued would shorten the length of time a father would need to support his son, and allow the son to be self-supporting a year or two earlier than would otherwise be the case. The age of priesting, twenty-three, would remain unchanged.[63] This requirement of the age of twenty-three, although canonical, had once allowed a dispensatory power to the archbishop of Canterbury, but this concession was disallowed by legislation introduced by Lord Ellenborough in 1804. Richard Watson, bishop of Llandaff, found this objectionable, and wished for a lower age, noting as his reason the many undergraduates he had known at University, especially the sons of clergymen, farmers and tradesmen, from which categories the Church obtained its ministers, whose families had struggled to provide for their education. Since the expense of a university education had increased, the number of such men had decreased and the Church had to find its supply elsewhere. He felt the bishops ought to have a discretion in this matter, while an earlier ordination would encourage more parents to accept the expense of a university education.[64] Ffoulkes, like Watson, clearly had in mind graduates, for he argued that this change would help parents consenting to their sons studying for the ministry, and prevent graduates from taking up scholastic work as an interim measure, which often resulted in them remaining in teaching and giving up any thoughts of ordination. He also considered that a man of twenty-one, presumably a graduate, was perfectly capable of taking up parochial duties, though in his early years he should assist but not preach, and be given time to learn pastoral work.[65]

T.E. Espin, a former head of Queen's College, Birmingham, a theological college, maintained that because of this age requirement many men had been lost to the Church. Bishop Ryle also had non-graduates in mind when he argued that many such men had entered the Nonconformist ministry or secular callings because of the pressure of family finances, being unable to "stand idle in the market-place". Even if a man of this background was inclined to the work of the ministry "the Church of England can find him nothing to do" until he reached a certain age.[66] Such a scheme was never effected, possibly because of the legislation required, but also due to the many objections made against it. These were that the age of twenty-one was too low, and no other profession allowed men to earn their living at this age; men should not pass directly from the University to ordination, and the cost of finding a stipend for the newly ordained deacon would be difficult for incumbents already financially hard-pressed.[67]

MOTIVES

What were the motives that induced men to offer themselves for ordination? Clearly, many were activated by spiritual considerations, a desire to preach the Gospel, and to serve Christ and their fellow men, and who saw the Ministry of the Church as a life rather than a career. But as a writer of 1832 maintained in a published letter to Bishop Copleston of Llandaff, many passed through a lifetime of ministry "with little lively apprehension" of the work to which they had been called.[68] In an attempt to remedy this ignorance Henry Owen, a chaplain to Bishop Barrington whilst he was bishop of Llandaff (1769-82), wrote his *Directions for Young Students in Divinity*, possibly, it is thought, for candidates for Holy Orders in that diocese. This book emphasised the need for a warm zeal for the glory of God, and the honour of religion, a tender concern for the welfare of souls, a life of self-discipline, and frequent meditation about the truth of religion and the importance of the pastoral office. It warned that those who were ordained without such concerns would find that their office would be a source of unhappiness to themselves and useless to the people of their parish.[69]

It is clear from the writings of many bishops and others that there were many who were ordained without giving much thought about the responsibilities of their calling. John Popkin, although a prejudiced witness, wrote that though the candidate might swear that he had been inwardly moved by the Holy Spirit to the office of priest or deacon, his motive might well be a desire for wealth, profit, gain, ease and honour in this world.[70] Bishop Basil Jones of St Davids in an ordination address argued that the temptation to seek Orders from some secondary motive was more powerful in his diocese than possibly elsewhere, and men could be blinded about the sacredness of the work they were about to undertake and seeing it as a career rather than a life.[71] Chancellor Ollivant, of Llandaff, son of the bishop, and S.L. Brown, warden of the Bangor Church Hostel, spoke of men drifting into the Church's ministry for want of something to do, without feeling any sense of vocation.[72]

In some instances a man deferred to family pressure or desire in seeking ordination, possibly because of a family living that would come his way. Hannah Moore, writing to Wilberforce in 1801, mentioned the rector of Chew Magna who was about to enter the army when this valuable living of £600 per annum was obtained for him. "He rather seems unacquainted with religion than hostile to it," she added.[73] Charles Darwin's father is said to have considered the Church for his son's career, considering that "an aimless son" would fit in nicely with that "haven for dullards and dawdlers", and in a profession where the risks of failure were low and the rewards high.[74] David Williams of Fairfield who had been vicar of Ystradyfodwg in the Rhondda Valley 1842-58, was said in his obituary to have had no inward calling to the Ministry, but was one of those sad cases who was ordained because his father had wished it. Significantly he resigned his living at the age of forty-one some eighteen months after his father's death, and thereafter acted as a member of the landed gentry.[75] A Pembrokeshire squarson, Thomas Gwynne Mortimer, had fallen in with his parents wishes that he should be ordained, although his inclination was to go to sea. Duly ordained, through family influence he obtained the living of Castlebythe in the patronage of the Lord Chancellor which he held until 1899.[76]

There were others who were attracted to the social position occupied by the clergy. John Morgan, rector of Llandudno, writing in 1892, complained that the bishops were admitting into Orders year after year "anybody and everybody" who had discovered a short cut to a better social position and easier life than would otherwise be the case. We reap what we sow, he added.[77] In a satirical comment, "an Oxford Tutor" wrote of several of his students who had been ordained in Wales. One, the son of a Nonconformist draper, had so progressed that from Thomas Richards he had become the Revd. T.T.Ll. Wynne-Richardes, having gone over to the Church whilst a student at the Nonconformist Brecon College. This tutor also suggested that those sons of the gentry who had been ordained in order to sustain "their butterfly life" would turn to other professions when and if disestablishment arrived.[78]

These were the exceptions, however, and even those who might have entered Holy Orders for more worldly than spiritual reasons often turned out to be fine pastors and guides to their congregations.

CHAPTER TWO: THE WELSH DILEMMA

It has been noted already that the four Welsh dioceses were part of the wider province of Canterbury and thus part of the Church of England, and that there were considerable differences between the northern and southern dioceses of Wales due to historic circumstances. The bishops of both Llandaff and St Davids were unable to obtain many university men, so they had to look for their supply for clergy elsewhere, while their fellow bishops in the north could take a more relaxed attitude. Bishop Warren of Bangor, during his episcopate 1783-1800, ordained only university men, 26 from Oxford and 6 from Cambridge,[1] whereas between 1750-99 only 45 graduates were ordained in the diocese of St Davids compared to 680 literates.[2] This position was continued for many years thereafter. It was not until 1843 that the first Lampeter man was made deacon in the diocese of Bangor, but it was not until 1870 that their number became substantial.[3] When Robert Roberts was looking for a title in this diocese during 1859, he discovered that Bishop Bethell objected to men trained at St Bees' College, and thus was forced to enter the diocese of St Asaph.[4] It needed a new bishop, Campbell, to reverse this trend. He ordained the first St Bees' man in his diocese in 1862, though their number thereafter increased dramatically so that all the deacons ordained at the Trinity 1872 ordination were products of this college.[5] It is said that the first bishop of modern times who accepted non-graduates in the diocese of St Asaph was William Cleaver, 1806-15. He did so as a reaction to the Calvinistic Methodist secession of 1811, when that denomination ordained its own men, as he wished to ensure that talented men of good character and spirituality, debarred from the Church's ministry because of lack of finance for a university education, should remain within the Church and not stray into Nonconformity.[6]

The vice-principal of St David's College, Lampeter, William Harrison Davey, speaking in 1879, indicated that the Welsh Church needed in its ministry those who were good Welshmen, good Englishmen, good Churchmen, good parish priests and good Christians.[7] Henry Edwards, then vicar of Caernarfon, was concerned that the clergy of the Church should be "the Priests of the people", embracing both palace and cottage. It was thus undesirable that the clergy of Wales should be drawn exclusively from one class, either from the upper classes (who were increasingly Anglicised) or from the working classes (who were almost exclusively Welsh-speaking).[8] Though most of his candidates for ordination came from Welsh-speaking parishes, Bishop Basil Jones was aware that with the increasing use of English in many parishes, clergy were needed who were fit "to minister to two races, mingled in various proportions".[9] The dilemma faced by the Welsh Church, especially in the southern dioceses, was how to find such a balance.

This dilemma was a historic question, one from which even the northern dioceses were not always immune, especially in previous centuries. When the archbishop of Canterbury, Sancroft, reminded his suffragans in 1686 about their responsibilities regarding ordination, Bishop William Lloyd of St Asaph informed him that his regulation that only graduates should be ordained was impracticable in a Welsh diocese: "We have a great many more cures of souls than we have graduates in this country; and as most of the people understand nothing but Welsh, we cannot supply the cures with any other than Welshmen".[10] By the eighteenth century it was argued that there were more non-graduates ordained in the diocese of St Davids than in the other three dioceses, men the writer regarded as of defective education and as incompetent clergymen. He argued that the reason for this large number of non-graduates was that university men would not accept the fatigue and trouble required to serve three or four churches for a trifling consideration.[11] Bishop Burgess of that diocese (1803-25) described it as "this dilapidated part of the Church of England", and was appalled at the want of polish, refinement and the extent of the ignorance of some of those who applied to him for ordination.[12]

The basic dilemma that faced the Welsh bishops was that the Welsh-speaking university men often elected to be ordained in English dioceses, where (as noted above) there were far better prospects than in Wales; those graduates who remained often did not speak sufficient Welsh for the needs of Welsh-speakers, while those who spoke Welsh were unable to afford a university education and whose education was thus limited as were their social skills. Bishop Joshua Hughes of St Asaph, a non-graduate himself, emphasised in 1871 that there was a comparatively small number of Welsh-speaking university men who entered the ministry of the northern dioceses.[13] It was probably far less in the southern dioceses. This concern was a constant theme of many of the Welsh bishops. Bishop Ollivant in his Primary Charge of 1851 put it this way:

> As the smallness of our preferment holds out little inducement to the higher classes to educate their sons for our service – who, if they are sent to the English universities, are under strong temptations to remain in England, where their talents may obtain a better reward – so is the proportion of persons in the other classes, who can afford to give them a suitable education, far too limited to allow of their yielding us an adequate supply. Those who, in spite of all difficulties, determine upon dedicating them to the Church, are too often obliged by their straightened means to restrict the outlay within the narrowest possible limits that are compatible with the attainment of their object.[14]

The position might be put in another way. David Howell argued that those who could speak Welsh were under-educated, and those who were well-educated were unable to preach effectively in Welsh.[15] Dean Edwards of Bangor wrote that "[w]hile the Bishops were laying hands upon unfit men, the natural Heaven-born teachers of Wales were influencing thousands in the Chapel and *Cymmanfa*. Of the clergy, those who were educated knew no Welsh, and those who knew Welsh were not educated; those who had something to say couldn't say it to the people, and those who could say it had nothing to say."[16] The Welsh that was required, according to David Howell, was not to be spoken nervously, stiffly, awkwardly, but fluently, with power, "using the limpid idiomatic Welsh of the common people". Only native-born speakers could do this, and sadly, these were the men who lacked the more academic and refined qualities demanded by the popular concept of a gentry and university educated ministry.[17]

There was thus a desperate need to supply this deficiency in the number of university men with others who might still be seen as fit and proper candidates for ordination. Yet the individual Welsh bishops could not afford to allow the standard for ministry to fall behind the other learned professions.[18] Ollivant reminded John Griffith that mere fluency of speech would not build up the Church unless it was accompanied by other qualities.[19] Bishop Campbell spoke of his concern in 1875 that the rising number of men ordained in his diocese could be the cause of weakness if those ordained were not raised by education and habits above "the common level".[20]

The men who supplied this need for Welsh-speaking clergymen were the so-called *gwerin* [literally, peasant but more folk] clergy. William Davey, as vice-principal of Lampeter, knew the breed extremely well, describing them as those drawn "mainly from one class only in society, and that a class which labours under special disadvantages, both socially and from an educational point of view." It was not from the upper or even from the middle classes in society, as was the case in England, that "the great bulk of the clergy in Wales is derived".[21] These were the "mountain clergy" in Conybeare's description, estimated by him to be about 700-800 in Wales and 200 or so in the north of England, the sons of farmers and small tradesmen who did not differ in habits or education from their parents and families. Such men, he declaimed, quite unjustly, were destitute of moral or social advantages, and the education of a national schoolmaster at St Mark's College was incomparably better than these men would have received.[22] John Griffith, when vicar of Aberdare, described them as "bullfrog clergy", who were "uneducated, unclipped", and as raw as their fathers' colts, for whom twenty or thirty pounds a year, "and the exclusive privilege of wearing black clothes, could not, of course, but be an advantage, and a matter of congratulation." He later described some of his curates at Merthyr Tydfil in the same way, and was bitterly attacked for his presumption.[23]

THE "INFERIOR" MEN

Such men as described above were deficient in education as well as in social skills. Canon Perowne, then vice-principal at Lampeter, wrote in the late 1860s that those who were admitted to his college were those whose parents either would not or could not afford the cost of keeping them in school long enough to gain any solid advantages: "they are sent to school late, they stay at school just long enough to get sufficient knowledge of Greek and Latin to pass one preliminary examination; and then they come to us for three years, and we are expected in that time to do all that is necessary to qualify them for their profession." There was the "profoundest ignorance" of the English language, English history and literature, and he felt, as did his predecessor, Rowland Williams, that the "germ of the evil", to use John Griffith's expression, rested clearly on the want of preparation before entering college.[24] It was a circular argument. William Morgan, ordained in 1886 after studying at Llandovery and Lampeter, being considered by his parents as the most intelligent of their sons, recalled that many Welsh boys of his day preparing for Orders, were more proficient in the ancient languages than in English.[25] As W.L. Bevan of Hay maintained, many of these men's English diction was not always "to the complete satisfaction" of their parishioners. This was an understatement.[26] Davey also spoke of the need of these Welshmen to possess "a fairly accurate acquaintance with English, if they are to minister respectably and without offence to those who – not less than their Welsh-speaking parishioners – are committed to their charge, and whose ears are fastidiously accurate in detecting faults in grammar, pronunciation, or ideas, as those of their Welsh hearers." The problem was that "[i]f Welsh, considered as a language, is often but imperfectly known by them, their knowledge of English is as a rule much more deficient." Such men laboured under the great difficulty of studying a language additional to their own which was not only essential for their preparation for Orders but also used in daily life.[27] His distinguished predecessor faced the same problem. In a letter to Bishop Short of 1851 Rowland Williams said of his Lampeter pupils, "Welsh they cannot write, and English they cannot speak."[28]

The need for men was often so desperate that, in the words of Bishop Ollivant, he was obliged to ordain men whose qualifications were inferior and whom he would not have ordained from choice. He had to insist that many of these men served as deacons for five years, were not permitted to serve cures on their own during this time, and needed to come up to the normal standard before being ordained priests. In his case quality had to be sacrificed for the sake of quantity or else the Church's mission in the coalfield might have come to an ignominious end. Writing in 1865 to Gilbert Harries, one of his incumbents, he pointed out that there were not a few clergy in his diocese whom he would not have ordained had he acted upon his convictions. To continue the present depressed and unsatisfactory condition of the Welsh clergy would be the death blow to the best interests of the Welsh Church.[29] In the 1870s, according to William Price's history of S David's College, that college was producing so few ordinands that Ollivant was forced to ordain from necessity literates and Scripture readers, who had had no suitable training for the ministry and, at the best, certified students from St Bees and Birmingham theological colleges, whose attainments fell far below his desired standard.[30]

Ollivant's successor, Richard Lewis, added that the intellectual attainments of these men were far from satisfactory.[31] In turn, his successor, J. Pritchard Hughes, in his Visitation Charge of 1907, argued that while the standards of admission had been lowered for ordination because of the need of men, this was the wrong policy and he had reversed it by raising the standard. He asked his incumbents who were waiting for curates to accept the temporary inconvenience rather than accept an incompetent man.[32]

John Griffith, writing in 1870, added that the bishops were compelled to ordain men who would not have had a chance of ordination in an English diocese. After a recent ordination when there were no university men admitted, a dignitary of the Church had suggested to him that hardly one these men was able to take charge of the little Baptist chapel opposite the cathedral. Many of these men had not thought of ordination until late in life; some were failed businessmen, and others had entered the Church to better their prospects.[33]

A report of 1870 written for the quarterly paper of the Church Pastoral-Aid Society noted that many Welsh-speakers had been ordained who "from want of early education were sadly deficient in English" and whilst able to minister to one part of the population were not qualified to minister to the other. It noted that in examining the testimonials of some of these men, in order to decide whether a grant for a curate might be given to an incumbent, they were "painfully sensible" that they were giving their sanction to nominations which if there had been more eligible candidates "they would have thought it their duty to withhold."[34] Vincent in his *Letters from Wales* wrote that with this need to obtain Welsh speakers it was inevitable that the ranks of the clergy would be filled by men of indifferent education and insufficiently trained, men who started life as farm labourers or quarrymen.[35] A speaker at the Llandaff diocesan conference of 1910 feared that some men who were ordained would never earn £120 in the secular world,[36] while Bishop Edwards of St Asaph noted that he often felt "a point was being stretched" in allowing a man to go forward to ordination.[37]

The social skills of these men were equally lacking. George Huntington, rector of Tenby 1867-1905, writes with some humour about some of these men who came to Abergwili to be examined by Bishop Thirlwall of St Davids prior to their ordination examination. They were probably as trying to the bishop as he was to them, for some of them were mere peasants, destitute of culture and ignorant of the usages of society. One, having arrived and offered some tea and bread and butter assumed that was his evening meal, and went to bed, only to be woken by a footman who told him that dinner was being served. Another drank the water in his finger glass and when the footman came to fill it a third time told him, "Please, I can't sup it three times."[38] Similar stories became part of the folklore of the Church.

There were those who defended such "inferior" men. Bishop Copleston of Llandaff was one. Writing to his examining chaplain in 1839 about a candidate whom Bruce Knight would have rejected, he stated that he was "decidedly of opinion that he ought to be received." The evidence obtained of his character, his knowledge of the Bible, his preaching talent, and the opinion of others, inclined the bishop to this opinion, but above all he took into account

> the field of duty in which he is to be employed – the foul and neglected part of the vineyard on which his labours are wanted, and the little chance there is of procuring men of more refined education and manners to devote themselves to that service. Besides which, the very defects you notice will not appear to be defects *there*. He is a Galilaean, about to preach in Galilee, where his speech will not bewray [sic] him; and although the Greek of St. Matthew's Gospel may be a *terra incognita* to him, so it probably was to St. Peter, and so I suspect it would be to many a divine now esteemed a learned and regularly-bred minister of our church. ... 'Go, thou, into the vineyard,' let us say to him, 'and whatever is just, that shalt thou receive.' I have little doubt but that at the day of reckoning he will be found as well entitled to his wages as the rest.[39]

John Griffith, though he might describe these men as the "bullfrog clergy", was prepared to defend them as well, especially when his bishop suggested that the cause of the inferiority of the Welsh clergy was that they came from a low social position. This Griffith granted:

> But, then, will his Lordship have the kindness to tell me, where would be the Church, not only in his diocese, but in all Wales, at the present moment, were it not for these men? Let him set these men on one side, and the clergy of an inferior [sic, superior?] origin on the other; let him ask whose churches have any congregation in them, and whose churches have not? Would there be any congregation at all in his diocese, or in any other diocese where Welsh is spoken, if it were not for these men of a *low* social position? Granted that many of them are rough, coarse, uneducated, you may say, and rude in their manners; still, they are the salt that has not lost its savour, and without them the Church in Wales would have descended to a lower depth still. I have the greatest respect

> possible for that class of clergy whom his lordship would fain see prevalent amongst us. Some of them are my best friends and intimates. They are everything that gentlemen and scholars and parish priests ought to be. They are laborious in their calling, anxious to do their duty, painstaking, and would be all that one can desire, were it not that they *lack one thing* and that is everything, - *a knowledge of the language of the people amongst whom they labour*. They have a bastard kind of knowledge, but not the knowledge sufficient to fill churches and save souls.

If the lower grade of clergy were inferior in other respects, yet they fulfilled "the necessities of the case better than the others do." The Church could not live without these men, and if their pulpits ceased "to resound in the land but for one year, ... the ... Welsh Church is throttled."[40] It was these men who managed to ensure that the Welsh Church remained intact after the Methodist secession of 1811, and whose ministry enabled the Church to survive and even compete with Nonconformity in the great industrial and valley parishes of the diocese of Llandaff.[41] Dean Edwards was at one with John Griffith in this respect. A clergy drawn from the lower middle and working classes would "influence the masses of people more powerfully than a Clergy who have only a professional acquaintance with their social atmosphere."[42]

Griffith went on to maintain that these Welsh clergy were seen as an underclass, to be "mere Ecclesiastical Helots", never to rise "above the condition of battered, ill-used, Clerical Serfs". The better livings, the honours of the Church, were denied them, so what encouragement did they have to "render themselves more accomplished, better educated, and better dressed", when a puddler in an iron works was better paid and sometimes better housed than these men.[43] Speaking at the Church Congress held at Swansea in 1879, Thomas Walters openly condemned the treatment of these "native clergy" by the Establishment. Its great Welsh preachers, such as Parry of Llywel or John Griffiths of Llandeilo, had received no recognition from their bishops, even though their preaching talents had raised the profile of the Church amongst Nonconformity and within the nation.[44]

THE LACK OF FINANCE
We have already identified that many Welsh-speaking men, or their families, were unable to provide a reasonable education for them, let alone a university course. It has

been suggested that it was the fathers who were the operative factors, for it was they who determined how the family finances would be used, and how much could or would be spent on a son's education if he was destined for Holy Orders, whether by his own choice or that of his father.[45] Rowland Williams suggested in 1851 that "[t]he first question of a Cardiganshire farmer is, whether he shall make his son a preacher of any denomination; and the next, what is the smallest expense at which the object can be effected."[46] Dean Edwards remembered the case of an avowed atheist who spent his savings in educating his son for Orders. Asked why he did so with his particular views, he replied he had "simply regarded the matter as an investment."[47] On the other hand parents, as noted earlier, would discourage their sons from seeking Orders if the future rewards were minimal, and they had to face the hardships, privations and disappointments of trying to obtain their own livings.[48]

Williams' concern regarding the minimum cost was echoed by many in Wales and beyond.[49] Ollivant, who had as vice-principal at Lampeter seen the position at first hand, believed that the outlay for the purpose was restricted within the "narrowest possible means" that was compatible with the attainment of their object. This meant taking a two-year course at some English institution like St Bees rather than the three-year course at Lampeter, designed with the Welsh Church in mind. It was a temptation that was inflicting a great evil "upon us", but the demand for Welsh candidates was such that the bishops were obliged to accept these St Bees' men, even though they fell below the desired standard.[50] He was not alone in his concern. It was shared by Campbell of Bangor and Basil Jones of St Davids.[51]

There was an equal concern about the number of men who were unable to afford the costs of training and thus lost to the Church. Eliezer Williams, preaching in 1807, argued that those who had little more than wealth and descent to recommend them had long been admitted to Orders, while those who had nothing besides their own merits were excluded.[52] His sentiments were repeated by many over that century. In 1882 Chancellor Phillips of St Davids argued that many suitable men were lost through a want of means, while Arthur Henderson, vicar of St John's, Cardiff, told the Llandaff Diocesan Conference in 1902 that there was no dearth of men wishing to be ordained, but what many of these men lacked was the necessary "cash qualification."[53] William Davey, presumably from his own experience at Lampeter, spoke of the possible ordination candidate who had to be withdrawn unwillingly from school in order to enter secular employment because his family's means had been strained to the utmost. With the prospect of an immediate occupation and an income in life he would never return to his earlier hopes.[54]

There were many who believed the Church needed to provide assistance to these candidates and expressed concern that many such men, deterred from Orders by reason of expense, would become Nonconformist ministers. Thirlwall of St Davids spoke in his 1848 Charge of those men of great promise who excluded from the service of the Church were "induced reluctantly to dedicate their talents to the cause of dissent."[55] Campbell of Bangor suggested that such men were likely "to dissent from our communion" if no adequate field for the exercise of their gifts was available in the Church.[56] Thomas Walters claimed he knew many men who had become Dissenting ministers because they found no other way open for them in their desire to preach to their fellow men.[57] Dean Edwards noted the contrast between "the naturally and eloquent son of a small farmer" or tradesman who was unable to be ordained because he and his friends had "no command of money", and "the dull, ungifted son of a neighbour" whose father scraped together some £200 or £300 to enable him to have the minimum training possible and who because of the shortage of clergy was able "to command the *forced* leniency of the Bishops' chaplains. Into what channel does that other youth throw his energies?" he asked. "Supported at some Dissenting college by the contributions of Dissenting congregations, he is in due time enabled to devote his energies, with an embittered spirit, to the irregular ministry of the Nonconformist pulpit, and to do much to weaken the influence of the Church which has practically denied him any sphere of usefulness." These men, he noted, had been endowed with gifts and powers of oratory that made them the natural teachers of the people. By this neglect, the Church had lost "the powerful forces of Welsh oratory, and of Welsh popular literature", and thereby, he hinted, almost lost the nation.[58] The fact that the Nonconformists would provide the finances for training if a man could not afford it added fuel to the fire.[59] Not only was that training free, stated John Griffith, it was also practical, and the students were sent out week by week to supply local pulpits and so gain valuable experience in preaching.[60] The Church needed to learn from its Nonconformist brethren.

For those who endeavoured to obtain the necessary finances sacrifice was all too often the order of the day. R.H. Parry tells the story of a fellow pupil at Pwllheli Grammar School, probably in the early 1900s, at a time when more scholarships were available than previously. In school he had received a tuition scholarship, and then gained a £30 scholarship to Aberystwyth University College. It was insufficient. His widowed mother sold her home and took rooms in Aberystwyth to assist him. He did well, gaining a scholarship to Oxford and winning the major Greek prize of the university, later becoming principal of a theological college. His name was not disclosed.[61]

A traditional route for obtaining the necessary finances for training was in school teaching, some finding work as an assistant in a church school, or even, before the days of National Schools, opening a small school of their own. One such man was David Rowlands, who died in 1820 having been appointed shortly before as vicar of Tregaron. Born the son of a poor glover, he opened a number of small schools at Tregaron and Llangeitho to obtain some of the money he needed to enter Ystrad Meurig College, and then tutoring pupils in his holidays in order to defray his expenses.[62] James Jones Morgan, writing in 1800, was acting as schoolmaster at Dolgellau in order to pay his debts to Jesus College, thus enabling him to take his degree and enter Holy Orders.[63] John Hughes, later archdeacon of Cardigan, who died in 1860, became an assistant master at a school in Putney in the hope of paying his way to Oxford. Unfortunately, he failed in his task, but was ordained as a literate by Bishop Cleaver of St Asaph in 1811.[64] Bishop Burgess, having found some monies to award candidates for Orders in his diocese, made it clear in his Charge of 1813 that he would not allow any of these men to keep a school. He emphasised that it was a great hindrance to the acquisition of their professional knowledge when they were engaged in the charge of instructing others before their own education had been completed. His exhibitions, which contributed a large portion of the expense of their education, were meant to enable them to continue in education until they were twenty-three, and thus left no excuse for such employment.[65]

Another method used to obtain finance for a theological training was to serve as a stipendiary lay assistant or reader in a parish. This became quite common by the early 1900s. It was an arrangement which offered these men practical experience, a curate's assistance with their academic preparation, and enabled them to find some of the monies required for their college expenses. Daniel Richards was one such man. Before he entered Lampeter for its biennial course in 1913, he had acted as a stipendiary lay reader in the parish of Pontypridd, earning twenty-five shillings a week, taking charge of the Welsh congregation, and receiving tuition from one of the curates. He had previously worked as a baker's roundsman.[66]

A number of individuals received assistance from friends or patrons. A number of Welsh literary clergymen, who had won eisteddfod competitions in their younger days, were recipients of funds organised by well-wishers to enable them to proceed to university or college preparatory to ordination. Amongst them were Evan Evans (Ieuan Glan Geirionydd, 1795-1855), who entered St Bees College, and John Blackwell (1797-1840) who studied at Jesus College. Both undertook preparatory studies at Berriew School under Thomas Richards.[67] Sarah Thomas wrote to Lord Bute's agent in 1848, pointing out that his lordship was assisting her son at Cowbridge Grammar School and that he was destined for the Church. She requested payment as she depended on it, especially as this son was about to advance to the divinity class and the fees were presumably higher. Ten pounds was authorised, to cover a fee of £15.[68] The vicar of Llanwnog, John James Ellis, ordained in 1886, having started life as a quarryman, had been tutored by John Owen, later bishop of St Davids, and won an exhibition of £10, probably to Lampeter. The parishioners of Llandegai organised a concert for his benefit which raised £40, and John Owen, then principal of Lampeter, persuaded Lord Penrhyn to pay for his college course.[69]

Not all candidates for ordination were in such a fortunate position. It was believed that the average Welsh boy had only one third of the educational endowments available to him compared to an average English boy,[70] and most of the closed university exhibitions and scholarships were said to have been confined to north Wales, although Cowbridge had a few at Jesus College, Oxford.[171] In addition, the sizarships or servitorships at the universities, by which a man received a free education in return for domestic duties rendered, were becoming obsolete by the turn of the nineteenth century, as we note later. The Powis exhibitions, established in memory of the earl of Powis who had master-minded the campaign to prevent the uniting of the two northern sees, offered a four-year scholarship of £60 per annum at one of the universities, but required candidates to sit an examination in classical languages and Welsh.[72] There were clerical societies in England that assisted men, mainly evangelicals, for their university course, but there was nothing similar in Wales.[73]

By the 1850s there were scholarships and exhibitions available at Lampeter, though to obtain one required a better educational background than the majority of its students had received. It is not surprising, therefore, that one of the major difficulties in Wales was not so much as providing the funding for a university education, though that did come into the equation, but rather for the licensed grammar schools and later for the preliminary training required to prepare a man for entry to Lampeter or to some other college. Robert Roberts, *Y Sgolor Mawr,* when teaching at Ruthin in 1855, faced an acute dilemma. He had no hope of an exhibition and was too old for a servitorship at one of the universities, his savings were insufficient for even the cheapest theological college, and how could he possibly borrow money when he could not afford to repay it on a curate's stipend?[74] Again and again the need for such financial provision was stated in visitation charges and at diocesan conferences.[75] Sir Henry Reichel, principal of University College, Bangor, expressed his concern as late as 1908 that far too often for want of finances a boy, preparing for university or Lampeter, had to do so within the restraints of a secular job, as his parents could not afford to keep him in school. As a result, many entered college at an older age, and had to "grapple painfully" with work a teenage boy would have readily accomplished in school.[76]

The first initiative came through Bishop Burgess. The fourth object of the Church Union Society established by his initiative in the diocese of St Davids was to promote clerical education. This objective would be achieved by the building of a seminary where men could be trained for the ministry of the Welsh Church. He resolved, however, not to commence building it until a sum of £2,000 had been obtained. Knowing that one great defect in the education of young men for Orders was their inability to remain in a school long enough to acquire the learning required of them, due to financial restraints, he allowed the interest arising on the money already obtained for his college to be used in offering twenty exhibitions of £10 per annum to those attending the licensed grammar schools of the diocese, thus allowing them eight years of education.[77] Presumably, these exhibitions continued until St David's College was opened in 1827.

The next initiative came significantly from the diocese of Llandaff, and came many years later, by which time that diocese was relying more and more on literates to supply its continuing demand for clergy. The Llandaff Church Extension Society, as it became known, was established during Ollivant's first year as bishop, and was designed to raise funds for the church's mission in that diocese whose population had more than doubled in thirty years, and where townships had risen where there was once barren land. Part of its remit was to provide exhibitions for those studying at the various grammar schools in the diocese who wished to proceed to St David's College.

Five exhibitions were made available at this college, two of £25, two of £20, and one of £10, tenable for three and a half years. These were awarded competitively to those who had spent two years at a grammar school in the diocese, and whose proficiency in Welsh had been tested and whose classical learning had been examined. In 1851 three of these exhibitions had been gained by pupils of Cowbridge School. Unfortunately, the funds were insufficient to award any new exhibitions after 1859, though they were re-established in 1871, but were now restricted to those undertaking preparatory work before entering Lampeter. A sum of £100 was made available for this purpose to award exhibitions not exceeding £20, conditional upon satisfactory progress and ability in the Welsh language. If more applied than funds permitted, then a competitive examination would be held. Candidates were not to be over the age of eighteen unless they were serving an apprenticeship as pupil teachers. The rules were gradually tightened though more finance was made available, so that by 1876 these exhibitions were restricted to Welsh-speaking youths aged between fifteen and eighteen, and were available at Cowbridge, Ystrad Meurig and Llandovery and other schools as approved, to prepare them for Lampeter or the universities with a view to taking Orders. Lasting for three years, and not exceeding £20 per annum, they were available by competitive examination involving a knowledge of Latin and Greek, of the Bible and doctrines of the Church, general intelligence, and an ability to speak and write both English and Welsh.

In addition to these exhibitions, there were also concessions available for those who held them, such as half fees at Cowbridge, while the warden of Llandovery made clear that his total fees were only six pounds and so above the amount of the exhibition, and school prizes and scholarships could easily make up the difference. There were also restricted university exhibitions available from some of these schools. John Griffith argued a man could pay his way by obtaining one of the Meyrick scholarships at Jesus College, or one of the numerous scholarships at Lampeter of between £30 and £50 per annum, together with one of the diocesan grants.[78] It appears that the diocesan funding ran out by 1878 and these exhibitions were discontinued.[79]

The revival of these Llandaff exhibitions in 1871 was a direct result of a remarkable conference held at Llanidloes in 1870, which had consequences for the other dioceses as well. It was apparently organised, or at least well-publicised, by John Griffith of Merthyr, following his public appeal in the *Western Mail* for clergy and lay, north and south, to come together to discuss the "crisis" in the supply of men for the Ministry of the Welsh Church. There were many young men who would be good candidates for ordination provided they had the financial resources required. Such men needed assistance not only to pay for a theological college training, at Lampeter or elsewhere, or for a university education, but also for their preliminary training in the existing grammar schools, such as Ystrad Meurig, Lampeter, Dolgellau and Llandovery, all of which had been invigorated by new masters. He considered that fifty boarders at Ystrad Meurig would hardly cost £1,000 per annum, and yet it could produce twenty lads annually "well trained and well-educated". If that sum seemed impossible, they might consider that Nonconformists were able to find £20,000 to establish one of their colleges. The result of the meeting was a resolution that each diocese should endeavour to provide exhibitions of between £20 and £25 for four years for suitable boys of promise of fifteen years of age towards the cost of their preliminary training, and further grants for four years for those attending a college such as Lampeter or one of the universities, or undertaking ministerial training. These expectations were far too high and were only partly achieved.

Dean Edwards, probably elaborating upon these concerns, suggested that a Diocesan Clergy Fund be established in each diocese, and each should appoint a board of examiners, "to examine and test not only the knowledge and intelligence, but also the other necessary ministerial aptitudes of youths desirous of being prepared for the ministry." Edwards believed each diocese could readily raise £1,000 for this work, maintaining 40 students at school and college, and allowing five "talented and well instructed candidates for Holy Orders" to present themselves each year in each diocese. Such a supply would enable bishops to reject candidates not duly qualified, and significantly raise the standard of clerical education. Furthermore, the recipients of this scheme would be drawn from the working classes and help "conciliate to the Church, by the workings of a popular ministry, the sympathy of the masses, and make her truly, what in many parishes she now is only in name, the Church of the people." The suggestion of a central council of all the Welsh dioceses was ignored, and the provision of spiritual training in theology previous to admission to Orders was neglected by all but one diocese.[80]

This diocese was Bangor, which like St Asaph before it, was now aware it needed to recruit men from another class of society than it had done hitherto. As a result of this conference, and Dean Edwards' powerful persuasions, the Bangor Clerical Education Society was formed. Its brief was almost identical to that proposed at the Llanidloes conference. In his 1872 Visitation Charge Campbell outlined the purposes and philosophy behind its origin. Those men already in grammar schools were probably able to obtain exhibitions at university and even if they had to struggle they could pave their way without the help of the society. His concern was with those who were shut out of Orders by want of educational advantages, who might well be tempted to become dissenters for the lack of an adequate field for the exercise of their gifts, and who would be found more in parishes than in schools, and who, he hinted, were already involved in parochial life. By 1875 he was encouraged as the superior efficiency of the grammar schools was beginning to be felt, so raising the standards of education and therefore the future tone of ministry. His 1878 Charge indicated a change in the rules of the Society occasioned by the realisation that it had been putting a disappropriate stress on educational as opposed to spiritual qualifications. These grants, Campbell noted in 1881, were never intended to assist those who had the means to educate themselves.

Dean Edwards is said to have raised £700 each year for the work of this society, and by 1884 it had assisted some of the most promising of the diocese's candidates to the English universities. These men, said Campbell in his 1884 charge, needed to receive preferential treatment in their own diocese, for its grantees were required to serve within it, and it was unfair to them and to the means taken by the Dean in cultivating and improving their gifts, if incumbents wanting curates advertised outside the diocese for them. By 1910 the scheme had given over 100 clergy to the diocese. The mention of the Dean's work above related to a scheme he devised for these men during their vacations, accommodating them in Bangor itself, allowing additional coaching in their theological, pastoralia and bilingual education, and enabling them to assist in the daily services of the cathedral. Particular attention was given to the reading of Welsh and the delivery of sermons "in a way that would be acceptable to the Welsh ear".[81] This work was continued, in a sense, by the creation of a Church Hostel at Bangor in 1886, which not only provided for Anglican students at the university college, but also for ordinands, with the warden offering them additional courses and practical training, in addition to continuing the so-called "summer gathering" of exhibitioners.[82]

The Church Hostel was a joint venture with the diocese of St Asaph, which had also established a similar society by 1871 for the assistance of "young men of promise but of limited means" in their preparation for Holy Orders. Called the Church

Extension Society it offered five college exhibitions of £20 per annum and three school exhibitions of £15 each. These were held by young men at Llandovery, Ystrad Meurig and Friar's School, Bangor, respectively. In 1874 seventeen candidates had presented themselves for examination, most of whom would have been eligible for assistance had the funds been available.[83] By 1906 the two dioceses were working together, and in that year St Asaph had six exhibitioners at Oxford colleges and three at schools, and Bangor had two at Oxford, three at Lampeter and four at Bangor. Between 1902-06, 25 exhibitions had been awarded.[84]

Although there was an Ordination Candidates Exhibition Fund for the Church of England, founded in the 1870s by the Assistant Curates' Society, which was only able to assist 33 out of 95 applicants in 1883, it is not known if it gave any assistance to men from the four Welsh dioceses.[85] But these Welsh schemes appear to be the first established by any diocese within the established Church, and although their work was restricted, it was nevertheless extremely significant. It was not until a resolution of the 1908 Lambeth Conference that each diocese should set up an ordination candidates' fund that most English dioceses did so, as did the diocese of Llandaff, thus resuming an activity that had been discontinued for thirty odd years.[86] I have failed to find any trace of such a fund in St Davids diocese. The disestablished Church in Wales set up its own scheme, administered by a central body but activated by diocesan committees. Thirty such scholarships were available for the whole province, ranging from between £40 to £100 per annum, of which the diocese of St Asaph had five. Competition was fierce, the examination taxing, as weight was given to a knowledge of Greek and Latin, and in 1930 it was said there were five candidates for every place available. Many did not come up to the standard required, mainly because many of the secondary schools in Wales did not teach Greek and sometimes not even Latin. It appears that the St Asaph Clerical Education Committee had retained its own exhibitions, but in 1935 it decided, in line with the diocese of St Davids, to award no more of its own exhibitions save, perhaps, at the end of training, but instead to offer a similar loan scheme to that of the county education authorities. Yet the old problems still remained, for there was still difficulty in obtaining Welsh-speaking candidates whose other qualifications were "satisfactory".[87]

THE ORDINANDS

The background and origins of the Welsh clergy, especially those from the two southern dioceses, was generally far different from the average English diocese, apart from those of the northern province, particularly the dioceses of Carlisle and Chester. A study of the diocese of Canterbury revealed that between 1750-80 the number of those from a plebeian background diminished in favour of those from gentry, clerical and professional backgrounds.[88] Between 1782-1808 there were 532 incumbents in the diocese of Worcester. Of those who could be identified 205 were gentry sons, 122 clergy sons, and 62 came from a plebeian background, 63 were literate and 448 university men.[89] By comparison in the diocese of Durham those ordained in the periods 1810-30 and 1900-20 were compared. The number from gentry families declined from 21.8% to 5.9%, those from clerical families from 44.9% to 23%, and those from the skilled working class increased from 7.7% to 26.4%.[90] Conybeare estimated in 1852 that of 100 clergy taken at random from the diocese of Bangor, clergy sons accounted for 29, gentry sons 30, sons of farmers and tradesmen 41. He believed the proportion in St Asaph to be the same, and thus claimed that two fifths of the north Wales clergy were from the lower classes, though probably a third of this number had received a university education, possibly as servitors at Jesus College. This, he noted, did not apply to south Wales where he felt that the majority of clergy came from a *gwerin* background.[91] In most dioceses the clergy were born within it or in a neighbouring one, as was the case in all the Welsh dioceses save for Llandaff, where in Glamorgan less than half of its clerical strength were natives of that county.[93] Jacob, who quotes these figures, also notes that in England many clergy came from urban rather than rural areas.[94] Again in Wales most candidates tended to be older than those from English dioceses, mainly because they entered college at a later age, due to the need to find secular employment to obtain the finances required for their training.[84] John Griffith maintained, however, that before Lampeter was opened, youngsters were often intended for the ministry from an early age, and were educated accordingly from boyhood to manhood, with parents holding no other object before their view. It was not for them, as was often the case at the present time, that the desire for ordination was an "after-thought".[95]

THE SOCIAL BACKGROUND

The scarcity of gentry sons has been noted already,[96] as has John Jones' remark of 1768 that because the Principality was separate from the metropolis Welsh families had little connection with those men of influence who could further the careers of their sons in commerce, the armed forces, or law. As a result, he argued that many gentry families brought up their eldest son to succeed to the family estate, and the second was sent to the University in order to be ordained. though he went on to state that many fathers, knowing that preferment was by interest rather than merit, felt it unwise to pay for a university education when their future reward might be a petty curacy of £20 or so.[97] The dioceses of St Asaph and Bangor continued to recruit such men, however, and in a sample of those 58 clerics instituted to benefices between 1750 and 1850 in the two deaneries of Pool in Montgomeryshire and Rhos in Denbighshire, 39 were university men (69%), and of the few whose backgrounds were identified by D.R. Thomas, 12 (20%) came from gentry families and five (8.6%) from clerical families.[98] Thomas's figures for the sons of clergy are probably accurate, that for gentry may be an underestimate. The diocese of Llandaff also had a number of gentry-clerics, who were the subject of Bishop Copleston's forceful and disparaging comments,[99] and Pembrokeshire also boasted of a number of gentlemen-parsons or squarsons.[100] By the 1850s the situation had changed, and might be summed up by the plea of *A Pauper Clergyman* who wrote a pamphlet in 1857 in which he noted a letter written by Bishop Short of St Asaph to the Marquess of Westminster. In this letter the bishop wrote that their school contemporaries who were ordained were already possessed of a private fortune, as was true for himself. But now, he added, this no longer applied and those entering Holy Orders would be found poorer than their contemporaries.[101]

A second category, already noted, comprised the sons of clergymen. This group always comprised a reasonably large percentage of those who were ordained, as noted above, and over the whole Church it was estimated that in the eighteenth century about a quarter to a third of the clergy were sons of the clergy.[102] By the 1850s there was concern about their diminishing number. Bishop Short wrote that the sons of the clergy rarely took Orders in the Welsh Church, and when they did, they were "not apt to show any great proficiency" in their native language, for it was "seldom spoken at home by the children of those above the rank of farmers."[103] The situation became even more acute by 1900, for as Bishop Edwards of St Asaph pointed out, the poverty of the clergy made it impossible for them to educate their sons for Orders. There were many such sons who had grown up in surroundings conducive to turning their thoughts to ordination, but who had been forced to give up in despair.[104]

There still remained some clerical dynasties, where sons had followed their fathers for two and more generations into the service of the Church. Bishop Edwards, whose comment is noted above, came from one such family. His father, William, was one of three brothers who were ordained, and he himself was one of five brothers who took Holy Orders.[105] Others were the Allens', the three sons of a Pembrokeshire rector. One, James, became dean of St Davids and another, John, was archdeacon of Salop, who died in 1886.[106] One example may suffice for the many clerical dynasties that came from the diocese of St Davids. This was the family of Thomas Davies of the Factory, Llansawel, in Carmarthenshire, whose four sons (the eldest was born in 1838) and four grandsons were ordained, while a descendant of the family claimed that it had produced over twenty-five clergymen over four generations, though this included sons-in-law![107]

A number of men who came from professional backgrounds may be noted as well, although their number was not substantial. In 1910 Canon Johnson, warden of St Michael's Theological College, Llandaff, that catered mainly for post-graduate training, bemoaned the fact that of 260 men who had been trained at that place, there had been hardly any whose fathers were in the professions with the single exception of clergymen. He appealed to tradesmen to offer their sons because the Church, wishing to minister to all classes of society, needed to draw from all its classes, from lower to upper.[108] Within the wider Church a number of men were ordained from a professional background, including Walsham How, the son of a prosperous Shrewsbury solicitor; while others were ordained after serving in one of the professions, such as William Thomas, vicar of Llangynwyd, Glamorgan, 1829-46, who had been an army ensign before proceeding to Jesus College and ordination; Edward Burnard Squire, vicar of Swansea 1846-76, had served as an officer in the Indian Navy, and John Evans, archdeacon of Merioneth, had commenced his career as a solicitor.[109]

It has been noted that the Llandaff Church Extension Society gave grants to those preparing for Orders up to a certain age, but exempted from this age limit those who were apprenticed as pupil teachers.[110] Nevertheless, many men were ordained into the Welsh dioceses who had been trained as schoolmasters. In fact, there had been many such students before that date. William Price, in analysing the 306 students at Lampeter between 1865-78 found that ten had been national schoolmasters, and others had attended training colleges.[111] Frances Knight notes that a large proportion of the 50 men ordained in 1874-5 had been schoolmasters or tutors before ordination.[112] In one ordination of 1875 in the diocese of St Davids two of the twelve ordained came into this category.[113] The historian of Trinity College, Carmarthen, a church training college for teachers, found that by 1887 twenty-five of its former students had been ordained, many leaving that college in order to study at Lampeter.[114] One of these men was J.A. Jackson, who after being head of the Pwllheli National School, entered Lampeter in 1868, and was later diocesan inspector for schools in the diocese of St Asaph. His biographer recorded that a previous vice-principal of Lampeter, Rowland Williams, had alleged that the education received at these training colleges was an excellent preparation for the Lampeter course.[115] It has even been suggested that the biennial course at Lampeter had been established in 1884 for elementary schoolmasters who wished to be ordained.[116]

Two other examples may be noted. Elias Owen, a noted historian and one of three brothers who were ordained, started his career as a pupil teacher before winning a Queen's Scholarship to Culham College, became headmaster of Llanllechid School, before proceeding to Trinity College, Dublin from which he graduated in 1871.[117] The most noted example was the unfortunate Robert Roberts, *Y Sgolor Mawr*, who trained at the Church training college at Caernarfon, and became schoolmaster at Castle Caereinion, Llanllechid, Amlwch and Ruthin, and was much involved in the lay life of the diocese of Bangor, before entering St Bees College in 1857 to be ordained two years later.[118]

A number of those ordained were the sons of artisans. Thomas Price, better known as *Carnhuanawc,* one of the Welsh literary clerics, was the son of a stonemason who was himself later ordained in 1787.[119] John Griffith, already mentioned on many occasions, was the son of a maltster, though in sufficient prosperous circumstances for his son to somewhat elevate his position.[120] Thomas Walters, already noted, was the son of a shoemaker, but rose to become lord of a manor.[121] Edward Thomas, vicar of Skewen until his death in 1897, had been brought up as a weaver, probably in a family business.[122]

The Llandaff Diocesan Conference of 1902 heard T. Jesse Jones describe how a young man from Bedlinog, D. Edwardes Davies, who had been brought up as a collier, had worked at his calling to find the finances for his course at Durham, having been tutored by a neighbouring curate. He was later bishop of Bangor. Five years later the same speaker proudly related how men from his mining parish of Gelligaer had been ordained after much sacrifice, having worked as colliers, a blacksmith and as a draper's assistant.[123] Griffith Edwards, rector of Llangadfan, Montgomeryshire, who died in 1893, started life as a quarryman, following his father, but was another cleric who managed to take his degree at Dublin.[124]

There was some bitterness expressed about the ordination of men who came from these commercial and artisan backgrounds, with what justification is not known, though Lady Llanover believed they were attracted by the "loaves and fishes" of the Church. At the Leeds Church Congress of 1872 John Griffith complained about those men who had emerged from such colleges at St Bees or Birmingham, or those who were literates, stating that they were often below the mark. They had not thought of Orders until late in life and as failed businessmen believed the Church would offer them better prospects. Dean Edwards is said to have referred to men who had failed in every trade who had crept into the ministry of the Church, while Lemuel James suggested to the 1904 Llandaff Diocesan Conference that when men who wished to enter the medical, legal, teaching or civil service failed their examinations they took Holy Orders.[125] The same complaint had been made a century and a half earlier by Erasmus Saunders, who complained about the men admitted to Orders to serve as cheap curates who had been previously schoolmasters, a gentleman's butler, and even a mounteback.[126]

THE MEN FROM CARMARTHENSHIRE AND CARDIGANSHIRE

In all probability the majority of those ordained into the Welsh Church, especially in the southern dioceses, came from farming stock, a class that William Davey considered laboured "under special disadvantages, both socially and from an educational point of view".[127] By far the greatest proportion of them men came from Cardiganshire and to a lesser extent Carmarthenshire. These were the *gwerin* clergy or those who came from the peasant classes. Bishop Burgess's apocryphal Cardiganshire ploughboy ordained at the age of twenty-three after a year's training at Ystrad Meurig would be of this background.[128] Bishop Basil Jones of St Davids in his 1880 Charge referred to the fact that all who knew the Church in Wales were aware that the county of Cardiganshire supplied a larger percentage of its clergy, especially those who were most acceptable to the Welsh people.[129]

This had been true since the eighteenth century. Bishop Horsley's domestic chaplain, W.H. Holcombe wrote to Isaac Williams of Llanrhystud in 1788: "So your countrymen are at their old tricks again. Half our titles of deacons from Cardiganshire. I could wish from my soul that the gentlemen of your county were less given to smuggling and divinity."[130] Rowland Williams asserted in 1850 that the first question a Cardiganshire farmer asked, in relation to his family, was whether he should make his son a preacher of any denomination, and what was the smallest amount required to effect his desire.[131] John Griffith referred to the county as "the Levitical county of Wales", and noted that one of its parishes with a population of less than 1,000 had produced 32 clergymen then actively serving in the Church.[132] The parishes of Llanrhystud with its 1,600 population produced 56 clergymen between 1820-90, and that of Llansawel, Carmarthenshire, a smaller parish, 29 over a similar period.[133] In the first seven years of J.J.S. Perowne's vice-principalship at Lampeter, 1862-9, 170 students had entered Lampeter. Sixty-one were from Cardiganshire and twenty-nine from Carmarthenshire (52% in all), while between 1892-97, during the principalship of John Owen, 100 of its 216 students (46%) – most of whom were destined for Orders – came from these two counties.[134] D. Gwynfor Lewis noted as late as 1954 that Cardiganshire clergy were found in nearly every deanery in Wales, and in his own deanery of 19 clerics eight had come from the "south".[135] This is hardly surprising for, as a letter writer in the *Western Mail* of 1870 wrote, the Welsh-speaking areas of the diocese of St Davids could not absorb them and so many migrated to north Wales, but he concluded it was a mystery how one county could produce so many clergymen.[136]

Some of these men who came from this *gwerin* Cardiganshire stock became distinguished leaders within the Church in Wales. One may be noted. David Jones, a farm labourer of Llangeitho, having prepared himself for entry to Lampeter, graduated, and migrated to the north, where he became vicar of Dwygyfylchi (or Penmaenmawr), and a prominent evangelical and diocesan figure. He died in 1909.[137] Evan E. Thomas, later rector of Marchwiel, in his novel *Where Eagles Fly,* wrote about a Cardiganshire cleric moving to the easy pastures of Montgomeryshire, and finding life much easier there than the hard life he had been accustomed to, when families denied themselves the very necessities of life in order to keep sons in school and to send them to college to become parsons.[138] These men were often rough and ready, and it is hardly surprising that there was often considerable criticism about their lack of social graces and their style of ministry. John Guest, a leading ironmaster, who built a church at Dowlais in 1823 for his working force, feared the appointment of a Cardiganshire man who might carelessly perform the duties of his office.[139] He might have had in mind some of the nonconformist tendencies of these men, for many came from Methodist stock, as we note in the concluding sub-section of this chapter.

A NONCONFORMIST BACKGROUND

The letter writer of 1870 who concluded it was a mystery how so many clergymen came from Cardiganshire, when that county was a stronghold of Welsh Methodism, might have been unaware of the extent to which many of its young men, brought up in Methodism, turned to the Church and successfully sought Holy Orders. It might almost be said that we cannot understand the nineteenth century Welsh Church without taking this phenomenon into account. It was remarked upon again and again, and became such a source of embarrassment to some Nonconformist leaders, especially during the disestablishment campaigns, that they sought to minimise its impact.

At the start of that campaign, Bishop Hughes of St Asaph argued that the claim of "deep seated hostility to the Church of their Fathers" was absurd, considering that so many men brought up in Nonconformity had found the means to be ordained in that Church. In that same year E.O. Phillips claimed that a large proportion of the younger clergy of the Church were the sons of dissenters, and as a result their parents were no longer opposed to the Church. Archdeacon Ffoulkes believed the Church had been strengthened when members of the working class, often dissenters, could say they had a son or brother who was a clergyman. Lord Dynevor, a cleric himself, observed in 1884 that many of the tenant farmers known to him had sons, brothers and other family relations who were clergymen, and while they themselves remained Nonconformists, they had no wish to disendow those relatives of whom they were proud.[140] There are numerous references to farmers, mainly but not exclusively from Cardiganshire, who while Nonconformists, endeavoured to bring up at least one son to the ministry of the Church.[141] In a satirical comment *Draig Glas* suggested their reasoning was that if you are spending hard-earned money on education for your son the Church offered better prospects and social status than the Nonconformist ministry, while it would be "a pity to cast such a finished pearl before the Nonconformist herd".[142] Lord Aberdare (H.A. Bruce) commented that doctrinal differences sat lightly on such people who believed that bringing "a son into the Ministry of the Church" was "a matter of business."[143]

The number of such men were clearly substantial, though when the question was asked about their number during the Royal Commission of 1911 the answer was returned that though the number was "many" or "considerable" it had never been enumerated.[144] From what figures are available, though chosen at random, the number in the two southern dioceses could be as high as one quarter to two fifths of those ordained in the second half of the nineteenth century.[145] Although the numbers seemed to have become substantial by the 1840s, or even a little earlier, there are indications that beforehand dissenters had been ordained. Dr Williams, headmaster of Cowbridge School, which held a divinity department, was accustomed to re-baptise those baptised by a dissenting minister, before they presented their papers to the bishop as candidates for ordination.[146] In 1847 it was reported that the Church was held in such high respect in Cardiganshire that many wealthy Nonconformists had brought up their sons to be clergymen. In an area twelve miles around Aberystwyth about thirty clergymen had come from such homes.[147]

Many observed that it was not unusual in one family for one son to be ordained and the other to be a Nonconformist minister.[148] This position, suggested Vincent in his *Letters from Wales* might well cause jealousy between the two brothers, as the social privileges obtained by the one were denied to the other.[149] The Cardiganshire farmer, wrote W.J. Wallis-Jones, was sufficiently shrewd to ensure that the eldest son was sent into trade, the next to Lampeter to qualify for Orders at some moderate cost, and the third was sent to Aberystwyth College in the expectation that with numerous scholarships, and probably assistance from his denomination, he might become a Nonconformist minister.[150]

The suggestion was made that the son chosen for the honour of ordination was not always the better candidate. H.C. Raikes, speaking at the Leeds Church Congress, described such a farmer with two sons whom he wished to push on in the world, both of whom were sincerely attached to religion. One had a deep desire to obtain influence over men leading to the salvation of souls, a fluency of speech and expression, a command of language, while his brother has less eloquence, less ambition, less activity of mind. The first is thus designated for the Nonconformist ministry, where his gifts will be recognised and rewarded. The second is ordained to become an "impeccable humdrum plodder" but with a certain income, a social advantage, and eventually a small benefice where he can use his small talents. He regretted the short-sighted policy of the bishops in making Lampeter the main feeder for the clergy of the Church, as it needed men of wider culture and more experience than farmers' sons could obtain in two or three years at that college.[151]

Nevertheless, some outstanding men entered the ministry of the Church from this background. Some examples would include Robert Jones, born in 1809 at Llanfyllin, and a member of an Independent chapel, served as curate of Connah's Quay before becoming vicar of All Saints' Church, Rotherhithe, and a leading member of the London Welsh community;[152] Daniel Evans, vicar of Caernarfon, and his brother Owen, warden of Llandovery College, who were the sons of a Calvinistic Methodist family which had "turned Church";[153] Grimaldi Davis, vicar of Welshpool and archdeacon of Montgomery, ordained in 1898, the son of a Blaenau Ffestiniog quarry worker who was brought up as a Welsh Methodist.[154] A further example is that of Stephen William Jenkins, ordained in 1878 after taking degrees at Lampeter and Oxford, and later rector of Oxwich, whose father was the renowned Baptist lay-preacher, Stephen Jenkins, whose exploits in the pulpit became part of the folk-lore of that denomination in Pembrokeshire.[155] A more recent example would be Euros Bowen, a crowned bard, who having studied for the Welsh Methodist ministry became an Anglican at Oxford and died in 1988 having served as a Merionethshire incumbent. Perhaps the two most important examples are David Howell, the son of an influential Welsh Methodist lay leader in Glamorgan, who regenerated the church in the parishes he served at Cardiff and Wrexham, dying as dean of St Davids in 1903,[156] and his bishop, John Owen, bishop of St Davids 1897-1926, who came from a similar background, though humbler, in Lleyn, Caernarfonshire.[157]

COMMENT AND CONCERN

The number of Methodist sons, even the sons of deacons and probably ministers, who were ordained into the Church, was sufficiently substantial to cause comment, concern and sometimes reprisals within that community. A newspaper letter of 1854 claimed that the Welsh Methodists in an attempt to prevent this loss were prepared to cashier any office holder in their denomination who brought up his son for the

Church. He did not believe this would stop the exodus, though he wondered if the Church benefited from it, for these men with their Methodist upbringing contributed to the Low Church nature of the Welsh Church.[158] These men, wrote "Towyn", were attracted to Church's ministry because their characters would not bear scrutiny for their own ministry, while the Church was seen as such an "easy and lazy life" that it was regarded as a secular calling. Such men, he continued, had abandoned the form of religion cherished by their parents and in which they had been brought up, with the result that the awful iniquity of dissent was forcibly brought to their conscience and pocket. Ambition beckoned: at Ystrad Meurig School "the morning star beamed upon his mind, in Lampeter the dappled dawn did rise, and in Jesus College, Oxford, the broad sunlight of perfect day shone into the chambers of his soul".[159]

The Nonconformist press made its own comments. Debates in *Y Goleuad* during the 1870s linked this secession with the lack of a settled pastoral ministry in the Welsh Methodist denomination, so that their elders who had sons drawn to the ministry felt that the ministry of their own church was far too precarious to offer a settled future for them. The result was that the number of these Nonconformist sons who had gone to the Church instead was "legion", too numerous to be counted, while those sons who had entered the ministry of their own denomination could be counted on the fingers of two hands. Other writers replied that those who so easily sacrificed the principles of the Connexion could be no asset to the Church of England, and in joining it were linking themselves to a body that ninety per cent of Wales regarded as an injustice. These men were "richly equipped with the grace of gullibility." Their motives were nothing more than social status and a good income, and it was impossible to believe that any could secede in the hope of obtaining a wider scope for ministry in the Church. Such men were no loss. Church officers who encouraged their sons into the ministry of the Church were a source of weakness to the denomination.[160]

The November 1886 of Thomas Gee's *Baner* warned: "[b]e it known to the swarms of curates who are brought up as Methodists and as Nonconformists in Cardiganshire and elsewhere that the days of the fatness of the Church are at an end". The *Genedl* of June in the same year argued that "The pulpits of the Church are filled with a flood of priests reared in the sheepfolds of the Dissenters, with men who follow the ways of Jeroboam, the son of Nebat, who made Israel to sin". These men were described as the prophets of Baal.[161] This was the time of a further flare up of the disestablishment controversy, and the Church's claim that the ordination of former Nonconformists indicated little hostility between Church and Nonconformity at a local level was deeply embarrassing to the latter. Furthermore, the argument that the Church was an English alien import was seriously weakened by the introduction of these Welsh-speakers into its ministry. David Davies of Penarth, an influential Baptist minister and writer, considered that the number of these men reflected little credit on the Church, as it showed it was unable to produce sufficient men of its own.[162]

It was also claimed that some of these men had been proselytised into the Church by local clergymen holding out inducements of educational advancement and social prestige. The father of Henry Richard, MP, Dr Edward Richard of Tregaron, refused to accept episcopal ordination being a Welsh Methodist, through pressed to do so by a relation of his wife, John Jones of Derry Ormond, whose influence in the Church would have secured him early preferment.[163] John Evans, Eglwys Bach, a leading preacher of the Wesleyan Methodists, was offered a pupil-teachership in his school by his vicar with the suggestion it could lead to Oxford and ordination.[164] It is hardly surprising that Thomas Ellis argued in 1885 that strong efforts were being made to attract Nonconformist university men into the Church by tempting them with promises and prospects.[165]

If these were the comments made about the sons of Nonconformist families entering the Church, we may well imagine that the strictures about those ministers who defected to the Church were even more severe. There were many. Chapel and parochial histories abound in instances where a minister left his charge and entered the Church to be subsequently ordained.[166] Some of these men were outstanding, such as Lodwick Edwards, ordained by Copleston, whose early death in 1856 brought to an end a ministry at Rhymney that laid the foundations of a vigorous Welsh-speaking Church,[167] and John Cunnick, formerly a Congregational minister at Aberdare. He resigned his pastorate in 1860 as a result of a split in the congregation, and was eventually ordained after a further pastorate at Gloucester. Later he became the Welsh secretary for the Church Pastoral-Aid Society.[168]

In the 1840s a complaint was made that Lampeter was being frequented by dissenting preachers who found a residence there was an easy way to promotion to the benefices of the Church without undergoing any change of sentiments. This was denied by Ollivant, then vice-principal, who made clear that between 1827-40 only four dissenting ministers had been admitted to the college, two of whom were serving in the diocese of Llandaff, one in Bangor, and another in Liverpool. One had printed and published a recantation of his former position, and the other had given oral satisfaction to the same effect.[169]

If the number of dissenting ministers who were ordained into the Church was said to be considerable,[170] (at one ordination in Llandaff in 1855 three of the six deacons were former Nonconformist ministers[171]), the number of those who were unsuccessful in their application for ordination was even more substantial. It was claimed by the bishop of Llandaff at the Rhyl Church Congress of 1891 that in eight years he had received forty such applications, some stating they wished to give up teaching what they now perceived to be errors and to enter into the true fold.[172] Dean Edwards alleged that there were "hundreds" of such letters in the possession of the bishops, and he had seen more than one in the last six months. He would not give names as otherwise these men would be persecuted.[173] Some were not up to the academic standard required, while others were unable to offer testimony that they had done nothing contrary to the doctrine and discipline of the Church for three years previously.[174] Possibly they had to bide their time, for Bishop Lewis of Llandaff required them to serve for some time as lay readers in populous parishes under selected incumbents before proceeding to training. In 1891 he had four such men, and another man at Lampeter.[175] These matters were frequently reported as a means of showing that many of the leaders of Nonconformity realised the superiority of the Church and its doctrinal and sacramental position, as against the "spurious ordinations" and ceremonies of dissent.[176]

It was hardly surprising that there were frequent protests about these claims, and that the ministers who had defected to the Church were thoroughly abused and their motives queried. After all, such secessions almost suggested that the validity of the nonconformist denominations was suspect. When Bishop Lewis of Llandaff stated in 1891 that several Welsh Methodist ministers had applied to him for ordination, the denomination's paper, *Y Goleuad,* published a solemn protest, signed by forty ministers, though one of them was later found to be one of these applicants, and taken before a "kangaroo" court, made the excuse that he was in ill health at that time. Principal Edwards of the Baptist College, Cardiff, replying to Bishop Edwards' assertion of 1898 that sixteen nonconformist ministers had applied to him for admission into the Church, argued he had drawn that number from his imagination, but then described such men, if they existed, as base traitors, hypocrites and cowards.[177]

R.H. Morgan (Towyn) claimed that the proselytising spirit of the Church enabled it to ordain nonconformist preachers and students without any proper enquiry into their lives and character or the reasons for their change of direction. Even if they were without reproach many simply wished to enter a profession that was regarded as an easy and lazy life. A footnote added that one minister who had been ordained had resigned rather than face charges of immorality, and another person, also ordained, had been rejected by the nonconformists because of ignorance.[178] David Davies of Penarth, though he conceded that some might have seceded for conscientious reasons, argued that many more did so because the Church was less competitive than dissent, for they had realised they had little change of succeeding against the more able men who entered the dissenting ministry. Such men were no loss.[179] John Williams, one of the most eminent preachers and leaders of the Calvinistic Methodist denomination, who had blotted his copybook by his recruitment campaign during the First World War, blotted it again by an address to the Synod in 1918 about the loss of ministers. He accepted that from time to time there were isolated cases where a minister decamped to the Church, but the movement was now much more general. While he accepted that some did so because they believed the Church "most nearly approaches the true ideal", he could not believe that the generality of "seceders" did so because the Church's ideals were more spiritual and her standard of conduct more spotless than Nonconformity. Rather it was for financial gain and social advancement."[180]

Were such men, either ministers or those men from nonconformist homes, activated by social and financial gain, or because of more genuine motives? It is not easy to identify the motives of individuals, though it must be noted that most bishops in taking on such men endeavoured to sort out the genuine from the ambitious.[181] Ollivant publicised the case of one of them, C.J.S. Russell, former minister of Wardrow Street Chapel, with a congregation of 700 or so, who was ordained by him to a curacy in his diocese, and who died aged forty as incumbent of St John's Church, Walthamstow. One wonders if Ollivant did so in order to address objections made to such ordinations and as a means of validating others. Russell, he noted, began to feel that the Church of England was the true position and proper sphere of work for a Christian minister. His faith in Nonconformity had been shaken by its voluntary principle, whereby each church had to pay its own way; his concern about the growth of papalism and the need for a strong Church to counteract it; the antagonism of dissent to the Established Church that he did not feel himself; the lack of order in Nonconformity and the need for episcopal authority, which he believed was sanctioned by the Epistles. Before ordination he had served for a year as a lay helper at St Mary's Church, Cardiff, presumably as a test of his vocation.[182] Evan Andrews of Dolgellau noted another case in the 1840s of a dissenting minister who was asked by his congregation to deliver a series of lectures against the Established Church. As a result he found the evidence on behalf of the Church so convincing that he gave up his calling, lost a family legacy, and was ordained priest by the bishop of St Davids after studying at one of the Oxford halls.[183] A former dissenter, William Ceidrych Thomas, in a paper delivered to a ruridecanal conference, said he was a Churchman by conviction whereas he was once a dissenter by tradition and force of circumstances.[184]

At a later date, in the 1920s, T.T. Lucius Morgan claimed that many had changed in order to enter a Church whose faith was more consistent with modern thought; to obtain a wider sphere of influence, and because they preferred the control of an "enlightened and fatherly episcopate" rather than lay control by the diaconate.[185] One such man was John Charles Jones, bishop of Bangor 1949-57, who became convinced, whilst studying for the Welsh Methodist ministry, of the catholicity of the Church in Wales, and relished its freedom as against the tyranny of the presbytery which demanded that men "toe the line".[186]

No doubt the claims made for the catholicity of the Church in Wales, its historic heritage and continuity with the early Church as well as its traditions and worship, its concern for the whole community rather than for a membership; its clear structure of leadership compared to what some felt was a closed and hypocritical system, and its breadth of vision embracing both languages and cultures (especially at a time when the Welsh language seemed to be in decline) found favour with many, but in the 1830s and probably until the 1860s there were two further factors. The first that, by and large, there was little doctrinal difference seen between Church and Chapel. K.O. Morgan suggests that as late as 1868 "many nonconformists were more aware of the links that bound them to the Anglican Church than of the elements that estranged them". Though the disestablishment campaign severed many of these links the legacy remained, so that D. Parry-Jones, ordained in 1914, remembered that when a young man signified his interest in entering the ministry in his part of Cardiganshire, it created no small stir in the community amongst all denominations, whose members would encourage him and take care to be present at his first sermon.[187]

The second factor is that until the late nineteenth century only the Church had a settled pastoral ministry. Dean Edwards alleged that most ministers had an income of £60 per annum (those who had more were few in number), so they were forced to combine their ministerial calling with more lucrative employment, such as in trade or farming. Though the Welsh Methodists were endeavouring to promote a resident pastorate of men entirely devoted to ministry, only the wealthiest congregations could afford to do so, and there were hardly any such pastorates in the rural areas.[188] John Owen, later bishop of St Davids, confirmed Edwards' statement in 1894 by noting that while Nonconformity wanted a settled pastorate, the voluntary principle which required a congregation to be self supporting, hardly allowed this save in the larger town churches.[189] Some years earlier, in 1888, it was claimed that while the Welsh Methodists had 569 ministers, only 366 of them were ministers "pure and simple", the remainder had secular jobs, presumably because their chapels could not afford a stipend for them.[190] Thus, if a man wished to devote his life to the ministry, without any distractions, he might well be drawn to the Church, whatever his background, while the fears of Methodist fathers about the precariousness of the Nonconformist ministry was not without foundation. Considering the close links and doctrinal similarities between Church and Chapel it is not surprising that so many men were drawn into the Church's ministries from Nonconformist backgrounds, especially those of the Welsh Methodist persuasion.

If Nonconformity disliked this exodus of its men into the arms of the Established Church in Wales, there was an equal disfavour within certain sections of that Church itself. The entrance of these men with their Methodist habits meant that the Church in Wales tended to remain low-church in many areas, thus inhibiting the advance in church life and practice many Anglo-Catholics desired.[191] Though this was written in 1915 this concern has been widespread for many years beforehand. A newspaper letter of 1854 argued the Church did not benefit from the introduction of such men into its ranks, as the low-church influences of many clergy were derived from this source.[192] Such men had introduced the habits and practices of Methodism into the life of the parishes in which they served, wrote John Griffith in 1846 under his pseudonym of *Cambro Sacerdos*. They ignored the rubrics of the Prayer Book, and brought extempore prayer and private meetings into their parishes. Services were abridged, a private system of discipline established which owed more to the chapel than the canons of the Church, and the service gabbled through in order to accommodate the "excitement" of the sermon. His statements about these "bullfrog" clergy were exaggerated, and some of his assertions far-fetched, such as his claim that the only articles such men had ever known were those of Geneva rather than the 39 Articles, or that before ordination few had seen anything but the inside of a dissenting chapel, although there was more than a grain of truth in some of his allegations.[193] Another writer, of 1853, protesting that in one parish in the diocese of Llandaff three of the five clergymen were former dissenting ministers, said the Church gained nothing from these "faded flowers from the irregular borders of Dissent."[194] Bishop Ollivant, preaching at Lampeter in 1880, suggested that the circumstances of their upbringing made these former dissenters (though he didn't use the phase) believe that the work of the ministry concentrated upon preaching. As a result these men had made the Established Church in many parts of Wales an integral part of Dissent.[195] These men had no real church principles, declared Canon Johnson of St Michael's College, Aberdare,[196] while Lemuel James claimed that the Nonconformist tradition in the Church was kept alive by those who came over from Dissent and forgot to leave their dissenting tradition behind them. It was these "churchmen" in name who would not allow the rest of the Church to be "faithful Churchmen".[197]

Yet it must be argued that these men were the backbone of the Church's mission in the industrial areas of south Wales, and managed to retain the Church population in the diocese of St Davids as well as that of Llandaff where they led the Church's mission in the more undesirable and unrewarding areas of the south Wales coalfield. They knew their people, they preached to them in the tones and mannerisms they preferred, and their extra-church activities kept their congregations together, even if they were based on Nonconformist precedents. With their Welsh background they enabled the Church to retain a Welsh presence in areas where that might have been lost, and so escape the accusation that it was an alien Church. Nonconformity fed the Church in Wales for many generations with men, and its decline, together with the depopulation of rural Wales, had a profound effect on the twentieth century Church in Wales.

CHAPTER THREE. THE EDUCATION OF THE FUTURE CLERGY:

Part one: from Grammar School to University

The table referred to in this chapter, on Clerical Education, will be found immediately after the contents page of this section.

It needs to be emphasised that no candidates were accepted for ordination as deacons until they had passed the bishop's examination, held generally a few days before or even on the eve of the ordination itself, though there were many ways of preparing for this examination, from self-preparation to graduation from a university. In addition, those who aspired to priest's orders faced a further examination.

In this chapter we examine the various places where a man could study in order to prepare himself for ordination, the courses they offered and the attitude of the bishops regarding these courses. We need to remember that there was no one route, and none of the institutions involved in this process of training was controlled entirely by the Church. At best, a bishop could influence a college's activities and work; at worst, he could decline to accept its men for ordination.

The table relating to Clerical Education lists what information is available regarding the places of clerical education for the wider Church and for individual dioceses within the Church in Wales. It is not exhaustive but selective, and all it can do effectively is to notice trends and make suggestions. It will be seen that in the eighteenth century both St Asaph and Llandaff dioceses managed to attract a reasonable number of graduates from the universities (distinguished here as Oxbridge), while St Davids was very different, for of those ordained in that diocese between 1750-1800 only about six per cent came into this category. The percentage of Oxbridge men serving in the ministry of the whole Church of England fell from 86 per cent in 1841 to 65 per cent twenty years later, but in 1865 while 78 per cent of those ordained in the province of Canterbury, excluding Wales, were of this distinction, in Wales it was but 25 per cent. Diocesan totals, taken from the published

Clergy Lists of those dioceses, show considerable differences between them, though it should be noted that while a bishop might decline to ordain non-graduates, he had little control over an incumbent taking such a person as a curate (rather than as a title for ordination) or of a patron nominating one to the parish whose advowson he held. In 1863 in the diocese of St Asaph 67 per cent of the clergy were graduates, including those of Trinity College, Dublin, 13.6 per cent were Lampeter men, and 9.3 per cent from St Bees College. There were a few men from other theological colleges, and 4.6 per cent were designated as literates. This term meant in its earlier context those who did not possess a university degree; it was later applied to those who had not attended either a university or a theological college.

Three years later Bangor had 56 per cent of its clergy as graduates, 18.5 per cent were Lampeter men, and nearly 10 per cent came from St Bees, with a number of men drawn from St Aidan's College, Birkenhead or Birmingham, though no literates were recorded. By contrast, in 1875 in the diocese of Llandaff, 43 per cent of its clergy had attended Oxbridge, a small number had attended other universities, 13.6 per cent had been at Lampeter, 8 per cent had attended a theological college, and 31 per cent were described as literates. Of the 39 men ordained in St Davids between 1886-9 Oxbridge graduates accounted for 30 per cent and 61 per cent had been to Lampeter. From the 1889 Clergy List for the same diocese we may note that 31.6 per cent had been to Oxbridge or Dublin, 44.5 per cent were Lampeter men, 11.4 per cent had been to a theological college (nearly half at St Bees), and 9 per cent were classified as literates. In a study of those made deacon at the September 1901 ordination in the diocese of Llandaff, four were Oxbridge men, two of whom had also attended St Michael's College for theological training, four had graduated at Lampeter of whom one had attended St Michael's College, four held the Lampeter licence in divinity, one had a London degree but had also studied at St Michael's College, three men had studied at Durham, and one each at Chichester and St Bees, these being theological colleges, while one was described as a literate.

By 1910 it was estimated that 29.6 per cent of the Welsh clergy were Oxbridge men, another 6.8 per cent had graduated at another university, including Dublin and Wales, 41 per cent were educated at Lampeter, 13 per cent had trained at a theological college, and 8.5 per cent were literates.[1] The theological college men were those who took their full training at these institutions, not those who went there for a post-graduate course. The general trends observable are the gradual reduction in literates, the immense significance of Lampeter to the diocese of St Davids and, to a lesser extent, the whole of the Church in Wales, the decline in the number of university men overall, and their replacement by those attending a theological college course. In addition, as noted above, a number of men continued their training at a theological college after taking their degree. The significance of St Bees College is obvious from the figures quoted in this connection.

The Welsh Church needed a large number of men each year to supply its needs, and as already noted, its requirement for a Welsh-speaking ministry made it increasingly dependent on men who came from a *gwerin* background. In 1877 Bishop Basil Jones of St Davids suggested that twenty-five years earlier the diocese needed at least ten new deacons each year to fill up vacancies, and in the past three and a half years he had ordained forty deacons, but that number was still insufficient.[2] Between 1883-1910 the number of deacons ordained for the diocese of Llandaff alone was 844, but it seems that number was still insufficient for its needs. This was an average of thirty per year, compared to St Davids diocese between 1874-88 when 196 deacons had been ordained, an average of thirteen a year.[3] Yet standards were rising. In 1880 Basil Jones announced he would ordain no more literates,[4] and Bishop Edwards of St Asaph noted in 1901 that for the ten years ending 1869, 60 per cent of those ordained for the diocese were graduates of the older universities. Between 1888-1901 it had dropped to 50 per cent, but for the previous three years it had increased to 80 per cent.[5] The Church needed not only a better qualified clerical body but it also needed more men. It was an uneasy position to say the least.

We proceed to note the various possibilities open to men for ordination training, noting first how literates coped, then the use of licensed grammar schools in the two southern dioceses, the universities, St David's College, Lampeter, and the various theological colleges, with particular reference to those which supplied men to the Welsh dioceses.

THE PRELIMINARIES

Many of the men who were ordained into the Welsh dioceses had received only an elementary education, and in order to be ordained needed to be prepared for the bishop's examination, or for a preliminary examination if they wished to enter Lampeter or a theological college. All these examinations required a knowledge of Latin and the Greek Testament as well as an understanding of the Bible and the doctrinal teachings of the Church. Bishop Burgess of St Davids made this perfectly plain in 1807. A minister of the Gospel, he stated to his clergy, who was incapable of reading the original languages of Scripture was ill-prepared to instruct and advise the people committed to his care, especially in a diocese abounding with dissenters, whose doctrinal differences rested on points of doubtful disputation which a clergyman might solve from the original records of Scripture.[6]

Though a number of men worked on their own, it was a hard and difficult labour. Eben Fardd (Ebenezer Thomas) schoolmaster and poet, was persuaded in the 1840s to prepare for the examination at St Bees and eventual ordination by the bishop of Chester by Thomas Thomas, vicar of Caernarfon. He managed to learn the rudiments of Latin and Greek before realising that the amount of work involved, his family and school commitments, together with a feeling of unfitness for ordination, necessitated abandoning his aim.[7] Robert Roberts, though he was successful in entering St Bees in 1857 found his preparation for entry to it a hard struggle, having to puzzle out for himself the obscurities of the classical languages.[8]

Many were assisted by local clergy. Indeed, their bishops often encouraged them to look out for likely men and young boys and assist them in this preparatory work. There is evidence that many curates maintained schools as a means of supplementing their income where young men were given the basic rudiments of a classical education. David Ellis, curate of Derwen, Denbighshire, was one, and in 1770 he acted as tutor for Edward Williams, who was later a celebrated Independent divine and teacher.[9] Francis Homfray, rector of Llanfair Cilgedin in Monmouthshire, 1813-31, also prepared men for ordination and for entry to the universities,[10] as did Joseph Prosser of Newchurch, Monmouthshire, a previous headmaster of Tewkesbury Grammar School, one of whose pupils, Cooper, was sent back to him for further study having failed his ordination examination. Another was Maurice Evans, rector of Llangeler, who established a school in 1820 known as Hen Golleg to assist men who wished to enter the ministry of the Church.[11]

At a later date there were men like Richard Bowen Jones, rector of Cilymaenllwyd, who informed the St Davids Diocesan Conference in 1882 that he trained young men in his parish for the ministry and gave them help especially in Latin, noting this cost comparatively little compared to the cost of education elsewhere.[12] Henry Morgan was coached by his vicar in classics to prepare for entry to Llandovery School. He later studied at Lampeter and eventually became vicar of

Eglwysilan.[13] Charles Hyde Brooke, vicar of Criggion in Montgomeryshire 1890-1900, is said to have taken in pupils to prepare them for ordination. They were known locally as his curates.[14] It is said that over thirty Welsh clergy owed the beginning of their higher education to Mrs Ann Walter Thomas, wife of the vicar of Llandygai, David Walter Thomas, who, with her husband, held classes for them in Bangor. She died in 1920.[15] It might be argued that many of the parishes that supplied the Church with numerous clergy did so because, as at Llangeler, the curates of the parish had given them the educational start they needed.[16]

A number were trained by their clerical brothers. John Lloyd Richards was probably prepared for entry to St Bees by his brother, Thomas, who kept a school at Berriew, Montgomeryshire between 1813-26. It was at this school that John Blackwell was prepared for university and Evan Evans, Ieuan Glan Geirionydd, for entry to St Bees.[17] Thomas's father, another Thomas, vicar of Darowen, is said to have coached a good number of young men for the ministry of the Church.[18] Daniel Richards, ordained in 1914, was helped at first by his elder brother Jenkin in obtaining a grounding of Latin and Greek, and was later assisted by Cyril Williams Miller, curate of Pontypridd, when he was stipendiary lay reader of that parish.[19] One assumes that some were prepared by their own clerical fathers.[20] William Williams, ordained in 1800 in the diocese of Llandaff, had been prepared for ordination by his brother-in-law, Isaac Morgan, vicar of Dingestow and had been under "his care and tuition" for a number of years.[21]

The wardens of the Church Hostel in Bangor assisted students who wished to be ordained by teaching them Greek and introducing them to pastoral studies, as did the then warden, Glyn Simon, in the 1930s.[22] At the same date others were able to make use of the facilities of the Workers' Education Movement and of its summer schools, or take correspondence courses in Latin and Greek, in order to prepare for entry to a college or university, as did David Rees Davies, who entered Lampeter in 1925 and became vicar of Llanwrtyd. He had started life in the pits at fourteen years of age.[23]

LITERATES

The number of literates, especially in the diocese of St Davids and Llandaff was considerable, especially in the former during the eighteenth and early nineteenth centuries. From Table One it will be noted that over ninety per cent of men ordained in that diocese between 1750-1800 came into this category, and it was only the opening of St David's College, by establishing a new category, that brought this number down. The same table reveals that this situation was not unique to Wales, though the number of literates was significantly less over the whole Church of England than in Wales.

Sadly, there is little recorded about these men, apart from their ordination papers. Many of them attended the grammar schools that are discussed in the next section, while others were possibly tutored by local clergy. One such man was Evan Rowlands. In a letter to John Griffith his bishop, Ollivant, took Griffith to task for not allowing Rowlands, who was employed at Merthyr Tydfil as a "reader", sufficient time to study for his examination and "self-improvement", in which he was probably helped by the curates of the parish. Though he had done well as a reader, his real purpose in the parish was his preparation for this examination, and he was allowed to use his spare time to act as a reader. As a result, he knew nothing of the Greek Testament. Ollivant was ordaining him with great reluctance, for it was a "great evil" that if one uninformed man was admitted others would assume "they might just as well". He would not be ordained priest without a competent knowledge of the Greek Testament and some knowledge of Latin. He was ordained to that parish in 1860 and was still there as a deacon in 1865.[24]

Those who prepared themselves for the ordination examination were required to have a reasonable acquaintance with the Greek Testament, some Latin texts, especially Grotius, and numerous standard books on theology, liturgy, doctrine and history. Thomas Beynon, later archdeacon of Carmarthen, ordained in 1768, compiled a manuscript list of the books he had read during 1763-7, which included not only the kind of books mentioned above but also fiction, Richelieu's *Art of Pleasing in Conversation*, *Welch Piety*, books of sermons, and a pocket companion to Oxford. A farmer's son, Beynon's ambition in this direction failed to materialise.[25]

It is not known if Beynon availed himself of Henry Owen's *Directions for Young Students in Divinity, with regard to those Attainments, which are necessary to qualify them for Holy Orders,* for its first edition was published in 1766, and went into five editions before 1800. Owen was examining chaplain to Bishop Barrington of Llandaff, 1769-82 (and rector of St Olave's, Hart St., in the city of London), and it is not unreasonable to suppose this book was designed with the ordination candidates of that diocese in mind who were, in Owen's phase, "unable to obtain a University education" and instead left to their own devices. While those at the universities would be directed in their studies by their respective tutors, he pointed out that if their classical education neglected Scriptural and theological learning they would be unfit for their future profession. After noting the moral, academic and spiritual qualifications for the ministry, he offered a substantial reading list of classical authors (mainly the moralists who needed to be read with care), works by Nelson, Taylor, Pearson, Clarke, Burnet, Stillingfleet, Gibson, Hooker, Wheatley and Tillotson, amongst others, these being the standard works of their day. The Scriptures were to be diligently studied, the New Testament read in Greek, and there should be a continual reading of the Ordination office in order "to strengthen resolve". His list combined elements of a classical liberal education with theological study, and he believed that most of these books could be readily borrowed. Owen also expressed his concern that while all other professions had a practical training, there was little pastoral training or preaching skills taught to those preparing for ordination, and his book-list endeavoured in part to remedy this deficiency. Owen also advised that two sermons should be read every Sunday from such standard Anglican divines as Tillotson, Sherlock and Secker.[26]

Richard Watson, who was bishop of Llandaff (1782-1816) and also regius professor of divinity at Cambridge, produced six volumes of theological tracts, mainly on apologetics, for the use of those preparing for ordination. In his case it seems his main target was university graduates who needed to prepare for their ordination examination and for their future calling. Too often such men concluded that having taken their degree they had completed their education. Their minds may have been "stocked with a great abundance of Classical Knowledge", or with natural philosophy or mathematics, but more was needed. Watson also had in mind those, who ordained from "county schools", were at a loss in their curacies as to what course of studies they should pursue. If these men, many of whom were in his diocese (as he pointed out in his 1788 Charge) were to instruct themselves through these works they would not disgrace any university in the world. Though their study would not make a man into a "deep divine", they would go a long way towards making "a well-informed Christian". Watson also noted that literates as well as university graduates were often in no position to purchase theological books, even if they knew how to make a proper selection. In these volumes Watson revealed his own religious liberalism, for the sacraments were never mentioned, and his tracts included a number of works by dissenters, while he made clear that it was the duty of the Christian teacher to distinguish between the Word of God and the additions men had made to it. As a result some of the bishops and the Archbishop of Canterbury were rather displeased by his publication.[27]

THE SCHOOLS

For those who wished to be ordained, and who were unable to afford a university education, the best available resource available to them were the various grammar and private schools which provided both a classical and also a theological education.[28] This was before the opening of St David's College, which had a profound effect on these schools. All these schools were private venture affairs, though sometimes regulated by trusts, and it was generally these that survived beyond the lifetime of their founders. The only control the Church had over them was for the bishops to regulate the conditions required for ordination.

The schools may be briefly mentioned, diocese by diocese, though there is little reference to schools in Bangor, possibly because most of the men ordained there were graduates. In St Asaph diocese Berriew school has been mentioned already, but this school did not appear to train men for ordination, only for entry into college. Ruthin School apparently did so, but evidence is scarce.[29]

The diocese of Llandaff possessed two so-called divinity schools. One was based at Cowbridge Grammar School, an old-established institution which was regulated by and had scholarships to Jesus College, Oxford, and the other school was at Usk. This, unlike Cowbridge, which also functioned as a grammar school, was dedicated to preparing men for ordination. When its head, Thomas Williams, was appointed minister of the new district of Holy Trinity, Abergavenny, in 1842, he moved his Divinity School to that place. It appears that Bishop Watson established, or authorised, these two divinity schools in 1812, for those for "whom poverty or lack of education made the universities inaccessible", and as a means of preparing men in a more orderly fashion for the service of the Church. Bishop Sumner later amended the curriculum and added to the reading list works by Beveridge, Henry Birkett and Doddridge. The headmasters, as was common in those days, were in Holy Orders.

The date of their foundation seems to be confirmed by a letter Bishop Copleston wrote to his father in 1828. In it he stated that until the two divinity schools were established there "was nothing like principle or system" in the training of ordinands in his new diocese. The two schools had twenty to twenty-four students between them, and each had to remain for four years until they were ordained. Though students had to live in lodgings, the towns were sufficiently small so that "no irregularity of conduct could escape notice". The candidates he had ordained from these schools seemed better prepared and fitter for the "humble and ill-paid duties" that would be their lot compared to the university men, though they were "quite as well-mannered and admissible into society" as these men.[30]

Bishop Copleston's good opinion did not last. In that same year he expressed some concern about these schools. Writing to Bruce Knight in 1828 he felt that the system of teaching at Lampeter, then newly opened, must be superior "to our seminaries, where the superintendence of the Divinity Students is an incidental and (in point of time and attention) a minor duty." Twelve years later Copleston wrote to Knight that he felt something ought to be done about Cowbridge Divinity School. Lampeter was so well conducted that he considered it should be the seminary for south Wales and he would be perfectly content to allow Cowbridge and Usk to "expire".[31]

Iolo Williams in his history of Cowbridge School prints "The Regulations for the Divinity Schools in the Diocese of Llandaff". These appear to have been drawn up at quite an early date, for it is clear that many of them were obsolete by the time of their closure. No-one was to be admitted a student under the age of seventeen or over the age of nineteen, and no-one was to be admitted as a candidate for orders who had not continued at the school from the time of his entrance to the time of his being of full age to be ordained, namely twenty-three. No person was to be admitted, without permission from the bishop, who was not born of parents resident within the diocese of Llandaff, or who for the most part had resided in it. An entrance examination required a knowledge of Latin and of the Greek Testament.[32]

As numbers declined in both schools, and as Lampeter exerted a stronger appeal, it is hardly surprising that Bishop Ollivant, a former vice-principal of Lampeter, was anxious not to let the new college "languish for want of our co-operation". Thus Ollivant, arriving in the diocese two years after the death of the headmaster of Cowbridge, Dr Williams, in 1847, without realising that Williams' successor, Dr Harper, a non-Welsh speaker, had different ideas about the future of the school, withdrew Cowbridge's privilege of being a divinity school. Announcing this in his 1851 Charge Ollivant made clear that Lampeter was not a diocesan college but one that would benefit the whole Church. He felt it unwise for a school to have two objects that could not be properly combined, and he thought the union of boys and young men undesirable. In 1866 Thomas Williams, the head of the Abergavenny school died, and Ollivant once again decided not to appoint a successor. This school had catered for the Welsh-speaking men of the diocese, although Benjamin Hall had claimed that neither of the two schools had given any instruction in Welsh to their students. Circumstances in the diocese had changed, Ollivant argued, in defence of his closure of the Abergavenny school. Small colleges were not desirable, and a school with ten to twelve pupils could not offer the necessary classical instruction upon which a theological education could be built. All it could do was to offer a narrow selection of theological subjects sufficient to allow a man to pass the ordination examinations, but it could give no solid foundation for that intellectual improvement in the clergy needed by the Church. The Abergavenny course by Ollivant's time had become spread over two years, and the temptation to take this shorter and cheaper course compared to Lampeter's three years was too strong for most men. The influence of these schools upon the church in his diocese had been "decidedly injurious", Ollivant concluded.[33]

Cowbridge School remained as a grammar school after the closure of its divinity school, and Rowland Williams claimed that it was one of the few schools that sent the "best class of students" to Lampeter.[34] In an obituary to Dr Williams it was stated that "many most respectable and useful clergymen" were "indebted to Cowbridge ... for their admission into holy orders".[35] The same might be said of those men trained at Usk and Abergavenny, such as David Howell and Thomas Walters, though Howell was not uncritical of the training he had received at Abergavenny, writing that whilst at the school he had never written a sermon, addressed a public meeting, knelt at a sick bedside, or performed any public religious function. Yet when he was ordained he was placed in sole charge of a district.[36]

The diocese of St Davids had a number of divinity schools, which were attached to grammar schools. Queen Elizabeth Grammar School, Carmarthen, was one such school. It appears that William Higgs-Barker, headmaster 1767-97, established the divinity course that was said to have given a higher tone to the school. In the 1820s the curriculum consisted of Latin, Greek, Hebrew, English and Welsh, apart from other studies, and boys were required to translate from Greek texts into Welsh, and *vice versa*. A graceful delivery of speech was also insisted upon, while pupils were required to speak in Latin whilst at school. At the annual examination several of the divinity class were required to deliver a sermon in Welsh, sometimes in English, from memory, before their examiners and members of the local clergy. The senior pupils were also known to have organised an extempore sermon class on their own initiative. The main criticism was that little attention was paid to mathematics, general science and English and Welsh literature. It was said that its theological training was more systematic and thorough than that of the universities. David Jones, Llangan, Peter Williams the Methodist cleric and editor of a Welsh Bible, together with his two sons, Eliezer and Peter Bailey Williams, W.T. Rees of Casgob, William Leigh of Eglwysilan, and David Parry of Llywel, all influential clerics in their day, were pupils of this school.[37]

Cardigan Grammar School was another similar school, though it does not appear to have had a separate divinity department. Nevertheless, it had a reputation for classical studies, and in 1821 its pupils enacted Euripides' *Medea* in the original Greek. David James, Panteg, a former pupil, was said to have been taught by its headmaster, Watkin William Thomas, a Cambridge B.D., Hebrew, Greek, Latin, French, English and Welsh. Archdeacon John Griffiths of Neath was another former pupil of this school.[38] Christ College, Brecon, in its heyday before the opening of Lampeter, had between forty to sixty pupils, who received a classical and theological education that prepared them for ordination.[39] Lampeter Grammar School, a private venture school, was opened by Eliezer Williams, noted above as having been educated at Carmarthen, in 1805. In 1819 it had eighty pupils, of whom fifteen were divinity students. They received a four or five year course of classical and general subjects before two or three years of theology during which they studied Hebrew and Greek texts, the Christian Fathers, Grotius, Burnet, Jewell, Hooker, Pearson and other standard works. They were also required to be competent in spoken and written Welsh. If the building was not very grand, its reputation was substantial, especially during the headship of John Williams, later archdeacon of Cardigan, regarded by Sir Walter Scott as the finest headmaster in Europe, and who brought him to Edinburgh in 1824 to be the first principal of its Academy.[40]

It is arguable that the most celebrated of these schools was Ystrad Meurig. It was this school that Bishop Burgess mentioned when he stated, without any justification, that the custom of Cardiganshire was that a man would follow the plough until he was twenty-two years of age when he entered this school for a year prior to ordination.[41] Founded around. 1757 by Edward Richard, it taught both classics and theology. The master, by its 1774 deed, was required to teach the Greek and Latin classics as taught in the principal grammar schools of England, so that boys could be prepared for entry to the universities. Though it originally catered for twelve poor boys of the parish in the principles of the Church of England, it had become a grammar school by 1771, with 32 pupils in 1774, and until 1812 when a schoolroom was built to accommodate its 150 pupils the school was held in the parish church. Like all these schools those pupils who did not live within walking distance of the school were required to live in licensed lodgings. Burgess through the Church Union Society offered its pupils under the age of twenty who passed an examination in the Greek Testament, Epictetus and Cicero's *Offices* a book prize worth one pound. An exhibition of £10 for four years was also awarded by the same society for the maintenance of a scholar at the school, but the examination consisted of specified classical and theological authors together with the Greek Testament. Its fees were four guineas per annum for day pupils, and twenty for boarders, and it is said that many of its students conducted their own schools during winter in order to pay for their summer's tuition, a practice eventually forbidden by Bishop Burgess.[42]

If Bishop Burgess's "one year" ploughboy could ever have been true, it would have been before the time of Samuel Horsley, bishop of St Davids 1788-94, who imposed order and regulation for ordination training in his diocese. Discovering that some men were being educated for the Church in schools run by Dissenters he promptly refused to accept any candidates from them, arguing that any training such places could give would be insufficient for the Church's requirements.

It appears that there were two major places of such training. The Carmarthen Presbyterian College or Academy was one of these schools, and was supported by the London Congregational and Presbyterian Boards, whose tutors by Horsley's time had a reputation for unorthodox if not Arian theological views. It trained men for the ministry of those churches, and had a high reputation. Amongst other requirements its students were expected to read the Psalms in Hebrew, translate into Latin unseen sections of the Greek Testament, and write a thesis proposed to them in Latin. Two previous bishops of the diocese, Anthony Ellis (1752-61) and Samuel Squire (1761-6), had been agreeably surprised at the proficiency of the men ordained from this college, and had expressed great satisfaction with its academic standard. The other school was a private venture school run by David Davis at his home Castell Hywel, which he commenced in 1782, combining this with ministering to a number of small

Arian churches in the neighbourhood. His reputation as a teacher was known throughout south Wales, and in his school theology, classics, Hebrew, Welsh grammar, mathematics and science were taught.

Horsley's refusal to ordain any men educated by a dissenting minister was not unchallenged. *Welsh Freeholder* in a letter to Horsley reminded him that many of his clergy and other gentlemen in his diocese would bear "honourable testimony" to their work, and that the Church had been indebted to them for "several ministers". However, David Evans claimed that Horsley had been forced to relax his rule regarding Davis's school when he realised the scarcity of other schools of a similar nature and as the number of his candidates diminished.[43]

Horsley insisted he would ordain no one without a university education unless they had studied for three years in a divinity class of a reputable grammar school. Although his concern was for the raising of clerical education and in order to supply the churches by "abler assistants and in a much more regular manner", it was also a consequence of his policy of raising the stipends of curates, thus allowing the incumbents who employed them to obtain a better quality of men. A better stipend, in his estimate, demanded that each candidate should have "a much greater share of knowledge and learning than has generally been insisted on here." He also insisted that no pupils were to be admitted to the divinity class until they were able "to construe the Greek Testament, and the common Latin authors with tolerable proficiency", and had attended classes in English. It appears the bishop felt that if candidates had not reached this proficiency by the age of twenty, it was not worth their while continuing. Those who had engaged in low and menial occupations, had speech defects or some "remarkable" deformity about their person, were to be excluded. A syllabus of standard theological works was prescribed based on Henry Owen's *Directions for Young Students in Divinity*. The Greek Testament was to be the chief object of study, and while Horsley considered it pedantic to insist that Greek should always be construed into Latin, or that the proper pronunciation of Latin be cultivated by reading Virgil and Juvenal, he considered that his book list, including Burnet on the Attributes, Pearson on the Creed, Wheatley on Common Prayer, Secker on the Catechism, Grotius' *De Veritate*, and others, would equip the newly ordained minister to teach his flock and defend his faith against the encroaching rationalism of the age.

Furthermore, a practical training was to be given by the masters of these schools. Pupils were to be exercised in reading the Common Prayer aloud, clearly and distinctly, "with proper stops and emphasis", and do the same with select sermons, while they were to make abstracts of the sermons they had heard which were to be examined by the master in order to help their compositional skills. Students, who had to find their own lodgings, were forbidden to lodge at inns or public houses. But, as Maber points out, there were two defects. The Welsh language appears to have been ignored, and, as he puts it, "anyone who could pass through so selective a social and academic net would be able to attain a more prestigious and less arduous course" at one of the universities. But Horsley preferred quality to quantity, and in the letter to the schoolmasters announcing these changes he accepted the fact that his rules might well cause some men to give up any thought of ordination. This was true. According to William Price, between 1750-87 the average number of men made deacon was twenty-five per annum, between 1788-99 six, and thereafter until 1825 eight. How far the schoolmasters were able to put these precepts into practice is not known, though they were required to account to the bishop for their divinity students each year, two months before the ordination, giving him their personal details and possibly updates of their academic progress.[44]

Bishop Burgess, equally appalled at the lamentable state of clerical education in his diocese, in spite of Horsley's reforms, further extended the requirements for ordination in his diocese, and in particular by licensing divinity classes at seven of the grammar schools in his diocese, namely Lampeter, Ystrad Meurig, Brecon, Carmarthen, Cardigan, Haverfordwest and St David's. Each school was said to have had upwards of seventy pupils, but this probably related to the whole school rather than the divinity students. He thus declined to ordain men educated at any other school and did so by refusing to accept the certificates of their masters regarding their pupils' progress and conduct. He also insisted on a seven-year course of study. Burgess had given a clear hint about his policy in his primary Charge of 1804, when he accepted that the principal schools of the diocese, "under proper regulations with *appropriate* methods of study", were sufficient for the elementary part of clerical education.

A speaker at the 1853 meeting of the Association of Welsh Clergy in the West Riding of Yorkshire claimed that, having discovered that some of the students at Ystrad Meurig were unable to express themselves fluently in English, the bishop gave directions that each candidate had to spend seven years in training before he would admit them to ordination. The speaker, Lewis Jones, claimed that this ruling caused many students in that school to depart for other dioceses, and greatly depleted the school. He may well have been one of those concerned in this exodus. Burgess offered his own justification for this policy in a sermon of 1812. The great defect in the training of men for Orders was their inability to remain in school long enough to be grounded sufficiently in the required subjects, and the lamentable consequences of this were seen during the ordination week. Though this had to some degree been obviated by requiring an attendance in the divinity class for the last four years of education, previous to the full age for deacon's orders, he still felt it little compensation for the lack of a regular course of instruction. He had in mind the foundation of a college, and went on to state that he would use the interest on the monies accumulated for this purpose for assisting poor parents with the means of keeping their sons in school longer than they could do otherwise. We need to remember, however, that these four years of divinity were in addition to the three years of classical training, hence the seven years mentioned earlier.

In a letter to these schoolmasters, attached to a reprint of Robert Nelson's *On the Advantages of Clerical Seminaries,* reprinted by him in 1813, Burgess made it clear that of all their duties the most important was the education of men destined for Holy Orders, and hoped that Nelson's paper "for an appropriate course of clerical instruction (though it can be fully executed only in a Seminary devoted to this purpose)" would be promoted by them in their schools. Nelson, in addition to the usual course of study, desired instruction in the care of the sick and dying, in performing the liturgy with "becoming gravity and devotion", in elocution, the art of preaching and deportment. In addition, the master should ensure that his pupils' piety and devotion be formulated and a zeal established for promoting the salvation of souls. Once again, as an anonymous writer of 1851 on Lampeter asserted, the standards required were as high as those that entitled a man to a degree in the universities.[45]

THE DEMISE OF THE SCHOOLS

John Banks Jenkinson, bishop of St Davids 1825-40, was the inheritor of Burgess's scheme of theological education based at St David's College, Lampeter, and realised that a college of that size - it was said to have room for eighty students - needed to be filled, especially if it was to cover its costs, though William Price suggests he was not worried whether parents could afford the cost of training, as like Horsley he wanted quality rather than quantity. It is possible he may have been deceived by the large number of men made deacon in 1825, twenty-five in all (excluding many rejections), twice as many as the diocese required. In his Charge of 1828 Jenkinson argued that while the local divinity schools had been established to rectify the lack of a university education, they had become utterly inadequate for the needs of the diocese, which required one institution conducted on a much larger scale and an expanded plan of education. The solid and liberal education it could provide would rescue the clergy of the diocese from a state of intellectual inferiority. It was his duty to encourage this new college which was well adapted to place the Church in their diocese on a more respectable footing, and thus he would look exclusively to St David's College for the supply of his candidates. He directed, therefore, that a four-year course was required at Lampeter, and admission could only be gained after a preparatory course at a grammar school had been undertaken.

A circular sent out to the various schools of the diocese in 1827 indicated that candidates for ordination were to make up what remained of their seven year training at Lampeter; but from the beginning of 1828 the minimum age of entry to that college would be twenty, and from the end of that year no candidate would be ordained from a school. The cost of the Lampeter course was estimated at £50 per annum, twice as much as the cost of tuition and board at one of these schools. The schools were now feeders for the college, and Jenkinson required their scholars to be well grounded in Latin and Greek, without which the college course would be futile, while he supplied them with a substantial book list.[46]

As a result of Jenkinson's decision, many men, discovering that to be ordained meant a further period of training at Lampeter that they had not anticipated, gave up thoughts of ordination or went elsewhere. One mentioned by D. Edwardes, a former headmaster of Denstone, was John Rowlands. He had been at Ystrad Meurig, but was now forced to go to north Wales where he assisted in a school at Bangor and later at St Asaph, and also worked as a land surveyor.[47] Others, specially those of more limited means, would have found it more convenient and certainly cheaper to remain at one of these schools and so qualify themselves for entry to St John's College, Cambridge, as sizars, to keep terms at Trinity College, Dublin, or to migrate to another diocese, where the only requirement was to satisfy the bishop's examining chaplains that one had sufficient learning for ordination, than "to struggle against all the difficulties and disadvantages" of Lampeter.[48]

It is hardly surprising that the number of men ordained in the diocese of St Davids dropped considerably. In 1823-5, 47 deacons were ordained, but between 1854-6, when the grammar schools had been closed to divinity students and Lampeter was at a low ebb, the number fell to 22, of whom only eight were from Lampeter, with fourteen graduates from the universities, including Dublin.[49] This reduction in number was said to be due to the cost involved for training a son for Orders being beyond the reach of most parents, unlike the former system. John Griffith was not alone in declaring that as a result the Church had lost its best recruits to the dissenting ministry or to secular employment. "The Church of their forefathers was for ever shut against them", he argued, as a result of this misguided policy.[50]

Jenkinson's decision, together with the opening of St David's College, paralysed the work of the grammar schools. Lewis Jones was one of many who complained that by depriving these schools of their licences Jenkinson had offered nothing in return. The consequence was disastrous. At that same meeting E.O. Phillips cast scorn on the teaching of most of the Welsh grammar schools, arguing that they now offered nothing to interest the young and busy mind, but concentrated instead on teaching Latin and Greek. Joseph Hughes remembered that many of these schools had an average attendance of seventy pupils and after seven years study they were regarded as competent to instruct people and take services through the medium of the Welsh language. This, he believed, was hardly the case with Lampeter.[51] There were others who asserted that these schools provided a far better grounding and education for the Ministry of the Church than Lampeter could, especially as some of the schools offered instruction in pastoralia and preaching.[52] Archdeacon Thorpe, who acted as examining chaplain on the last occasion when grammar school men were admitted for ordination, said that neither Oxford nor Cambridge could produce an equal number of candidates better qualified in every respect … that those he had examined and recommended for ordination.[53] These men, declared a newspaper "portrait" of David Parry, had been trained from boyhood to manhood for the ministry, and were far superior to the products of Lampeter in every way.[54]

Not all agreed about the value of these schools. Thomas Rees in 1815 declared that while the Welsh clergy were at one with their English brethren for respectability of character and devotion to their calling, many of them were exceedingly ignorant.

He believed this was due to the education in these schools, where few pupils went beyond acquiring sufficient Greek and Latin in order to satisfy the bishops' examination chaplains.[55] Ollivant, in his first Charge of 1851, noting the condition of the schools in the diocese of St Davids, argued that the remedy for the difficulty in providing an adequate and Welsh-speaking ministry did not lie in the revival of these schools, which were "part of a system that was unsound in principle, and injurious in effects".[56] Conybeare repeated these allegations with added sarcasm. In such a school, he wrote, a man learnt to talk broken English, and perhaps to construe Caesar. "There too he gained the power of stumbling through a chapter of his Greek Testament, and was crammed with such a store of theology as satisfied the easy requirements of a Welsh examining chaplain".[57] Others replied stating that these later comments reflected the schools as they were at the time of writing. The schools as they existed before the foundation of St David's College were far superior, "flourishing and active" even to the standard of that College's work in the 1850s and 60s.[58]

The schools, of course, declined, Griffith writing that it only needed three years to ruin a school. Haverfordwest had had a large divinity class, but after these events, numbers rapidly declined. Carmarthen, with 64 pupils in 1824, was reduced to 25 ten years later. Brecon, with seven pupils in 1838 compared to 40 to 60 before, soon collapsed, to be revived later as a public school.[59] Thirlwall, visiting Ystrad Meurig in 1843, met a former pupil who was now working on his father's farm. He had retained a little smattering of Latin and Greek, but his knowledge of English was very imperfect. This meeting prepared him for his visit to the school. Though it was well endowed, he accepted it could never regain the reputation it possessed before Lampeter was opened.[60] In many cases the lower school provided pupils for the divinity class, so if the latter suffered, so did the former, while parents, unable to find the necessary costs for Lampeter, declined to send their sons to these schools.[61]

Another factor which concerned John Griffith of Merthyr was that since the grammar schools had closed, the Church no longer attracted into its ranks men from the poorer classes, as compared to Nonconformity, as they could not afford the cost. It was these men, predominantly Welsh speakers, who were required for work in the industrial parishes of south Wales, for they alone could preach the Gospel to their own sort of people in the language and style they found acceptable. The priority, he hinted, was for Welsh speakers, rather than classical scholars. The old grammar schools, cheap because men boarded (and sometimes were allowed to go home during the weekends), were admirable for this purpose, as they trained men from boyhood to manhood in a rigorous, disciplined and effective manner. They had catered for Welsh-speaking men, and if they received a veneer of English, it was not at the expense of their background. Lampeter, he claimed, paid lip service to the Welsh language. Griffith's nostalgia knew no bounds. His early education had been at Ystrad Meurig, and even forty years after the opening of Lampeter he still grieved over those days, writing in 1869:

> The true, old Ystradmeurig man, and his congeners from Carmarthen, Haverfordwest, Cowbridge, Usk, and Abergavenny, were as different to the general run of Lampeter men, as an officer on the quarter-deck is to seamen before the mast … Revive the old grammar schools. Let the bishops restore them their old privileges, and I will answer for it, it will be better, not only for the Church, but for St. David's College, Lampeter. It will not then have the humiliation of taking men in after twenty years of age who do not know their *hic, haec, hoc*; and who would never have entered in there at all had they not failed in something else. … The bishops of North and South Wales, in those days, never ordained a man who had not gone through a regular curriculum at the Grammar Schools, having begun his *hic, haec, hoc* at eight, when every man ought to, if he ever means to be well disciplined. The difference between such men and the man who has never known anything but a "three years' residence at Lampeter" it is easy to see. The one is a trained man from his youth, the other a ploughboy all his life. No surplice or gown can ever cover his defects.

A storm of criticism met these remarks. Ollivant pointed out that in closing the divinity school at Cowbridge he had allowed its master to concentrate on its work as a grammar school. Many others, including the Lampeter College staff, reminded him that the education given at Lampeter was far superior to the old system, and the number of ordinands required by the Church justified a centralised system. But Griffith's concern was the lack of a preliminary and affordable education as a preparation for ordination training, a concern the staff at Lampeter knew all too well. Presumably he wanted the grammar schools to be revived in order to act as a sort of preliminary seminary.[62]

Griffith was not alone. In an open letter to Lord John Russell of 1850 *Golifer* argued that Lampeter had not only caused the ruin of the old Welsh grammar schools, but had also closed the gates of theological education to natives of the Principality. There were now few candidates for ordination who were qualified to teach in their native tongue. Consequently, the Church was unable to compete with dissenting teachers in the favour of the native population.[63] At an archdeacon's visitation at Swansea in 1858 it was reported that the college had only 29 students (it was the time of the Rowland Williams controversy), and it was then argued that the revival of the old grammar schools would supply a class of men sufficiently educated to meet the needs of the Welsh Church.[64]

Yet the schools may not have been all that pious reminiscences recalled. They were as good as their headmasters. Some were outstanding, others not so. Many offered no pastoral or pulpit training, which a writer of 1851 suggested caused "a chilling and extinguishing effect upon many of those who might, under different circumstances, have become shining lights in the Church of Wales". He also claimed that compared to the universities they offered a meagre course in divinity.[65] The schools were not residential, and Jenkinson claimed that some of them lodged in inns and private houses, "where they have necessarily witnessed scenes, and associated with company exposing them to the danger, and unless they are endowed with great strength of character, to the certainty of acquiring tastes and contracting habits utterly incompatible with the profession for which they are destined." By contrast, men in a residential college would be placed under constant supervision.[66] Memories may be selective, and some pupils better than others, but it is clear that by and large these grammar schools provided a cheap and sufficient education for the prospective clergy of the Welsh Church. The best of their students almost rivalled university men, and the better schools offered an education that their replacement, St David's College, was unable to offer, and for a far greater number of men.

THE UNIVERSITIES

A university degree from Oxford or Cambridge was regarded as a sufficient preparation for Orders on its own until the early years of the twentieth century. Men were required to attend the college chapel and were supervised by tutors, most of whom were in Orders themselves. Table One notes how in 1841 eighty-six per cent of the clergy in England and Wales had been educated at either Oxford or Cambridge.

By 1861 the percentage had dropped to sixty-five. This was not because there was a diminution in the number of those graduating but rather that the number of clergy in the country had risen in order to accommodate the needs of the new industrialised towns and the expansion of the cities.[67] It will also be noted that while the dioceses of Bangor and St Asaph were able to obtain a reasonable number of Oxbridge men, this was not the case in the southern dioceses, especially that of St Davids, mainly because of the expense required.[68] The fear has been noted elsewhere that those Welshmen who attended the universities would not return to their homeland, feeling that an English benefice offered a more lucrative reward for their academic exertions and social pretensions. Frances Knight, however, considers that about a quarter of the Welsh clergy during the nineteenth century were educated at these universities, and these men generally obtained the better livings.[69]

The universities, that is Oxford and Cambridge, were regarded as the ideal place for educating men for the Church's ministry, though not all survived the course. A substantial number of undergraduates took pass degrees, as opposed to an honours degree, these being established in the 1800s. Between 1851-1916 one third of Cambridge students took a pass degree, but over one quarter never graduated.[70] Here they mixed with the laity, and so did not become an exclusive caste, obtained a veneer of culture and polite manners, and acquired a broader education as well as a unique knowledge of men, but this in turn had its limitations as their education would distance them from the lower classes. Bishop Sumner of Winchester in 1858 claimed that their teaching was unaffected by the teachings of any particular theological school, unlike some of the theological colleges. It was felt, therefore, that even with a restricted amount of theological teaching and a lack of pastoral training these benefits outweighed any more practical instruction. The principal of Wycliffe Hall, Oxford, a graduate theological college, told the Church Congress in 1879 that a university education developed manliness, independence, courtesy and forbearance, besides other essential qualifications for the ministry.[71] Yet on the other hand as early as 1770 there were complaints that those who returned from the universities were little improved in learning and morals, and there was a constant fear that men would pick up bad habits from their more worldly contemporaries.[72]

Trinity College, Dublin, was frequented by a number of men, especially in Wales and Lancashire, because it was easily accessible by sea. Haig suggests it was regarded as providing a lesser education and was attended by men of lower status than the English universities.[73] It was clearly not popular with many in the Church of England, possibly because the Church of Ireland was Low Church. The *Ecclesiastic* could assert that the "refuse" of Dublin, unable to obtain their testimonials from that college for ordination in Ireland, migrated to dioceses on the mainland because of the lax examination of certain English bishops. Its degree, said an exiled Welshman in Yorkshire, was merely a certificate of learning.[74]

Though the cost of a university education could be expensive,[75] many men were able to pay their way by acting as sizars or servitors, that is, acting as servants to their fellow undergraduates or to their college in general. Unfortunately, for reasons still unclear, these sizarships were becoming less and less common by the early nineteenth century and as a result the universities were catering more for the upper classes rather than for a mixture of all classes in society.[76] One of these sizars was the eldest brother of Price, Carnhuanawc, J. Rice Price, who was a servitor at Wadham College, Oxford, and in 1808 he allowed his brother to spend several months with him at Oxford, hoping in some way "to supply the want of that university training" he was debarred from by poverty.[77] Conybeare, writing in 1855, estimated that about fifty clergy in north Wales had been educated as servitors at Jesus College, though he made it clear that this route was not applicable to those from south Wales, while Haig suggested that in 1852 there were still 143 sizars at Cambridge, most at Trinity and St John's Colleges, though by then the term related more to scholarship and humility than to service. Haig also notes that the Oxford Halls were relatively cheap, though they offered little academic potential.[78] Frances Knight makes an ironic point about those who held these sizarships: "Men who sometimes had been treated as the lowest form of academic life in Oxford, were regarded as the highest form of clerical life when they returned to Wales."[79]

The traditional college for Welshmen was Jesus College, Oxford, whose Meyrick foundation offered 20 scholarships of £80 and 30 exhibitions of 40 per annum, tenable for five years, to those resident in Wales. It also had a number of restricted scholarships attached to some of the Welsh grammar schools, notably Cowbridge and the north Wales schools.[80] There is a legend attached to the college, dating from the eighteenth century, that as many of them travelled home on foot they would keep students in other colleges awake on the last night of term as they tinkered their hobnailed boots ready for that journey.[81] As late as 1878 a large proportion of the sixty in residence at the college were described by its vice-principal as "the sons of ambitious Welsh countrymen", who had come to Oxford intending in most cases to be ordained and serve in Welsh parishes, "and who were not accustomed to general society."[82]

We may note a constant concern from the bishops and other interested parties that the courses provided for future clergy at the universities were not particularly suited for their future vocation, and their desire that the divinity courses should be properly regulated and examined, so that men, when they came to be ordained, had some clear knowledge of the subject they were required to teach in their parochial ministries.[83] Bishop Porteus of Chester thus claimed in 1778 that university men entered the Church "with so little knowledge of their profession as to be very moderately qualified for discharging the common duties of the smallest country cure".[84] Connop Thirlwall, then a fellow of Trinity College, Cambridge, argued in 1834 that the universities were not theological institutions. The lectures given communicated knowledge rather than offered any particular purposes of religion, while the examinations asked questions about grammar, chronology, geography and history, but almost without exception there was no question about a point of doctrine.[85] Alfred Ollivant, in his introductory lecture to his lectures as regius professor of Divinity at Cambridge, pointed out that the preparatory course of instruction in the university absorbed all the undergraduate's energies, and there was little time left for the student of divinity to acquire the professional knowledge indispensable for ministers of God and stewards of the mysteries of Christ. The university's education was too secular he claimed, with the result that divinity was neglected.[86] As late as 1879 the principal of the Oxford theological college, Wycliffe Hall, R.B. Girdlestone, complained that a university man might well be lost when asked to minister to the sick or asked "what must I do to be saved?"[87]

Others expressed concern that the curriculum was limited and men only studied those areas in which they would be examined,[88] while there was equal concern that no training was offered in pastoral work, in the conduct of worship or in the composition and preaching of sermons.[89] A more serious concern for others, especially Tractarians and evangelicals, was that the universities did not offer the discipline required for a priestly or ministerial life, or enable their students to apply their theological knowledge into their daily lives.[90] Nevertheless, William Ince, later the regius professor of Divinity, claimed in 1862 that the Oxford arts degree represented a general liberal education, suitable for every profession. It was never designed to be the specific training of a clergyman.[91]

By 1800 Oxford held regular examinations for its degrees, previous to which undergraduates were required to take part in disputations, where they would be required to debate a subject given to them. Even in the 1810s the examinations were regarded as farcical as failures were almost unknown.[92] In one set of collections or terminal examinations an undergraduate complained he had been asked the names of the twelve apostles, but he only knew those of the four evangelists.[93] The subject matter for the Oxford pass degree included the Greek Gospels, some books from the English Bible, the elements of religion and the 39 Articles. Fifty years later the university's first public examination demanded a paper on the four Gospels in Greek, and in the second public examination more of the Greek Testament was included, together with books of the old Testament, the evidences for Christianity, and the 39 Articles. In 1824 Cambridge introduced what became known as "the previous examination", a preliminary one that enabled a man to proceed to the final examinations. This was designed to reduce the stress given to mathematics at the university and included the study of classical authors, one of the four Gospels or the Acts of the Apostles in Greek and Paley's *Evidences of Christianity*. The final examinations for the ordinary or pass degree included some aspects of Church History, a more extensive knowledge of the Greek Testament, and Paley's *Moral Philosophy*.[94]

At Cambridge, though tuition was probably given by the individual colleges, there were hardly any lectures in theology offered by the various divinity professors, save for the Norrisian professor who was required to give fifty lectures per annum. It was not until the 1790s when the bishops started to require Cambridge candidates to obtain certificates of having attended these lectures that they started to be well attended. The lectures of J.B. Hollingworth, professor 1824-38, were described as a mere reading of Pearson on the Creed, so that few attended. His lectures were repeated each year; his hearers were not examined, so that many read newspapers and novels in his lecture room instead. Herbert Marsh, then Lady Margaret Professor and later bishop of Llandaff, was the first to give his lectures in English rather than Latin. This was in 1807.[95]

Following concerns expressed by Charles Perry of Trinity College,[96] Cambridge in 1842 established the voluntary post-graduate Theological examination. Taken after a degree had been obtained, when most men were too young to be ordained, it consisted of parts of the Greek Testament, assigned portions of the early Fathers, ecclesiastical history, the 39 Articles and the Church's liturgy. There was an optional paper in Hebrew. Few took it, as it required further study, more expense, and probably two or three terms of preparation, until a circular letter was written to the bishops asking them to require candidates for ordination to present a certificate that they had passed it. The examination thus ceased to be voluntary, ceased to be a distinction, became a pass rather than an honours examination, and thus the standard was lowered so it was possible for students to "cram" for it. Examining chaplains frequently complained that while men passed this examination, they had to reject them, as it was easy to tell the difference between real and simulated knowledge. By 1873 it was regarded as a failure and ended. It was replaced by an honour tripos in theology. Oxford followed suit in 1869-70 with an honours school in theology.[97]

Oxford was slow to follow the lead initially set by Cambridge. Charles Ogilivie was appointed the first regius professor of Pastoral Theology in 1842, and charged with giving instruction in "Ministerial duties, composition and delivery of sermons, Knowledge and History of Liturgy, Rubrics, and the like". Four years later a series of divinity lectures were established in Oxford for postgraduates, but they were irregularly held and attendance was not compulsory. Some bishops required it of their candidates, and some heads of colleges made attendance a condition of obtaining a college testimonial, but many did not.[98]

Admirable as these changes were, they were regarded by many as insufficient, especially as candidates had to avail themselves voluntarily of the facilities, unless a bishop required a certificate of lectures attended or an examination passed. Within the universities individuals offered assistance to ordination candidates, of whom the best known was Charles Simeon (1759-1836). He held sermon classes in his rooms at Trinity College, Cambridge, and on alternative weeks an open forum for discussion.[99] Edward Bickersteth, later dean of Lichfield, concerned that the system of education at the universities was far too classical and thus promoted national pride and love of earthly glory, offered not only a course of private study for those preparing for the ministry in his *The Christian Student*, but also advice about cultivating spirituality together with moral cautions.[100] A much later development was the Oxford Pastorate, an evangelical organisation designed to work amongst undergraduates. In the 1900s it offered courses of doctrinal instruction for ordination candidates, especially as it was still possible for graduates to proceed to ordination without any intervening pastoral or theological training.[101]

The need for a more formalised post-graduate training was being clearly articulated by the 1830s. George Townsend, prebendary of Durham, objected to one of the objects of the Church Reformation Society, an organisation he disliked in any case. This was the necessity for a course of strictly professional study and a period of probation for candidates for Holy Orders, "so as to secure ministers duly qualified for their sacred and responsible office". His objection was not that this was unnecessary, but that this work was a matter for the universities and not for private organisations.[102]

As early as 1854 Thomas Briscoe of Jesus College suggested to the Cathedral Commissioners, a government body of enquiry, that one remedy for the lack of theological training was to insist that candidates after their eighth term should spend a year outside the university in theological and pastoral pursuits. At the end of the year they should be able to proceed to the BA degree provided they passed a further examination, but without any further residence being required.[103] The lower house of Convocation supported a similar proposal in 1865, requesting that the universities should offer an additional year after the BA degree had been awarded for the study of divinity, or that the university course be supplemented by time spent in a theological college.[104] Specific colleges for post-graduate work had been started in the 1840s, and though regarded with much suspicion, gradually became accepted within the wider Church, especially as the bishops were realising the need for the training they offered. Cuddeston was probably the most significant, while Wycliffe in Oxford and Ridley at Cambridge were evangelical colleges based in a university setting. St Michael's College, then at Aberdare, was not opened until 1892 and was designed specifically for Welsh graduates, including those of Lampeter. As a consequence, by 1891, about half of those who graduated from the ancient universities attended a theological college for a period of time.[105] These colleges will be noted in the following chapter.

THE NEW UNIVERSITIES

Bishop Chavasse of Liverpool speaking at the Manchester Church Congress of 1908 expressed pleasure that the "provincial" universities were providing an education for those unable to enter the older universities. Sir Henry Reichel, principal of Bangor University College, suggested that the fees at these places were £40 per annum, which included the cost of residence, and consequently much lower than the older universities.[106] Expressing concern, at a later date, that the University of Wales had excluded theology from its remit, he managed by 1922 to establish a compromise. This enabled a new theological faculty to be started, modelled on the Manchester one, which incorporated teachers appointed by the university and those on the staff of affiliated theological colleges, who would act as special lecturers and be paid through their colleges. It was entirely his own work, and redressed a resolution of 1892-3, which he alone opposed, that no provision be made for theology in the university. Reichel believed this was due to sectarian feeling, and because the Nonconformist theological colleges felt their position might be undermined by such a radical departure.[107] The Church Hostel at Bangor gave additional training to ordinands at the University College there, as noted before, and after the date of disestablishment a reasonable number of Welsh ordinands took degrees in the University of Wales and then went onto St Michael's College for more specialised training. By the 1950s the Welsh bench of bishops were discouraging Welsh ordinands from attending Oxford or Cambridge, a position Bishop J.C. Jones of Bangor regarded as deplorable as he believed the Welsh Church needed to look beyond its own borders.[108]

CHAPTER FOUR:
THE EDUCATION OF THE FUTURE CLERGY
PART TWO: ST DAVID'S COLLEGE, LAMPETER

There can be little doubt that when Thomas Burgess became bishop of St Davids in 1803 he received a culture shock when he met his clergy and discovered that one of the great defects of his diocese was the financial impossibility of those destined for Orders to remain in school long enough to be sufficiently grounded "in the elements of grammatical learning". The great want of such education was "seen and lamented in the consequences of the ordination week". This was stated in a sermon of 1812, by which time he had established the Church Union Society, whose fourth object was the promotion of clerical education, establishing a fund for a seminary, and allowing the interest on the capital obtained to be used for exhibitions to enable candidates to remain in school for the seven years study he now required.[1] His grand object was to establish a college to educate men for the ministry whose resources precluded them from a university education, and where they would employ their time "in strictly professional studies for four years prior to their ordination."[2]

Burgess's initial plan was to establish residential accommodation at Ystrad Meurig, but it appears a row with its master ended that suggestion. A seminary at St Davids appears to have been considered, but eventually Llanddewi Brefi was preferred, as it formed part of the episcopal estate, and had a large church. Although on average only eight deacons were ordained each year, this new college would accommodate thirty men. They were expected to have studied for four years at one of the licensed grammar schools before admission at the age of nineteen, and have a good knowledge of Greek, Latin and Hebrew, an understanding of some theological books, be able to write an English composition, and have a grasp of some more conventional subjects. The syllabus of the new college extended this knowledge, together with the study of doctrine, writing compositions in Latin, Greek and Welsh, a daily transcription of a chapter of the Bible in the original language, together with logic and Euclid in the first year, Christian evidences and history in the second, and Church History, canon law, pastoralia, and the Thirty Nine Articles in the third. In addition elocution and the duties of the clerical profession were to be taught. During the vacations students were expected to copy out sermons. The annual charge was set at £30 per annum, including board and lodging. Compared to the universities this was a small expense, declared Richard Evans, and the location such that it would be "without the dangers incident to a more populous situation". If they were too young to be ordained when the course was finished, men would be employed as catechists within the diocese.

Donations came from the diocese of St Davids, but more substantial sums came from George IV and a Treasury grant of £400 per annum. The offer of land at Lampeter meant the new college was built there and opened in 1827, with room for sixty students, and three professional staff.[3] By 1836 the test for admission was "a slight preparatory examination" in Latin and Greek, but the four year syllabus that had to be completed before the Colleges Testimonial was awarded – required for ordination – included two and a half years study of the classics, Welsh (if appropriate), logic and Euclid, and if the students passed the necessary examination in these subjects the remaining time was spent in the divinity class. Here men studied the Greek Testament, parts of the Hebrew Bible, and specified theological and apologetical books, analysed a section of Burnet's *Thirty Nine Articles* each week, while the Welsh students were required to compose a Welsh theme and in turn deliver an English lecture each Saturday in the college hall. They were also required to read the lessons at the daily services, which were conducted bilingually.[4]

Bishop Jenkinson, in whose episcopate the college was opened, declared that the new college would be useful and effective, in comparison to the "local institutions" it was replacing, as it was established on a much larger scale and had a more expanded plan of education. Though the Welsh clergy previously had "fallen behind" other dioceses regarding their literary and theological attainments through lack of opportunity, now they had before them "the inestimable advantages of a solid and liberal education" and the ability to rescue themselves from a state of intellectual inferiority. As it was his duty to place the Church in his diocese on a more respectable footing, he would encourage this new institution by looking to it exclusively together with the universities for the supply of candidates for ordination.[5] Nevertheless, there were dissenting voices. Some felt that the endowments collected for the new college would have been far better used as scholarships for Welsh students at Oxford and Cambridge.[6]

The aims of the college might be stated to unite to some degree the advantages of a university education, living a communal life as in an Oxford college, together with a moral discipline. At a later date Ollivant, a former vice-principal, suggested the college's aim was to encourage a conception of ministry that was more than simply preaching and to obtain a clerical body, which if not of high birth, nevertheless had refinement and the grace of a sound education so as to be an influence amongst both upper and lower classes.[7] Jenkinson in a letter of 1826 put matters in a more negative way. In the context of the difficulties of the grammar schools whose pupils boarded in somewhat unsavoury places, he argued "for these evils and abuses the College will prove the best and only effectual remedy, and the only adequate security against the admission of improper persons to the profession".[8] Equally, in 1849, Sir Thomas Phillips hoped that the college would accustom the students "to habits of self-respect" and inculcate a taste for "liberal studies" so as to preserve them from intemperance and the indolent apathy that was the lot of many isolated Welsh clergymen.[9] John Owen, Principal 1893-7, put it this way: to teach students theology and humanities, to polish their manners, broaden their outlook, and to deepen their characters.[10] Principal Bebb in the 1900s was said to have extended this concept by ensuring that his students became respected gentlemen, good Tories, moderate Anglicans, keen sportsmen and committed supporters of the Establishment.[11] It was the idea of the gentleman parson, able to hold his own with the better educated of his profession, though this was hardly the requirement for a man in a Welsh-speaking rural or industrial parish.

At first the other Welsh bishops believed that the college was an exclusively diocesan seminary, and thus declined to accept men from the college into their dioceses.[12] Gradually, over a period of some considerable time, the Welsh and some English bishops began to accept Lampeter as a place of training for ordination. Van Mildert of Llandaff did so in 1827, stating that it offered to its students "many of the peculiar advantages of academical discipline".[13] Copleston, his successor, wrote to his father in 1828 that the college at Lampeter, "for divinity students", was flourishing and had assumed "quite an academical form". Writing to Bruce Knight, his diocesan confident, in 1832 he declared that the benefit of the college was "even greater than I had expected". Eight years later he felt it ought to be "the seminary for Wales" and he should require a residence there as the qualification for ordination, without resorting to schools "nearer home".[14] By 1837 Lampeter men were being ordained in the dioceses of Sodor and Man, York, Norwich, Lichfield and Chester.[15]

THE DIFFICULTY OF IMPOSING A STANDARD FOR ADMISSION

Did the college live up to these high expectations? The answer is that it probably did not. Many of the first students had been pupils of the old grammar schools and had been well prepared, and it seemed, in the words of one writer, that the "first fruits" promised a rich harvest.[16] Others questioned this assertion. Rice Rees, professor of Welsh, in a letter of March 1827 to his uncle, William Jenkin Rees of Casgob, acknowledged that the standard of admission had been fixed far too high, and so they were obliged to lower it to a level he had never even contemplated. The examination had eventually consisted of three verses of the Greek Testament and two stanzas of Horace. Some candidates confessed that having read divinity in the grammar schools for the previous three years they had forgotten their classics, and at first these were admitted for fear of terrifying the rest. Then it became apparent it was unjust to reject others who were of a similar standard. There were hardly twenty decent scholars out of forty-six, and though these men were divided into three classes, they really needed twelve to do justice to their age range and abilities.[17] When Joseph Romilly visited the college in 1837 he found 45 students with accommodation available for 70, three professors instead of the five he considered necessary, and while the college itself was "neat" it was in a miserable place and was far from flourishing.[18]

The first students were mainly local men, nearly all from St Davids diocese. Up to 1849 there were 462 students, of whom 350 were from that diocese, 14 from the diocese of Llandaff, in spite of Copleston's admiration for the college, and 18 from north Wales, mainly from Montgomeryshire. Farmers' sons remained the largest single category. It was clear to Rowland Williams that most of the students would be from the poorer classes. "The question is not," he wrote, what sort of wood you might prefer cutting your tool from (for that has been determined by circumstances beyond our control), but into what sort of instrument you will fashion it".[19]

Ollivant accepted in 1842 that the college was not as useful to the Church as it might have been,[20] while Bishop Thirlwall in a letter of 1847 accepted that the transition from the old system of grammar schools to the present one had produced problems which had interfered with the well-being of the college, and which had not been foreseen at the time.[21] This was a recognition that in insisting that no candidates for ordination could proceed directly to ordination from a grammar school, these schools had declined and as a result were unable to be effective feeders for the college. Numbers at the college declined, and in an attempt to remedy this the admission standard was again lowered, with an anonymous critic alleging that men were admitted who were not fit for the higher classes of a common national school. The four year course was reduced to three and a half years in 1841, and the rule none be admitted unless they had received two years education in a grammar school was ended. It is hardly surprising that it was said that the standard of scholarship had shrunk far below that of the old grammar schools, though the expenses had doubled. Nevertheless, by 1839 numbers had risen to 60 from the 36 of 1833. In 1847 a further attempt was made to raise the standards of the college, and the minimum admission requirement was increased to two years attendance at a good grammar school, while external examiners were appointed from the two universities. But numbers dropped again: in 1856 to 34.[22]

The reasons adduced for this state of affairs was that the College was poorly endowed, its want of good management, its scarcity of scholarships, its lack of degree status, and because it had to cater for students who had little scholastic background. The need was for the grammar schools to rise to the college's level, not for the college to sink to their level. It was believed that if degree status could be obtained the standard of entry would rise.[23] This was eventually achieved, and the grant of degree status (BD in 1852, requiring an additional term, and BA in 1865) allowed Bishop Thirlwall, preaching at the college's commemoration day, to assert that this new status had lifted the college above those which were considered equal to it, even though they had a shorter course.[24] William Price, in his history of the college, suggests that there was a crisis of confidence about it by the Welsh bishops in the 1870s, with the sole exception of Thirlwall. Their concern was the lack of candidates, and Ollivant added that because of this he was forced to ordain men who were certified students from colleges such as St Bees or Birmingham, or even literates, who fell far below his standards. One of the reasons adduced for this lack of numbers was the cost of attending the college, and it appears that the Welsh bishops were successful in obtaining a reduction in the tuition fees.[25]

The great difficulties faced by the college until the introduction of the new intermediate schools of the 1890s was the insufficient preparation of those who entered it, for it was noted that many parents could not afford to pay the fees for a grammar school education. There was also a lack of general knowledge and an imperfect acquaintance with English, and even of Biblical knowledge, so instead of educating men at an advanced level the tutors had to do the work of schoolmasters.[26] Rowland Williams said of his pupils that as they entered the college they "know *no* language, but are engaged in acquiring the rudiments of several. Welsh they cannot write and English they cannot speak". Indeed, if their fathers asked "how little can I pay", their sons asked "how little may I learn". It might have been charitable to have lectured in Welsh, but the difficulties of doing so and the prejudices this would cause made this an impossibility. Williams wrote descriptions of several of his pupils. One had frequently failed at Oxford and found Lampeter a place of refuge; another Thomas Thomas, was strangely ignorant but had a power of preaching, and John George, a former tailor, thirty-one at entry, was "wonderfully ignorant, rude and simple", but reported to be eloquent in Welsh. He was fitter to be a shepherd of sheep than of men. He smoked to excess, but was still ordained by Bishop Ollivant. Amongst these men, in his words, were men advanced in years, broken down farmers, blacksmiths, Wesleyan preachers, of whom many came from their own homes without any previous preparation.[27] As late as 1870 Perowne made the same complaint. Boys entered school at sixteen and over and stayed just long enough to get sufficient knowledge of Latin and Greek to pass the entry examination.[28]

With these problems constantly before him, Rowland Williams, vice-principal 1850-62, endeavoured to reform the whole system by imposing a more stringent entrance examination and a more demanding and satisfactory curriculum. In a review of Bishop Ollivant's Charge, attached to his pamphlet *Christian Freedom in the Council of Jerusalem,* Williams made clear that he wished to establish a finesse of tone and discipline, a systematic instruction in doctrine, and as large an education as circumstances permitted. The tone, he suggested, might be described as "old Anglican, with new life in it". The college calendar of 1857 notes that candidates for admission were required to have spent at least two years at a grammar school, and the entrance examination consisted of Latin and English composition, Biblical and general history, geography, arithmetic, Euclid, and some Greek and Latin classical texts.

Though there were many complaints that the balance was wrong, too much attention was paid to classical studies and too little to pastoral experience or matters of doctrine, Williams defended his course by pointing out that one third of the period was devoted to theology in the divinity class, admission to which was by a further examination in the work of the previous terms. Here the Hebrew Scriptures or a Latin substitute were taught, together with the epistles in Greek, and the standard theological texts and books on the Articles and Prayer Book. These, Williams pointed out, would be the requirements of a bishop's chaplain. In addition, Welsh and elocution were taught, and assistance was given in sermon writing while students also had some experience in a national school. English analysis and composition were also taught and there was a weekly Welsh exercise class, but he hoped that in matters of preaching and prayer students would learn by example. If a student failed his final examination he was not allowed to resit for another two terms. The college had the same examiners as the universities, nor was Lampeter more expensive than the older universities (another frequent complaint), for the annual expenses should not exceed £70, this sum including dress, travelling and books. As Williams wrote in his *Lampeter Theology*, he was laying the foundations in three years for a lifetime of service, and forming habits that would be consistent with the spirit of Christ. To make good divines, he noted elsewhere, you first needed good scholars.[29] The standard of admission had been raised over the past four years "by much trouble and anxiety ... but the *degree* of raising is hardly perceptible ... as compared to the difficulty there has been in enforcing it". It is hardly surprising that with all these difficulties, namely the lack of preparation in men, the want of cheap classical schools, the competition from other seminaries with shorter courses, Williams wondered whether his experiment in raising standards would ever be successful.[30]

Unfortunately, this new system meant that many failed the entrance examination (in 1852 during one term four out of ten did so), and the three year course became so notorious for its academic weight that many men looked elsewhere, discovering that some of the English theological colleges offered a much easier, and even better, two year course. Williams' hope was that the Welsh bishops would refuse to ordain men from these other colleges, but he was disappointed. When Bishop Campbell in 1859 accepted students from Birmingham that Williams had rejected he "felt the hour of darkness had triumphed". Even men whose entry to Lampeter had been postponed for further reading took the hint and departed elsewhere "for a shorter and easier cut", and these other colleges seldom hesitated to admit any candidates whom he had rejected as incompetent. Bishop Short of St Asaph's encouragement of St Bees' men into his diocese had the same effect, and youths, "from that area of country which

Lampeter might be expected to sweep, ... have gone there [St Bees] because the requirements for admission were less, and the period of study shorter". As a result numbers had dropped by one third and they were likely to remain that way.[31] Yet Williams made clear it was kinder to reject deficient candidates at the start rather than allow them to spend time and money for some years in a fruitless attempt at ordination.[32] He also expressed concern that the university examiners for the college were unaware of its difficulties and either asked too much or too little of the candidates.[33]

Williams was also unfortunate in that some of his published writings were regarded as "heretical" by the evangelical clergy, and alleged that his views further depleted entry to the college. However, in denying this, he affirmed that while some of his students were frightened by his examinations none were by his theology.[34]

It needed a new principal and a vigorous shake up of the old order for the institution to revive, a matter clearly hinted by Bishop Basil Jones in his 1880 Charge, when he noted that under Principal Jayne the college had entered upon a new career of usefulness, though he still bemoaned the insufficient preparation of those who entered it.[35] Until then J.J.S. Perowne, as vice principal, had a justified complaint that the college was expected in three years to provide all the education and training a man needed to qualify him for his profession, which could not be done without cutting corners and accepting a course that the tutors felt inadequate.[36] By 1883 Basil Jones was declaring that Lampeter not only gave men specific theological instruction but also a general education similar to that of the ancient universities. Theological colleges could not do this, and he greatly depreciated the common practice of sending young men to such institutions in the north of England and elsewhere when they could obtain a more liberal education closer to home. Three years later the bishop declared that the college was the chief nursery for clergy in the Church in Wales, and that the new principal had not only developed its educational system but also had doubled the number of students.[37]

A QUESTION OF THE WELSH LANGUAGE

The tensions between reality and expectations are quite clear, and soon began to surface. The Church wanted more and more clergy, and one section of it wanted Welsh-speaking men who would be akin to the nonconformist preacher as preaching seemed to be the way to win back dissent. The college authorities wanted to give their students a well-rounded education to enable them to serve the whole Church, both upper classes and peasants, and believed the ministry was a learned profession rather than a gifted trade. The bishops were torn between the need for clergy in a numerical sense and their desire for a well-educated body of men. The college had been established to provide clergy and offer then an education akin to that of the universities and provide them with resources for future intellectual development. The latter was generally forgotten by those who criticised it for not producing sufficient men. There were other criticisms that were not unfair, namely that the Welsh language and culture was generally ignored by the College, and that it failed to give its students an adequate pastoral training. Many of these criticisms surrounded the work of Rowland Williams and J.J.S. Perowne as vice principals, for they were the real leaders of the college, whereas the principal, Llewelyn Lewellin (1827-78) was also vicar of Lampeter and dean of St Davids, and apart from teaching, his role in the scholastic side of the college seemed rather minimal. Even Thirlwall, visitor of the college, felt he could not support a petition of 1847 asking for it to receive degree status "until steps had been taken to raise the character of the college".[38]

Two of the most vigorous of the assailants of the college were John Williams, archdeacon of Cardigan, a prominent educationalist and a former headmaster of Lampeter Grammar school, and Sir Benjamin Hall, MP, later Lord Llanover, together with his wife, who were leading proponents of the need for the Church to be Welsh-orientated.[39] Williams may well have been activated by jealousy as he had assumed he might have been principal himself rather than Lewellin. In a letter to the London *Times* of 1851 he alleged that St David's College was "a blight and a curse upon the spiritual and intellectual energies of the Principality", and that it was "the slaughter house of the rising talent of his country." His assertions were vigorously denied.[40]

Augusta Hall in many letters made accusation after accusation about this apparent lack of Welsh in the college. She alleged in 1847 that the bishop of St Davids had rejected every candidate for ordination from the college the previous year for deficiencies in Welsh and the classical languages. She complained there was no Welsh professor in the college, though its charter required one, that there had been one Welsh lecture in three years and that the principal hated "Welsh in his heart". Lampeter was a sink of corruption.[41] Further allegations followed in 1851: the bishop of Llandaff had sent back to the principal the Welsh exercises submitted to his Welsh examining chaplain by the Lampeter men as "quite disgraceful". Benjamin Hall

89

discovered this and made a complaint to the prime minister, Lord John Russell. Thirlwall, writing as visitor, explained that Ollivant had sent these papers back as it would have a good effect if the students realised that such notice was taken of their work. While there were deficiencies in their spelling and writing, these would not interfere with their practical usefulness, for their ability to read and speak the language correctly was not impaired and would make them useful and efficient Welsh pastors. Hall accused the Welsh bishops of not having sufficient Welsh to understand the position and being unsympathetic to the language. He demanded an enquiry into the conduct of the college. Around the same time *Giraldus* (John Rowland) alleged that men trained at Lampeter had to pay Nonconformist ministers to write sermons for them.[42] An editorial in the *Cardiff and Merthyr Guardian* of 1870 noted that the college's Welsh professor was "a nominal appointment" and had produced no results, and the college had neglected the opportunity of strengthening the Welsh Church by enabling its men to meet the Welsh people on their own ground.[43]

A writer in the *Ecclesiastic* of 1846 considered that Lampeter together with St Bees College witnessed to the Church's wants rather than supplying them. Both colleges were conducted on a "most miserable starving scale" and excluded "the doctrines and disciplines of the Church", by which the writer meant Tractarian teachings.[44] His initial statements were not unfair, and testified to the continuing problems faced by their authorities. In 1851 *Giraldus* was quoted by the writer of *St. David's College, Lampeter. Its Assailants and Defenders*, in which he reviewed the history of the college and the evidence for its malfunctioning. Its students, Giraldus claimed, were crammed to get through their examinations; the trial of twenty-three years indicated the college had entirely failed its purpose, and it would be better for it to become a two-year theological college and for its students to obtain their preliminary education elsewhere.[45] The Association of Welsh Clergy in the West Riding of Yorkshire castigated the college for its over-emphasis on classics, its lack of Welsh and of a pastoral and practical training. What was the point, it was asked, of sending a minister to the Welsh hill country who could render the classics into equally eloquent English? A man could fail Welsh and still be ordained, but not if he failed the examiners in Latin or Greek. The Welsh dissenting minister was far better equipped to serve his congregation than the Anglican pastor.[46] In a memoir of J.A. Jackson, later a diocesan inspector of schools and a student at Lampeter in 1868, William Hughes noted his concern that Welsh as a subject could not be offered for the pass degree. Though there were Welsh lectures the fact that the subject was not examined meant that men concentrated on other subjects.[47]

These accusations were vigorously denied. Rowland Williams declared that the assertions about academic failure were not supported by the external examiners, while they used the same books as the English universities, and he declared that Welsh was taught in the college, as we have already seen. With regard to pastoralia he felt that preaching and prayer would be learnt by example. English, he pointed out, was required of every gentleman, and was the medium through which almost all the educated classes obtained their knowledge.[48] Joshua Hughes, then vicar of Llandovery, argued that to make "Welsh everything" as the Llanover party wanted, would be wasting precious time required for more important knowledge. After all, the English clergy did not go to Cambridge to learn English.[49] Perowne, as vice-principal, argued that while the study of the Welsh language was encouraged by the college, it was not by the study of that language that "the advancement of the Welsh Church would be secured, but by a higher cultivation of the English tongue".[50] It is perhaps not surprising that when Thomas Phillips, a retired surgeon, wished to endow a Welsh chair at the college in 1848 it was rejected, and instead he founded a new public school at Llandovery.[51]

A further accusation gained some prominence in the 1900s, namely that the college was an Anglicising influence, and as Howard Evans asserted, was "used as a means of stifling Welsh feelings and flouting Welsh national sentiments". This may have been a reference to Principal Bebb, but it was still related to the claim that the college was not sufficiently concerned with the Welsh language or culture.[52] Evans was not alone in his sentiments. The Liberal MP, Lord Rendel, described the college as "the spawn of the English establishment".[53] Bebb redeemed himself, however, by writing in his annual report of 1904 that he wished Welsh to have a full share of time and attention, and the appointment of E. Lorimer Thomas in 1904 to a full chair in Welsh - it was previously held with history – was the result.[54]

Thus Lampeter was embroiled in the midst of a national dilemma, rather than one of its own making, between the need for English as the language of advancement and that of Welsh as the language of the hearth and soul. Lampeter was not alone in this matter, however. The Welsh language disappeared from the syllabus of many of the dissenting theological colleges in Wales: Brecon Memorial College in the 1860s, the Presbyterian College, Carmarthen until 1894, while Pontypool Baptist College had abolished Welsh, and English was thought to be the official language of Bala College in Lewis Edwards' time.[55]

A CONCERN FOR PASTORALIA AND SPIRITUALITY

The allegations and complaints continued. Joshua Hughes in his primary charge of 1881 bemoaned the fact that the college's supply of ordinands was unable to meet the needs of the Church in Wales, and that it lacked a chair in pastoral theology and training in parochial work.[56] Yet five years later, James Rice Buckley, ordained in 1872, later archdeacon of Llandaff, could inform the Llandaff Diocesan Conference that in his time at the college it offered pastoral addresses and instruction in pastoralia and preaching.[57] Writing of Buckley's contemporaries and those who followed him, Canon Mason, the archbishop of Canterbury's missioner, was not so complacent. In a report to Archbishop Benson he concluded, from his own observations and from many conversations with incumbents during his mission work in Wales, that the college "did not give to young men a sufficiently practical training for Holy Orders". The younger clergy seemed to conclude that their duties were over when the services had ended, so there was little pastoral work, but they also exhibited in their reading of the service and preaching "a want of intelligence."[58] It is not surprising that on the appointment of Herbert Ryle as principal in 1886, Benson wrote to him pointing out that the college preserved too much the "stiff dry type of religion" that prevailed in the universities at the date of its foundation. He also felt the lack of pastoral teaching and the poor spirituality of the college needed to be addressed.[59]

Speaking to the Llandaff Diocesan Conference in 1892, H.R. Johnson, principal of the theological college at Aberdare, argued that while they did not look in vain to Lampeter for their future clergymen, its training needed to be supplemented. Claiming that as many of its men lacked Church principles as they came from dissenting backgrounds, and as the college's purpose was more academic, he felt they had little time or opportunity for deepening their spiritual life, while the large number of students made personal influence impossible. Such men needed a further course in a theological college to equip them for their future role, and such a place was his own college.[60] By the early 1900s the position had been somewhat remedied, as lectures in pastoralia and social problems, and lessons in intoning and preaching, were started, but no devotional training was given.[61]

THE BIENNIAL STUDENTS

There was another class of students at Lampeter of whom no mention has yet been made. In 1850 it was agreed that persons recommended by their bishops, and after passing a suitable examination, could be admitted to the college as theological students. After two years residence they would be allowed to present themselves before the board of college examiners for the award of the college certificate. Gaining this they would be allowed to offer themselves for Orders in the diocese of their recommending bishop. It seems this was an unusual procedure, and confined to older men. But precedent almost became a right, and one assumes that some of Rowland Williams' strictures related to this category of student.[62] In 1884 the Welsh bishops insisted on a reorganisation of this course. The class of certified non-graduate students was abolished, and in its place a new course, with a higher standard, for biennial students was commenced. Those who completed the course successfully were allowed the accolade of Lic.Div. It was stipulated that this course was for those over twenty-one years of age, was to be set at pass degree standard, and it was understood that those admitted to it lacked the finance to do more than six terms rather than the ability to take a degree. In all probability these men were former schoolmasters, who would have found the necessary classical requirements for the degree course extremely difficult. It was anticipated that the course would encourage men to enter St David's College rather than attend St Bees or other similar colleges.

Once again the course was abused, as Basil Jones alleged in his Charge of 1892. Though the course was designed to meet exceptional cases it had "worked itself into a more prominent position in the system of the college than was either intended or desirable." This was surprising, for the course was far more demanding than equivalent courses at other colleges or the "voluntary examination" now required by many bishops. Though the bishops of St Asaph and Bangor disapproved of this course, the external examiners found it valuable as it meant that the standard of the degree could be maintained without affecting college numbers.[63] Certificates in theology and Welsh were also available by 1900. The theological certificate was for those who had taken their degree in other subjects and required an examination in two Gospels and the Acts of the Apostles in Greek, Old Testament subjects, the history and contents of the Prayer Book and Articles, early church history and pastoralia. A tenth term was required for it.[64]

There had been expectations that the college would become a constituent college of the University of Wales, founded in 1893, as were the Aberystwyth, Bangor and Cardiff colleges. But the refusal of Lampeter to give up the teaching of theology undermined the concept of a secular university, and added to this the Nonconformist dislike of a Church institution meant this desire was frustrated.[65] In 1908 Principal Reichel of Bangor had proposed, and Bishop Edwards of St Asaph had supported, a scheme whereby the college became a theological college for those men who had taken an initial degree in the University of Wales. Reichel noted that the Nonconformist colleges had given up their secular teaching for theology, sending their men for a university education first at public cost. The original position of St David's College in providing both secular and theological training was now outdated. When he had first come to Wales Lampeter had turned out a better class of men than these colleges, but the position was now reversed as the Nonconformist colleges had brought themselves into the university movement. Their five-year course had to be condensed into three at Lampeter. If the college was founded today it would have imitated these other colleges. If they continued the present system they would be condemning the bulk of ordinands to a shorter and less adequate course than that obtained by most Nonconformist minsters.[66] However, the realisation that the college's endowments were linked to its art courses effectively ended these discussions. Turning Lampeter into a pure theological college was not a new idea, for it had been suggested in 1856 by the Welsh clergy in the West Riding, with Christ College, Brecon, being given degree status, and also by David Howell of Wrexham in 1888.[67]

Gilbert Joyce, principal 1916-22, proposed that a new college be established at Aberystwyth, linked to Lampeter, where men would take their initial degree. They would then proceed to Lampeter for a two-year theological course, and then for a final year to St Michael's College, Llandaff, for a year of preparation before ordination. The debate over these proposals continued over many years, though it was soon realised that a six-year course was not financially viable. Eventually, the college authorities convened a committee chaired by Lord Justice Sankey. This committee examined these proposals of Joyce and the whole position of Lampeter. It discovered that in the late 1890s it drew from such schools as Brecon and Llandovery, so that many students were of the usual age, but between 1901-13 there were a large number of men of a more mature age. Both the Lampeter College School (established by

Jayne) and Ystrad Meurig had adult classes that helped swell these numbers, but as the majority of secondary schools no longer taught Greek, essential for entry to the college, the committee's report questioned if it was worth the effort of making this a requirement. In addition, it suggested that the degree course was not in itself sufficient preparation for ordination, and the college should be adapted to provide post-graduate training as well. Its main recommendation was the continuation of the college as a degree-giving institution.[68]

Maurice Jones as the new principal (1923-38) brought new life to the college after the aridity of Joyce's tenure of office. For the first time the college attracted the majority of its students from the county schools, and there were now fewer from the public schools or older men. Over 95 per cent of the intake in the 1920s and 1930s were ordained so that it became the power house of the now disestablished Church in Wales.[69]

Until the 1930s, when the University of Wales became popular, St David's College was the main source of ordination candidates for most of the Welsh dioceses, as Bishop Pritchard Hughes of Llandaff maintained.[70] In 1905 Principal Bebb, writing to Archbishop Davidson, asked for his support for the college, it being one of the strategic points of the Church in Wales. More than two thousand clergymen had been trained there, of whom 900 were still working in England and Wales.[71] William Price calculated that in 1927 830 of the 1250 clerics in Wales had been trained, whole or in part, at Lampeter, 66 per cent of the total, though the number had dropped to 57 per cent by 1939 because of the number graduating at the University of Wales.[72]

The social status of the college's alumni remained unfairly low. H.C. Raikes, a Breconshire landowner, was typical of his class when he argued at the 1872 Leeds Church Congress that there was a need to find men of more culture and wider experience than could be obtained in two or three years by a farmer's son at Lampeter.[73] *Golifer* in 1850 wrote that these Welsh-speaking products of Lampeter would face "a course of humiliating indigence under the discouraging scorn or contemptuous neglect of their ecclesiastical superiors".[74] A newspaper letter of 1874 argued that while the minimum requirements for the pass men at the old universities was below that of Lampeter, yet its men were seen as the workhorses of the Church. They were not the ones who received the best curacies, parishes, or canonries.[75] Though Judge Sankey stated at the Governing Body of the Church in Wales in 1922 that Lampeter had supplied the "bread and butter" to the Church in Wales, to applause, there must have been many alumni who wished there had been some jam laid on it as well.[76] It was these "workhorses" of the Church, who had replaced the earlier literate clergy, who continued to ensure that the Church in Wales remained a bilingual Church and enabled its presence to remain in its rural heartlands of Cardiganshire and Carmarthenshire, and to advance its mission in the mining areas of south Wales.

CHAPTER FIVE:
THE EDUCATION OF THE FUTURE CLERGY
THE THEOLOGICAL COLLEGES AND PRIVATE ENTERPRISE ESTABLISHMENTS

St David's College, Lampeter, was generally assumed to be a theological college, but its charter indicated it was more, and the charter permitting it to grant the BD and then the BA degree consolidated this position. If it trained men for Holy Orders it also offered them a classical and liberal education. Lampeter was founded because of the continuing need for ordained men in the Church in the diocese of St Davids and beyond, men who found the cost and even the requirements of a university impossible to fulfil. For men with a similar background other colleges were established, some by dioceses, as at Chichester or Wells, others supported if not founded by bishops, as St Bees, and others established by private enterprise, such as St Aidan's in Birkenhead. A few were meant to be graduate colleges, such as Cuddeston, founded by Bishop Wilberforce, but not all managed to retain that distinction and soon permitted non-graduates to enter their fold. Although the movement only started in the nineteenth century, it was not a new concept. Robert Nelson had advocated such a seminary to teach a post-graduate course in pastoralia, liturgy, and personal spirituality, and he noted the precedent of Bishop Wilson's early-eighteenth century and short-lived seminary on the Isle of Man for non-graduates.[1] Bishop Burnet of Salisbury (died 1715) established a seminary in his diocese, but the lack of favour shown it by his clergy and his own attitude to his ordinands made it short-lived.[2]

The first initiatives of the nineteenth century were for non-graduates. St Bees, Cumberland, was opened in 1816 with the active support of Bishop Law of Chester, and St Aidan's Birkenhead in the same diocese of Chester in 1846. Bishop Blomfield of Chester and later of London proposed the creation of seminaries for graduate training, and in 1833 E.B. Pusey suggested that such colleges be linked with cathedrals. This was apposite as the cathedrals were anxious not to lose their endowments to the Ecclesiastical Commission, which was proposing to re-distribute the income of the Church in favour of the industrial areas. It was claimed that the cathedrals, where appropriate, would be able to furnish pastoral opportunities, the students would be removed from distracting influences, and the diocesan bishop would have more input into their training. Durham, fearful of losing its wealth, established a university, and diocesan colleges were founded at Chichester in 1839, Wells in 1840, and Cuddesdon in 1854. The first college to accept graduates and non-graduates was Lichfield, founded in 1857.[3]

These theological colleges for non-graduates were established to provide the Church with the curates it needed for an expanding population. The universities could not supply the need, and so these courses arose from sheer necessity, as T.E. Espin maintained in the 1860s from his own experience as head of Queen's College, Birmingham. He believed that his and other similar colleges – he probably included Lampeter in this total - supplied about a quarter to a third of the clergy, and in some dioceses more than half. If bishops insisted on graduate clergy then half the curacies in many dioceses would remain unfilled.[4]

There was a great concern by the Welsh bishops that because of the complexities and time-scale of the Lampeter course, noted earlier, men would enrol at other colleges, with a shorter course and lesser academic demands. Bishop Ollivant articulated this concern on many occasions. His 1866 and 1869 Charges expressed his hope that if men could not afford the universities then they should choose Lampeter, instead of being tempted by the small savings of expense offered by a two year course elsewhere over a three year course of study. These other places were "decidedly injurious" and inflicted a "great evil", especially on the Welsh-speaking candidates, for he could not believe that in two years they could attain a theological and general education together with a perfect knowledge of the English language.[5] Too many candidates, he wrote, would not spend a shilling on their education if they thought they could be ordained without it.[6] Bishop Basil Jones of St Davids reiterated this concern, as has been noted already.[7]

Yet these colleges continued to attract men from Wales. The table on clerical education indicates that St Bees in particular supplied just under ten per cent of the clergy in the diocese of St Asaph in 1863, and almost the same proportion for Bangor in 1866. In 1890 the college supplied nearly eight per cent of the incumbents of the Welsh Church, while in that year two and a half per cent had been trained at St Aidans and three per cent at Birmingham. As John Griffith alleged in 1872, not entirely accurately, the great bulk of Welsh ordinands came not from the universities or Lampeter but from St Bees and Birmingham or were literates.[8]

The Welsh bishops may have disliked these colleges because they took away men from St David's College, but in the Church at large, still dominated by a mentality that saw the universities as the rightful place of training and the parson as a gentleman, there were attitudes that ranged from disquieted acceptance to downright hostility. Many of the colleges were private venture establishments. W.J. Conybeare fumigated against them in such far-fetched words as these:

> A clergyman begins by taking a few pupils, whom he prepares for ministerial functions by a course of parochial visiting, and "Pearson on the Creed". After a time he persuades a bishop to ordain one or two of these pupils without requiring them to take a university degree. The next step is to call his parsonage "The College of St. Ignotus", and to advertise it in the newspapers as a new theological seminary. If a good-natured bishop will consent to be nominated as "visitor", the scheme is complete. Candidates for cheap ordination flock to the halls of St. Ignotus; the projector dubs himself Provost, Warden, or President; and a self-created dignitary is added to the Church. We do not say this is always done from unworthy motives; it may be well to supply an urgent need by irregular means. But the wants of the Church ought to be met by the deliberate and collective action of her official authorities, not left to the chance-medley of individual speculation.[9]

Four concerns were expressed about these colleges. The attempt to train graduate with non-graduate clergy had not been a success.[10] The need for men was such that the bishops' desire to raise the standards for ordination had been frustrated. All these colleges lacked a liberal education and concentrated on those subjects required for the bishops' examinations, accepting as the norm the minimum standards required by the examining chaplains. Most were small in number, with twenty or so students, so that the tutorial staff was insufficient and the principal was often able to train men in his own image – reproductions of his own opinions and peculiarities - and perhaps even mould them into a priestly caste, especially as they had little contact with lay people. They had no general oversight, apart possibly from the diocesan bishop, and a number were designed as party colleges so that the theological breadth of a university was lost.[11] A report of 1893 indicated that some of these colleges possessed no common life and others provided little in the way of spiritual development.[12] It was also alleged that by allowing men of a lower status into Orders through these colleges, men of a better social position and of higher cultivation would be repelled from seeking ordination.[13]

In the 1850s Conybeare claimed that the education of national schoolmasters at St Mark's College, Chelsea, was incomparably better than that obtained by three quarters of these men.[14] Yet in 1864 a *Times* leader admitted that in the episcopal examinations these men did better than many graduates and that in their theological attainments they were generally superior to university men.[15] The majority of these colleges catered for older candidates, and it was claimed that it was difficult to do much for a person who began to learn Greek at the age when he should be ordained. It is not surprising, therefore, that there were constant calls for the requirements of Latin and Greek to be modified for these older men.[16] In a Welsh context John Griffith called for Welsh preachers, not classical scholars. A far different style of training was required.[17] There was also a call that the colleges should be linked to a university and its students subjected to its examination system.[18]

One of the difficulties faced by those who desired to regulate these colleges was that they had different emphases and catered for different kinds of men. Cuddeston, an all-graduate college, emphasised a devotional training with practical work in a parish, together with theological study.[19] Other Tractarian colleges believed their main aim was training a man in spiritual character and devotional habits. They were not enamoured of pastoralia, and wished their men to be removed from ordinary life and immersed in an exclusive devotional and ecclesiastical atmosphere.[20] R.B. Girdlestone, speaking in 1879 as principal of the evangelical college, Wycliffe Hall, Oxford, an all-graduate establishment, suggested his aims were that during his training a man's faith should be confirmed, his enthusiasm kindled, and his sympathies quietened. He also stressed the need for social concern and practical work.[21] His successor, W.H. Griffith Thomas, wanted colleges to be affiliated to the universities, an amalgamation of the smaller colleges, their courses to be obligatory, and combine intellectual work, especially on the Bible and Anglican theology, with pastoral preparation. His concern was to develop a man's personality.[22]

Standards were gradually enforced by the bishops and other interested parties, and the long-standing complaint that these non-graduate colleges were deprived of recognition and support from the Church was partly remedied as noted below.[23] The snobbery against them persisted, together with the belief that their products were not "gentlemen".[24] But their admission to these colleges indicated that the Church was slowly accepting the role within it of the lower middle class and perhaps redressing the lack of the old sizarships that allowed many men from this background to obtain a university degree.

One of the major concerns of many within the Church was that the system of examining candidates over the few days before ordination gave no time for devotional and spiritual preparation. To counteract this, Brooke Foss Westcott, then regius professor of divinity at Cambridge, later bishop of Durham, suggested a common examination that would replace that of the individual dioceses, though leaving the bishops the task of examining a candidate's doctrinal and spiritual position. Known as the preliminary examination it commenced in 1874, and by 1880 was accepted by twenty-four of the diocesan bishops. By 1884 all but two bishops had accepted it. The examination was supported by the theological faculties of the two older universities, and was held twice a year at different centres. It never attracted many graduates, and theological college principals felt it was not only too scholastic for their non-graduates, but also was too linguistic and historical in scope, but were forced to make their students cram for it, though about fifty per cent of their men failed it at their first attempt.[25] Saunarez Smith, principal of St Aidan's, expressed concern about these examinations. Though he accepted they would exclude unfit candidates, he also believed they might exclude working men who would find such an examination difficult to pass, but who from intelligence and their general capacity were fit to be ordained. These were the men, he stated, who would be able to minister to the middle class people.[26] Basil Jones, bishop of St Davids, announced in 1883 that he would require that all candidates for ordination in his diocese who had been students at a theological college should have passed this examination, but exempted Lampeter men from this requirement as they had been examined by external examiners.[27] Nevertheless, this new departure was a great gain, even though dioceses differed as to whether passing this examination gave exemption to certain parts of the bishops' own examinations.[28] The colleges as well as the universities had long complained about the frustrating disparities of the diocesan examinations, for a man needed to find a title or curacy, and would only then discover what the diocese he was entering into required for its own examination.[29]

In 1881 a conference was held at Oxford to which heads of theological colleges, examining chaplains, and those who held theological chairs at Oxbridge were invited. Its purpose was an attempt to regulate ordination training, as it was recognised that the colleges were under no general system and oversight apart from the diocesan bishops. It met every three years, and made many recommendations: of financial assistance for candidates in 1891, and two years later that graduates should undertake a year in theological study and training and non-graduates three years. Unfortunately, neither was effected, and the only result was the imposition of a common entrance examination for non-graduates to theological colleges. This examination consisted of translations of Latin and Greek, and questions on the Bible, English History, Euclid and elementary logic. Called the Central Ordination Examination its effect was to close three theological colleges, including St Bees, possibly because those without a grammar school background where classics were taught were almost excluded from taking it.

It was not until 1906 that the Upper House of the Canterbury Convocation requested that candidates for ordination should have a degree and follow a one year post-graduate course of specific training, the cost of which should be met by the Church. Following a recommendation of the 1908 Lambeth Conference a committee of bishops of the Upper House agreed to these proposals which were to be enforced from 1917, but were postponed because of the outbreak of War to 1920, and thereafter quietly shelved as a consequence of the War and the number of service men who wished to be ordained. However, a Central Advisory Council for the Training for the Ministry had been established in 1912, thus taking the matter of training out of episcopal hands. Its role was to inspect colleges and supervise the courses. It was this body that eventually replaced the preliminary examination with the General Ordination Examination in 1921, taken in two parts, though Oxbridge theological graduates who had achieved a class two or above were exempt as they were not required to reside at a theological college.[30] Nevertheless, each diocese still retained the right to examine candidates in particular subjects.

It is not clear whether the Church in Wales was part of this Central Advisory Council after disestablishment, but in 1938 it made its own regulations. Training for ordination should follow secular training, meaning in most cases graduation, and all candidates were to be vetted before they commenced this training, nor (it was hinted) were any to describe themselves as ordinands until they had been accepted for training. Pastoral and practical training were to be given during the diaconate, for it was accepted that this was not the main work of theological colleges. Wardens of ordinands were to be appointed in each diocese and they would oversee candidates, visit colleges and provide training days for ordinands. The Report noted that part two of the General Ordination Examination placed heavy demands on candidates, and not all were able to complete it whilst at college and so had to spend time and expense doing so at home, while those in college received their results far too near the date of ordination giving them anxiety and too little time to devote to spiritual preparation. Equally, the attempt to cram the General Ordination Examination syllabus into a year was said to have led to devotional starvation, with the path to ordination dominated by examinations.[31]

THE THEOLOGICAL COLLEGES

The cathedrals were seen as natural places for ordination training. It was claimed that this was intended by Archbishop Cranmer at the Reformation, and that the cathedral canons could be appointed to take on this work without much additional expense.[32] Bishop Phillipotts of Exeter made the first suggestion in 1833, having in mind a course of study for men between leaving university and ordination. The Ecclesiastical Commission's review of cathedral establishments endorsed this suggestion two years later, as did E.B. Pusey who believed it would invigorate the cathedral bodies. Pusey was also concerned that the university course at Oxford gave a totally inadequate preparation for ministry as regards the teaching of doctrine and pastoralia. Archdeacon Manning followed up this suggestion in 1842 by hinting that the 33 cathedral establishments should train those unable to obtain a university education, but who were needed by a Church facing unprecedented population growth.[33] At first the majority of colleges linked to cathedrals were for graduates, as were Chichester and Wells, but later others, such as Lichfield, catered for non-graduates.

It has been noted already that the Welsh bishops were deeply concerned at the number of Welshmen who entered English theological colleges rather than Lampeter. Bishop Ollivant in a letter to Rowland Williams expressed his bemusement that Welshmen had been flying in every direction but the one he would have wished, namely Lampeter, and named St Bees, Dublin and Birkenhead especially. Bishop Basil Jones of St Davids told his diocesan conference in 1882 it was not so much because of the expense that men went elsewhere but because it was so much easier to get into St Bees than Lampeter. It was not a question of pocket but of brain, he sarcastically added. This clarified an earlier statement of his, namely that these colleges were unsuitable and not well adapted for ordinary Welsh students or for the ministry of the Church in Wales. It is hardly surprising that John Griffith of Merthyr had his own comments to make about these colleges and about St Bees in particular. Some had even entered the latter before they had become members of the Church. Those who were ordained from these colleges lacked any specific training in Welsh preaching and pastoralia – though this was true of Lampeter in his day – and he compared such men to a cavalry officer who had all the items of his equipment but had forgotten the need for a horse.[34]

ST BEES COLLEGE

St Bees College, Cumberland, was founded in 1817 by William Ainger with the co-operation of the evangelical Bishop Law of Chester, his diocesan. Chester was a diocese with similar problems to St Davids about recruiting clergy. Ainger had been licensed as perpetual curate of the parish the previous year, and it appears that the college was run in conjunction with a grammar school. It was readily accessible by sea from Wales, offered a two-year course, required its students to lodge in approved houses in the town, and was cheap. Its standard of entry was said to be low (so low in fact that when a common entrance examination was imposed by the bishops it was forced to close), and it attracted a large number of Welshmen, as we have noted from Table One. The Welsh seemed to have formed a group of their own in the college. In 1826 John Lloyd Richards found many Welsh students there, as did Robert Roberts who entered in 1857, having wasted his time as a schoolmaster at Ruthin when he should have been preparing for Oxford. Roberts, who was intellectually bright but pathetically poor, managed to pay his way by acting as librarian and tutoring the less academic students, often burning the midnight oil to cover all his commitments. He claimed its costs were between £60 and £80 per year. Roberts disliked the loss of a communal life and the lack of fellowship with the principal and tutors, all of whom had parishes of their own. While Bishop Bethell of Bangor declined to take men from this college, his colleague at St Asaph, Short, had no such qualms and is said to have favoured the place and thus Roberts was ordained into that diocese. Yet the Welsh students were often placed at a disadvantage. Evan Evans, admitted 1823, had to hide his Calvinistic beliefs from his principal, and his deficiencies in the English language (as with many other Welshmen there) hampered him greatly, though he received help with his English pronunciation and hoped to lose his Welsh twang.[35]

The entrance examination, according to Cecil Wray, consisted of reading and construing parts of the Greek Testament "readily and grammatically at sight", , an acquaintance with Grotius's *de Veritate*, and a correct knowledge of the rudiments of Latin composition. The subjects taught were those required for the bishops' examinations, together with Latin and English compositions and the writing of sermons, examined by the principal. George Huntington, later rector of Tenby, recalled that to stand well one was required to cite the Articles and Creeds in Latin and English.[36] John Allan, archdeacon of Salop, was highly critical of the college, complaining he had rejected as an examining chaplain two of its men who had received the college testimonial, one as he could not spell, the other because he could not answer questions a National schoolchild could have answered. Almost a year later it was suggested that while at one time the college was the resort of scholars and gentlemen of limited means, "the Scripture-reader class, tailors and shoemakers" had "crept in".[37] Robert Roberts, for example, discovered his contempories there included turncoat dissenting ministers, blockheads for whom the college offered the only chance of taking Orders, failed Oxonians who scoffed at the college, and long-haired, raw-wristed Welshmen, as wild as their ponies, clad in black-dress coats, corduroy breeches and Belcher handkerchiefs. They were fond of beer and Welsh singing. There was also an exclusive religious set that Roberts rather despised, and the studious set to which he belonged.[38] Arthur Burns noted that about half the number of a selected sample of its students were ordained in the diocese of Chester. It was the largest of the colleges, with sometimes well over 100 students, and in 1870 three quarters of all those ordained from a theological college came from St Bees and in 1890 over half. The majority of its students were destined for the northern province and Wales.[39] Many of those ordained in the Welsh dioceses were required to accept a three year diaconate, though Daniel Evans, later vicar of Caernarfon, took a public examination at Lampeter which enabled him to be priested a year after he was made deacon.[40]

THE OTHER COLLEGES

St Aidan's College, Birkenhead, had been founded by Dr Baylee in 1846 as a residential college for non-graduates. It was there to provide the Church with "ordinary" pastors, trained in parochial and pastoral work (they were linked to parishes in Liverpool where they spent so many afternoons per week), in public reading and prayers, the composition of sermons, and in theological and general instruction, including Greek and Hebrew. He defended this syllabus by arguing that such a course was far more congenial and useful than one of heathen classics and natural science, but basically it was a course designed to cram men for the bishops' examinations together with his forte, pastoral work, that seemed to override the academic work of the college. Baylee was evasive about the social background of his men, most of who were in their mid-twenties and had worked previously in clerical jobs, who he endeavoured to mould as evangelical pastors. Many of them were plunged out of their depth because of inadequate preparation, though he recognised this by holding a preparatory class for the preliminary or common entrance examination.[41]

Both Durham (1832) and King's College, London (1828), offered a theological and professional course, leading after two years' study to a licence in theology or associateship of the college. King's College also permitted men to study through evening classes before a year of residential training. They were also degree-giving bodies.[42]

A number of these colleges had established a probationer status for those who wished to enter as students. At Chichester they were required to spend two years continuing their secular work while being engaged in regular church work. They were also required to study a number of books and pass a series of examinations before being admitted.[43] Lichfield Theological College had a similar system apparently started by Bishop Selwyn, with selected men working and studying under the direction of their incumbents, and if found satisfactory after two years work and six monthly examinations would enter the college for a final year of study. A title had to be found in that diocese, however.[44] The Scholae Episcopi at Manchester, founded in 1890, was a non-residential college. It was a two-year course, and men were admitted at the age of twenty-five and were prepared for the preliminary examination while they worked as lay readers in parishes for a small stipend.[45]

However, bishops were becoming more selective. St Asaph refused to accept theological college men from 1872, and St Davids would only accept graduates,[46] while Ollivant privately determined not to accept any St Bees men even for a five-year diaconate as he believed their education was worth very little.[47]

THE CONCERN FOR PASTORAL TRAINING

If St Aidan's College scored on anything, it was on the pastoral training its students received.[48] By and large this was an exception, and there was deep concern within the Church that the more practical requirements for ministry were almost totally neglected, as has been noted already in respect of the universities and Lampeter. The concept that men should acquire these pastoral and preaching skills from their incumbent during their first curacy was a non-starter in most cases, for many newly ordained men were required to take sole charge of a parish, or were placed in such a large parish that there was little time for such personal training, a fact admitted by Bishop Lewis of Llandaff in 1900. This was hindsight, for his Second Charge of 1888 made clear that he expected the incumbents of new deacons to offer them systematic training in their parochial work and to encourage them to continue their reading, together with offering them an example of devotion in the discharge of their sacred duties.[49] For many it just wasn't true. As John Griffith declared of men placed in sole charge of parishes or districts from the day of their ordination, "[t]here they are the whole year through from Sunday to Sunday", and he added, "they never hear any voice but their own". Griffith was a little dishonest. The curates of his own parish had their own districts and often had to sink or swim. It was not always so, he claimed, rather ingeniously. In previous years men served as assistant curates under an experienced incumbent and so had examples and good models before them, "good and faithful preachers to stimulate them and lead them on".[50]

This concern about the lack of adequate pastoral and spiritual training was particularly acute where university men were ordained, and this is why some of the theological colleges specialised in post-graduate training, though once again the emphasis of some colleges, such as Cuddeston, was not so much on pastoralia but about an interior spiritual development. Another problem was that these colleges required an extra year of expense, and until this was made compulsory many men declined to attend them or their fathers to support them for that extra year. (The same applied to the facility the universities provided of a post-graduate year in attending the divinity lectures). By comparison many of the other colleges were more concerned to offer those courses which would enable men to get through the bishops' examinations, thus excluding pastoralia, or making it a very poor second.[51] David Howell, trained at Abergavenny, spoke later in his life about the defects of his training. For until he was placed in charge of a large district as a deacon, he had never written a sermon, addressed a public audience, knelt at a sick bedside, or performed any public religious function.[52] As late as 1871 Bishop Hughes of St Asaph bemoaned the fact that Lampeter had no chair of pastoral theology and offered no training in the work of a parish.[53] He did not stand alone in his concern.

It is not surprising that the contrast between the Church and other professions was made. It was strange, Bishop Hughes of St Asaph declared, that "of all callings – and one most difficult in exercise and important in its issues", the ministry of the Church was destitute of special training, and he held this was the source "of our greatest weakness". His successor, A.G. Edwards, declared that the Church seemed to be a profession for which the least amount of specialised training and equipment was given.[54] An unknown writer held that young men were ordained without any mature thought of what they were entering, without having digested what they had learnt in divine things, and without exhibiting a settled holiness of character. His suggested course of post-graduate study would have embraced several years of study, combining a study of the Scriptures in their original languages with a correct, reverential and impressive manner of reading the liturgy, not forgetting psalmody, a right view of pastoral duties and the delivery of sermons.[55] Another writer in the *Church Quarterly Review* of 1885 suggested that those at the universities who were not reading for theological degrees were as ignorant of religious truth as when they were mere boys at school, and it was as absurd for them to offer themselves for ordination within a year of graduating as it was to offer them books to read when what they needed was practical and spiritual training.[56] Dean Vaughan of Llandaff considered in 1886 that a special training for the ministry to supplement the general education of the universities was "one of the most urgent needs of the Church at the present time". On an earlier occasion he had asserted that forty years earlier in his younger days

> there was practically no place of clerical preparation for the graduate of the University. We must not exaggerate the evil. Men, of intellect, men of genius, thought and read for themselves, and they escaped the dwarfing influences, if they also missed the elevation. The good seed sprang and grew up, if other men – if the man himself – knew not how. It was not the choicer spirits of the Church that the destitution of special preparation showed itself. In the rank and file of the ministry it showed itself disastrously. The oversight of souls was a mere

guesswork and haphazard. The entrance upon a parish was a mere leap into darkness.

But such first-rate men are not common, Vaughan added, and most men were rather of the average and thus needed pastoral and spiritual preparation for their own sakes as well as that of the Church.[57]

An equal contrast was made with the Nonconformist ministry, especially in Wales. John Griffith declared in 1872 that the Welsh dissenting minister was selected as a youth, trained at the cost of his denomination, taught Greek and Latin and preaching skills, and sent out to preach, whilst at college, every Sunday. By the time of ordination these men were "full-blown" preachers. Alas, he added, our men blundered their way through manuscript sermons.[58]

This need was continually stressed. Chancellor Phillips, speaking to the St Davids diocesan conference of 1882 felt that before ordination candidates ought to have had a previous training in pastoralia, the culture of the voice, extempore preaching and homiletic skills, too much of which was taken for granted.[59] An 1893 report presented to Archbishop Benson made it clear that while these one-year courses for graduates were valuable, they should not be spent on the acquisition of knowledge but on direct preparation considering the seriousness of their calling.[60] Davey, vice-principal of Lampeter, added his own voice to this concern in 1879. Not only should there be "an acquaintance, theoretical, and to some extent, practical, with the public and private duties of our Christian ministry", but also men should be trained to be good Christians, "God-fearing men, who know in their own souls the terrors and mercies of our God", who were "striving to live the life that they are commissioned to commend to others, and by their example, not less than by their words, to win souls to God".[61] Expense made it difficult to translate wishes into action, as no doubt the members of the Llandaff Diocesan Conference of 1892 accepted when they passed a resolution that all candidates for ordination should, whenever possible, undergo a period of special training between the completion of their academical training and their ordination.[62]

Apart from requiring men to attend a theological college there were other suggestions. Bishop Campbell of Bangor suggested in 1872 that candidates for ordination should, a year before their ordination, be used as lay clerks in the cathedral, and be trained in pastoral work. It was a suggestion taken later, in part, by Dean

Edwards.[63] He ensured that the ordinands of that diocese should meet for training at Bangor for a week or so of their vacation. One of his main concerns was to ensure that the offensive tone of speaking Welsh, a "stiff, stereotyped, unanimated tone", often acquired during their training, was replaced by a more acceptable style.[64] Chancellor Phillips of St Davids also suggested a similar scheme for St David's Cathedral, though this was never effected.[65] Others suggested men should place themselves with an experienced clergyman in order to gain this experience,[66] a point that will be taken up later, though in the diocese of Llandaff men who had completed their training but were too young to be ordained or had failed to obtain a title were given such experience and a small stipend as lay readers.[67]

PRE-ORDINATION PAROCHIAL TRAINING

An alternative method of obtaining post-graduate training for the work of the ministry was through hands-on experience in a parish, with a certain amount of doctrinal and other teaching given by its incumbent. During the nineteenth century this was much more common than has been thought, and there are numerous references to this practice, though, with two exceptions, in England rather than in Wales (one of these exceptions was Dean Edwards' vacation courses at Bangor, already mentioned, perhaps following a precedent in the diocese of Chester[68]). One of the first references to this practice occurred in 1832, when "A Clergyman" argued that as many men realised a lack of preparation for the work that lay before them a solution might be found if they passed a year in the home of some clergyman in the active discharge of parochial duty.[69] The dean of Canterbury, Henry Alford, in suggesting this expedient in 1864, argued it would make theological colleges redundant.[70] Dean Vaughan of Llandaff, whose work is noted below, speaking at the annual meeting of the Llandaff Church Extension Society in 1879 suggested there were many clergy who could give bed and board to some "young disciple" who could work under their oversight and so assist his training.[71] The bishops in Convocation in 1900 agreed that "in some cases" such training would be equivalent to training at a theological college.[72]

Those who offered training in their own parishes included W.H. Havergal, canon of Worcester, who between 1820-45 had eighty odd pupils, of whom forty-one were ordinands;[73] Samuel Wilberforce, then rector of Alverstoke 1841-5 and later bishop of Oxford,[74] Ashton Oxenden of Ashford, Kent, and Archdeacon Sandford of Bromsgrove.[75] Edward Girdlestone of Deane, Lancastershire said he had been engaged in this work for 25 years and treated his students as members of his family, giving them an hour's theological instruction each day and responsibility for a district in his parish,[76] Bishop Lightfoot of Durham (1879-90) had six to eight men staying with him as his guests, who became known as the Auckland Brotherhood or more unofficially as his "lambs",[77] while in the 1900s Armitage Robinson, dean of Westminster, performed the same role.[78]

A number of incumbents and others even advertised their services. One was W.T. Barry of Uley, Gloucestershire, who was not its incumbent nor appears to have been in orders. In 1858 he advertised that he accepted graduate students at ten guineas a month and offered preparation for the episcopal examinations. Whether any pastoral training was offered is not known. Adam Clark Smith, incumbent of St John's, Middlesborough, also offered his services to those who wished to enter the Christian ministry and needed experience of parish work. They would live with the clergy of the parish in an united community, be taught divinity, Latin, Greek and Hebrew, in return for assistance in parochial work. It may well be he was targeting non-graduates.[79] It is doubtful if any Welsh ordinands trained at these establishments, but the same was not to apply to Vaughan's "doves".

Charles John Vaughan, a former headmaster of Harrow, commenced what was regarded as the major work of his life. While he was vicar of Doncaster he preached the University sermon at Cambridge on Trinity Sunday 1861. Stating that theology was well taught at the University, he felt that the art of ministry required practical training in a parish setting. This he provided at Doncaster. Addressing some of his former students at Salisbury in 1875 he noted that practical training was not the normal position for candidates for Orders, unlike the medical and legal professions. But to continue this position was to hand over one parish after another to be experimented upon by an untaught person, and to prevent one clergyman after another from ever rising out of the awkwardness of a perpetual beginner, or, at best, the eccentricities and mannerisms of a self-instructed genius. Vaughan continued this work of training men for the pastoral ministry when he became master (or chaplain) of the Temple (1869) and dean of Llandaff (1879), offices he held together for many years.

His men were known as "Doves", for a reason no longer known, though Vaughan disliked the term as he wished his men to retain their individuality and not to be labelled. Most of them were a type not generally considered as burning with zeal for the Gospel, namely public school and university men of good family, often men set apart from birth for the family living.

By the date of his death in 1897 Vaughan had trained over 450 men, whose ministry and character was said to have been largely shaped by his example and teaching and his desire that they should belong to Christ's party alone. He declined to interfere with any man's theological inclinations unless they were doctrinally unsound. Taking at first nine each year, and later fourteen, he charged no fee, spent time with them in the exposition and study of the Greek Testament, which he regarded as the true preparation for ministry, required his students to write a weekly sermon which was judged in an open session, taught preaching and taking services by his personal example, advised about their reading for the bishops' examinations, and offered advice about the selection of a diocese and title. At Llandaff they attended the daily services of the cathedral and generally formed half the congregation. They took services and preached in some of the schoolrooms attached to the parish, and read the lessons in the cathedral at Sunday evensongs. The men lived in lodgings, and migrated with him between Llandaff and the Temple. Pastoral experience was found for them in the poorer parts of Cardiff and the east end of London. If a man seemed unfitted for the work, Vaughan, according to James Rice Buckley, would tell him, "You do not seem very happy among us, perhaps you had better go." There was one drawback, namely lack of a communal life, though they were invited to dine with Vaughan and his wife on a frequent basis, and this allowed those who lacked some social graces to remedy that deficiency. One of his students, Robert Hugh Benson, placed there by his father, the archbishop, because of Vaughan's personality and high spirituality, remembered not only the training but also the football they played on a frequent basis.

Vaughan, speaking at the Swansea Church Congress in 1879, said this about this work:

> Another experiment has been tried. It sets up no rival to the theological college. It has a different scope, a different idea, and a different material. It deals with the case of graduates only, and of graduates whose college career has been satisfactory. It is inapplicable to men who require either discipline to make sure of their conduct or tuition to make sure of their reading. There is here no common home, common table, or common study. The students take care of

themselves as to their lodging and maintenance, and there is no "account of giving or receiving" between them and their chief. He, on his part, gives them free access to his parochial meetings, whether of school teachers, district visitors, communicants, or Bible-readers; assigns them districts among the poorer people, classes in his Sunday-school, places in his choir; reads with them daily in the Greek Testament, sets them texts for sermons, subjects for essays on doctrine; looks over, comments upon, suggests alternatives of idea, arrangement of, and treatment; counsels them as to their future ministrations in the Church offices, and in the various departments of parochial visitation; advises and assists them in their negotiations for curacies, and seeks to turn them thus, and their endeavours, into channels which his larger experience has shown him to be wise, right, and true. When through change of position he has himself been without a parish, he has supplied through others this part of the work, keeping a general supervision over all, and seeking to maintain in everything that personal charge of influence which is the keynote of the whole system. In the course of the last eighteen years some 200 men have passed through this course under one person.

When asked if it was not impossible for others to continue his example, and make this form of training an alternative to the more conventional training, Vaughan advised his hearers that it needed "no extra-ordinary gifts of scholarship, no remarkable store of knowledge; the devotional study of Scripture is always more than the exegetical; the pious influence of an experienced pastor is far more valuable for his purpose than any brilliancy of speech or any profundity of learning. If a man who can do nothing else would open his quiet parsonage to one young candidate of small means and modest attainments, make him one of his household, and train him into a minister, he would be doing more for his Church than any of us."

In the Davidson papers at Lambeth there is a list of Vaughan's "Doves". Amongst them are six men who served in Wales: F.H. Archer, vicar of Christ Church, Monmouth, in 1867; F.G. Pelham, honorary canon of Bangor, in 1868; H.H. Stewart, rector of Porthceri and Barry in 1871; J.H. Wynne-Jones, vicar of Caernarfon in 1874; A.W. Adams-Williams, then curate of Caerleon, in 1889, and Edward Sunderland, curate of Canton, Cardiff, in 1895. Archbishop Davidson was Vaughan's most distinguished "dove". Most of these men remembered Vaughan's teaching and dignity of holiness to the end of their lives, from the morning prayers and Bible study in his dining room, or his studies in the Greek Testament, where they began to realise that his great learning was "subordinate to his belief that through the Scriptures God is still speaking directly to anyone who will humble and reverently listen". And they knew he would keep in touch with them to the end of his life. H.M. Butler, his successor at Harrow, in his funeral sermon suggested he saw these men as his children and sons. In his addresses to them at their various gatherings he found "the pith, the salt, the subtle humour that made the charm of his style, but all fused and mellowed by the deepest human affection, such as Paul might have felt for Timothy, together with profound thanks to God for having provided him with this untrodden and now well-furrowed field of gratuitous and delightful labour".[80]

Though the ancient universities provided an additional year of teaching and attending lectures after graduation, this was regarded as not particularly satisfactory, as no pastoral training could be given.[81] Equally, theological colleges that catered for both graduates and non-graduates were thought to be equally unsatisfactory, as too often the courses catered for the lowest denominator, though it was hoped that where the two groups mixed, those without university credentials might gain from those who possessed them.[82] The other problem was that as graduates were not required to attend a theological college, many did not do so, especially as many fathers declined to pay for an additional, and to them an unessential, year.[83] Yet it was felt essential that graduate candidates for ordination should have some training in pastoral work and homiletics, intellectual development and devotional preparation. As Lord Hugh Cecil put it when he spoke at St Michael's College, Llandaff, courses were needed which would turn out cultivated men who would be suitable for the ministry of God.[84] By 1902 it was said that about half the graduates were now taking a theological college course of one year, though this meant that another half were entering parish life with little preparation.[85]

POST-GRADUATE TRAINING

As Lampeter served the requirements of the Welsh dioceses by offering a classical and theological course in a Welsh environment, the need was also felt for a post-graduate theological college for Wales, offering the pastoral and devotional training that Lampeter felt unable to offer because of its particular nature and size. It eventually came in the shape of St Michael's College, Llandaff, but this was a college founded in the Tractarian tradition that was unrepresentative of the Welsh Church as a whole at that time.

Many ideas and suggestions had been put forward previously. We have noted already the scheme of Thomas Briscoe, vice-principal of Jesus College, who, concerned that the graduates of his university had a very inadequate knowledge of their future duties and a modicum of Biblical and theological knowledge, informed the Cathedral Commissioners in 1854 that he had prepared a scheme for Wales. His scheme would enable Welsh ordination candidates studying at the university to spend a year outside the university, hopefully in Wales, and after a successful examination be entitled to the degree of BA without further residence. This, he argued, would allow a spiritual preparation, enable men to dissociate themselves from the bad habits formed at Oxford, and set a good tone of feeling, though he recognised the cost would be prohibitive and was well aware that the university would never consent to this plan.[86] Other plans may have been suggested over the years, but the bishops were probably more sympathetic to Bishop Ollivant's antipathy to any such venture, probably feeling that Lampeter needed their fullest support.[87]

A year after Briscoe's suggestion, Lewis Evans, vicar of Llanfihangel-y-Creuddyn, Cardiganshire, wrote to Isaac Williams about what he had heard from another early Tractarian leader, Lewis Gilbertson. Criticising St David's College where things were getting worse and there was little hope of improvement, and accepting that the grammar schools had been paralysed by the system, he proposed establishing a school in his parish (which had produced numerous clergymen) that would act as a rival to Lampeter, though he needed Williams' assistance as its tutor. Clearly, it was not a graduate college, but it never got off the ground because Williams was taken seriously ill. Basil Jones, later bishop of St Davids and then a fellow of Queen's College, Oxford, may have heard of these plans, for in May 1846 he proposed a more substantial scheme, with six or eight persons forming a voluntary college in the diocese of St Davids, based on the model of an Oxford college. He felt there was a great want of clerical education in the county (in spite of Lampeter) and that such a plan would be well received in south Wales. A bishop would be required to patronise it, and he believed its location could be Brecon, central to three counties, and could be the means of preserving its collegiate church from destruction. As he feared, Bishop Thirlwall of St Davids "put an extinquisher" on the idea, though it was accepted that he could do little else considering his position as visitor of St David's College.[88]

Describing St David's College as a small Welsh university, Canon Neville, vicar of Great Yarmouth, and a member of a prominent Llanelli family, suggested in 1872 that the Welsh Church needed a similar college to Cuddeston in Wales itself. His particular concern was that it should teach the distinctiveness of the Church as against the tenets of Welsh Nonconformity.[89] Thomas Walters, David Howell, David Jones of Dwygyfylchi and J. Allan Smith, vicar of Swansea 1884-1901, as evangelical leaders in Wales, all hoped for an evangelical theological college in Wales, similar to the evangelical Wycliffe Hall at Oxford or Ridley Hall at Cambridge, and argued that its lack meant many Welsh evangelicals went to England for their training and remained there. They did so with more urgency when St Michael's College had opened, recognising that its Tractarian influence might contaminate the Welsh Church, though Howell more generously stated that St Michael's College was doing a great work in south Wales.[90]

The failure of St Michael's College to promote the Welsh language and culture caused Stephen Jackson to suggest in 1907 that a thoroughly Welsh-speaking theological college should be opened in north Wales.[91] He might have known of an earlier venture by Watkin Williams when he was dean of St Asaph 1892-8 and before he became bishop of Bangor. A wealthy man, he built the Dean's Library opposite the cathedral as the first part of a possible theological college. The idea never materialised possibly because the Church Hostel at Bangor was the greater priority.[92]

R.J. Beck, vicar of Roath and a leading Tractarian in the diocese, hoped that the bishop of Llandaff, Richard Lewis, whose sympathies lay with that movement, would follow the example of Bishop Wilberforce of Oxford who opened a theological college alongside his palace gates, namely Cuddeston, and so replicate in a more formal sense what Dean Vaughan was doing for graduates. This was in 1886.[93] Six years later his dream became reality with the opening of St Michael's College, Aberdare.

St Michael's College, Aberdare, was established with the help of two sisters, Olivia and Emily Talbot of Margam Castle, daughters of a man described as one of the wealthiest commoners in the kingdom. Their brother, Theodore, who died young, was a disciple of Fr. Stanton of St Alban's, Holborn, a leading London Tractarian church. Concerned that a theological college was needed for the diocese of Llandaff offering graduates an intellectual, practical and devotional training before ordination, they gave generously towards its cost of approximately £1,500 per annum together with a substantial endowment fund. It was a Tractarian foundation, and vestments were worn from the first day it opened in 1892, with room for twenty-five students. Miss Emily insisted that the college should remain in Wales and be seen as more a resource for the whole Church in Wales rather than for one diocese. Its first warden was Henry Robert Johnson, then a curate at Aberdare who had been trained at Cuddeston, and who gave his services without recompense.[94] An additional aim was to ensure that its products were "cultivated men", for as Emily Talbot wrote to Archbishop Davidson, the Welsh clergy were "in need of civilising influences as well as instruction in their spiritual and parochial duties"[95] Johnson himself stated that he looked upon the college as a place where men could take a year between graduating and ordination, during which they might deepen their spiritual life and be trained as priests. In a pamphlet of 1908 Johnson offered his philosophy: if we would win Welshmen back to the Church, ... we can only hope to do so by offering them a higher spirituality than which the chapels ... can supply them". For many of a previous generation, it was preaching that would win back the masses. For Johnson it was priestly service. Wilfred de Winton, a banker and a leading lay High Churchman, also suggested that the average Welsh ordinand had no sense of vocation or any distinctive theological views. He could not see the need for any further professional qualifications once his degree had been obtained. The college's task was to give these men discipline and devotional habits, as well as an understanding that Holy Orders was not a profession but a vocation.[96] By 1898 the number of students who had been ordained from the college was 88; 52 per cent had come from Lampeter, 14 per cent from Oxbridge, and others from provincial universities or who had studied at other theological colleges (15 per cent) while eight were non-graduates undertaking the two-year course. Of this total half were ordained in the diocese of Llandaff, roughly fifteen per cent each to the dioceses of St Davids and St Asaph, nearly seven per cent to Bangor but, apart from two who went to overseas dioceses, over twelve per cent went to English dioceses.[97]

Few men could afford the cost of this extra year, with the result that many students were admitted free of charge to enable them to take advantage of its training.[98] In addition, when the General Ordination Examination was introduced in

1921, a year's course was not always sufficient for it, and some men were forced to study at home for Part II after their course had ended.[99]

The premises at Aberdare were rented, and the lease expired in 1899, and thereafter it was allowed on a grace and favour basis until new premises could be found. Eventually, through the good offices of de Winton, a site was obtained in Llandaff itself, and the building cost of £30,000 was solicited by him from his friends although he gave a substantial portion of it himself.[100]

The bishop of Llandaff, Pritchard Hughes, was an evangelical, and in a letter of 1907 to Archbishop Davidson he expressed his concerns about the legal and ecclesiastical position of St Michael's College. Considerable pressure had been put on his predecessor by the promoters of the college, and while there was nothing in the Trust Deed to indicate its theological nature, the Council was all of one school and filled up vacancies themselves. He also felt that an indirect pressure was put on Welsh candidates to go there, and noted that about half of the Welsh ordinands did so.[101] Hughes was hardly alone in his concern. Sir Henry Lewis wrote in 1914 that not one layman in a thousand knew what was taught there, and maintained it was a place of advanced sacerdotalism and uncongenial to freedom and inquiry.[102] He was not unfair. In an inspection report of 1914 the college was said to be "distinctive of one school of thought in the Church".[103]

According to a former warden, writing in 1982, J.G. Hughes, the archbishop claimed that Bishop Lewis of Llandaff, before he died, urged him to visit the new college and dedicate the buildings. The archbishop, taking note of Hughes's concerns and the fact the college would be on his doorstep, made clear he could only do so if the bishop had full oversight of the college. Its Council disliked the idea and, with the solitary exception of the bishop, refused to change the Trust Deed by substituting for itself the bishop as the chief authority for the college, claiming that the college was for the whole of Wales rather than for one diocese. This cut little ice with the archbishop. Cuddesdon and other colleges could say the same, but they were under the authority of their diocesan bishops. Nor would the Council accept a compromise offered by the bishop under which the college chapel would be placed under the bishop's control and he would have what amounted to a veto over the appointment of a new warden. This requirement that the diocesan bishop should be more than just the visitor but instead possess the overriding authority over the college was clearly the desire of both archbishop and Bishop Hughes and in accordance with policy at that time. As a result, the archbishop declined to attend the opening ceremony. Indeed, as he wrote earlier, had he known the situation before, he would have sent a strong remonstrance against a constitution that deprived the diocesan bishop of any effective control over the college. It was unacceptable for the bishop to have the appearance of responsibility with its reality.[104]

Speaking to the 1910 Llandaff Diocesan Conference, the warden, H.R. Johnson, expressed his grief at the lack of the support for his college by the general public of the diocese, and also that out of the 133 men recently ordained in Wales only 26 had fulfilled what was regarded as the ideal by the bishops, namely taking a year's additional training. If the cost seemed prohibitive bursaries were available, but perhaps many men saw little need for that additional year. Johnson clearly felt that the indifference of Lampeter men to his invitation to attend the college was deplorable. By the time, after eighteen years, there had been 268 students, though it was noted that a few non-graduates had also been admitted, about thirteen per cent of the total.[105] Although the college expected its students to serve in the Church in Wales for at least five years, not all did so, and these received the castigation of the warden. "The difficulties of the Church in Wales", he wrote, "are overwhelming enough without being made a training ground for the comparatively raw recruit … It is rather pitiable to find so much patriotism which ends in mere vague affection for everything Welsh, except work in a Welsh diocese." Johnson also expected his men to stay in their first curacy for at least two years and then only move at the request of their incumbent. Too frequent moves, he claimed, encouraged the idea that the only duty of the clergy was to preach with the result that when a man has said all he had to say, he would move on and reuse the sermons he had already written.[106] By 1933 there were forty men in residence, all of whom were graduates.[107]

St Michael's College still exists to serve the Church in Wales, but it is seen as a provincial responsibility and as such has quietly subdued its Tractarian character.

CHAPTER SIX: THE FINAL HURDLE

The requirements for ordination were carefully laid down by the 1603 Canons. Canon 35 stated that before a man was admitted to Holy Orders the bishop was to diligently examine him in the presence of those ministers who would assist him at the imposition of hands, though the exact nature of this examination was not specified. In addition, care was to be taken that no person with an impediment, either physical or moral, was to be ordained.[1] By tradition ordination was restricted to the four Ember seasons, Advent, Lent, Trinity and Michaelmas. Thomas Secker was one of many archbishops of Canterbury who endeavoured to establish a uniform policy. In 1759 he issued directions to the bishops of his province about the papers required from candidates. University men who had resided away from the university for a considerable amount of time should not be admitted unless they had enclosed a Si Quis notice that had been read in their parish church on some Sunday a month before the ordination, and that no objections had been made. The bishops should ensure that care was taken with letters testimonial and that no college testimonial should be accepted unless it was properly signed and sealed. No candidate should be admitted on letters dimissory unless it been had granted by the bishop of the diocese or a guardian of spiritualities; and the archbishop should be informed if any candidate was rejected for immorality so he could warn the other bishops.[2]

As the Ember seasons approached the advertisements or notices from bishops about their forthcoming ordinations would appear in the press. Those who wished to apply to a bishop as candidates for the next ordination were required to send their papers to the diocesan secretary one month before the date of ordination, offering the bishop details of their age, usual residence and place of education. In addition they were required to provide a birth certificate, a college testimonial and certificates, Letters Testimony (signed by three incumbents certifying the candidate's good life and conversation), a Si Quis, indicating that the intention of the candidate to be ordained had been read out in his parish church and no objections had been made, and a nomination to a curacy, described as a title. The examining chaplain would also write to the candidate giving details of the examination syllabus and of the ordination itself.³ These syllabi, until 1884 when the preliminary ordination examination was introduced, as noted previously, varied from diocese to diocese, and only when a man had obtained a title would he know the subjects and books on which he would be examined.⁴ (It is said that examining chaplains knew all "too well the frequent appeal, 'I did not know until a month ago I was coming to this diocese'."⁵ Finding a title was a complex business which added further to the pressures placed on a prospective candidate.⁶ At a later date incumbents were required to inform the bishop about the duties and stipend of their new curate, by which time the procedures had become even more rigorous, with the papers being carefully scrutinised.⁷

Bishop Short of St Asaph by 1863 required written application to be made to him three months before the ordination date, together with the names of three referees, clergy or "other persons of respectability", to whom the bishop could apply "by searching letters of inquiry" for further information. Such matters being in order, the bishop would interview the candidate, require him to sit a preliminary examination, and when the candidate had been accepted he could then seek a title in his diocese. The bishop of St Davids had a similar policy by 1889 though instead of the need for referees, the candidate would receive a paper of questions he was required to answer.⁸ Yet in many other cases the first time a bishop and his examining chaplains would meet the candidates would be on the occasion of their ordination examination.⁹

Many bishops felt the responsibility of selecting men for ordination to be a heavy one. Bishop Burnet of Salisbury (1689-1715) said these Ember weeks were the burden and grief of his life. Bishop Burgess said much the same,¹⁰ as did Basil Jones of St Davids who added it was not sufficient that there was nothing against a man, he wanted to know what positive evidence was in his favour and that he was well qualified to be a minister. He added that he rejected or discouraged men from ordination if he found this was not the case.¹¹

Bishops also imposed their own rules about whom they would ordain. Many of the English bishops would only ordain graduates of the ancient universities, but this option was hardly available to the south Walian bishops. Bishop Horsley, as noted before, declined to ordain those educated at a dissenting academy.¹² Bishop Burgess declined to ordain those grammar-school men who had not been resident for seven years prior to the canonical age for ordination, though he did advise men who fell short of this requirement that they could get a title in another diocese such as Hereford or Llandaff.[13] Bishop Marsh, when he was bishop of Peterborough, devised a series of eighty-seven questions to ask candidates, known as "the cobwebs to catch Calvinists", whom he refused to ordain. As he had been bishop of Llandaff previously (1816-19) he might well have tested them out on his Welsh candidates.[14] When he was bishop of Chester, Charles James Blomfield (1824-8) declined to ordain former tradesmen, military or naval personal - he suspected they wanted houses to live in, or Irish candidates. He expected his candidates to come from either the universities or St Bees College, as did Van Mildert of Durham (1826-36).[15]

A debate in the upper house of Convocation of 1872 revealed that the bishops had different policies about whom they would accept. The bishop of Ely would only accept graduates of Oxbridge or Durham, his colleague at Bath and Wells would accept those who had studied for two years in a theological college, and the bishop of St Asaph added he had made up his mind not to accept candidates from an English theological college nor any biennial student from Lampeter.[16]

Basil Jones in 1880 described how he was often requested to ordain a literate because he had been denied the opportunity of receiving a proper education, or had some especial fitness for the ministry. But soon an exception would became a rule, and he thus announced he would only accept graduates of the universities or Lampeter, certified students of that college, or of some recognised theological college (and three years later he required them to have passed the preliminary theological examination). He claimed in 1886 that the other Welsh bishops had similar policies and one an even stricter rule.[17]

By the 1900s, with the acceptance of the need for a specialised and professional training, the bishops endeavoured to insist that by 1917 all those graduates wishing to be ordained should have undertaken a year of training in a theological college. However, as noted earlier, it was never implemented and many declined this extra year,[18] so that in 1911 it was claimed that of 133 men ordained in the diocese of Llandaff during the previous nine years, only 26 had undertaken this additional year, while 63 had taken degrees at Lampeter and might have been expected to have gone on to St Michael's College but had not done so.[19]

A bishop, however, might widen the circle of those he was prepared to ordain. Bishop Short of St Asaph (1846-70) was obliged, said his biographer, to "admit persons to orders who had not had the advantage of university training". His successor, Joshua Hughes, pointed out that if he insisted on a degree as a requirement for ordination many churches would be "unserved".[20] Thus Bishop Campbell of Bangor accepted candidates from Queen's College, Birmingham, in 1859, to the consternation of Rowland Williams of Lampeter as many men opted for its shorter course rather than the longer one at Lampeter.[21]

A number of bishops would not take candidates over a certain age. Pinnock, who wrote a handbook for the clergy, said this age was thirty, as it was assumed that some previous pursuits might not be compatible with a due preparation for Holy Orders.[22] However, many of those ordained in the south Walian dioceses were not far from this age, and generally six years older than their English counterparts.[23] There was one particular case of a man being ordained at the age of twenty, having used the baptismal certificate of a decreased brother who had the same name as himself. This was in 1764, and John Crowe the younger, "pretended" curate of Michel Troy, Monmouth, pleaded that his father, the incumbent, was ill and wished him to assist him. As a result, he was found guilty of forging his ordination papers and required to pay the costs of the case. Whether he subsequently served in the Church is not known.[24]

With the applications sent in, the bishops would then start their enquiries, though at least one letter of Bishop Carey of St Asaph indicates he had no candidates to hand. Writing to Thomas Griffith Roberts in 1833, rector of Llanwrst and his examining chaplain, he explained he had not yet heard of any candidates for Orders but there was still time for papers to be sent in.[25]

The clergy of the lower house of Convocation in 1865 applauded those bishops who had a personal interview with the candidates some months previous to the ordination in order to ascertain their fitness.[26] In fact, this was already taking place in many dioceses by the 1850s, when in addition to this interview with the bishop, a preliminary examination took place some months before the ordination itself. Surprisingly, this had been the practice of Bishop Bull of St Davids (1705-10), which gave him time to enquire into the candidates' papers and characters. He would ask questions about their faith, whether they were inwardly moved to offer themselves for ordination, while he emphasised the nature and dignity of the clerical calling, and advised them to spend time in prayer, fasting and in considering the vows they would be making.[27] Bishop Burgess of Salisbury may have re-started the trend in the early 1800s. Candidates were required to bring abridgements of such books as Pearson on the Creed and Burnet's *Pastoral Care*, and read aloud the morning service in the bishop's chapel. The candidate was only permitted to proceed to the main examination if these tasks were performed satisfactorily.[28]

Elias Owen, in a newspaper article entitled "Anecdotes of Bishop Short" of St Asaph, notes that he held a preliminary examination a few months before the ordination, when having made certain enquiries about the candidate, would invite him to the palace for a few days. The 1863 diocesan directory described this examination as "of a general nature" in the Greek Testament and Scripture history, plus some special subject set by the bishop "upon which a large part of the examination will turn". The bishop conducted an informal examination, and if satisfactory, the candidates were informed that if they could procure titles, they might present themselves for examination by his chaplains. If they failed to reach the standard required by the bishop they were advised to place themselves under the tuition of some able clergymen and present themselves again for examination at a later date. In this way, stated Owen, the disgrace of being plucked was avoided. The bishop manner of conducting this examination varied considerably. Though the subjects were usually the same as those of the main examination by the chaplains, there was no routine or syllabus, though the bishop, claims Owen, was able to form from their answers a correct estimate of their character and fitness for ministry. On one occasion he asked two young graduates what they would do if they found themselves in a pulpit without their sermon. According to Owen one candidate stated it would be a serious affair if he found himself "in such a fix", and thus the conversation proceeded:

> "Mr. J.," said the bishop, "you are at this very moment in that very fix; you are in the pulpit and you have lost your sermon, and I am the congregation; and now, Mr. J., proceed."
> After a prolonged silence, Mr. J., said, "Really, my lord" –
> "No, no," said the bishop, interrupting him, "you must preach to the congregation."
> To this remark there was no response, and by-and-bye the bishop, who was seated on a sofa, with his eyes closed, said –
> The congregation is waiting."
> But still there was no sermon forthcoming. Then, after another long pause, the bishop said –
> "The congregation is waiting very patiently."

Even this hint that the episcopal patience was exhausted failed to assist the bewildered Mr. J., and he had nothing to say. His colleague, however, was equal to the occasion. Short sometimes threw out riddles to the consternation of his candidates, or would tell them that he was an old woman and that they were paying him a ministerial visit. What had they to say to him? Or he might be a Socinian and then an infidel, and they were asked to controvert his views, and finally to give a reason for the faith they possessed. By these means Short tested their pastoral and theological attainments. Sometimes the candidates were too clever for him. One insisted that Moses had entered the land of Canaan, and when asked to explain himself stated he had done so on the Mount of Transfiguration. It was not the answer the bishop expected. A favourite question was "Who is the best cobbler in the parish?" He would answer it himself, "he who makes the best use of the materials he has got to work with", and would then apply it to those candidates, many of whom would be entering areas very different from the college life they had previously enjoyed.[29]

Evan Glanley, a Durham graduate ordained in 1864, who was rector of Ystradgynlais, wrote about the questions asked a friend of his by an unidentified bishop upon such as occasion. One was how many children had Abraham. He answered "eight" three times, to the bishop's deep annoyance and description of him as "a perfect ignoramus". However, he proved the correctness of his answer with names and relationships, whereupon the bishop, stating he didn't know that much information, apologised and expressed his willingness to give him "everything". This could well have been Short.[30]

In the disestablished Church in Wales candidates for ordination had to appear before a diocesan selection committee as well as meet their bishops, while their incumbents were required to write reports about them during their time in training. In addition only graduates of the universities or Lampeter were acceptable unless they were mature men.[31]

TESTIMONIALS AND TITLES

The bishops constantly used their visitation charges to remind their incumbents of the need to take care in signing testimonials for candidates. These testimonials stated that the candidate was morally sound and fit to be ordained and had to be signed by three beneficed clergymen. That they were personally checked by the bishops is affirmed by Bishop Barrington of Llandaff in 1776 querying Thomas Davies' signing the testimonials for a Mr Aldridge, for as he lived fifty miles away from his place of residence how could he know he had lived piously, soberly and honestly? Davies replied that he had known him since he had been curate of Llangorse and his motive in signing was for the glory of God and the good of immortal souls.[32]

It appears that Bishop Burgess threatened those clergymen who had signed testimonials contrary to their knowledge of the facts with a reprimand for the first offence and with suspension if they repeated their offence.[32] Bishop Jenkinson of St Davids (1825-40) regarded these testimonials as a sacred trust. They were not to be signed at random, nor if those who signed them could not confirm from their personal knowledge that the candidate was of a pious, sober and honest life, had diligently applied himself to his studies, was qualified for office, and his voice and manner was suited for a public assembly. They should not allow the entreaties of friends, an unwillingness to hurt feelings, or the dread of obloquy if they refused, to influence their opinion.[34] His successor, Basil Jones, in his 1877 charge, advised his clergy that under the influence of an ill-advised good nature many souls might be ruined by signing a statement that was not true. He appealed to the corporate spirit of the clergy that they should repel unworthy applicants for admission to their ranks. Campbell of Bangor, in 1875, reminded his clergy that in signing these testimonials it was not enough for them to know nothing against the candidate, they needed to know whether he was worthy of the position he desired to fill.[35] Yet R. Camber Williams, then diocesan missioner for St Davids' diocese, argued in 1909 that many clergymen found it impossible to tell a leading layman that his son was unfit for ordination and so signed his testimonial. He felt a candidate needed to he approved by either the local congregation, as in Nonconformity, or by a local panel of laity and clergy.[36]

There was a similar concern about college testimonials. Norman Sykes records that in the eighteenth century they were given unsealed and conveyed little sense of any personal knowledge of the candidate.[37] A writer in the *Quarterly Review* of 1862 regarded these testimonials as "almost worthless",[38] and Archbishop Benson in the 1880s expressed concern that some men who had been refused their college testimonial on moral grounds had still been ordained.[39] Forged testimonials were not unknown. In 1757-8 the archbishop of Canterbury warned the bishop of Llandaff not to admit into Holy Orders several men, including Lewis Thomas of Bonvilston and a native of Lampeter, who had forged testimonials.[40] Jacob suggests that the eighteenth century bishops had to cope with forged documents but were diligent in trying to make the system work.[40]

The titles (or curacies) of those to be ordained were carefully scrutinised and checked to see they were in order and the required stipend would be paid. This had been fixed by statute of 1813, and was £80 rising to £150 depending on the population of a parish.[41] Previously, bishops had tried to ensure that a reasonable stipend was provided and that men were not offered a title in order to be ordained in return for giving their services free for a year. Bishop Bull of St Davids (1705-10) refused the term "competent salary" used by many on the appropriate form, and insisted on a proper sum being mentioned. He also checked whether the benefice could maintain an incumbent and a curate with the stated salary.[42] William Fleetwood of St Asaph (1708-15) claimed that he knew that half the benefices in his diocese could not afford a curate, so their clergy should not "pretend" to offer a false title. He wished to guard the Church against overstocking it with labourers.[43] A letter of 1788 from Bishop Horsley's agent in the diocese of St Davids, William Holcombe, noted a number of sham titles, including a man who had told the bishop he was starving as his "time was out".[44]

Fleetwood's concern was echoed by Bishop Jenkinson of St Davids, who in his primary Charge of 1828 refused to ordain on any short-term or temporary title because the profession was already over-crowded, and he insisted that incumbents used those already ordained who were without clerical employment. Fictitious titles in which no stipend was allowed, were fraudulent and simoniacal, and those who presented them would be refused ordination.[45] Bishop Copleston of Llandaff in 1833 considered titles for one year "too common" and queried his examining chaplain's comment that a two-year title was uncommon. Writing to his father in 1828 he stated there "a great dealing of jobbing and collusion" regarding these titles in his new diocese. In another letter of 1836 he queried a title offered to one Farquhar at Kemeys Commander, believing a bargain had taken place for him to receive less than the due stipend as he lived a mile from the parish. The incumbent, Lewis Williams, questioned, excused himself by saying he had resisted offers of money for a title, including a sum of £50 on one occasion. The bishop required the full stipend to be paid.[46] Conybeare, writing in the 1850s about a period thirty years earlier, believed that while incumbent and candidate were required to make and sign a solemn declaration that the one would give and the other receive the stipulated legal stipend, regarded these as "too often deliberately false". He had heard of instances where a sum of £5 had been paid when £50 had been stipulated, and added that "these frauds were unblushingly avowed, and treated as a matter of course".[47]

Bishop Basil Jones in his 1877 charge depreciated those incumbents, literates themselves, who would prefer to employ literates as curates rather than duly qualified candidates, generally because they had a fluency of speech that would appeal to congregations more than "the crude compositions of a young man fresh from college".[48] Bishop Campbell in his 1884 charge expressed dismay that many of his clergy were advertising for curates in the church press, rather than asking him whether there were men awaiting ordination who needed a title. These were the men who had received exhibitions from the diocese for their education and who had attended the diocesan vacation courses, with the result they were known to the diocese and had promised to serve within it.[49] Another problem soon manifested itself. Incumbents, especially those of large industrial parishes, who were required to find the money for their curates' stipends, often from their own pockets, found themselves unable to obtain sufficient funding, with the result that the number of titles available became restricted. This was also noted by Watkin Williams, bishop of Bangor, in 1900.[50]

The various requirements laid down by the archbishops included one that all those candidates for ordination on the forthcoming Ember Sunday should meet on the previous Wednesday night or Thursday morning at the bishop's palace for their examination and receive whatever preparation was available. They would remain until the ordination on Sunday, providing they had passed successfully. Bishop Sumner of Llandaff (1826-8) took the *Cardiff Arms* for the exclusive use, it seems, of himself, guests, chaplains and candidates, all of whom dined with him for the three days of examination. At that time there was no episcopal residence at Llandaff.[51] George Roberts in his *Speculum Episcopi* of 1848 suggested candidates would stay at a hotel, possibly have lunch at the palace, then with the examinations over by the Saturday afternoon, they would individually meet the bishop, probably for the first time, listen to his charge, and be invited to dine with him the following day.[52] At St Asaph candidates used to stay at the Mostyn Arms, until Bishop Short lodged them in his palace, perhaps for the sake of decorum.[53] The candidates were also expected to attend the daily cathedral services and to be properly dressed.[54] For example, Price, Carnhuanawr was advised by his clerical brother to wear black breeches and shoes rather than pantaloons and boots when he went for his ordination examination in 1811, probably at Abergwili, the bishop of St Davids' palace.[55]

During these proceedings, generally on the day before the actual ordination, the bishop would give a charge to the successful candidates. At Llandaff during Copleston's time this took place on the Saturday before the ordination, and in a letter of 1836 he requested Bruce Knight to ensure the candidates were in the cathedral by 2.00 pm, and that no-one was to be admitted once the charge had begun.[56]

The successful candidates dined with the bishop after the ordination itself. Sumner held his in the Chapter House of Llandaff Cathedral and assigned to those newly ordained different parts of the evening service, at which he preached.[57] Copleston of Llandaff frequently mentions these occasions in his letters to Bruce Knight. He did not wish to offer his candidates more than one dinner, and probably the Sunday was more convenient to them than the Saturday. Otherwise they would have to fend for themselves.[58]

With the bishops holding such a light view about this time of preparation, it is hardly surprising that many of their candidates idled away their spare hours. George Roberts suggests that while there were many earnest candidates, others saw the taking of orders rather like taking a degree. Though well behaved before the bishop, at their evenings in their inn the "college leaven" would emerge and it would be spent in cigars, drink and gossip, hardly the preparation for a solemn event, he remarked. He complained that while the bishop might examine a man's testimonials he hardly ever examined the man's heart, his motives or his character.[59] Edward Williams, a noted Presbyterian leader of his day, in the early 1770s was preparing for Oxford and ordination but changed direction when, having decided to attend an ordination service at St Asaph, he was horrified to discover that some of the men about to be ordained were the foul-mouthed young men he had met at an inn prior to the service.[60] Henry Arthur Morgan, son of a vicar of Conway, ordained at Ely in 1859, not only remembered that the bishop's one talk with his candidates when they were assembled in a semi-circle in front of him, was to hear his announcement that dinner was about to be served, but also that some of his fellow ordinands in the inn where they were staying were told by the waiter that "his lordship" didn't like "the young gentlemen to play cards" on these occasions.[61] The bishop's stable boy at Llandaff recalled that the ordinands used the harness room as their smoking room in the 1880s or thereabouts.[62]

Such was the laxity in which many men spent the time immediately before the solemn occasion of their ordination.

THE ORDINATION EXAMINATION

As noted in a previous chapter most dioceses had similar requirements for the ordination examination as deacon. It consisted of the Greek Testament, some Latin texts, especially Grotius, knowledge of the bible, prayer book and the theology of the Church of England. Jenkinson in 1836 specified some of the books required for the examination. They included Pearson on the Creed, Paley's Evidences of Christianity, Burnet on the 39 Articles and his Pastoral Care, Wheatley or Mant on the Prayer Book, Butler's Analogy, Hooker's Ecclesiastical Policy, and Bishop Bull's Advice to Candidates for Holy Orders.[63] Many of these books would have been standard texts at the universities or at Lampeter. Books on ecclesiastical history and on the Scriptures tended to vary according to the episcopal taste. Bishop Short of St Asaph specified in 1863 that candidates would be examined on the Greek text of certain specified books, be required to explain any part of the Bible as well as the doctrines of the Church as contained in the catechism, Prayer Book and Articles. The object of the examination, it was stated, was to discover whether the candidate was prepared for the work he wished to enter, and possessed that knowledge that would enable him to fulfil his new duties. A caution was added. Candidates needed to remember that the real concern was about their understanding rather than how far they had committed things to memory.[64] At Llandaff in 1875 a competent acquaintance with the Greek Testament as well as the rest of the Bible was required. The bishop did not insist upon Hebrew, but would be pleased by any indication it had been cultivated. Specific areas for Biblical study included the evangelical prophecies and theology of the Old Testament, the miracles of the Jewish and Christian dispensations, the parables and discourses of the Lord, and subjects treated in the various epistles. In addition to these they would be examined in the evidences for the Christian religion, the history of the Church in its first three centuries, the history of the Church in England in selected areas, the Book of Common Prayer, and the doctrines and polity of the Church. By 1896 the examination included the writing of a sermon on a subject chosen by the bishop.[65]

By 1911 the subjects had been narrowed down a little for Llandaff ordinands, so that only the gospel of Matthew, the letter to the Ephesians and Revelation chapters 1-3, were required in Greek, but in addition a second part had been added, including reading lessons and the liturgy, exposition and delivery of sermons, extempore speaking, and a patristic book studied in the original Greek. Bangor ordinands were also examined on a book exploring the relationship beween Church and dissent.[66]

It was not unknown for weak candidates to take the examination of the diocese with the lowest standard of examination. It was even alleged that the principal of a theological college advised one candidate to go to a particular diocese as it was "the easiest in the kingdom". Ripon was said to offer a relatively easy examination, while Oxford under Bishop Wilberforce (1845-70) was regarded as extremely difficult.[67] Possibly this also happened in Wales for the standard of Llandaff, by necessity, was lower than that of the other Welsh dioceses. John Gott, vicar of Leeds, complained in 1878 that many candidates knew that the former examination papers were recycled in a circle and these papers lacked freshness and vitality. He was probably referring to James Fraser, bishop of Manchester, who in that year wrote to W.H. Davey about his examination subjects and mentioned that he was reusing some sets of papers. He didn't want this to become known, as it would encourage men to begin a system of cramming.[68] It was also generally accepted that many candidates crammed, or were crammed by their theological colleges, for these examinations. This was especially true of the Latin and Greek texts the bishops expected them to know reasonably well.

Bishop Copleston in 1832 received a petition from one Yoreth, who had been made deacon but was hoping to be ordained priest, which required a further examination. He asked that he might be allowed to write a sermon instead of bring examined in the classics in which he had been found wanting. The bishop was inclined to allow his ordination as priest if he could manage the Greek Testament tolerably well, adding that classics would never do him or his hearers any good, and being already in deacon's orders there was "no retreat". Yoreth's request appears to have been allowed, but as his bishop remarked "a readiness in composing sermons does not belong to him". He had spent four hours producing one page of the "most ordinary stuff" upon a New Testament text.[69]

THE FINAL SCENE

Candidates, as we have noted, generally arrived at the episcopal palace or other place of meeting on the Thursday morning. They would then be examined by the examining chaplains, sometimes in a written test, often orally, in their theological knowledge, and then they might have a personal interview with the bishop. This tended to be the norm by the mid-nineteenth century, although in many cases this was a revival of the procedures of some bishops a century earlier. Thomas Scott, for example, the commentator, ordained by John Green, bishop of Lincoln in 1772, was tested in long interviews by two clergymen, presumably examining chaplains, and then by the bishop himself, who asked Scott his motives for ordination amongst many other questions.

Some bishops were much more thorough than others. Bishop Horsley of St Davids (1788-94) examined candidates personally as to their vocation and fitness.[71] Others interviewed men with the deliberate aim of excluding Methodists or evangelicals from ordination. Bishop Marsh has been noted in this connection already. Bishop Burgess personally examined men, requiring in those he accepted an accurate Biblical knowledge, competent acquaintance with the Greek Testament, a facility in English composition, an understanding of the Articles of Religion, while he encouraged a study of Hebrew. He impressed upon each candidate the need for a true and sound piety, enquired into their motives for ordination, offered "such admonitions as were likely to produce the most beneficial effect", and published several tracts for their use, one being *The Importance and Difficulty of the Pastoral Office, and the danger of rashly undertaking it*.[72] Bishop Sumner of Llandaff (1826-8) would counsel his candidates collectively to introduce family prayers into the lodgings where many would reside, and then individually would ask them about their inducements for seeking Holy Orders, about the chief doctrines that should animate their pastoral teaching, and how much of their duty would they consider discharged after they had performed their Sunday services. One candidate remarked on Sumner's ability to put men at their ease and bring forth their confidence. After this interview Bruce Knight, as examining chaplain, examined them individually for two hours orally, and then got them to write a Latin essay on a subject he gave them.[73]

Copleston of Llandaff (1828-49) left the examination and interviews to his examining chaplains, probably because he was generally resident in London as dean of St Paul's and on his parliamentary duties. He would "lay willing hands upon all the candidates you recommend" he wrote to Bruce Knight, his examining chaplain, in 1833. Later he was prepared to examine those Monmouthshire candidates himself if they could come to London for the ordination, but as a general rule Knight was to examine all candidates.[74] This was probably the case with many bishops of that time, but due to the influence of Bishop Wilberforce of Oxford (1845-70), who was the great reformer of the system and insisted on a period of intense personal contact between himself and the candidates,[75] most bishops followed his example. Archbishop Temple required candidates to read aloud to him in his study one passage, 2 Kings 19, verses 20-34, an extremely difficult passage that would test a man's powers of reading and intelligence.[76] Hughes of St Asaph strongly impressed some of his candidates by engaging in prayer with them.[77]

When Robert Roberts was examined by Bishop Short of St Asaph in 1859 he recorded his experience in some detail. Advised to wear a white tie as he would give offence to the bishop if he appeared in a coloured choker, he was greeted by a footman who he felt had "undisguised contempt" for him. The examination took place in the bishop's study, filled with books, and Roberts described the subsequent interview:

> How he plied me with rapid questions, often not waiting for the answer to the first question before another was launched: where had I been educated, what my parents were, what my previous profession, etc.? Coming to Greek, he trots off to one of the book-cases and brings a Xenophon Cyropaedia, which he opens at random and tells me to construe the first paragraph. "When I want to know if candidates know any Greek I always try them with Xenophon, it's such Greek Greek." I had never read a line of the Cyr, but I had happened to light on a plain passage and got thorough pretty creditably. "That will do – you don't seem quite to see the force of it, but never mind – let's try the Greek Testament." A few verses of St. John's Gospel were read and construed. "Very well: hardly the salvation: have you heard of a distributed middle?" Yes. So we went rapidly over logic, history, geography, and I don't know what besides; myself sitting in my chair, and his Lordship walking backwards and forwards between the desk and the waste-basket, sometimes taking short runs at me when he had a special question to ask, and giving me a gentle kick, then running back to the desk, lecturing away with great rapidity. The end of it was that he expressed himself satisfied with my acquirements. I might send in my papers to the registry, and come up next term. Suddenly he said – "Why did you go to St. Bees?" I told him the reason – want of funds to go to a University. "Ah, it's a pity, you should have gone to Oxford. You would have learnt something at Oxford. You would have found better men than yourself at Oxford. At St. Bees you were the 'cock

of the walk.' It does not do a man any good to feel himself the 'cock of the walk.'[78]

Examining chaplains were often even more demanding. William Gibson notes that by the late seventeenth century most bishops had delegated the examination of candidates to their chaplains, thus giving them the name "examining chaplains". As a result the standards tended to rise by the next century.[79] The celebrated diarist, Parson Woodforde, in 1763 during a half-hour oral examination was asked to construe a passage from Romans, and was asked a good many "hard and deep questions" that could not be answered with "yes or no" but made it clear whether a man was well read or not.[80] Lewis Evans, ordained to a curacy in Cardiganshire in 1792, was told by the chaplain when he came for his examination as a priest that he was the most illiterate person in the diocese, one of "fatheaded dullness". He felt as though he had put his hand to the ark improperly, like Uzziah, though he was eventually successful.[81] Bishop van Mildert of Llandaff and his examining chaplain, Bruce Knight, are said to have steadily increased the stringency of the examination, testing religious, moral and academic fitness.[82] One interview that has gone down into history was that of Edward White Benson, later archbishop of Canterbury (1883-96). Benson in his examination became embroiled in a dispute with the chaplain about the doctrine found in a particular passage in the Greek Testament. Both lost their tempers and the chaplain told him he could not recommend to the bishop a man as deficient as he was in so important a subject. The examiner proceeded to write his report, asking Benson his name, college and if he had any university distinctions. He had: fellow of Trinity, eighth wrangler, chancellor's gold medal in classics. Realising he was about to pluck the senior classic of his year, the examiner commented, "let us look at this passage again, Mr Benson".[83]

In many cases these examinations were conducted orally, as was the case with Thomas Coke, who became the first Methodist bishop in America. Ordained in 1770 his deacon's examinations at Abergwili and his priest's at Oxford were both conducted orally, when he was required to translate a Latin article into English and asked some general questions in divinity.[84] One assumes also that David Davies, ordained in 1801 at St Asaph Cathedral, had an oral examination, as he was required to appear on the Friday before the Sunday ordination, was examined on that day and during the following day signed the Articles of Religion and listened to an excellent

Charge given by the bishop.[85] Written examinations were not unknown, as seen above in the example of Fraser of Manchester's second-hand papers and other references. Edward Boys Ellman, a first class honours man, was examined by John Allan, of a Welsh clerical family, later archdeacon of Salop and a notoriously lax examiner, who told him his bishop was wrong to allow him to be ordained on letters dismissory. Ellman was later placed in an empty house for seven hours to answer three questions Allan had hastily written down. Allan had disappeared and was not to be found until the next day, when Ellman was reproved for the length of his answers, and then given another paper of questions to answer that morning. Allan's biographer alleged he never asked questions that a well-informed cleric could not readily answer without reference to books, as that would make men cram facts, and for the same reason he never examined church history.[86] That written examinations were required by some of the Welsh bishops is indicated by a story told by G.C. Coulton about a local incumbent invigilating a government examination at Llandovery. The inspector, suspecting some of cheating, asked for his comments. Horrified, he replied that schoolboys could always try again, while if those taking the examination for Holy Orders were to fail they would be ruined for life.[87]

There is one reference to a Welsh cleric receiving prizes for his ordination examination. This was David James, Panteg, ordained in 1826 into the diocese of St Davids. His biographer stated he had the first prize in classics, prizes for the best abridgement of a sermon, the best specimen of Hebrew calligraphy, and the best knowledge of music. As there is no other record of prizes being awarded one may be doubtful of these claims, somewhat typical of their day.[88]

A further examination concerned the Welsh language. It was an English bishop of Llandaff, van Mildert, who in the 1820s along with his Welsh-speaking examining chaplain, Bruce Knight, insisted on a Welsh examination for candidates, without which proficiency their "sphere of usefulness" would be much diminished.[89] He may have followed the example of Bishop Burgess of St Davids who, according to Archdeacon Bevan, was the first to require every candidate to be examined in colloquial and literary Welsh.[90] Later in the century there were many protests by the Welsh clergy that the Welsh examination required of Welsh-speakers counted "for nothing". Benjamin Hall bitterly complained that no candidate had presented himself for a Welsh examination since Ollivant had become bishop twelve months before.[91] In the diocese of Llandaff Peter Williams of Troedyrhiw said in 1910 that while other languages counted, Welsh did not, and that the Welsh examining chaplain, Canon Lewis of Ystradyfodwg, had never failed a man and his predecessor only once, thus making the examination a "farce".[92] Archdeacon John Griffiths, the Welsh examining chaplain to Bishop Ollivant, defended himself from similar allegations in 1879, stating that when he had told the bishop he had passed some candidates though there was much room for improvement because of the need for Welsh-speaking clergy, the bishop asked him why he was not faithful to his duties. If a man was not properly qualified, he would not proceed further.[93] Basil Jones of St Davids complained in 1882 that those examined in Welsh in his diocese often had an insufficient grammatical and literary knowledge of the language.[94] Paradoxically, Alfred George Edwards, later the first archbishop of Wales, as a result of his Welsh examination in the diocese of St Davids was informed he was not to be licensed to preach in Welsh before a further examination, though he might read prayers. His reading and preaching was declared to be fair, his Old Testament examination "fair and full" but in the New Testament it was "fair but vague".[95] The diocese of Bangor, according to its Directory of 1896, also had an examination in Welsh, its grammar and exposition, and in reading and speaking the language,[96] though *Draig Glas* commented that the English duty of many of these men was lost because of their Welsh accents.[97]

As far as is known these examinations, with the exception of the Welsh examination, were conducted in English, which possibly put many Welsh-speaking candidates at a disadvantage.[98]

Another deep concern was that while the bishops tested the academic knowledge of these candidates, few were concerned about their moral fitness or spiritual aptitude for ordination. John Wesley, indignant that Bishop Louth of London had failed a candidate for lack of a formal education, asked if he enquired about their spiritual qualifications and accused him of sending to America men who knew the classics but knew nothing about saving souls.[99] R.M. Beverley in 1831 pointed out that the apostles were not chosen for their knowledge of Greek or their skill in metres, but because it had pleased God to have called them, not to reward but to suffering for the sake of the Gospel.[100] In addition, many felt that the examination ought to be more practical in scope. Archdeacon Ffoulkes of Montgomery suggested an examination in preaching, for example, while John Griffith sarcastically remarked that there was no enquiry made whether a candidate could preach, and it was taken for granted that the passing of examinations in the classics was a sufficient warrant for office.[101]

Significantly, the deposited canons of 1874 and 1879, never enacted, required candidates to be examined in the usual subjects (though Latin and Greek Testament could be dispensed with in the case of older men provided they had other spiritual qualifications), but said nothing regarding personal fitness or pastoral experience.[102]

The position did change, however, as seen from some of the episcopal examples above. When Frederick Temple was bishop of Exeter (1869-85) he personally set questions on a pastoral theology paper. The questions included such subjects as ministry to the sick, appointment of churchwardens, visitation of a parish, or how to deal with a person who had moral scruples about receiving communion. He also asked candidates about their vocation to the ministry. Some were staggered when he asked if they believed that the work of the ministry was what God intended them to do.[103] In 1900 Bishop John Owen of St Davids made clear that the qualification of the heart was even more important than of the intellect, though it was better to have a combination of both.[104]

Many incidents were recorded about the superficial examinations conducted by the examining chaplains, particularly in English dioceses. George Spencer, son of Earl Spencer, ordained in 1822, was told by an examining chaplain that he could not even entertain any idea of subjecting "a gentleman with whose talents and good qualities I am so well acquainted as I am with you to any examination", but as a matter of form he asked him to turn into Latin a verse of the Greek Testament and one of the Articles. Admittedly, Spencer had a certificate of attendance at the university divinity lectures.[105] Two early examples may be related of Welsh dioceses, though the first may be a matter of gossip. William Bulkeley, an Anglesey squire, recorded in his diary for 30 June 1734 that Owen Bulkeley preached in his church that day. Five years ago he was but a common labourer and nothing of a scholar. Through the influence of Owen Lloyd of Llansadwrn, an absentee incumbent who wanted a cheap curate at £14 per year, he was ordained by Bishop Sherlock, but the squire refused to believe he could have been examined as otherwise it would have been impossible for him to be ordained.[106] Erasmus Saunders argued in 1721 that persons "very meanly qualified" found an easy access to be ordained in the diocese of St Davids, and were readily admitted on the recommendation of an impropriator who wanted a cheap chaplain or who desired to "pack off" a useless servant. Such a position, he added, offered no encouragement for others to go to the trouble and expense of a decent education.[107]

The standard of examination in Wales was known to be low. Ollivant explained in 1866 that the bishops would gladly raise the standards if circumstances allowed. He inferred if they did so the supply would considerably diminish. Ollivant's high ideal of the clerical calling, of clergymen distinguished by a professional ability and knowledge, true piety and Christian character, able to mould and challenge public opinion, and rescue not only individuals but the nation from judgment, had rather a hollow ring about it when faced with the actual circumstances. This was a point accepted by Basil Jones, who realised it was hard to raise standards without a very serious displacement of candidates, though he was later encouraged by the improvement in the academic abilities and tone of his ordinands.[108]

As late as 1899 Bishop Edwards of St Asaph complained that no bishop could force up a standard that necessity dictated, but he later agreed he could not allow the standard in his diocese to fall behind that of the other learned professions. Yet he observed that he and his chaplains often had to stretch a point to allow a man forward who might be otherwise qualified, rather than raise the standard to a more difficult level, which they were desirous of doing but knew that men were urgently required for the parochial ministry. It was said of Archdeacon Bevan of Hay, examining chaplain in the diocese of St Davids, that he would often make allowances for some shortcomings if he saw tokens of self sacrifice and practical fitness in candidates.[109] On the other hand Bishop Lewis of Llandaff argued there was not the slightest foundation for the belief that many of those ordained in his diocese, especially men from Lampeter, would not be seen as fit for ordination by an English bishop.[110] His successor, Pritchard Hughes, declined to ease the standard as requested by his incumbents, desperate for curates, to enable more men to be ordained. Rather he requested them to be patient as he wished to raise the standard and felt it better for them to have good men rather than those who were incompetent.[111]

Nevertheless, standards rose throughout the nineteenth century. Basil Jones of St Davids in 1877 claimed that the minimum standard in his diocese had never fallen below that which he endeavoured to maintain as an examining chaplain in an English diocese. In this case it was York, though its standard was not particularly high compared to some of the other English dioceses.[112] As noted above, bishops later became more selective in the men they would accept as candidates for Holy Orders, insisting on some academic status if a man was not a graduate.

Candidates were rejected, often it seems without mercy, not only for ordination as deacons, but also for admission to priest's orders, for by the nineteenth century a further examination was required for priesting. Walsham How recalled a boy in a church school being asked what were the Ember weeks replied it was when they prayed for the young gentlemen who were afraid of not passing their examination.[113] Bishop Burgess of St Davids, at his first ordination in 1803 is said to have rejected five out of twenty of the candidates, one of whom, found peculiarly ignorant and incompetent, had been a former livery servant. He was said to be inflexible in withholding Orders from those he found incompetent in their examinations, some of which he himself conducted, mainly in Latin and Greek composition and translation.[114] Bishop Jenkinson, writing to his predecessor in 1826 remarked he had rejected a number of men at his last ordination as they had not been at a grammar school for the required seven years, others for want of a title and another for insufficiency, who the next month enlisted as a common soldier. Another of those rejected had married instead a Llandeilo alehouse keeper.[115] A story, of an unknown date and possibly apocryphal, is told of a schoolmaster from Llanbadarn who came to the bishop to be examined. Asked what he could do he informed an amazed bishop he could jump like a buck and accordingly did so over a table. "Quite so," said the bishop, "admirably done, you can go on jumping like a buck", and declined to admit him as a candidate for Orders.[116]

In the Llandaff Diocesan Memorandum Books a list of those ordained and those rejected was maintained year by year. In the December ordination of 1868 three deacons were ordained but two men rejected. In February 1869 two men were rejected from the diaconate, and two deacons from the priesthood, one of whom was a Cambridge man, and in September 1882 four deacons were denied priests' orders. Most of those rejected from the diaconate were from St Bees or Queen's College, Birmingham, and in 1882 reasons are given, such as ignorant of the Greek Testament, ill-equipped in Old Testament, or shamefully ignorant of the Catechism.[117] Gilbert Harries of Gelligaer was reminded by Ollivant that he should ensure his curates had time to prepare for their priests' examination, and suggested he formed a Greek Testament study group with them.[118] No doubt men were turned down because of their moral life, but no examples are known from Wales, though Bishop Wilberforce of Oxford did so on several occasions.[119]

Basil Jones in his 1877 Charge referred to the care shown in his selection of candidates. To prove his point he told his clergy he and his chaplains had in three and a half years rejected three men who wished for deacons' orders and four from priests orders, while eighteen others had been refused upon enquiry previous to the examination by himself. Twelve years later he pointed out that some of those he had rejected were not allowed to present themselves again, and others were rejected at their first enquiry. This did not imply a moral fault, only a want of aptitude for the work of the ministry. It was his duty as a bishop to ensure only fit candidates were ordained. He realised it meant bitter disappointment for those rejected, especially after money had been spent on their education. He would give these men he had initially accepted for ordination his reason for their rejection, but not those who had lost out at the first hurdle.[120] Concern was expressed in 1910 that men who had passed their theological college examinations were for some reason failing in the ordination examination, yet the failures of one diocese were readily accepted in another.[121]

At the March 1870 ordination at Llandaff one man, Herbert W. Davies, voluntarily withdrew. It was his "third vain attempt".[122] It had probably happened before on many occasions, as when an unknown candidate appeared before Bishop Ewer of Llandaff in 1763, as described by William Thomas in his diary. The man went dumb and could not answer at any time, so the bishop told him to come in the evening, but he did not attend and had done the same thing before the bishop of St Davids.[123] The bishops generally sent lists to each other of those they had rejected and the grounds for their rejection.[124]

Those who were not outright failures, or perhaps showed some sign of promise, or whose qualifications were inferior to what the bishop expected, were from necessity ordained, but on the understanding they would remain deacons for five years. As Bishop Ollivant explained in 1870 these men were not allowed to take sole charge of a parish, and if they wished to be priested before the expiry of this time they were required to present themselves before the examiners of St David's College and pass an examination in classics, logic and mathematics. Those who remained deacons for the required time had to show they had acquired the knowledge required of candidates for the office of priest. These were only ordained because of the desperate need for Welsh-speaking clergy.[125] This was the case with John George in 1855 and James Jones in 1877 who "made a very bad examination", while in two ordinations of 1860 five of the nine deacons ordained were five-year men. Several were given a two-year diaconate, for such reasons as not being well acquainted with the Scriptures or because they needed to be examined again in Welsh reading. Many of these men had been biennial students at Lampeter.[126] The same position applied to the diocese of St Davids, where Archdeacon Henry de Winton, examining chaplain to Bishop Basil Jones of St Davids was scathing about St Bees candidates, many of whom came before him in their examination for priests' orders after a five year diaconate.[127]

A letter written by Bishop Short of St Asaph to a candidate who had been turned down survives. It appears the unsuccessful candidate asked an intermediary to see the bishop and ask the reason, and also to suggest if he might be more successful in another diocese. He met with a reply that must have astonished him for its honesty and yet compassion. In his letter Short wrote as follows:

> So far from having any objection to your offering yourself as a candidate for orders in the diocese of ----, I myself believe that it would be best for you to do so – best I mean for your future prospects of clerical usefulness. If you come to St. Asaph, you must come before my chaplains and myself under an unpleasant prepossession against you, which no preparation can obviate, and the feeling this on your part would create perhaps in your manner towards us a fresh suspicion of that which was the real cause which made me decline to proceed with your ordination.
>
> My reason for writing to you is, to put you as far as I can in possession of your own real defects, with the hope that the knowledge of them may go some way to cure them. It was not that we found you insuperably ignorant on any one or more points, but that you were generally defective in all. The few first questions were superficially answered. Wherever the examination became deeper, it was found there was nothing below the surface. Instead of having learnt that which a young clergyman need to know, you had crammed yourself as to that which an examiner would probably ask. When you had papers to write on subjects on which you had little or no knowledge, instead of admitting your ignorance by silence, you showed by a profuse use of words that you were not at all aware how ignorant you really were. When a bishop ordains, he takes on himself the responsibility of sending into the Church of God a minister who will promote the cause of Christ, or who will allow those who are committed to his charge to perish for lack of knowledge.

> How could I send forth one to teach who did not seem to know that which he was to teach? When I last examined you … I selected those articles of our Church which pertain to the salvation of souls, which pertain to Christians as individuals, which form the basis and groundwork of our Christian hopes, by which we and our hearers must be saved or perish. I examined you as to the fundamentals of Christianity. Now, in those cases when you knew what the article said, you did not seem to understand the meaning of it, the doctrine which you were to teach, nor to be aware that upon your teaching the salvation of souls might, humanly speaking, depend. For I cannot but repeat to you, that there appeared to me to be an unbecoming levity of manner. It may have been mere manner, but manner is a great index of the state of the heart.
>
> What I should advise you to read are works of piety. I gave you "Law's Serious Call;" read books of that sort, and go on making yourself master of the subjects which you have before studied. Study your Bible with prayer. Prayer will do more for you than any cramming.
>
> You deem yourself harshly dealt with in having your ordination delayed. I believe that if you employ your time wisely it may prove the greatest blessing which ever happened to you. It may make you *think* of what you are doing, have done, and are to do, and if so, it will prove a blessing to you to all eternity, which that God in mercy may grant is the prayer of your sincere friend.[128]

We do not know if this person benefited from this advice.

THE ORDINATION

Candidates were generally told whether they had been passed or rejected for ordination the day before the ordination. Even for those who were successful, the ordination was far from a spiritual climax, for their senses had probably been dulled by the examination process and the fears and anxieties it had caused. Even the ordination itself could seem like an anti-climax, for there was little spiritual and devotional preparation for it, and the service itself could be a hasty and undignified affair, squeezed in between the main services of the cathedral church. Bishop Westcott of Durham, ordained at Manchester in 1851, grieved at the undevotional character of the proceedings and the lack of any fatherly sympathy by the bishop.[129] Bishop Walsham How, ordained in 1846 at Worcester, was told the ordination was conducted in a "very indecorous, off-hand, careless way …".[130] It was remarked by Basil Jones that very few had actually attended an ordination service, and he wondered, amongst the candidates he was addressing, whether one in five of them had been present at such a service. In fact, he almost argued, how could that be, when ordinations in his diocese had been held at Abergwili, probably in the bishop's private chapel, or in the chapel of St David's College, Lampeter, until his predecessor had made them more public.[131]

Much concern was being shown in the 1860s and beyond about this state of affairs when the bishops' examinations were held in the ordination week, and men not told their result until a day or so before the ordination. One ordinand, albeit at York, made deacon in 1880, wrote that the examination lasted from Tuesday till Saturday morning, and only then, during that afternoon, were they told whether they had passed or not. The ordination was the next day.[132] It was clear that this was causing much anxiety and distress to many, and distracting from the solemnity of the occasion.[133] Walsham How as an examining chaplain pleaded in 1878 that the last two days before the ordination be given over to devotional exercises, and that men be told of their fate on Thursday at the latest, for those who feared failure could not enjoy acts of devotion. He knew that candidates longed for this spiritual assistance and even for a time of retreat, and he remembered a man telling him about the time of examination that it was so cold: "Oh, if I could have had only a squeeze of the hand and a 'God bless you!'"[134]

The bishops changed their practices slowly. Some of the English bishops put their examinations some weeks before the ordination, enabling them to come together with their bishop in the days before the ordination for a devotional preparation.[135] As Edgar Gibson, then principal of Wells Theological College and afterwards bishop of Gloucester put it, men ought to be preparing for ordination not examinations.[136] Campbell of Bangor felt unable to hold his examination some weeks before the ordination because of the distances candidates had to travel, but decided in 1881 to hold the examination on Monday morning to Wednesday evening, thus allowing two days for religious exercises and private meditation and prayer. He had realised, perhaps a little belatedly, that the feeling of "strain and anxiety" caused by the examination and waiting for the result, was "likely to interfere with that free play of devotional feeling, which ought to accompany the dedication of the life to God's service".[137] The bishops of St Asaph surprisingly seemed to have retained this older system until 1897 or thereabouts, for at the diocesan conference of that year it was suggested the examination should be separated from the ordination week in order to allow devotional and private preparation.[138] St Davids diocese adopted the same procedures some time in the 1880s. In his memoir of Archdeacon Bevan of Hay, examining chaplain to Bishop Basil Jones of St Davids, Gregory Smith made it clear that once again distances made it impossible to hold two separate events, but as the results of the examination were announced on the Thursday morning the rest of the week was undisturbed by anxieties. There were daily services in the chapel twice a day, spiritual addresses in the evening on Ember topics, one at the close of the week by the bishop, Holy Communion on the Saturday, as well as quiet walks with or evening visits to the chaplains who were able to confer with the candidates and offer advice.[139] Yet the same situation Campbell was endeavouring to avoid repeated itself in the 1930s, when a Church in Wales report argued that the results of the then standard examination, the General Ordination Examination, were received far too close to the date of the ordination for candidates not to feel anxiety and have too little time to devote to spiritual matters.[140]

Thus for two days or more the candidates were given time to prepare for their ordination, with services, addresses, the charge of the bishop, and private time for themselves. Walsham How was one of many examining chaplains called upon to give these devotional and pastoral addresses.[141] Basil Jones's ordination addresses were published after his death, in which he asked men to examine their motives, to see that ordination was not about entering a profession but rather a life, together with other fatherly exhortations.[142]

While bishops of the late seventeenth century held ordinations in their dioceses, Humphrey Humphreys of Bangor during 1690-7 holding them in its parish churches,[143] it was quite common thereafter until the 1840s for bishops to send their candidates to another diocese for ordination, either because there were too few candidates to hold one themselves, or because of their other duties. Frances Knight records of one ordination held at Ely Cathedral in 1836 when fifty-three men were ordained to the diaconate or priesthood. But forty-four of these came from the neighbouring dioceses of Peterborough and Norwich.[144] Bishop Warburton of Gloucester wrote about a little Welsh deacon whom he ordained in 1769 on letters dimissory, "who flew hither from his native mountains by accident, like a woodcock in a mist". One hopes this little Welsh curate was examined by his own bishop, for

Warburton was a fierce examiner and his examinations were described as "a kind of execution".[145] Thomas Jones of Creaton was sent by the bishop of St Davids to his colleague at Hereford for his ordination in 1774, having passed a successful examination before his own bishop. When he waited on the bishop of Hereford he was told he had slept too late, for the ordination had taken place that morning. Telling the bishop that this would be a serious disappointment to his new incumbent as he was much in want of an assistant, Jones asked if he might be allowed a private ordination. At first he refused, but a servant called back a dejected Jones as he left the palace to say he would be ordained the next morning.[146] Richard Bassett, curate of Colwinston and an earnest evangelical in his day, was ordained in 1801 at Gloucester on letters dimissory from Bishop Watson of Llandaff. Its bishop complimented him on his classical proficiency.[147] When James, Bruce Knight's curate, desired to be priested, he asked if the bishop of Bristol ordained at Bristol or not. Copleston, his bishop, replied his own ordination service would be in London but was unsure of the date. It might be better, he wrote, if he were to take advantage of the bishop of Rochester's ordination at St Paul's in early February. Around the same time the son of the vicar of Matharn, Thomas Lewis Williams, claming he knew nothing of Copleston's ordination day, requested letters dimissory to allow him to be ordained by another bishop. Have the goodness to examine him, the bishop asked Bruce Knight.[148] As late as 1868 Ollivant had sent two of his candidates to be ordained by the bishop of Hereford.[149]

George Roberts in 1848 bitterly complained about these ordinations held in London to suit the convenience of some of the bishops. Twenty to thirty men would come up, lodge in hotels, be surrounded by the gaiety and temptations of the metropolis, face a service at 8.15 am without a sermon which had to be completed by 10.30 for the Sunday services, and when the admonition to the "good people" was read there were no representatives of the dioceses present. All this, he exclaimed, when men were undertaking the most solemn act of their lives.[150]

Other bishops held their ordinations where it was most convenient for them. Daniel Rowland, the Welsh revivalist, is said to have walked to London from his native Cardiganshire to be made deacon by his own bishop at Duke Street Chapel in Westminster in 1734.[151] A.I. Pryce records that many Bangor clergy in the mid-eighteenth century were ordained in London by English bishops, though Bishop Zackary Pearce (1748-56) appears to have held most of his ordinations at Bangor.[152]

Bishop John Harris of Llandaff (1729-39) held his ordinations at Duke Street Chapel or St Margaret's, Westminster; Tyssherst in Sussex, St Mary's Abergavenny, Llantilio Pertholey and Trelech, Monmouthshire, as well as Llandaff and Hereford Cathedrals.[153] Bishop Burgess held his ordinations either at St Peter's Carmarthen, the parish church at Abergwili, alongside his palace or in its chapel. Ordinations were not held in St Davids Cathedral until the end of the nineteenth century.[154] Archdeacon David Evans alleged that William Williams, vicar of Llansanffraid Glan Conwy (1837-67) had had to walk to Windermere in order to be ordained by his diocesan, Bishop Watson of Llandaff.[155] Copleston of Llandaff was also dean of St Paul's and he often arranged for candidates from his diocese to be ordained there. One of them was James, Bruce Knight's curate at Margam, already mentioned, and Copleston wrote a very unfavourable account of him in December 1831. It was for him alone that he as dean and bishop had arranged the service at St Paul's as early as light would allow, 8.30 am, so James should have been there at 8.00, as was Tyler, his chaplain. Mr Bunder, the registrar's clerk, arrived some time later, but James not until 8.35 or so, with a choir service taking place at 9.00 am. It seems the ordination took less than twenty minutes to perform. "All this comes of calculating upon the last moment", Copleston wrote, and it was only because Knight needed him for his services that he did not make him come back another day.[156]

Candidates in 1843 were given a choice of the place of ordination. Some could come to him in London, or go to the other bishops, but Copleston did not wish to send more than two to any bishop so as to "make an equitable distribution".[157] It was only towards the end of his episcopate that Copleston started to use Llandaff Cathedral for his ordinations, though to be fair to him it was in a rather ruinous state for most that time. With that cathedral under repair in 1847 he held the service at St John's Cardiff where he had seventeen candidates. He was gratified that there was a large congregation, and all those present seemed deeply interested. There was never a large congregation in the cathedral.[158] Basil Jones of St Davids apologised to his clergy in 1880 that he had to hold his ordinations in London – he probably used one of the larger churches – because of his duties there. He was then the junior bishop sitting in the House of Lords and it was his duty to take the morning prayers.[159]

Bishop Ollivant held his ordinations in the Lady Chapel of Llandaff Cathedral until the whole cathedral had been restored. A newspaper report of 1851 recorded the service in this chapel, noted a crowded congregation, many of them being natives of

Cardiff.[160] His successor sometimes took the services around the diocese. A letter from Frederic Edmondes to Bishop Lewis of December 1887 stated that the ordination service held at Bridgend that month was very impressive and the deacons had been much liked by their hosts who presumably had given them accommodation.[161]

Nearly all the ordination services in Wales were conducted in the English language. The bishop of Bangor defended this practice in 1911 stating that it was likely there were some candidates who did not understand Welsh.[162] It was not until Trinity Sunday 1901 that Bishop John Owen of St Davids held an ordination service in Welsh. At least one person believed this was the first time it had ever happened in that diocese.[163] In fact, when the Welsh Book of Common Prayer was being revised in 1838, the delegates of the Oxford University Press wished to omit the Ordination Service on grounds of cost. It was eventually included when the revisers protested. The delegates may well have been briefed how little the service was used, if at all.[164]

A sermon was generally preached at these ordinations, though possibly not at the rather *ad hoc* ones arranged by some of the bishops. John Jones, later archdeacon of Bangor, preached the ordination sermon at Bangor Cathedral in September 1800, reminding himself (for remarkably he was also a candidate) and those being ordained that they had been called to a dignified office and were engaged in the immediate service of God. He exhorted himself and his fellow ordinands about the need for holiness of life, constant prayer, and purity of sentiment, especially as they were called to bring back those who had strayed from the flock. Four years later Rowland Williams, senior, followed his example, arguing that dissent had been caused because of the neglect by the clergy of their spiritual duties.[165] Bishop Sumner of Llandaff (1826-8) preached himself at the evening service after one of his ordinations, when the newly ordained were present.[166]

The old system may be said to have lasted until the 1930s in at least one Welsh diocese. Eryl Thomas, later bishop of Llandaff, recalled his own ordination at St Asaph in December 1933, conducted by the eighty-six year old Archbishop Edwards. He and his colleagues stayed overnight at the Palace, and between tea and dinner had an interview with the archbishop. Thomas had never met him before, and the interview was rather short. "Ah, yes, Thomas, I believe you have a streak of obstinacy in you … A little obstinacy is a very good thing, my boy, but should not be carried to extremes. Always remember that, my son", and that was it. At dinner there was no sign of the archbishop nor of Mrs Edwards, and some of the young men got bored and started a pillow fight. The butler stopped it and told them that the archbishop was not feeling well and so the ordination would be at ten the next morning and not at eight. A score of people sat in the congregation for it, but were too far away from the high altar to see or hear anything. And thus the inaudible and invisible service ended at 12.40 pm because the archbishop kept losing his place and going back over the service. Nor was there any music whatsoever.[167]

Prior to the ordination the candidates were required to subscribe to the 39 Articles, make the oaths of allegiance and supremacy, and the declaration of conformity to the liturgy. After it they received their letters of ordination and licence to officiate. This was not a part of the service itself, and thus a fee was exacted from them by the bishop's secretary, who pocketed it. Some dioceses charged ten shillings for the licence and between fifty and sixty shillings for the letter of orders, justified by one officer because of the considerable trouble he had taken on their behalf.[168]

The ordinands are now at the end of their travail, and probably out of pocket as they travel to their designated parishes. We shall follow them there in the next section.

ENDNOTES TO SECTION ONE: THE ROUTE TO ORDINATION

CHAPTER ONE: INTRODUCTION

1. *Report of the St David's Diocesan Conference,* 1882, p. 47. His name is misspelt as Beavan.
2. As noted in the *Bangor Diocesan Calendar and Clergy List* 1907, pp. 270-1. This was especially so, as the Church was losing its hold on education.
3. *Report of the Royal Commission, 1911,* I.I, 43.
4. Philip Jenkins in Gregory and Chamberlain, *The National Church in Local Perspective,* p. 268.
5. Conybeare, *Essays Ecclesiastical and Social,* pp. 9-11, 17, 20.
6. Noted by O.W. Jones in Walker, *A History of the Church in Wales,* p. 117.
7. Russell, *The Country Parish,* p. 226.
8. *Quarterly Review,* III (1862), p. 413. The article was on the training of the clergy.
9. Quoted by Toman, *Kilvert: the Homeless Heart,* p. 123, and Andrea Jones, *A Thousand Years of the English Parish,* p. 225. See also Haig, *Victorian Clergy,* pp. 141-3.
10. Heeney, *A Different Kind of Gentleman,* p. 96; Andrea Jones, *A Thousand Years of the English Parish,* pp. 225-6; Owen Chadwick notes that both Bishops Wilberforce and Stubbs regretted the erosion of this concept: *The Spirit of the Oxford Movement,* pp. 212-3.
11. Quoted by Chadwick, *The Victorian Church,* II. 250-1.
12. W. Hale, *Proposals for the Extension of the Ministry in the Church of England* (London, 1864), p. 115.
13. *Quarterly Review,* 123 (1867), 227-8. The article is on the Church and her Curates. Haig, *Victorian Clergy,* pp. 145-6, notes that J.H. Blunt and Bishop Stubbs made similar comments.
14. Dowland, *Nineteenth-Century Anglican Theological Training,* pp. 131-2; R. Towler and A.P.M. Coxon, *The Fate of the Anglican Clergy* (London, 1978), p. 23.
15. *Report of the Church Congress, Cambridge,* 1861, pp. 105-8. He suggested a permanent diaconate drawn from the ranks of the lower classes.
16. Dowland, *Anglican Theological Training,* p. 131.
17. Vincent, *Letters from Wales,* pp. 223-4, cf. Hart and Carpenter, who illustrate the same point in their *Nineteenth Century Country Parson,* p. 6.
18. A. Ollivant, *A Sermon Preached in the Chapel of St David's College, Lampeter, on the 24th June 1880, when the Chapel was re-opened* (London, 1880), p. 8.
19. Edwards, *Wales and the Welsh Church,* pp. 379-80. He added that the main qualification at the present time was the ability to pay for the necessary training and education.
20. Morgan, "The Diocese of St David's", Part C, pp. 51-2.
21. L.E. Elliott-Binns, *Religion in the Victorian Era* (London, 1953), p. 446.
22. See Heeney, *A Different kind of Gentleman,* pp. 4-8, 93-8; Russell, *The Clerical Profession,* pp. 200-2; Percy, *Clergy: the Origin of Species,* pp. 26-9; Jacob, *The Clerical Profession,* pp. 1-3; Burns, *The Diocesan Revival,* pp. 102-3. Parsons, in *Religion in Victorian Britain,* I, 185, is more sceptical, and suggests that the other professions might have imitated the clergy rather than the other way about.
23. R.R. Williams, *The Word of Life,* pp. 116-8. He was referring in particular to the sacerdotal tendencies of the Tractarian movement.
24. Haig, *Victorian Clergy,* p. 3.
25. Brown, *John Griffith,* pp. 89-90.
26. Lewis, *Charge (Llandaff),* 1888, p. 3.
24. *Llandaff Diocesan Church Calendar and Clergy List,* 1911, p. 141.

28 NLW. MS 22721, Edward Copleston to his father, 2 September 1828.
29 Jenkinson, *Charge (St Davids) 1828,* pp. 31-2;
30 Basil Jones, *Charges (St Davids)*, 1877, pp. 23-5; 1880, pp. 25-7. Numbers were still "holding up" in 1892 (though he noted his had been assisted by the immigration of 26 curates from other dioceses): *Charge, 1892*, pp. 12-13. See also *Report of the St David's Diocesan Conference*, 1882, p. 47.
31 Basil Jones, *Charge*, 1886, p.16; Lewis, *Charge*, 1885, p. 11; *Report of the St David's Diocesan Conference*, 1882, p. 61.
32 To give but one example: *Proceedings of the St Asaph Diocesan Conferences*, 1881, 1887, 1899 and 1903.
33 Reported in the *CDH*, 28 October 1898, p. 3.
34 As noted by Harold Browne at the Oxford Church Congress, 1862: *Report*, p. 49; Espin, *Our Want of Clergy*, pp. 1-2 (though he was referring to university men): he also noted that if a northern bishop insisted on University men half his curacies would be unfilled: *ibid*, p. 5.
35 Quoted in Short, *Sketch of the History of the Church of England*, p. lxvii.
36 Vincent, *The Church in the Diocese of Bangor*, p. 9, cf. J.F. Durey, "Ecclesiastical Patronage in Trollope's Novels and Victoria's England", *Churchman*, 109 (1995), 269.
37 John Jones, *Consideration on the Illegality and Impropriety of Preferring Clergymen*, pp. 43-6; cf. *Proceedings of the St Asaph Diocesan Conference*, 1899, p. 9, which noted that many deferred ordination as they were aware they would not obtain a sufficient income for the needs of their families.
38 Conybeare, *Essays Ecclesiastical and Social,* p. 9.
39 *Report of the Llandaff Diocesan Conference*, 1900, pp. 10-11. Bishop Lewis continued that because of the fall in the tithe rent charge many men were compelled by prudence to turn their thoughts elsewhere, fearing that the Church would be unable to provide a decent maintenance for themselves and their families, who, in the event oft their death, might become dependent on charity.
40 *Report of the Llandaff Diocesan Conference*, 1907, pp. 18, 24.
41 *Report of the St David's Diocesan Conference*, 1882, p. 32; *Report of the Llandaff Diocesan Conference,* 1907, pp. 21, 26; *Chronicles of Convocation*, 1900, p. 362.
42 *Report of the Bangor Diocesan Conference*, 1910, p. 7.
43 *Chronicles of Convocation,* 1900, pp. 373-4.
44 See for example: Basil Jones, *Charge (St Davids)*, 1877, pp. 23-4; Lewis, *Seventh Charge (Llandaff)*, 1903, pp. 5-7; *Proceedings of the St Asaph Diocesan Conference*, 1899, p. 9, and 1907, pp. 11-12; *Report of the Llandaff Diocesan Conference*, 1902, pp. 66-7; *Report of the Church Congress, Swansea*, 1909, pp. 202-3; *Ecclesiastic,* 22 (1860), pp. 549-52, noting Bishop Wilberforce's remarks; *Guardian*, 2 February 1881, pp. 156-7; Chadwick, *The Spirit of the Oxford Movement*, pp. 207-10; Haig, *Victorian Clergy*, pp. 7-12, 42, 52-3; Albert Marrin, *The Last Crusade* (Durham, North Carolina, 1974), p. 21, who quotes Randall Davidson's concern about the objections of parents on financial grounds to the ordination of a son.
45 *Church in Wales: Report of the Revisory Sub-Committee*, p. 50.
46 *Report of the Association of Welsh Clergy*, 1853, pp. 27, 34; 1855, pp. 5, 18; E.W. Williamson, *The Church in Wales (reprinted from 'Theology')* (Cardiff, 1948), pp. 10-11; Gibson and Morgan-Guy, *Religion and Society in the Diocese of St Davids,* p. 218 (noting the better stipends in England and that few returned to Wales). Ollivant asked those Welsh-speaking clergy serving in English curacies to consider whether they were deserting the post to which they had been called: *Charge (Llandaff),* 1851, pp. 50-1.
47 Durey, "Ecclesiastical Patronage", p. 269.
48 Conybeare, *Essays Ecclesiastical and Social*, p. 5.
49 Thomas Arnold, *Principles of Church Reform* (4th. Edn., London, 1833), pp. 55-6.
50 *Report of the Church Congress, Leeds,*1872, p. 445.

51   Short, *History of the Church of England*, p. lxvi. He added that the bulk of the Welsh population were Nonconformists.

52   Writing as *Cambro Sacerdos* in *CMG*, 24 October 1846, p. 3; Brown, *John Griffith*, pp. 30-1, 219-20.

53   Ollivant, *Charge (Llandaff)*, 1866, p. 10; John Evans, *A Charge delivered to the Clergy of the Archdeaconry of Carmarthen*, 1864, pp. 31-2; John Owen, *Church Reform and Church Progress, A Charge* (Carmarthen, 1900), pp. 42-3; *Reports of Diocesan Conferences*, Llandaff, 1910, p. 78; St Davids, 1882, p. 37; St Asaph, 1903, p. 19; 1907, p. 9. Archdeacon Ffoulkes stated at the Stoke on Trent Church Congress that he always put the case for ordination before his confirmation candidates: *Report*, 1875, p. 427. Some clergy were prepared to discourage possible candidates, as did John Hughes of Llanbadarn Fawr, Cards., who told the village schoolmaster he was more fit for the plough than to be a minister of the Church, and that he should think no more of ordination. It was said he later became a Roman Catholic priest: "Cambrian Soldier", *The Established Church. A Letter to H.T. Edwards, vicar of Carnarvon* (Pwllheli, n.d.), pp. 17-18.

54   Wynford Vaughan-Thomas, *Trust to Talk* (London, 1980), p. 82.

55   See, for example, *Chronicles of Convocation*, 1862, pp. 853-60, 923-37; 1866, pp. 330-45; 1880, pp. 55-7; 1884, xii, 42-62, 84-97, 123-8, 132-6, and *Report on the Diaconate*, no. 181; 1904, pp.110-13: *Reports of Church Congresses*, Cambridge, 1861, pp. 107-8 (such procedures might disabuse the public mind that Latin and Greek made a clergyman, and give artisans the rough and ready teacher they require); *Oxford*, 1862, pp. 53-63; *Stoke on Trent*, 1875, pp. 320-8; *Croydon*, 1877, pp. 556-8; *Sheffield*, 1878, p. 541; *Derby*, 1882, pp. 352-69; *Shrewsbury*, 1896, 104-29: *Church Quarterly Review*, 25 (1887-8) 286-318: *The Churchman*, II (1880) 161-8: W. Hale, *Proposals for the Extension of the Ministry in the Church of England* (London, 1864), p. 114-21; Ryle, *Church Reform Papers* (London 1870), pp. 121-3: *Report of the St David's Diocesan Conference*, 1882, pp. 40, 53-4: *Proceedings of the St Asaph Diocesan Conference*, 1881, pp. 25-6, 29; 1884, p. 8; 1885, p. 17: A North Wales Incumbent, *A Letter to the Rt. Rev. Bishops of St Asaph and Bangor, on matters relating to the well-being of the Church in their Lordships' respective Dioceses* (London, 1851), pp. 17-19; W. Trevor Parkins, *The United Action of the Laity and Clergy in the Church* (Oswestry, 1876), p. 13.

56   *CMG*, 9 January 1869, p. 8.

57   Brown, *John Griffith*, p. 219; Davies, *Henry Phillpotts, Bishop of Exeter*, p. 283.

58   *Report of the Llandaff Diocesan Conference*, 1890, pp. 36-42.

59   *Report of the Llandaff Diocesan Conference*, 1884, pp. 55-70, esp. pp. 63-5.

60   *Minutes of the Cardiff Deanery Chapter* for 14 July 1885.

61   Campbell, *Charge (Bangor)*, 1884, pp. 51-6. He supported the concept of the lay-diaconate in 1854: *CMG*, 14 April 1854, p. 3.

62   *Proceedings of the St Asaph Diocesan Conference*, 1887, pp.15 and 2-3, cf. Ffoulkes in *ibid.*, 1881, p. 30.

63   *Chronicles of Convocation*, 1904, p. 242; *Report of the Church Congress, Sheffield*, 1878, p. 538; *Proceedings of the St Asaph Diocesan Conference*, 1887, pp. 13-14.

64   Watson, *Anecdotes of the Life of Richard Watson*, II, 199-202.

65   *Chronicles of Convocation*, 1879, pp.133-4; *Reports of Church Congresses, Stoke on Trent*, 1875, pp. 427-8, and *Croydon*, 1877, pp. 556-8. Ffoulkes probably influenced the Newtown Clerical Association in 1877, which argued for this possibility even though some men might have to wait for some years before being ordained priest: Brown, "The Newtown Clerical Association", p. 82.

66   *Report of the Church Congress, Swansea*, 1879, p. 550; Ryle, *Church Reform Papers*, pp. 116-7.

67   *Chronicles of Convocation*, 1879, pp. 134-40.

68   "A Clergyman", *On Clerical Education. A Letter...*, 1st letter, p. 8.

69   Owen, *Directions for Young Students in Divinity*, pp. 13-27.

70 Popkin, *Observations on the Nature of the House of God*, pp. 15-16. This was a reply to Bishop Burgess's 1804 Charge. See also Beverley, *On the Present Corrupt State of the Church of England*, pp. 26-9.
71 W. Basil Jones, *Some Ordination Addresses*, pp. 40-1.
72 *Report of the Diocesan Conferences,* Llandaff, 1902, p. 66; Bangor, 1910, p. 6.
73 Quoted by Anne Stott in M. Smith and S. Taylor (eds.), *Evangelicalism in the Church of England* (Church of England Record Society 12, 2004), pp. 39-40.
74 Quoted by Percy, *Clergy: the Origin of Species*, p. 81.
75 *Llandaff Diocesan Magazine*, July 1914, pp. 163-4; Prichard, *Representative Bodies*, pp. 112-4.
76 Francis Jones writing in *Pembrokeshire History*, 5 (1974), 102-7.
77 John Morgan to John Owen, 1 March 1892, in NLW, John Owen Papers, bundle 23 in file on his early days. Vincent in his *Letters from Wales* (p. 54) noted how dissenters disliked their young men being persuaded to enter the Church in order to gain social status.
78 'An Oxford Tutor', "The Making of Welsh Parsons", *Cymru Fydd,* III (1890), 513-24, especially pp. 514, 522.

CHAPTER TWO: THE WELSH DILEMMA

1 M.L. Clarke, "John Warren, Bishop of Bangor 1783-1800", *T.Caerns.HS*, 41 (1980), 97; Pryce, *The Diocese of Bangor*, pp. xii, lii. He notes that nearly all those presented to benefices in that diocese were university men
2 F.W.D. Fenn and J.B. Sinclair, "Continuity and Change: A Welsh Border Parish and its Clergy 1750-1900", *T.Radns.S.*, 57 (1987), 65.
3 Pryce, *The Diocese of Bangor*, p. lxxxiv-vi; O.W. Jones, in Walker, *History of the Church in Wales*, p. 146 (he gives an incorrect date).
4 Davies, *The Life and Opinions of Robert Roberts*, p. 375.
5 O.W. Jones, in Walker, *History of the Church in Wales*, p. 146; Pryce, *The Diocese of Bangor*, p. lxxxiv.
6 Brown, *Evangelicals in the Church in Wales*, p. 94.
7 *Report of the Church Congress, Swansea,* 1879, p. 261.
8 Edwards, *Wales and the Welsh Church*, pp. 373-7.
9 Basil Jones, *Charge (St Davids),* 1877, p. 24; cf. *Report of the Bangor Diocesan Conference,* 1910, p. 7.
10 Quoted by O.W. Jones in Jones and Walker, *Links with the Past*, pp. 166-7; Jacob, in Williams, *The Welsh Church*, p. 88. He notes Lloyd's comment that the best scholars were not always graduates.
11 *A Letter to the ... the Lord Bishop of St. David's concerning the Admission of Unqualified Persons into Holy Orders* (London, n.d., probably linked with Bishop Horsley, 1877-94), p. 4. Many of these graduates were said to have gone to the north Wales dioceses instead: Price, *David's University College*, I, 5. Nevertheless, between 1687-99 a large number of graduates were ordained in the diocese: in 1688 30%, 1685 76%, 1698 28% and in 1699 66%: Gibson and Morgan-Guy, *Religion and Society in the Diocese of St Davids*, p. 112.
12 Price, *St David's University College,* I, 3.
13 Hughes, *Charge (St Asaph),* 1871, p. 13.
14 Ollivant, *Charge (Llandaff),* 1851, pp. 46-7. See also Campbell, *Charge (Bangor)*, 1872, pp. 29-30; Thomas Walters, *Church Pastoral-Aid Society: Abstract of Report and Speeches*, 1869, p. 18; O.W. Jones, "Thomas Walters", p. 65; Bevan, *The Case of the Church in Wales*, p. 40; *CMG*, 1 September 1854, p. 2 for a speech by Ollivant.
15 *Substance of Speeches at the Annual Meeting of the Llandaff Church Extension Society*, 17 April 1879, p. 17; Griffith, *The Welsh Church Congress*, pp. 7-9, *CMG*, 5 March 1870, p. 5.
16 Edwards, *Wales and the Welsh Church,* pp. 343-4.

17 David Howell, *Vernacular Preaching: A paper to the Manchester Church Congress* (separately published, 1888), p. 3.
18 A point made by A.G. Edwards, *Proceedings of the St Asaph Diocesan Conference*, 1899, p. 7.
19 Ollivant to John Griffith, 21 July 1871, in South Glamorgan Library, Cardiff Ms. 3,508.
20 Campbell, *Charge (Bangor)*, 1875, p. 22.
21 *Report of the Church Congress, Swansea*, 1879, p. 262.
22 Conybeare, *Essays Ecclesiastical and Social*, pp. 9-12, 17-21, 201. Using the prejudiced reports of the 1847 Blue Books into Welsh education, Conybeare unjustly suggested that the farming homes from which many of these men came were brutalised and course, and that immorality was ripe within them. For want of refinement they would be exposed to temptation, especially to that of the alehouse.
23 *CMG*, 21 November 1846, p. 3, and 28 November 1846, p. 3; Brown, *John Griffith*, pp. 22-3, 122-3. Part of his concern was that these men introduced Methodist habits into the churches they served.
24 Quoted by Griffith, *The Welsh Church Congress*, pp. 6-7. The same position was found in the diocese of Chester, though at a much earlier period. In 1743 Archbishop Herring was warned about the low calibre of clergy in that diocese, who were described as "a whole Colony of poor Raw Boys taken from the home-bred insignificant schools of this County". Many of them sought their fortunes in the diocese of York as low-priced curates: quoted by Snape, *The Church of England in Industrialising Society*, p. 164.
25 W.G. Curtis Morgan, *My Life through Six Reigns* (Risca, 1983), p. 7.
26 Bevan, *The Case of the Church in Wales*, p. 40.
27 *Report of the Church Congress, Swansea*, 1879, pp. 259-60. In a newspaper article, probably by John Griffith, the gwerin clergy of west Wales were described as having no other language but their own and being totally ignorant of the world and the sphere in which a clergyman was supposed to move in: *CMG*, 7 November 1846, p. 3. As late as 1938 the same point was made by Maurice Jones, principal of Lampeter, who wrote that the best Welsh speakers were "sadly deficient" in the knowledge of English: *Church in Wales: Report of the Revisory Sub-Committee*, p. 5.
28 Williams, *Roland Williams*, I, 200.
29 *Chronicles of Convocation,* 1870, p. 504 (he noted many such men came from farming stock), Ollivant to Harries, 24 January and 28 November 1865, in NLW, Church in Wales Records, John Morgan (Llandaff) Papers, Box 10. There was a similar concern in the diocese of Durham: Lee, *The Church of England and the Durham Coalfield, 1810-1926*, p. 55.
30 Price, *St David's University College*, I, 122.
31 Lewis, *Charge (Llandaff)*, 1885, p. 13.
32 Hughes, *Charge (Llandaff)*, 1907, pp. 28-9. He believed his policy was producing more candidates.
33 At the Leeds Church Congress, 1872: *Report*, pp. 461-3.
34 *Church Pastoral-Aid Society Quarterly Paper,* lxxxix, April 1870, pp. 4-5. The remark was qualified in so far as it related to the piety and soundness of views expressed by the candidate, rather than his ability for the work of the ministry. It was thus a party statement.
35 Vincent, *Letters from Wales*, pp. 7, 223-4.
36 *Report of the Llandaff Diocesan Conference*, 1910, p. 90.
37 *Proceedings of the St Asaph Diocesan Conference*, 1897, p. 8.
38 Huntington, *Random Recollections*, pp. 89-90. Thirlwall's predecessor is said to have sent such men to dine in the kitchen: O.W. Jones in Jones and Walker, *Links with the Past,* p. 165.
39 Copleston, *Edward Copleston*, pp. 165-6.
40 *CMG*, 5 March 1870, p. 5. Griffith was speaking in the context of Ystrad Meurig School
41 Brown, *Evangelicals in the Church in Wales*, pp. 128-9.
42 Edwards, *Wales and the Welsh Church*, pp. 376-7.
43 Quoted Brown, *John Griffith*, p. 235.

44 *Report of the Church Congress, Swansea,* 1879, pp. 367-8.
45 A point made by Bullock, *Training for the Ministry 1800-1874*, p. 144, cf. Ian Green in W.J. Shiels and D. Wood (eds.), *Studies in Church History, vol. 26: The Ministry: Clerical and Lay* (Oxford, 1989), p. 265.
46 Williams, *Rowland Williams*, p. 193.
47 Edwards, *Wales and the Welsh Church*, p. 380.
48 *The Position and Prospects of Stipendiary Curates: A Paper* (Curates Augmentation, Fund, 5th. Ed., London, 1869), p. 8, cf. "The Church and her Curates", *Quarterly Review*, 123 (1867) 229.
49 *Reports of Church Congresses: Oxford,* 1862, p. 6; *Folkstone,* 1892, p. 464 (though this related to an extra year for theological training for university graduates).
50 Ollivant, *Charges (Llandaff),* 1851, p. 46; 1869, pp. 9-10; 1869, pp. 14-15; *Chronicles of Convocation,* 1872, p. 197.
51 Campbell, *Charge (Bangor),* 1872, pp. 30-1; Basil Jones in *Report of the St Davids Diocesan Conference,* 1882, p. 63. Campbell added that these men applied for ordination at the first opportunity because of their inability to maintain themselves from their own resources.
52 Eliezer Williams, *A Sermon Preached before the Society for Promoting Christian Knowledge and Church Unity in the Diocese of St. David's* (Carmarthen, 1807), p. 34.
53 *Report of the St Davids Diocesan Conference,* 1882, p. 32; *Report of the Llandaff Diocesan Conference,* 1902, p. 68, cf. *ibid*, 1907, pp, 21, 26. *Proceedings of the St Asaph Diocesan Conference,* 1903, p. 21. Many observed that the new theological colleges, attached to religious houses, at Kelham and Mirfield, offered a free education to those who could not afford to pay for it, and were oversubscribed, Mirfield having to reject 90 out of 100 applicants. This showed that there was no lack of men, only a lack of money: *Chronicles of Convocation,* 1904, pp. 236-8; *Report of the Church Congress, Liverpool,* 1904, pp. 266-7; Lloyd, *The Church of England*, p. 149.
54 *Report of the Church Congress, Swansea,* 1879, p. 263.
55 Perowne, *Remains of Connop Thirlwall*, I. 94.
56 Campbell, *Charge (Bangor),* pp. 33-4.
57 *Report of the St Davids Diocesan Conference,* 1882, p. 44; *Church Pastoral-Aid Society: Abstract of Report and Speeches,* 1869, p. 18.
58 Edwards, *Wales and the Welsh Church*, pp. 377-80.
59 *Report of the St Davids Diocesan Conference,* 1882, p. 43; *Reports of the Llandaff Diocesan Conference,* 1902, p. 69, and 1910, p. 85.
60 *Report of the Church Congress, Leeds,* 1872, p. 462.
61 R.H. Parry, *Within Life's Span* (Ilfracombe, n.d.), pp. 83-4.
62 John Rowlands, *Historical Notes* (Cardiff, 1866), pp. 48-9.
63 James Jones Morgan, *Epistolary Correspondence ... to the Rt. Rev. Dr Warren, Bishop of Bangor* (Birmingham, 1800), pp. 1-8, 50, 55. At a later date, graduates often taught in school to obtain money for their theological course: *Report of the Church Congress, Folkstone,* 1892, p. 464. In addition, men taught between the completion of a college course and the date of their ordination, especially if they finished their education before the canonical age of ordination: *Report of the Llandaff Diocesan Conference,* 1892, p. 65. This was the case with John Griffiths (1820-97), later archdeacon of Llandaff, who became headmaster of Cardigan Grammar School, of which he had been a pupil, after completing his Lampeter course: Brown, *Ten Clerical Lives*, pp. 104-5.
64 Jane Ross, *A Light upon the Road: Archdeacon John Hughes of Aberystwyth (1787-1860)* (Aberystwyth, 1989), p. 3. See also Brown, *John Griffith*, p. 214.
65 Burgess, *Charge (St Davids)*, 1813, pp. 51-2.
66 Richards, *Honest to Self*, pp. 60-1; *Swansea Parish Magazine*, February 1906, p. 27, for another example.
67 Park, *St Bees College*, p. 21; Blackwell, *Beauties of Alun*, pp. 22-33.
68 Sarah Thomas to J.P. Richards, 19 May 1848, in Glamorgan Record Office, D/DA/32, item 31.

69 J. Ellis to Mrs John Owen, 17 December 1929, in John Owen Papers, early days file, bundle 1.
70 Edwards, *Wales and the Welsh Church*, p. 326.
71 Eighteen Meyrick scholarships were available at Jesus College of £80 per year, and 30 exhibitions of £40, all restricted to natives of Wales: Griffith, *The Welsh Church Congress,* pp. 12-13.
72 *Ecclesiastical Gazette,* 1852-3, p. 45.
73 The Elland Clerical Society had been founded in 1777. Similar societies were at Bristol, 1795, Creaton, c. 1812, and London 1816: Owen, *Thomas Jones*, pp. 196-8; Jacob, *The Clerical Profession*, pp. 55-6.
74 Davies, *The Life and Opinions of Robert Roberts*, p. 351.
75 See, for example, *Report of the Llandaff Diocesan Conference,* 1910, p. 78; *Report of the Church Congress, Cardiff,* 1889, pp. 158-9; *Report of the Pan-Anglican Conference 1908:* IV, 12-13; Vincent, *The Church in the Diocese of Bangor*, p. 10.
76 *Report of the Church Congress, Manchester*, 1908, p. 171.
77 Burgess, *Tracts on the Ancient British Church*, pp. 146, 152-4.
78 A newspaper letter from John Griffith pasted into the flyleaf of a diocesan minute book: Glamorgan Archives Service, D/DF/95.
79 For details of these exhibitions see: *Substance of Speeches ... at Meetings for Providing Additional Pastoral Superintendence and Church Accommodation within the Diocese of Llandaff* (London, 1850), p. 9; *Reports of the Llandaff Church Extension Society*, 1853, p. 7, 1858, 1871, 1876, pp. 11-13; Ollivant, *Charge (Llandaff)*, 1851, p. 48; *CMG*, 14 December 1850, p. 3, 20 December 1851, p. 6, 9 April 1853, p. 4; *Report of the Church Conference, Leeds*, 1872, pp. 444-5. It noted there were 28 candidates for six exhibitions.
80 Griffith, *The Welsh Church Congress,* pp. 9-14; Edwards, *Wales and the Welsh Church,* pp. 381-5; Notes of a follow-up meeting held at Bangor in January 1871, in South Glamorgan Library, Cardiff Ms. 3,505; *Chronicles of Convocation*, 1871, p. 70; Brown, *John Griffith*, pp. 217-8. As a result of this meeting it seems the Welsh bishops forced Lampeter to reduce its fees, as they were sufficiently high to drive men to English colleges such as St Bees and Birmingham, whose attainments were far below the required standard.
81 Campbell, *Charges (Bangor),* 1872, pp. 28-35; 1875, pp. 21-2; 1881, pp. 14-17; Edwards, *Wales and the Welsh Church*, pp. 76-7; R.O. Roberts, "The Life and Works of Dean Edwards", *T.Caerns.HS.,* 40 (1979), 144-5; *Bangor Diocesan Calendar*, 1907, pp. 270-1; *Report of the Bangor Diocesan Conference*, 1910, p. 9.
82 *Reports of the Church Hostel,* 1906 and 1907; Barry Morgan, *The History of the Church Hostel, Bangor* (Cardiff, 1986).
83 Hughes, *Charges (St Asaph),* 1871, pp. 12-14; 1874, p. 8; Robert Wickham, *A Charge delivered to the Clergy and Churchwardens of the Archdeaconry of St Asaph*, 1875, pp. 11-12; Thomas, *St Asaph*, I, 204-5; and SA/DR/53, fol. 32.
84 *Report of the Church Hostel*, 1906. The society was funded by subscriptions and parochial collections. Between 1902-6 twenty five exhibitions had been awarded by the two dioceses, and between 1877-1902 eighty six Bangor exhibitioners had been ordained: *ibid*, p. 6.
85 Chadwick, *The Victorian Church,* II, 248n.; Haig, *Victorian Clergy*, pp. 69-70.
86 *Report of the Llandaff Diocesan Conference*, 1909, p. 91.
87 Brush, *Thesis*, p. 126; *St Asaph Diocesan Calendar*, 1936, pp. 70, 81-2; Lewis, *The Church in Wales*, p. 16.
88 Jeremy Gregory (ed.), *The Speculum of Archbishop Thomas Secker* (Church of England Record Society, Woodbridge, 1995), p. xv.
89 M. Ransome (ed.), *The State of the Bishopric of Worcester 1782-1808* (Worcestershire H.S., n.s. 6, 1968), pp. 7-8: she suggests that the term "literates" could include those who studied at a university but had not graduated. See also Jacob, *The Clerical Profession*, p. 40.
90 Lee, *The Church of England and the Durham Coalfield*, p. 50-1.
91 Conybeare, *Essays Ecclesiastical and Social*, p. 10n.

92 Jacob, *The Clerical Profession*, p. 38. Although these figures relate to the 18th century, they are probably applicable for the early 19th century as well. One of the reasons for the number of local men in English dioceses may be the family patronage of livings.
93 Jacob, *Lay People and Religion*, pp. 31-2.
94 *Report of the Church Congress, Swansea*, 1909, p. 209. Frances Knight in studying a cohort of those ordained in the diocese of St Davids 1874-5 noted that the average age when made deacon was 30 years and 3 months. The Oxbridge and Lampeter men were slightly below this age, but the literates on average were aged 32: Knight, in Williams, *The Welsh Church*, p.p. 344-5.
95 Griffith, *The Welsh Church Congress*, p. 14.
96 This, of course applied to the whole Church of England, as Harold Browne remarked at the Oxford Church Congress of 1862 (*Report,* p. 49). Jacob suggests that the number of gentry sons ordained might well have been over-estimated, for by the 18th century the title was fluid and would include the sons of the professional and merchant classes whose wealth earned them the status of gentlemen: *The Clerical Profession*, p. 41. Those who used the university lists as a guide to parental status might well have been misled because as William Jones wrote, many of his contemporaries at Jesus College incorrectly described themselves in the college registers as the sons of gentlemen rather than the sons of plebeians: O.F. Christie (ed.,), *The Diary of the Revd. William Jones, 1772-1821* (London, 1929), p. 231. Russell, who suggests that the decline in the number of gentry sons by the mid-19th century was due to the lack of career structures in the Church, also noted that wealthy families could influence the process by purchasing an advowson or the right of presentation to a living for a sum of £1000 to £1500: *Clerical Profession*, p. 245. Walsham How's father purchased the next presentation of the benefice of Whittington in the late 1840s on behalf of his son: Brown, *Parochial Lives*, p. 56.
97 John Jones, *Consideration of the Illegality and Impropriety of Preferring Clergymen,* p. 43-6. This was still the case in 1898 when it was stated fathers were not prepared to pay £1,000 to educate their sons for a living of £100: *Report of the St David's Diocesan Conference*, 1898, p. 21.
98 Thomas, *St Asaph*, III, 127-232. I have ignored perpetual curacies.
99 Brown, *The Letters of Edward Copleston*, for such men as Edwardes, Gronow, Robert Knight, Lisle, and also the bishop's correspondent, J.M. Traherne.
100 *Pembrokeshire Historian,* 5 (1974), 101; Vaughan, *The South Wales Squires*, pp. 111-27.
101 Quoted by "A Pauper Clergyman", *How to Make Better Provision for the Cure of Souls,* pp. 4-5.
102 Jacob, *Lay People and Religion*, p. 31.
103 Short, *Sketch of the History of the Church of England*, p. lxvii. Using the 1911 census returns Peter Meurig Jones notes that 115 of the clergy wives in the diocese of St Asaph were monoglot English speakers, though 92 of their husbands were bilingual, and only 49 clergy wives were bilingual: "The Diocese of St Asaph on the eve of the Great War", *T.Denb.HS.,* 61 (2013), 112.
104 *Chronicles of Convocation*, 1900, pp. 373-4.
105 Lerry, *Alfred George Edwards*, pp. 12-16.
106 Grier, *John Allen*, pp. 4-13. Another clerical dynasty was the Myddleton's of Wrexham: A.N. Palmer, *History of the Town of Wrexham* (Wrexham, repr. 1982), at p. 28.
107 Brown, *The Followers of Jeroboam*, in passim; Evan Jones, *Adgofion*, p. 48; *Yr Haul,* 1906, pp. 112-16.
108 *Report of the Llandaff Diocesan Conference*, 1910, p. 90.
109 Brown, *Parochial Lives*, pp.54-5, 182-3; SA/DR/54, fol. 336; R.R.L. Jones, *Vicars of Llangynwyd* (1994), p. 24. Some officers were ordained by the bishops of St Asaph and Hereford in 1783 at the end of the American Revolutionary War, to the distaste of many: M.D. George, "Some Caricatures of Wales and Welshmen", *NLW.Jnl.,* 5 (1947-8), 11. William Corbett noted that after the Napoleonic Wars many officers were ordained but retained their half-pay, indicating their willingness for further service: *Legacy to Parsons*, pp. 113-4, and cf. Malcolm Johnson, *Bustling Intermeddler?* pp. 24-5.
110 *Report of the Llandaff Diocesan Church Extension Society,*1876, p. 12.

111　Price, *St David's University College*, I, 127-8.
112　Williams, *The Welsh Church*, p. 342.
113　SD/MISC B/80, for June and July 1875; Knight, in Williams, *The Welsh Church*, p. 342.
114　Russell Grigg, *History of Trinity College, Carmarthen 1848-1998* (Cardiff, 1998), p. 52.
115　Hughes, *Memoir of the Rev. J.A. Jackson*, pp. 10-11.
116　Glyn M. Jones and Elfyn Scourfield, *Sully* (Sully, 1986), p. 35, in noticing a former rector of that parish, John Williams (1898-1929), who had been educated at Trinity College, Carmarthen, and later took the Lampeter course.
117　*MC*, 31 (1900), 201.
118　Davies, *The Life and Opinions of Robert Roberts*, in passim. He lost his curacy due to alcoholism.
119　Jane Williams, *Thomas Price, Carnhuanawc*, II, 3-5.
120　Brown, *John Griffith*, p. 8.
121　Brown, *Ten Clerical Lives*, p.188.
122　J.R. Richards, *Ecclesiastical Parish of Skewen: Historical Survey* (1950), p. 11.
123　*Reports of the Llandaff Diocesan Conferences*, 1902, p. 60, and 1907, p. 28. Another example of a former collier who was ordained in the 1900s is given by David Williams, *Y Wladfa Fach Fynyddy* (1963), pp. 44-5. For earlier examples see Denning, *The Diary of William Thomas, 1762-1795*, pp. 189, 217 (recording the ordinations in 1767 and 1769 of a former shop clerk and the son of a weaver), and Blackwell, *The Beauties of Alun*, p. 10 (noting that he had started life as a shoemaker. He was ordained in 1829).
124　*MC*, 27 (1893), 220-1. Vincent in his *Letters from Wales* (p. 224) notes that a number of quarrymen were ordained in the diocese of Bangor during the late nineteenth century.
125　*Report of the Church Congress, Leeds*, 1872, pp. 461-3; John Jones, "Dean Edwards", *Red Dragon*, 6 (1884), 399; *Report of the Llandaff Diocesan Conference*, 1904, p. 48.
126　Saunders, *A View of the State of Religion*, p. 60.
127　As alleged by Ollivant in *Chronicles of Convocation*, 1870, p. 504 (he added their qualifications were so inferior he would not have ordained them had he a choice); Davey was speaking at the Swansea Church Congress: *Report*, 1879, p. 262.
128　Harford, *Bishop Burgess*, pp. 225-6.
129　Basil Jones, *Charge (St Davids)*, 1880, p. 37.
130　Quoted by O.W. Jones in Jones and Walker, *Links with the Past*, p. 175; cf. *A Letter to the Bishop of St David's concerning the Admission of Unqualified Persons into Holy Orders*, p. 4.
131　Williams, *Rowland Williams*, I, 193.
132　*CMG*, 5 March 1870, p. 5; Brown, *John Griffith*, p. 210.
133　Brown, *Evangelicals in the Church in Wales*, p. 128; Brown, *The Followers of Jeroboam*, pp. 6-7. Brown notes (p. 7), from selected years of ordination papers at the NLW, that the number of Cardiganshire born men ordained in St Davids diocese in 1853 comprised 32% of the total (3 in all), 1865 20% (3), 1877 21% (3), 1878 6% (1), and in Llandaff diocese, 1865 21% (3), 1894 16% (6). St Padarn's Church at Pennant, Cards., has a memorial to its 14 sons who were ordained: Thomas Lloyd, et.al., *The Buildings of Wales: Carmarthenshire and Ceredigion* (Yale, 2006), p. 554. Between 1897-1938 the parish of Llanbadarn Trefeglwys produced 14 clergy, including Bishop Timothy Rees of Llandaff: Richards, *Honest Memories*, p. 47.
134　Griffith, *The Welsh Church Congress*, p. 4; Price, *St David's University College*, I, 169-70.
135　D. Gwynfor Lewis, "Over Two Countries", *Province*, 5 (1954), 129.
136　*WM*, 19 January 1870; John Griffith suggested that if one examined Wales district by district the number of Cardiganshire clergymen would seem "almost incredible": *The Welsh Church Congress*, p. 5. Peter Meurig Jones notes that in 1913, 31% of the clergy of St Asaph were Cardiganshire men, and 17% from Carmarthenshire, 140 in all: "The Diocese of St Asaph on the eve of the Great War", *T.Denb.HS.*, 61 (2013), 109.
137　Brown, *Parochial Lives*, pp. 79-81.

138 E.E. Thomas, *Where Eagles Fly ... no Bird Sing* (Liverpool, 1961), pp. 137-8; cf. Vincent, *Letters from Wales*, pp. 162-3.

139 Huw Williams, *A History of the Church in Dowlais 1827-1977* (1977), p. 9.

140 Hughes, *Charge (St Asaph)*, 1871, pp. 13-14; Phillips in *Chronicles of Convocation*, 1871, pp. 70-1, and *Church Pastoral-Aid Society Abstract of Reports and Speeches*, 1871, p. 13; Ffoulkes in *Report of the Church Congress, Stoke on Trent*, 1875, pp. 427-8; Lord Dynevor in *Report of the St Davids Diocesan Conference*, 1884, p. 22. See also Edwards, *The Position and Resources of the National Church*, pp. 11-12.

141 Conybeare, *Essays Ecclesiastical and Social*, pp. 11-12; Vincent, *Letters from Wales*, pp. 123-5, 163, 172; T.J. Jones, *The Church in Wales not Alien* (Cardiff, 1906), p. 67; *Record*, 6 April 1894, p. 314 (Llangwm).

142 Draig Glas (A.T. Johnson), *The Perfidious Welshman* (London, c. 1900), p. 44.

143 Quoted by T.G. Williams, *The University Movement in Wales*, p. 75.

144 *Report of the Royal Commission, 1911*, III (1911), 98, and IV (1911), 430; *CMG*, 24 April 1847, p. 4; SA/DR/54, fol. 349.

145 Brown, *Followers of Jeroboam*, p. 7, notes some figures in a random selection of ordination papers. For the diocese of St Davids, 1 out of 7 made deacon in 1853 had a Nonconformist baptism, in 1865 4 of 15 (26%), 1877 8 of 14 (56%), 1878 7 of 16 (43%, the figure included one baptised as a Roman Catholic); for Llandaff in 1865 5 of 14 (35%), and in 1894 7 of 36 (19%). George Huntington estimated a figure of 25% throughout the Church of England, and it was noted that the diocese of Ripon drew heavily on such people: Haig, *Victorian Clergy*, pp. 200, 204.

146 Brown, *Letters of Edward Copleston*, p. 138. When the Baptist David Davies joined the Church he was baptised by immersion at Llanidloes. He was later vicar of Dylife until his death in 1865: Richard Williams, *Montgomeryshire Worthies* (Newtown, 1884), p. 13.

147 *CMG*, 24 April 1847, p.4.

148 *Report of the St Davids Diocesan Conference*, 1894, p. 17; and noted by G.H. Jenkins and I.G. Jones (eds.), *Cardiganshire County History* (Cardiff, 1998), III, 486. One example may be given: Daniel Lewis, vicar of Caerphilly, was brother to Wyndham Lewis, a Nonconformist minister at Carmarthen: *Bye-Gones*, 20 February 1895, p. 27.

149 Vincent, *Letters from Wales*, pp.124, 163-4.

150 W.J. Wallis-Jones, *Welsh Characteristics* (London, 1898), p. 49.

151 *Report of the Church Congress, Leeds*, 1872, pp. 6-8.

152 Brynley F. Roberts, "Robert Jones, Rotherhithe", *NLW.Jnl.*, 31 (1999), 135, 138.

153 Evan Jones, *Adgofion*, pp. 27-30.

154 J.E. Davies, "Three Welshpool Vicars", *MC*, 76 (1988), 121.

155 J. R. Hughes, *Humour Sanctified* (Tonypandy, 1902), pp. 46-7.

156 Brown, *David Howell*, in passim.

157 Owen, *The Early Life of Bishop Owen*, pp. 11-13.

158 *CMG*, 28 January 1854, p. 4: Letter of "Cadvan" of Towyn. T.M. Bassett notes in the 18th century that taking a child to be baptised in the parish church or raising a son for the ministry of the Established Church or Wesleyan Methodism was a matter for church discipline in the Baptist denomination: *The Welsh Baptists* (Swansea 1977), p. 79.

159 R. H. Morgan (Towyn), *Disestablishment*, pp. 35, 40. David Griffith Davies, vicar of Pontypridd 1884-7, a former London draper's assistant, was censured in that having been educated at great expense by the Unitarian Church for its ministry, involving study at the Presbyterian College, Carmarthen, and at Queen's College, Cambridge, he turned "Church" immediately he took his degree: R.J. Jones, *The Unitarian Students at the Presbyterian College, Carmarthen, in the Nineteenth Century* (Aberdare, 1901), pp. 81-2. See also 'An Oxford Tutor', "The Making of Welsh Parsons", *Cymru Fydd*, III (1890), pp. 523-4. The writer insinuated that many men having wasted their education knew that their own denomination would never accept them and so "turned Church".

160   R.B. Knox, *Wales and "Y Goleuad" 1869-79* (Caernarvon, 1969), pp. 71-3, 131-6.

161   Quoted by and translated in Vincent, *Letters from Wales*, pp. 123-5.

162   Davies, *The Ancient Celtic Church of Wales*, p. 182.

163   H.R. Evans, "Dr Edward Richard of Tregaron and Finchingfield", *THSC*, 1962, p. 101.

164   John Humphreys, *John Evans, Eglwys Bach* (London, 1913), pp. 22-4, cf. Morgan (Towyn), *Disestablishment*, p. 35, and David Davies, *Reminiscences of my Country and People* (London, 1925), pp. 35-6, 67-8, for a general background.

165   N. Masterman, *The Forerunner* (Llandybie, 1972), p. 58.

166   See for example the following chosen at random: T. Glanville Jones, *Windsor Road United Reformed Church, Barry* (1990), p. 20; Herbert Hughes, "Bethesda Chapel, Merthyr Tydfil", *Merthyr Historian*, 14 (2002), 78, noting that Peniel Rees, its minister left in 1855 to join the Church at Penydarren, and was not allowed to preach a farewell sermon; Hughes, *Pwllheli Church*, p. 25, for Daniel Jones, vicar 1864-5, a former Congregational minister at Merthyr Tydfil; N. Evans and K. Gravelle, *The English Congregational Church, Carmarthen* (1998), p. 11, whose minister, E.Z. Little resigned in 1869 as the church was unable to increase his stipend and was later ordained; J.V. Davies, *A History of Tabernacle C.M. Chapel, Penclawdd* (1936), pp. 36, 39, for Thomas John and Hugh Prys James. Evan Jones mentions "Williams Myddfai" who died young, and was a former Calvinistic Methodist minister. When asked by his deacons why he went to St David's College, Lampeter, and whether he had known the Gospel before, he replied he now knew more than St Paul, as he was now out of the body, that is the *corff*, a name given to that denomination: *Adgofion*, pp. 10-11.

See also D. Rhys Phillips, *A Forgotten Welsh Historian* (Swansea, 1916), pp. 36-7 for D. Lloyd Isaac, a Baptist minister at Neath, later rector of Llangamarch, who died in 1876; Brown, *Letters of Edward Copleston*, p. 112, referring to Jones of Treforest, a nonconformist minister considered but eventually rejected for ordination because of his irregular education; E.R. Horsfall-Turner, *A Municipal History of Llanidloes* (Llanidloes, 1908), p. 118, for John Jones, Idrisyn, a Wesleyan local preacher and printer, later vicar of Llandysiliogogo, who died 1887; D.E. Davies, "The Baptist Students of the Presbyterian College, Carmarthen", *Trafodion Cymdeithas Hanes Bedyddwyr Cymru*, 1976-7, p. 20; J. R. Richards, *Ecclesiastical Parish of Skewen* (1950), p. 14, notes a previous vicar of that parish, T.C. Phillips, 1897-1915, was formerly a Welsh Methodist minister at Abercarn; *Llandaff Diocesan Magazine*, 1900, p. 205, has an obituary of the Revd. Samuel Griffiths, a former Congregationalist minister at Swansea, who was ordained in 1892 at a late age and though he had little change of preferment was "content to serve the Church patiently"; J.T. Evans, *The Church Plate of Carmarthenshire* (London, 1907), p. 7. A more celebrated case was that of J.M. Jones, later vicar of Brynaman, a Congregational minister who brought with him 200 of his congregation into the Church fold with the result that his chapel at Penrhiwgaled had to be shut: Peter Jones, "A Chapel Split with a Difference", *The Carmarthenshire Antiquary*, 51 (2015), 87-90.

167   Brown, *The Letters of Edward Copleston*, p. 160; and Brown, *Evangelicals in the Church in Wales*, p. 173.

168   D.M. Richards, *History of the Tabernacle English Congregational Church, Aberdare* (Aberdare, 1893), pp. 18, 24, (and see pp. 27-8 for another example).

169   Ollivant, *A Vindication of St. David's College*, pp. 16, 20, 23-5. Burgess appears to have made similar requirements about proof of intent: Harford, *Thomas Burgess*, pp. 546-50. However, Lady Hall (later Lady Llanover) claimed Lampeter offered a short route into Orders for such men: Lady Hall to J. Hughes, 30 March 1851, NLW, *Letters from the Llanbadarnfawr parish Chest*, p. 45. The number of former dissenting ministers studying at Lampeter appears to have been quite low. Of the 306 students who entered the college between 1865-78 only six were in this category: Price, *St David's University College*, I, 128.

170   *Report of the Special Meeting of the St Davids Diocesan Conference*, 1894, p. 13; Lewis, *Charge (Llandaff)*, 1897, p. 9 (he ordained three such men); D.W. Thomas, *The Church in Wales, Past*

and Present; Facts and Suggestions (London, 1870), p.19. For a general discussion of this topic as it related to the whole Church of England see Haig, *Victorian Clergy*, pp. 200-2.

171 Llandaff Diocesan Memorandum Book 1849-68. In June and July 1875 two former nonconformist ministers were amongst the twelve ordained in the diocese of St Davids: SD/MISC B/80.

172 *Report of the Church Congress, Rhyl,* 1891, p. 75. He claimed he had eight such letters in hand.

173 Edwards, *The Position and Resources of the National Church*, pp. 11-12.

174 *Report of the Church Congress, Leeds,* 1872, p. 444; *Chronicles of Convocation,*1872, p. 198.

175 Lewis, *Charge (Llandaff),* 1891, p. 8; *Report of the Church Congress, Rhyl*, 1891, p. 75. It was alleged that some men had given up stipends of £200-250 to serve as lay readers for £50.

176 The description is from Thomas Jones of Creaton: Jenkins, *Thomas Charles of Bala*, III, 306-10; Burgess ridiculed the dissenting claim that self appointed ministers were equal to those lawfully ordained, or that the ability to preach constituted a call to ministry: *A Charge*, 1813, pp. 29-32, and Dean Edwards, a High Churchman, disputed both dissenting ordination and also its sacramental life: *Wales and the Welsh Church*, pp. 367-8.

177 *Mr. W.E. Helm's Reply to the Rev. W. Edwards: Two Addresses* (London,1893), pp. 37-9. Theophilus Jones, who died 1829, was a Welsh Methodist minister whose request to Bishop Burgess for ordination was turned down on account of his age. His action was looked upon with great disfavour and only the intervention of friends prevented his suspension: Joseph Evans, *Biographical Dictionary of Ministers and Preachers of the Welsh Calvinistic Methodist Body* (Carnarvon, 1907), pp. 180-2.

178 Morgan (Towyn), *Disestablishment*, p. 35.

179 Davies, *The Ancient Celtic Church of Wales*, pp. 181-2.

180 *Cymro,* 18 September 1918, quoted by T.T. Lucius Morgan, *Rupert of Glamorgan* (Dolgelly, 1920), pp. 106-7.

181 Llandaff Cathedral, Copleston Correspondence, letter 278 to Bruce Knight, 13 June 1836 (not quoted by Brown), in which the bishop stated of one candidate that there was slender evidence of conscientious charge or of preference for our Church founded on principle. His position regarding Lodwick Edwards is noted in the text.

182 A. Ollivant, *Reasons for Withdrawing from the Dissenting Ministry and seeking Ordination in the Church* (London, 1862), in passim.

183 Evan Andrews ("The Curate of Dolgellau"), *Church and State: A Controversy* (Dolgellau, 1845), p. 46n. A printed circular regarding one W. Jones of the 1830s is in South Glamorgan Libraries, Cardiff Ms. 4,154. Formerly Baptist minister at Cardigan, and known throughout the Principality for his religious deportment and popular abilities, he had lately been convinced of his duty to conform to the Church of England. Subscriptions to assist him in his course at Lampeter were solicited, and all three of the academic staff at that college had contributed, including Ollivant.

184 William Ceidrych Thomas, *The Church in Wales: Shall we Mend or End it?* (Birmingham, 1893), pp. 3-5.

185 T.T. Lucius Morgan, *Rupert of Glamorgan* (Dolgelly, 1920), pp. 111, 116, 119.

186 Lewis, *John Bangor*, pp. 13-19.

187 Brown, *Followers of Jeroboam*, pp. 34-6; K.O. Morgan, *Freedom or Sacrilege* (Penarth, 1965), p. 31; D. Parry-Jones, *My Own Folk* (Llandysul, 1972), p. 151.

188 Edwards, *Wales and the Welsh Church*, pp. 274-5.

189 *Report of the Special Meeting of the St Davids Diocesan Conference*, 1894, p. 15.

190 *Report of the Church Congress, Manchester*, 1888, p.91.

191 Pugsley, *Church life and Thought in Swansea*, p. 64.

192 *CMG*, 28 January 1854, p. 4: letter of Cadvan.

193 *CMG*, 21 November 1846, p. 3 and 28 November 1846, p. 3; Brown, *John Griffith*, pp. 22-4.

194 *CMG*, 3 December 1853, p. 3. Letter of Laicus; cf. ibid, 2 March 1866, p. 8, in which Leoline Jenkins wrote that since the closure of Cowbridge Divinity School short cuts for Nonconformist ministers to enter the Church had been justified by necessity.

195 Ollivant, *A Sermon preached in the Chapel of St. David's College, 1880*, pp. 6-7.

196 *Report of the Llandaff Diocesan Conference*, 1892, p. 65.

197 Lemuel J. James, *A Defence of Conformity to the Church of England* (London, 1903), p. 31.

CHAPTER THREE: THE EDUCATION OF THE FUTURE CLERGY
PART ONE: FROM GRAMMAR SCHOOL TO UNIVERSITY

1   The figures for 1901 are from *Yr Haul*, p. 471. By comparison the bishop of Llandaff in 1858 made deacons four Oxbridge men, a London BA, a Lampeter man and a St Bees man, and a literate: *Yr Haul*, 1858, p. 317. In 1929 21.5% of the clergy of the Church in Wales were Oxbridge educated, 46.4% were Lampeter men, excluding 3.4% who had proceeded from there to Oxbridge for a further degree, 16.5% had been to a provincial university, and 12.1% had had no university education. This was at a time when university education was being stressed as a necessary condition for ordination: P.M.K. Morris, "Facts and Figures: The state of the Clergy in the Province of Wales", *Province*, 9 (1958), 79-84.

2   Basil Jones, *Charges (St Davids)*, 1877, pp. 24-5; 1880, pp. 25-7.

3   *Llandaff Diocesan Calendar and Clergy List*, 1911, p. 141; *St David's Diocesan Directory*, 1889, pp. 160-1.

4   Basil Jones, *Charge (St Davids)*, 1883, pp. 27-8.

5   *Proceedings of the St Asaph Diocesan Conference*, 1901, p. 7.

6   Burgess, *Charge (St Davids)*, 1807, pp. 17-18. As late as 1949 Ewart Lewis was stressing the need for Latin and Greek as indispensable for anyone acquainted with Catholic theology: *The Church in Wales*, p. 16.

7   E.G. Millward, *Detholion o Ddyddiadur Eben Fardd* (Cardiff 1968), pp. 134, 140.

8   Davies, *The Life and Opinions of Robert Roberts*, pp. 303-4.

9   W.T. Owen, *Edward Williams, D.D.* (Cardiff, 1963), p. 6.

10 Davies, "The Education of the Clergy in the Diocese of Llandaff", p. 62. John Pugh (1690-1763), curate at Motygido, Llanarth, achieved a high reputation for tutoring boys for the university: S.C. Passmore, "The Revd. John Pugh ... and his School", *Ceredigion*, 12/4 (1996), 33-48. A similar classical school was kept by the curate of Builth, and attended by Thomas Price, Carnhuanawc, before he entered Christ College, Brecon, in 1805: Williams, *Thomas Price, Carnhuanawc*, II, 17. Lewis Evans, curate of Llanfihangel Genau'r Glyn, kept a school from 1800 at Castle Hill. One of his pupils, Evan Morgan, was ordained by Bishop Majendie in the diocese of Bangor in 1810, the first non-graduate for many years. The bishop, he claimed, stated that Morgan had the advantage over all the other candidates both in knowledge and his ability: R.L. Brown, "A Cardiganshire Incumbent writes to his London Relations", *Ceredigion*, 13/4 (2000), 27. Copleston noted in a letter of 1834 that one Prosser of Newchurch took pupils for the ordination examinations: Brown, *Letters of Edward Copleston*, p. 178. *Bye-Gones* notes a curate at Wellington who taught men Latin from scratch to prepare them for ordination in the 1810s: 6 November 1912, pp. 284-5.

11 A.O. Evans, *Welsh Book of Common Prayer*, III, 300. It was continued by his successor, John Griffiths, and supported by Alfred Ollivant, who as vice-principal of Lampeter was the sinecure rector of the parish.

12 *Report of the St Davids Diocesan Conference*, 1882, pp. 46-7.

13 Henry Morgan (1855-1934), "Reminiscences of Cilycwm", *Carmarthenshire Antiquary Society*, 23 (1987), 71. David Jones of Dwygyfylchi was probably assisted in the same way in his home parish: Brown, *Parochial Lives*, pp. 80, as was Griffith Edwards, who was assisted by Peter Bailey Williams, rector of Llanrug: *MC*, 27 (1893), 221.

14 Joan Shaw, *Borderline* (Meifod, 1996), p. 22.
15 W. Glynn Williams, *Memoir of Mrs Ann Walter Thomas* (Holywell, 1919), pp. 19-20, 34-5.
16 A.O. Evans, *Welsh Book of Common Prayer*, III, 300.
17 Mary Ellis, A Llanwddyn Diary", *MC*, 59 (1965-6), 152; Robert Jones, "Dewi Silin", *MC*, 11 (1878), 131; Blackwell, *Beauties of Alun*, pp. 22-3; Roger L. Brown, "John Blackwell, Thomas Richards and Berriew School", *MC*, 104 (2016), 73-6. Another pupil was David Davies in 1791, whose parents were advised to send him there for a liberal education by the rector of Mallwyd, but the expense was too great. Later, through assistance he went to Shrewsbury School and Cambridge: David Davies, *Twenty-one Practical and Familiar Sermons*, pp. ix-xiii
18 A.O. Evans, *Welsh Book of Common Prayer*, III, 321.
19 Richards, *Honest to Self*, pp. 59-60.
20 An English example is found in John Longe, vicar of Coddenham, 1763-1834, who prepared his son Henry for ordination: M. Stone (ed.), *The Diary of John Longe* (Suffolk Record Society, LI, 2008), p. xxxiv.
21 Davies, "The Education of the Clergy in the Diocese of Llandaff", p. 62.
22 O.W. Jones, *Glyn Simon*, pp. 30-1.
23 B.H. Jones, "David Rees Davies, B.A.", *Welsh Church Life*, August 2000, pp. 7-9.
24 Ollivant to John Griffith, 22 September 1860, in South Glamorgan Libraries, Cardiff Ms. 3,508.
25 R.G. Thomas, "The Complete Reading List of a Carmarthenshire Student", *NLW.Jnl.*, 9 (1955-6), 354-63.
26 Owen, *Directions for Young Students in Divinity*, pp. v-ix. See also Jacob, *The Clerical Profession*, pp. 57-8 (he notes other works on pp.54-5); W.K. Lowther Clarke, *Eighteenth Century Piety* (London, 1945), pp. 23-5; Alan Davies, "Training the Clergy of a somewhat drowsy Church", *Province*, 14 (1963), 29-30; Davies, "The Education of the Clergy in the Diocese of Llandaff", pp. 54-6.
27 Richard Watson, *A Collection of Theological Tracts* (6 vols., London, 1785), I, v-ix. See also Richard Watson, *Charge (Llandaff)*, 1788, pp. 6-8; Watson, *Anecdotes of the Life of Richard Watson*, I, 222-7; Davies, "The Education of the Clergy in the Diocese of Llandaff", pp. 57-8.
28 Many of the clergy in Lancashire, then in the diocese of Chester, were educated exclusively in similar grammar schools: Snape, *The Church of England in Industrialising Society*, pp. 166-7. This was also true of the Ise of Man: Yates, *Eighteenth-Century Britain*, p. 131.
29 Jones in Walker, *History of the Church in Wales*, p. 145; D.C. Osborne-Jones, *Edward Richard of Ystradmeurig* (Carmarthen, 1934), p. 68.
30 Copleston to his father, 2 September 1828, in NLW, Ms. 22721; Iolo Williams, *A Certaine Schoole*, pp. 67-70; Davies, "The Education of the Clergy in the Diocese of Llandaff", pp. 60-1. Bishop Sumner found no books at all in one of the schools, and in the other the only books referred to were D'Oyly and Mant's Bible and Wheatley on the Common Prayer, the last of which had been locked up as a student had injured it: Sumner, *Charles Richard Sumner*, pp. 129-30n.
31 Brown, *Letters of Edward Copleston*, pp. 65, 249.
32 Iolo Williams, *A Certaine Schoole*, pp. 69-70; Davies, "The Education of the Clergy in the Diocese of Llandaff", pp. 60-1.
33 Ollivant, *Charges (Llandaff)*, 1851, pp. 48-50; 1866, pp. 4-7; Iolo Williams, *A Certaine Schoole*, p. 70; *CMG*, 2 March 1866, p. 8; Benjamin Hall, *A Letter to the Bishop of Llandaff*, p.5. Rowland Williams claimed that because of his doctrinal teaching, Ollivant had opened Abergavenny to students from the diocese of St Davids, so relaxing his stringent rule: Williams, *An Earnestly Respectful Letter*, p. 2.
34 Williams, *Rowland Williams*, I, 178.
35 Iolo Williams, *A Certaine Schoole*, p. 68.
36 Brown, *David Howell*, pp. 16-17.
37 Martin Evans, *An Early History of Queen Elizabeth Grammar School, Carmarthen 1576-1800*, (Carmarthen, 1986), pp. 41-3, 83; A.G. Prys-Jones, "Queen Elizabeth Grammar School,

Carmarthen", *Carmarthenshire Historian*, 2 (1962), 26; *St. David's College, its Assailants and Defenders*, pp. 4-5; Morgan, "The Diocese of St David's", Part C, p. 46; *Weekly Mail*, 31 January 1874, p. 5.

38   Morgan, *David James*, pp. 4-6; Brown, *Ten Clerical Lives*, pp. 104-5.

39   E.G. Parry, *Christ College, Brecon* (1991), pp. 11-12; *Christ's College, Brecon, its Past History and Present Capabilities Considered* (London, 1853), p. 10.

40   Malcolm Seaborne, *Schools in Wales 1500-1900* (Denbigh, 1992), pp. 144-6; O.W. Jones in Jones and Walker, *Links with the Past*, p. 179; St George A. Williams, *The English Works of Eliezer Williams* (London, 1840), p. cxii.

41   Harford, *Thomas Burgess*, pp. 225-6.

42   Osborne-Jones, *Edward Richard*, in passim, and pp. 68-9; W.H. Howells, "The Library of Edward Richard, Ystradmeurig", *Ceredigion*, 9 (1982), 239-40; Malcolm Seaborne, *Schools in Wales 1500-1900* (Denbigh, 1992), pp. 78-80, 146; W. Gareth Evans, "The Aberdare Report and Cardiganshire", *Ceredigion*, 9 (1982), 196-7. The school continued until the 1970s as a preparatory school for colleges and Lampeter in particular. John Jones, headmaster 1870-1915, regarded himself as a teacher of future clergymen.

43   H.P. Roberts, "Nonconformist Academies in Wales, 1662-1882", *THSC*, 1928-9, pp. 16-17, 23 (he notes on pp. 50-1 Dr Thomas Phillips' school at Neuaddlwyd, Cards., 1796-1842, and states that several of its pupils were ordained into the Established Church, possibly after further study elsewhere); W.S. Jones, "St David's College, Lampeter, and the Presbyterian College, Carmarthen", *Ceredigion*, I (1951) 194-6; D.L. Baker-Jones, "Castell Hywel", *Carmarthenshire Antiquity*, 32 (1996), 56-7; Welsh Freeholder, *Letter to the ... Bishop of St David's on the Charge he lately Delivered*, p. 29 (Horsley makes no reference to these schools in this Charge: *The Charges of Samuel Horsley*, pp. 1-46); David Evans, *Welsh Unitarians as Schoolmasters* (Llandysul, n.d.), pp. 7-8; *A Letter to the Lord Bishop of St David's ... concerning the Admission of Unqualified Persons into Holy Orders*, p. 6. This letter may have drawn Horsley's attention to these schools. Horsley's action was thoroughly condemned by Thomas Rees in his *The Beauties of England and Wales*, vol. XVII (London, 1815), p. 488.

A further seminary in St Davids diocese was Trefeca College, Brecs. This was established in 1768 by the Countess of Huntington in order to train men as preachers for the "Methodist" chapels of her denomination, which formally separated from the Established Church in 1779. Men were taught over two years the basic classical skills, but the main emphasis was in spiritual development, apologetics and preaching skills. Nuttall suggests that about seven of the men trained here were ordained into the Established Church, though probably after further study elsewhere, and none, apart possibly from one, in Wales: G.F. Nuttall, "The Students of Trevecca College 1768-1791", *THSC*, 1967, pp. 249-77; Alan Harding, *The Countess of Huntingdon's Connexion* (Oxford, 2003), pp. 173-232.

44   Maber, *High Church Prophet*, pp. 175-7; O.W. Jones in Jones and Walker, *Links with the Past*, pp. 172-7; Price, *St David's University College*, I, 5-6.

45   Burgess, *Tracts on the Ancient British Church*, in which his 1812 sermon is contained, pp. 152-4; Burgess, *Charge 1804* (Durham, 1805), pp. 34-5; Robert Nelson, *On the Advantages of Clerical Seminaries ...* (repr. Carmarthen, 1813), pp. 3f, and in passim; *Report of the Association of Welsh Clergy*, 1853, p. 34; *St David's College, Lampeter, its Assailants and Defenders*, p. 7; Harford, *Thomas Burgess*, p. 226 (he added that while some masters were incompetent Burgess achieved some beneficial changes through his regulations); Price, *St David's University College*, I, 9. O.W. Jones in Jones and Walker, *Links with the Past*, p. 177, notes that Whitton and Rhayader schools were also found acceptable.

46   Jenkinson, *Charge (St Davids)*, 1828, pp. 52-9; Price, *St David's University College*, I,29-32, 39-40, 53; Harford, *Thomas Burgess*, pp. 383-6.

47   *Reminiscences of the Rev. D. Edwardes* (Shrewsbury, 1914), pp. 9-10; *Report of the Association of Welsh Clergy*, 1853, p. 34.

48 *Report of the Association of Welsh Clergy*, 1854, pp. 43-4; *CMG,* 24 Dec. 1869, p. 5; Price, *St David's University College*, I, 52-3.
49 Morgan, "The Diocese of St David's", Part C, pp. 49-50.
50 Quoted Brown, *John Griffith*, pp. 214-5; *St. David's College, its Assailants and Defenders*, pp. 10-11.
51 *Reports of the Association of Welsh Clergy*, 1854, pp. 43-5, 47-9; 1855, pp. 15-16, and 1856, p. 63.
52 *St. David's College, its Assailants and Defenders*, p. 16; Price, *St David's University College,* p. 8; Morgan, "The Diocese of St David's", Part C, notes disparagingly on p. 49 that Lampeter made a parson in half the time the grammar schools required.
53 Quoted by Price, *St David's University College*, p. 82n.
54 *Weekly Mail,* 31 January 1874, p. 5.
55 Thomas Rees, *The Beauties of England and Wales*, vol. XVII (London, 1815), pp. 484-5.
56 Ollivant, *Charge (Llandaff),* 1851, p. 49.
57 Conybeare, *Essays Ecclesiastical and Social*, pp. 12-13.
58 *CMG,* 24 December 1869, p. 5.
59 O.W. Jones, *Rowland Williams*, p. 27; A.G. Prys-Jones, "Queen Elizabeth Grammar School, Carmarthen", *Carmarthenshire Historian,* 2 (1962), p. 27; E.G. Parry, *Christ College, Brecon* (1991), p.11-12; *CMG,* 24 December 1869, p. 5.
60 Perowne and Stokes, *Letters of Connop Thirlwall* (London, 1881), pp. 186-7; cf. Osborne-Jones, *Edward Richards*, p. 99 (the school never regained its old glory). Phillips, *Wales*, pp. 356-8, quotes the unfavourable report given of the school by the Educational Commissioners in 1847.
61 Noted by Lewis Evans in 1845: O.W. Jones, *Isaac Williams*, p. 101.Evans proposed the setting up of an alternative college to Lampeter, based on Tractarian lines, claiming that Lampeter was failing in its work and the grammar schools had been reduced to "a state of infancy".
62 Brown, *John Griffith*, pp. 213-7; *WM,* 23 December 1869, p. 3; *CMG,* 24 December 1869, p. 2 (letter of John Griffith); *St. David's College, its Assailants and Defenders*, p. 11, claimed that had Jenkinson allowed the grammar schools to be effective feeders to the college, it could have provided a shorter and less expensive course.
63 Golifer, *Diocese of Llandaff,* p. 6.
64 *CMG,* 16 October 1858, p. 6.
65 *St. David's College, its Assailants and Defenders*, pp. 5-6.
66 Harford, *Thomas Burgess*, p. 385. Price, *Bishop Burgess and Lampeter College*, p. 51, claimed that the position was the same in Burgess's day, offering him another reason for licensing the schools.
67 Virgin, *The Church in an Age of Negligence*, pp. 134-6, 283; Chadwick, *The Victorian Church*, II, 248-9.
68 During the ten years ending 1869 sixty per cent of those ordained in St Asaph were Oxbridge graduates, between 1888-1898 fifty per cent, but for the years 1898-1901 eighty per cent: *Proceedings of the St Asaph Diocesan Conference*, 1901, p. 7.
69 Knight, "The Education of Welsh Ordinands", p. 21. Guy, in his 1983 thesis, makes it clear that the wealthier and better livings in the diocese of Llandaff were reserved for graduates: *Thesis,* pp. 342, 348. See also in this connection Morgan, *A Study in Nationality*, pp. 274-5, where he notes the same.
70 Dowland, *Anglican Theological Training,* p. 197.
71 *Chronicles of Convocation*, 1900, p. 369; *Report of the Llandaff Diocesan Conference*, 1886, p. 69; *Report of the Church Congress, Swansea,* 1879, p. 540; Atherstone, *Oxford's Protestant Spy*, quotes Sumner's charge on p. 198.
72 *Letters from Snowdon* (London, 1770), pp. 35-6; 'An Oxford Tutor', "The Making of Welsh Parsons", *Cymru Fydd,* III (1890), 517-24.
73 Haig, *The Victorian Clergy*, p. 119. Durham University, founded in 1832, attracted a small number of Welshmen.

74 *Ecclesiastic*, I (1846), 89; *Report of the Association of Welsh Clergy*, 1852, p. 44.

75 David Davies, *Twenty-one Practical and Familiar Sermons*, p. xxiii, wrote that by 1803 his parents had helped him with £250 to assist his Cambridge education. He was probably a sizar as well.

76 McClatchey, *Oxfordshire Clergy*, pp. 25-7; Haig, *Victorian Clergy*, p. 36. Jacob, in Williams, *The Welsh Church*, notes on p. 119 that between 1690-1732 many of those matriculated at Jesus College described themselves as plebeians or as sons of poor men. They probably acted as servitors. Many of them did not graduate.

77 Williams, *Thomas Price, Carnhuanawc*, I, 26.

78 Conybeare, *Essays Ecclesiastical and Social*, p. 10n; Haig, *Victorian Clergy*, pp. 40-1, 44, 60; Jacob, *Clerical Profession*, p.46. Robert Roberts regarded himself in 1855 as too old to obtain a sizarship: Davies, *The Life and Opinions of Robert Roberts*, p. 351.

79 Knight, "The Education of Welsh Ordinands", p. 22.

80 It was feared that these endowments, specific to Wales, would be lost in the late 1870s and a campaign was mounted to save them by John Griffith and Dean Edwards. Both were mistaken: Brown, *John Griffith*, pp. 174-7.

81 Helen Ramage, *Portrait of an Island* (Llangefni, 1987), p. 213.

82 *Jesus College*, a reprint from the *Victorian History of Oxfordshire*, III, 219.

83 Bullock, *Training for the Ministry 1800-1874*, pp. 37-40; *An Appeal to the Lords Spiritual and Temporal upon the necessity of Measures to Increase the Efficiency of the Established Church* (London, n.d.), p. 3; *Church Quarterly Review*, 20 (1885), pp. 359-66.

84 Quoted by Snape, *The Church of England in Industrialising Society*, p.168.

85 Connop Thirlwall, *A Letter ... on the Admission of Dissenters to Academical Degrees* (Cambridge, 1834), pp. 63-5.

86 Alfred Ollivant, *The Introductory Lecture to the Course delivered before the University of Cambridge in Lent Term, 1844* (Cambridge, 1844), p. 8. Thomas Briscoe, vice-principal of Jesus College, agreed. The extent of theological knowledge most men received before entering upon their parochial duties consisted of Old Testament History, the Gospels and the Acts of the Apostles, and the 39 Articles: *First Report of the Cathedral Commission, Appendix* (London, 1854), pp. 813-6.

87 *Report of the Church Congress, Swansea*, 1879, pp. 540.

88 *Report of the Church Congress, Bath,* 1873, p. 140. Areas of the Bible, Prayer Book, church history and doctrine were ignored and men read the minimum of what was required.

89 *Reports of the Church Congresses, Oxford*, 1862, p.6, *Manchester*, 1863, pp. 80-1, *Bristol*, 1864, pp. 201-14; "A Clergyman", *On Clerical Education, a Letter* (1832), pp. 6-7; Miller, *Defective Ministerial Training*, pp. 29-36, 42. Haig suggests that the young men grew into the work: *Victorian Clergy*, p. 73.

90 Dowland, *Anglican Theological Training*, p. 129.

91 Bullock, *Training for the Ministry 1800-1874,* pp. 100-1. Yet Jacob in his *Clerical Profession*, (pp. 48-53), describes significant theological training at Oxford during the eighteenth century. However, in 1792 Herbert Marsh claimed that theological learning formed "no necessary part of our academical training": Bullock, *Training for the Ministry, 598-1799*, pp. 112-3.

92 Popkin, *Observations on the Nature of the House of God*, pp. 23-4; Jacob, *Clerical Profession*, p. 51. The pass degrees were not regarded as a searching test of knowledge: *Report of the Church Congress, Nottingham*, 1897, p. 400.

93 B.M. Lodwick, *Henry Hey Knight* (Neath, 2012), p. 53.

94 Bullock, *Training for the Ministry 1800-1874*, pp. 35-6, 49-50; Dowland, *Anglican Theological Training*, p. 182. The syllabus changed over the years.

95 Bullock, *A History of Training 598-1799*, pp. 114-5 (he notes that some Oxford professors also gave lectures, and cites John Randolph, who gave lectures on ministerial duty and character: pp. 116-7); Bullock, *A History of Training 1800-1874,* pp. 33-5, 51-3. There are many references to the non-attention of men at these divinity lectures: *Proceedings of the St Asaph Diocesan*

Conference, 1897, p. 5; *Report of the Llandaff Diocesan Conference*, 1886, p. 61, when Beck of Roath remembered this inattention at Mozley's lectures at Oxford. A certificate of attendance for these lectures is noted in a letter of Copleston to Bruce Knight of 1836: Brown, *Letters of Edward Copleston*, p. 205.

96 Charles Perry, then a fellow of Trinity College, Cambridge, and later bishop of Melbourne and canon of Llandaff, argued that the education of the clergy should be confined to the existing universities, as the most trustworthy and appropriate institutions for that task, but they needed to provide a suitable course of instruction: Bullock, *A History of Training 1800-74*, pp. 66-8; Haig, *The Victorian Clergy*, pp. 74-5.

97 Bullock, *A History of Training 1800-1874*, pp. 70-1, 80-2, 101-4; Bullock, *Ridley Hall, Cambridge*, I, 30-4; Dowland, *Anglican Theological Training*, pp. 192-3. A special examination in theology was established at Cambridge in 1865. Taken at the end of the third year it consisted of selected books of the Old Testament in English, one of the Gospels and two epistles in the Greek text, the history of the Church of England to 1688, and an optional paper in Hebrew.

98 Dowland, *Anglican Theological Training*, p. 183; Bullock, *A History of Training 1800-1874*, p. 77.

99 Handley Moule, *Charles Simeon* (London, 1965), pp. 131-47. Canon Christopher, vicar of St Aldate's, Oxford (1859-1905), followed Simeon's example: J.S. Reynolds, *Canon Christopher* (Abington, 1967), pp. 111-2.

100 Edward Bickersteth, *The Christian Student* (4th edn., London, 1844), see especially pp. 185-96, 367-70.

101 G.I.F. Thomson, *The Oxford Pastorate* (London, 1946), p. 67.

102 George Townsend, *A Plan for Abolishing Pluralities, and Non-Residence, in the Church of England* (London, 1833), p. 89.

103 *First Report of the Cathedral Commissioners, Appendix*, p. 815.

104 *Chronicles of Convocation*, 1865, pp. 1872-3; *Report of the Church Congress, Oxford*, 1862, p. 50; *Ecclesiastical Gazette*, June 1864, pp. 309-10. This was similar to proposals put forward by Bishop Edmund Gibson of Lincoln and London (died 1748), but the failure of Bishop Burnet's seminary at Salisbury after five years meant Gibson's proposal was never implemented: Stephen Taylor (ed.), *From Cranmer to Davidson* (CERS, Woodbridge, 1999), p. 194.

105 Haig, *Victorian Clergy*, pp. 87-8.

106 *Report of the Church Congress, Manchester*, 1908, pp. 167, 170; *Proceedings of the St Asaph Diocesan Conference*, 1903, pp. 19-20.

107 R. Tudur Jones, *Theology in Bangor 1922-1992* (Cardiff, 1972), pp. 119-20, 137-40; J.E. Lloyd (ed.), *Sir Harry Reichel* (Cardiff, 1934), pp. 25, 142, 144, 156-9; H.R. Reichel, *The Development of Theological Education in the University of Wales, an Address* (Bangor, 1917), and *The Development of Theological Study at Bangor* (Newtown, 1922), p. 4.

108 Lewis, *John Bangor*, p. 112.

CHAPTER FOUR: THE EDUCATION OF THE FUTURE CLERGY
PART TWO: ST DAVID'S COLLEGE, LAMPETER

1 Burgess, *Tracts on the Ancient British Church*, pp. 146, 152-3.

2 Harford, *Thomas Burgess*, pp. 227-9. There were precedents. Burgess may have been aware of two abortive schemes to establish such a collegiate school in Carmarthen in 1760 and 1797: Price, *St David's University College*, I, 6; a similar scheme had been proposed to Horsley by the writer of *A Letter ... concerning the Admission of Unqualified Persons to Holy Orders*, pp. 4-9. Burgess also wrote to the schoolmasters enclosing a reprint of an early 18th century scheme by Robert Nelson for a seminary: *On the advantages of Clerical Seminaries*, 1813. See also *Letters from Snowdon* (London, 1770), p. 36.

3 Burgess, *Charge (St Davids)*, 1807, pp. 24-9; Thomas Rees was extremely critical of this college to be built "in the midst of impassable deserts": *The Beauties of England and Wales*, vol. XVII

(London, 1815), pp. 486-7n. Popkin made an even more radical criticism of Burgess' proposals for a college at Llanddewi Breifi: *Observations on the Nature of the House of God*, pp. 5-6, 13-14.

4 *The St. David's College Calendar for 1836* (Llandovery, 1836), pp. 15-19.

5 Jenkinson, *Charge*, 1828, pp. 52-9.

6 Perowne and Stokes, *Letters of Connop Thirlwall*, p. 341; Price, *St David's University College*, p. 29. Lord Cawdor would not support the college as he believed education should be left to the universities: Cragoe, *An Anglican Aristocracy*, p. 241.

7 Ollivant's submission to the Cathedral Commission: *CMG*, 1 September 1854, supp. p. 2; his *The Principles that should influence a Christian Student, A Sermon Preached in the Chapel of St David's College* (Llandovery, 1841), pp. 6, 20-2, and his *A Sermon Preached in the Chapel of St David's College, 1880*, pp. 6-8.

8 Quoted by Harford, *Thomas Burgess*, p. 385.

9 Phillips, *Wales*, p. 326.

10 Owen, *The Early Life of Bishop Owen*, p. 128. Dowland suggests its aim was to polish the manners of the rough young men from the mountains: *Anglican Theological Training*, p. 208.

11 Quoted by Price, *St David's University College*, II, 35-6.

12 Quoted by Dowland from a report of the Charity Commissioners of 1839: *Anglican Theological Training*, p. 166.

13 Varley, *The Last of the Prince Bishops*, p. 93. Llandaff, it was said, became the safety valve for the unqualified destitute: quoted by Price, *St David's University College*, p. 82.

14 Copleston to his father, 2 September 1828, NLW, Ms. 22721; Brown, *Letters of Edward Copleston*, pp. 92, 245, 249.

15 Price, *Bishop Burgess and Lampeter College*, p. 67.

16 *St. David's College, Lampeter, its Assailants and Defenders*, pp. 8-9, 13.

17 Price, *St David's University College*, I, 42-3; Evans, *Lampeter*, pp. 91-3.

18 Morris, *Romilly's Visits to South Wales*, p. 56.

19 Quoted by and details from Price, *St David's University College*, I, 48-9. Of 306 students admitted between 1865-78, 115 were the sons of farmers, 36 sons of clergymen, and 220 came from the diocese of St Davids (178 from Cardiganshire and Carmarthenshire); most were aged between 19-21 on arrival: cf. for the period 1892-7 when there were similar figures for localities but the sons of farmers numbered 48 out of 216 students and there were only 34 clergy sons: *ibid*, pp. 126-7, 169-70.

20 Ollivant, *A Vindication of St. David's College*, p. 16. There were other problems relating to the administration of the college.

21 Thirlwall to J. Hughes, 22 February 1847, NLW. Transcript, *Letters from Llanbadarnfawr Parish Chest*, p. 3. In 1868 Thirlwall stated again that the college had never adequately answered the purpose for which it was founded, namely to provide a sufficient number of clergy for his diocese: *CMG*, 8 August 1868, p.

22 *St. David's College, Lampeter, its Assailants and Defenders*, pp. 10-17, 49; *Report of the Association of Welsh Clergy*, 1855, pp. 15-17 and 1856, p. 65; Morgan, "Diocese of St David's", C, p. 49. In contrast to this alleged poor teaching we may cite E.H. Browne's publication of his lecture notes on the 39 Articles given at Lampeter when he was vice-principal which ran to thirteen editions.

23 Phillips, *Wales*, pp. 319-21, quoting the report of the Charity Commissioners of 1836 that also felt the college had not lived up to its first expectations; Price, *St David's University* College, I. 57, 84-5; Evans, *Lampeter*, pp. 162-3. The *Report of the Association of Welsh Clergy*, 1856, pp. 66-70, noted a lack of vigilant visitorial inspection, the heretical views of Rowland Williams and the expense of education. There was a concern that the endowments of Christ College, Brecon, should have been given to Lampeter: *Edinburgh Review*, 77 (1850), pp. 358-9; *Report of the Association of Welsh Clergy*, 1856, pp. 67-70; *CMG*, 1 September 1854, Supp. p. 2; Price, *St David's University College*, I, 91-6.

24 *CMG*, 8 August 1868. Price notes that the movement to obtain degree status owed much to the Association of Welsh Clergy in the West Riding: *St David's University College*, I, 85; and see *Report of the Association of Welsh Clergy*, 1852, p. 43; 1853, p. 34-5. In a letter of June 1852 to the prime minister, the earl of Derby, Bishop Ollivant requested the granting of the BD degree. He pointed out that while the number of students were less than expected, the Welsh Church looked towards the college for its clergy, and its numbers were not sufficient for its needs. The class from which the clergy were recruited needed an inducement to subject themselves to the expense of the college, while those who managed to attend the universities to obtain a distinction denied at home remained in England for the want of good livings in Wales: *A Sermon preached in the Chapel of St. David's College*, 1880, pp. 24-6. See also J.G. Williams, *The University Movement in Wales*, p.7, where he notes Ollivant's assertion that its original charter indicated it was more akin to a university than a theological college, while to give degree status to Durham was unjust to Lampeter. We should note that while St David's College was seen until recent times as an institution for training for the ministry of the Church, its charter offered a much wider remit.

25 Price, *St David's University College*, I, 121-3. The cost was said to be about £42 per annum in 1864, with a number of exhibitions of between £10 and £50: John Evans, *A Charge delivered to the Clergy of the Archdeaconry of Carmarthen*, 1864, p. 31-2. It was argued that the fees of £45-50 in 1850 would hardly suffice at the universities for maintenance, yet alone tuition and other expenses: *CMG*, 14 December 1850, p. 3.

26 Rowland Williams, *A Sermon preached at the Visitation of the Lord Bishop of St David's at Cardigan* and *A Sermon Preached in St. David's College Chapel, Lampeter, with Some Account of the actual working of the College*, pp. xi-xii, 47-8; ibid, *Christian Freedom*, p. 103; *St. David's College, Lampeter, its Assailants and Defenders*, pp. 11, 13, 16; Williams, *Rowland Williams*, I, 167, 219. The need for better feeder schools was made by many, including the Association of Welsh Clergy in the West Riding: *Reports*, 1855, p. 45; *WM*, 8 January 1870, p. 5. The position continued thereafter: Basil Jones. *Charge (St Davids)*, 1877, pp. 25-7: W. Gareth Evans, "The Aberdare Report and Cardiganshire", *Ceredigion*, 9 (1982), p. 215, quotes Jayne's similar testimony of 1881. Sir Henry Reichel noted at the Manchester Church Congress of 1908 the difference these new schools had made: *Report*, pp. 170-1.

27 Williams, *Rowland Williams*, I, 167, 193, 200; Price, *St David's University College*, I, 105-7. Evan Jones, a Lampeter student wrote of Rowland Williams' kindness in assisting his students to a greater proficiency in English, and advised Jones to read such books as *Arabian Nights* and Miss Edgeworth's *Essays* to the great annoyance of Professor North: *Adgofion*, pp. 9-10.

28 Jones in Jones and Walker, *Links with the Past*, p. 183. Between 1863-70 of 170 students who entered the college 37 had been educated at institutions that were not grammar schools.

29 Rowland Williams, *A Sermon preached at the Visitation*, in passim (especially pp. 47-69);and his *Lampeter Theology* (London, 1856), pp. v, 1-27 (especially pp. 23-4); *Some Account of the Actual Working of St. David's College, Lampeter*, pp. 46-7, and *Christian Freedom*, pp. 101-5; Williams, *Rowland Williams*, I, 167, 192-3, 204, 219-20; *The St. David's College Calendar* (1857), pp. 7-10; Price, *St David's University College*, I, 82-5; Rowland Williams to Ollivant, 2 November 1853, LL/Ch/1796.

30 Williams, *Rowland Williams*, I, 219-20, 282-3. Williams was tempted to reduce the course but the new degree status, the external university examiners, the cheapness of the college, and the countenance of the south Wales bishops, sustained him in his efforts to retain the classical element of the course.

31 Rowland Williams, *An Earnestly Respectful Letter*, pp. 2-3n.; ibid, *Christian Freedom*, p. 104; Williams, *Rowland Williams*, I, 168, 192-3, 219.

32 Rowland Williams, *Christian Freedom*, pp. 104-5.

33 *CMG*, 22 January 1879, p. 5.

34 Williams, *An Earnestly Respectful Letter*, p. 7. He felt Thirlwall was being pushed by Ollivant and some of the evangelical clergy of Llandaff: ibid, pp. 2, 12. See also *Ecclesiastic*, 18 (1856),

255-62. Nigel Yates in his study of this controversy indicates the bishops had no wish to make Williams a martyr, or to compromise the revival of the Church by doctrinal disputes, while Thirlwall, though sympathetic, believed that those charged with the training of clergy did not have the luxury of engaging in speculative theology: "Rowland Williams and his Episcopal Critics", *WJRH*, I (2006), 1-13, especially pp. 12-13. See also Gibson and Morgan-Guy, *Religion and Society in the Diocese of St Davids*, pp. 86-8.

35 Basil Jones, *Charge (St Davids)*, 1880, pp. 32-6. He also noted its new statutes and its affiliation to the university of Oxford. John Owen, a later principal of the college, also attributed the revival of the college to Jayne's work, and said that this enabled Bishop Basil Jones to raise the educational standards for the ministry and thus increase the number of clergy: *Church Reform and Church Progress*, p. 30.

36 Quoted by O.W. Jones in Jones and Walker, *Links with the Past*, p. 183.

37 Basil Jones, *Charges (St Davids)*, 1883, p. 30; 1886, p. 18.

38 Thirlwall to J. Hughes, 22 February 1847, *Letters from the Llanbadarnfawr Parish Chest*, pp. 3-4.

39 Fraser, "Sir Benjamin Hall in Parliament", pp. 79-80. He was also concerned that a parliamentary grant of £400 per annum was no longer justified as the college's endowments had increased.

40 The various letters are printed in *St. David's College, its Assailants and Defenders*, pp. 37-44 Hall claimed there were better Welsh scholars at the Jesuit College in St Asaph than at Lampeter. A protest from the local MPs, laymen and clergy stating that Williams' allegations were entirely groundless is in *Letters from the Llanbadarnfawr Parish Chest*, p. 178.

41 Letters of 11 April and 4 May 1847, 30 March and 1 May 1851, in *Letters from the Llanbadarnfawr Parish Chest*, pp.12, 14, 44-6, 54-6, 60-1. The chair of Welsh was vacant from 1843-54.

42 *St. David's College, its Assailants and Defenders*, pp. 25-6; Thirlwall to Lord John Russell, 17 January 1851, and Hall to Lord John Russell, 23 January and February 1851, in British Archives, Lord John Russell Papers, 30/22/9a/144, 206, and 9b/48; Price, *St David's University College*, I, 81-2.

43 Editorial in *CMG*, 15 January 1870, p. 5.

44 *Ecclesiastic*, I (1846), 89.

45 *St. David's College, its Assailants and Defenders*, pp. 16-17.

46 Brown, *'Welsh Patriotism' and 'Justice to Wales'*, p. 26. Evan Jones, writing of the 1850s, made the same criticism, stating there was only one Welsh lesson each week and little grammar was taught. Pastoralia consisted of reading the lessons in chapel and a fortnightly visit to day school to give religious instruction: *Adgofion*, p. 13.

47 Hughes, *Memoir of the Rev. J.A. Jackson*, pp. 22-4. Hughes claimed that when the attempt was made to include Welsh in the pass degree papers, one of the external examiners objected, and Thirlwall as visitor upheld his objection. Welsh was first included in the ordinary degree in 1887. See also Morgan, "The Diocese of St. David's", Part C, p. 51.

48 Rowland Williams, *A Sermon preached at the Visitation*, pp.47-50, 55-67, 70; O.W. Jones, *Rowland Williams*, pp. 34-6.

49 Quoted Fraser, "Sir Benjamin Hall in Parliament", pp. 78-9.

50 Lambeth Palace Library, Perowne Ms. 1961, a cutting of the *Carmarthen Journal* of July 1868.

51 W. Gareth Evans, *A History of Llandovery College* (Llandovery, 1981), pp. 6-8. Lewellin's antipathy to the Welsh language was well known, but Thirlwall might have been more anxious to have a good grammar school as a feeder to the college than a Welsh chair when he believed that its students already had a good knowledge of Welsh. Lewellin also rejected a Welsh prize offered by Archdeacon Beynon on the grounds it would create tension in the college. As a result Beynon withdrew some of his prospective endowment: K. Robbins and J. Morgan-Guy (eds.), *A Bold Imagining* (Lampeter, 2003), pp. 67-8.

52 Howard Evans, *The Case for Disestablishment in Wales*, p. 47.

53 *The Personal Papers of Lord Rendel* (London, 1931), pp. 7-8. W.L. Bevan of Hay denied these assertions. Lampeter was a thoroughly Welsh institution, drawing nearly all its students from Wales, so it was hardly a department of the English establishment, as Stuart Rendel, MP, maintained: *Is the Church in Wales an* alien *Institution* (London, n.d.), p. 10-11.

54 K. Robbins and J. Morgan-Guy (eds.), *A Bold Imagining* (Lampeter, 2003), pp. 71-2.

55 R. Tudur Jones in Jenkins, *The Welsh Language and its Social Domains*, pp. 247-50. The families of Nonconformist ministers were said to be accustomed to speak English at home during this period: G. Parry and M.A. Williams, *The Welsh Language and the 1891 Census* (Cardiff, 1999), p. 411.

56 Hughes, *Charge (St Asaph)*, 1871, pp. 14-15.

57 *Report of the Llandaff Diocesan Conference*, 1886, pp. 67-8.

58 Report of 9 November 1889 in Lambeth Palace Library, Benson Ms. 170, fols. 235-6; Lady Llanover to Benson, 31 May 1886, Benson Ms. 39, fol. 241, in which she stated that those entering the college at seventeen were not fitted to supply the Welsh Church when they left it.

59 M.H. Fitzgerald, *A Memoir of Herbert Edward Ryle* (London, 1928), pp. 71-2.

60 *Report of the Llandaff Diocesan Conference,* 1892, pp. 65-7. A letter to W.H. Davey rejoicing about his appointment as vice-principal from Walsham How, 28 January 1873, indicated that the moral tone of the college was bad, and there was a need to raise the spiritual tone of the clergy: Lambeth Palace Library, Davey papers, fol. 112. J. G. Gauntlett of St Davids diocese suggested that after the Lampeter course men might be trained in homiletics and pastoralia at St David's Cathedral under the instruction of one of its canons: *Report of the St Davids Diocesan Conference*, 1882, p. 41. Nigel Yates in his *Lampeter, Wales and the Oxford Movement* (Trivium occasional papers 4, Lampeter, 2004), suggests that many of the college tutors were sympathetic to the Tractarian movement, and Davey managed to change the high-dry churchmanship on his appointment as vice-principal in 1872. Tyrrell Green, Evan Lorimer Thomas, and W.H. Harris, as members of staff, ensured that eventually a daily communion service was held by 1925, and vestments introduced in 1933 and made compulsory the following year: *ibid.,* pp. 5-6, 31-2. These innovations were welcomed by the Society of St David, which had been founded in the college in 1910: W.G.H. Thomas, *Society of St. David: History of the first 25 Years* (1972)

61 Price, *A History of Saint David's College*, II, 30-1. J.R. Lloyd Thomas notes that practical training was given in parochialia, elocution, choral singing, and assisting in services and preaching at some of the local mission churches: "Training for Orders, 1900", *Province*, 12/4 (1961), 138.

62 Williams, *Rowland Williams*, I, 187-8; *Ecclesiastical Gazette*, 13 (1850-1), 170. Ollivant noted the course in 1850 as a two year course for men of talent at a meeting of his archdeacons and rural deans: papers of 8 November 1856 in NLW. Church in Wales papers, John Morgan (Llandaff) Papers, box 10. Price notes a shorter course of two and a half years for former Nonconformist ministers in the 1850s, regarded by some as a bribe to increase the number of Welsh-speaking clergymen: *St David's University College*, I, 87, 140.

63 Basil Jones, *Charges (St Davids),* 1886, pp. 16-7; 1892, pp. 42-3; Price, *St David's University College,* I, 87, 140-1, II. 6. He notes that between 1884-1937 498 divinity licences were awarded.

64 J.R. Lloyd Thomas, "Training for Orders, 1900", *Province*, 12/4 (1961), 134-9.

65 Price, *St David's University College*, II, 16-21; Owen, *Early Life of Bishop Owen*, pp. 155-69; J.G. Williams, *The University Movement in Wales*, p. 32. An earlier link to the new college at Aberystwyth in 1872 also proved abortive. A hint is given that another objection was that the college was "the home of retrogressive clericalism and of fossilised Toryism": *Young Wales*, 2 (1896), 204.

66 Price, *St David's University College*, II, 18-21; *Report of the Church Congress, Manchester,* 1908, pp. 172-4; H.R. Reichel, *The Supply and Training of Candidates for Holy Orders. A further paper* (1909), pp. 1-8; F. Witton Davies in T. Stephens (ed.), *Wales: Today and Tomorrow* (Cardiff, 1907), p. 230; Lewis, *Is Disestablishment Just?* pp. 33-4.

67 *Report of the Association of Welsh Clergy*, 1856, pp. 40-1; *St David's College, its Assailants and Defenders*, p. 17 (its writer suggested the revival of the grammar schools as the preparatory colleges); David Howell speaking at the 1888 Manchester Church Congress: *Report*, p. 75.

68 *Report of the Committee to Survey the Situation of St. David's College (The Sankey Report: 1923)*, pp. 7-8, 31; Price, *St David's University College*, II, 45-63. The two year post-graduate course for the Diploma in Theology had few takers as the Welsh bishops only required a one year study for the General Ordination Examination: Price, *ibid*, p. 90. In the 1938 *Church in Wales: Report of the Revisory Sub-Committee on Training for the Ministry*, Maurice Jones argued that the minimum standard of training for the ministry in the Church in Wales since Disestablishment was higher than that of England: p. 28.

69 Price, "The Contribution of St David's College to the Church in Wales", pp. 63-4.

70 *Report of the Llandaff Diocesan Conference*, 1905, p. 14.

71 Bebb to Davidson, 14 November 1905: Lambeth Palace Library, Davidson Papers 105, fol. 202.

72 Price, "The Contribution of St David's College to the Church in Wales", p. 64. Of the 231 incumbents in the diocese of St Davids in 1928, 159 had attended Lampeter: Gibson and Morgan Guy, *Religion and Society in the Diocese of St Davids*, p. 205. By 1952, 850 former students were serving in the Church in Wales and 650 in the Church of England: Price, *St David's University College*, II, 173n.

73 *Report of the Church Congress, Leeds*, 1872, p.432.

74 Golifer, *The Diocese of Llandaff*, p. 6.

75 *WM*, 7 September 1874, p. 8 (letter of Viator), and 13 September 1874, p. 7 (where it is stated that dozens of men have had their hearts broken there, wishing they had gone to Oxford, as all the good curacies and livings, and canonries, went to Oxford men).

76 Price, "The Contribution of St David's College to the Church in Wales", p. 81.

CHAPTER FIVE: THE EDUCATION OF THE FUTURE CLERGY
PART THREE: THE THEOLOGICAL COLLEGES AND PRIVATE ENTERPRISES

1 Nelson, *On the Advantages of Clerical Seminaries*, pp. 5-9, 13; and Nelson, *The Life of Bishop Bull*, pp. 16-18.

2 Gregory and Chamberlain, *The National Church in its Local Perspective*, p. 132.

3 Burns, *The Diocesan Revival*, pp. 151-6; Bullock, *Training for the Ministry 1800-74*, pp. 42-5.

4 Espin, *Our Want of Clergy*, pp. 4-5, 9; *Report of the Church Congress, Barrow-in-Furness*, 1906, p.344. The report stated that in 1846 graduate candidates were 89% of the total, 1865 72%, 1885 65% and 1905 57%. These figures included all universities and probably Lampeter. See also Haig, *Victorian Clergy*, pp. 118-9, who notes that in 1859 that men from theological colleges averaged about one sixth of those from the older universities in the southern dioceses, though in the northern dioceses it was two thirds.

5 Ollivant, *Charges (Llandaff)*, 1866, pp. 7-9; 1869, pp. 14-15; Ollivant said much the same at Convocation in 1872: *Chronicles of Convocation*, 1872, p. 197.

6 Ollivant to Gilbert Harries, 24 January 1865: NLW, Church in Wales Records, John Morgan (Llandaff) Papers, Box 10.

7 Basil Jones, *Charge (St Davids)*, 1883, pp. 30-1.

8 *Report of the Church Congress, Leeds*, 1872, p. 462. He also claimed that these men were not "up to the mark", and not having thought of Orders until later in life assumed the Church offered better prospects for them.

9 Conybeare, *Essays Ecclesiastical and Social*, p. 202.

10 *Report of the Church Congress, Folkstone*, 1892, p. 451.

11 Espin, *Our Want of Clergy*, pp. 4-5, 9-13; *Ecclesiastic*, I (1846), 94-5; Basil Jones, *Charge (St Davids)*, 1883, p. 28; *Reports of the Church Congresses, Oxford*, 1862, pp. 10-11, and *Sheffield*, 1878, p. 542 (of Ryle); *Report of the Llandaff Diocesan Conference*, 1886, pp. 80, 84; Miller,

The Defective Ministerial Training of our Universities, pp. viii-xxii, 38-40. It was claimed that Archdeacon Allen, who had complained bitterly about these colleges, notoriously had the lowest standard of examination: Haig, *Victorian Clergy*, p. 139. Bishop Sumner of Winchester in his Charge of 1858 expressed concern about the influence of their principals: quoted Atherstone, *Oxford's Protestant Spy*, p. 198. Similar concerns were expressed about Nonconformist colleges: K.D. Brown, *A Social History of the Nonconformist Ministry in England and Wales 1800-1930* (Oxford, 1988), pp. 94-101. Suggestions were frequently made that these small colleges should be amalgamated but this was never fulfilled until the mid-20th century: Espin, op.cit., p. 27; Miller, *Defective Ministerial Training*, p. 40, and *Chronicles of Convocation*, 1901, pp. 62, 66; *Proceedings of the St Asaph Diocesan Conference*, 1897, p.6.

12 Lambeth Palace Library, Benson Papers, 120, fols. 6, 14; *CDH,* 28 October 1898, p. 3.
13 *Report of the Church Congress, Oxford,* 1862, p. 50.
14 Conybeare, *Essays Ecclesiastical and Social*, p. 201.
15 Haig, *Victorian Clergy*, pp. 139-41; Dowland, *Anglican Theological Training,* p. 175; Park, *St Bees College*, p. 60.
16 *Report of the Llandaff Diocesan Conference*, 1907, p. 11. J.C. Ryle, later bishop of Liverpool, also depreciated the requirement for Latin and Greek for older men: *Church Reform Papers*, pp. 117-8. See also Haig, *Victorian Clergy*, p. 140, and Dowland, referring to St Aidans, *Anglican Theological Training*, pp. 82-4, 104-5. The Newtown Clerical Association in 1877 questioned the need for Latin, but suggested Greek and Hebrew were more appropriate: Roger L. Brown, "The Newtown Clerical Association", *MC*, 104 (2016), 82.
17 Brown, *John Griffith*, p.213.
18 *Report of the Church Congress, Bristol*, 1864, p. 206.
19 Brown, *A History of the English Clergy*, p. 247. H.P.Liddon, then vice-principal, is said to have considered piety more important than academic work: Chadwick, *The Spirit of the Oxford Movement*, pp. 228-32.
20 Heeney, *A Different Kind of Gentleman,* pp. 101-2; Dowland, *Anglican Theological Training*, pp. 128-9.
21 *Report of the Church Congress, Swansea*, 1879, pp. 542-3.
22 *Report of the Pan-Anglican Conference: Appendix, paper S.C.1, of W. H. Griffith Thomas*, 1908; cf. *Report of the Church Congress, Nottingham,* 1897, p.409, where his predecessor, F.J. Chavasse, felt that one of the roles of these colleges was to help men break with old habits and associations.
23 Haig, *Victorian Clergy*, p. 148.
24 Haig, *Victorian Clergy*, pp. 142-3; Leeming, *Church Scandals and their Cures*, p. 80-1.
25 Haig, *Victorian Clergy*, pp. 154-7; Dowland, *Anglican Theological Training*, pp. 60-1; *Guardian,* 30 September 1874, pp. 1239-40; Bullock, *Training for the Ministry 1875-1974*, pp. 21-2, notes the subjects of the examination as the Greek Testament, Latin texts, the contents of the Bible, Book of Common Prayer, Creeds and Articles. This was criticised as being a most unsatisfactory standard: *Report of the Church Congress, Swansea*, 1909, p. 196.
26 Dowland, *Anglican Theological Training*, pp. 104-5.
27 Basil Jones, *Charge (St Davids),* 1883, p. 29.
28 Haig, *Victorian Clergy*, p. 190; Bullock, *Training for the Ministry 1875-1974*, p. 21; *Guardian,* 19 August 1874, p. 1063.
29 Dowland, *Anglican Theological Training*, p. 187; Bullock, *History of Training 1875-1974*, p. 22; *Report of the Church Congress, Bath*, 1873, p. 140.
30 Bullock, *Training for the Ministry 1875-1974*, pp. 23, 49-60, 85-6; Haig, *Victorian Clergy*, pp. 160; O.W. Jones, *St Michael's College, Llandaff*, p. 39; *Guardian*, 4 May 1881, pp. 625-6 and 11 May 1881, p. 657; *Report of the Church Congress, Swansea,* 1909, pp. 198-9; *Chronicles of Convocation,* 1900, p.389, when the Bishop of St Davids, during a discussion on this topic, asked for a longer time to consider the question as it affected in particular the sons of clergy, and

ibid., 1906, p. 264, when the Bishop of Llandaff appears to have claimed an exemption for Lampeter graduates as they had done two years theology in their degree.

A promise had been made in 1916 by the archbishop of York that no soldier fit for ordination would be denied it because of lack of finance. As a result, a special college was established at the former Knutsford Prison, Cheshire, in 1919, for men who came into this category and who had found a vocation in the trenches. Its aim was to prepare men to enter a theological college, and in 1926 the college transferred to the Old Rectory, Hawarden. Between 1922-37 it trained 365 men, 180 of whom entered a university and 136 a theological college as non-graduates. The college closed in 1940: T.W. Pritchard, *A History of the Old Parish of Hawarden* (Wrexham, 2002), pp. 131-2; Lloyd, *The Church of England*, p. 339, states it trained overall 675 men out of 1039 service candidates of whom 435 were eventually ordained.

31 *Church in Wales: Report of the Revisory Sub-Committee*, pp. 10, 39, 45-6, 67, 74.

32 Bullock, *Training for the Ministry 1800-1875*, pp.49-51, 90-4; Jacob, *Clerical Profession*, pp. 59-60; William Palmer, *An Enquiry into the possibility of obtaining the means for Church Extension without Parliamentary grants* (London, 1841), p. 38; *Ecclesiastic*, 19 (1857), 51-2; *Quarterly Review*, 3 (1862), 439-41; *Report of the Church Congress, Nottingham*, 1871, pp. 298-303.

33 Bullock, *Training for the Ministry 1800-74*, pp. 49-51, 56-7; Burn, *Diocesan Revival*, pp. 152-6; Davies, *Henry Phillpotts*, pp. 147, 175-6, 326.

34 Williams, *Rowland Williams*, I, 198n; *Report of the St Davids Diocesan Conference*, 1882, p. 63; Ollivant in *Chronicles of Convocation*, 1872, p. 197; Brown, *John Griffith*, p. 214; Dowland, *Anglican Theological Training*, pp. 165-6.

35 Park, *St Bees College*, pp. 18-23, 86, 92; Haig, *Victorian Clergy*, pp. 124-34; Bullock, *Training for the Ministry 1800-1874*, pp. 30-1; Davies, *The life and Opinions of Robert Roberts*, pp. 352-74; John Breay, *A Fellside Parson* (Norwich, 1995), pp. 11-12, 15-16; Conybeare, *Essays Ecclesiastical and Social*, p. 45; Mary Ellis, "A Llanwddyn Diary", *MC*, 59 (1965-6), 152; O.W. Jones, "Theological Training in the Nineteenth Century", *Province*, 8 (1957), 102. In his 2nd edition (2005) Park notes that in 1874 the Welsh students at St Bees held a St David's day dinner, when it was resolved that it was unfair for the Welsh students at St Bees to have to remain five years' in deacon's orders in three of the four Welsh dioceses. He notes too that in 1868 Daniel Owen Davies, a St Bees man, in his priest's examination was placed higher than a Cambridge wrangler and an Oxford honours man: *ibid*, p. 127.

36 Cecil Wray (ed.), *Four Years of Pastoral Work: being a Sketch of the Ministerial Labours of the Rev .Edward John Rees Hughes* (London, 1854), pp. 24-5; Brown, *Ten Clerical Lives*, p. 141.

37 *Guardian*, 27 September 1865, pp. 952-3; 4 October 1865, p. 999; 18 October 1865, p. 1051, and 17 September 1866, p. 963.

38 Park, *St Bees College*, p. 92; Davies, *Life and Opinions of Robert Roberts*, pp. 360-8.

39 Burns, *Diocesan Revival*, p. 152; Haig, *Victorian Clergy*, p. 126, 136; Parsons, *Religion in Victorian Britain*, II, 265. Bishop van Mildert of Durham would only accept, with few exceptions, Oxbridge graduates and men from St Bees: Varley, *The Last of the Prince Bishops*, p. 119. Many St Bees men found their way to ordination in the diocese of York where they formed over 10 per cent of those ordained between 1863-90: H. Kirk-Smith, *William Thomson, Archbishop of York* (London, 1958), p. 54.

40 Evan Jones, *Adgofion*, p. 30.

41 F.B. Heiser, *The Story of St Aidan's College, Birkenhead, 1847-1947* (Chester, 1947); *Report of the Church Congress, Bristol*, 1864, p. 216-20; Heeney, *A Different kind of Gentleman*, pp. 104-7; Haig, *Victorian Clergy*, p. 134; Dowland, *Anglican Theological Training*, pp. 64-106, 169-71.

42 Dowland, *Anglican Theological Training*, pp. 46-53; Bullock, *Training for the Ministry 1800-1874*, pp. 62-3, 83.

43 *Report of the St Davids Diocesan Conference*, 1882, pp. 48-9. This probationer status was introduced as the colleges were unable to obtain sufficient numbers of graduate students: Haig, *Victorian Clergy*, pp. 134-5.

44 *Report of the Church Congress, Stoke on Trent*, 1875, pp. 412-4 (one third of the college were graduates but approximately one in six had "drifted out"); *Report of the Church Congress, Sheffield*, 1878, p. 538, for Walsham How's commendation.

45 *Report of the Church Congress, Northampton*, 1902, p. 396.

46 *Chronicles of Convocation*, 1872, pp. 196-7.

47 Ollivant to Gilbert Harris, 9 February 1865, in NLW, Church in Wales records, John Morgan (Llandaff) Papers, box 10.

48 Even in the 1900s there was concern expressed by many incumbents that the theological colleges were too academic and detached from parochial life, and they complained that their new deacons had been taught nothing about their future work in the parish: Lloyd, *The Church of England*, p. 151.

49 Richard Lewis, *Charge (Llandaff)*, 1888, p. 4; *Reports of Church Congresses, Exeter*, 1894, p.563, and *Barrow in Furness*, 1906, p. 351; *Chronicles of Convocation*, 1900, p. 362 – speech of Bishop Lewis; *CMG*, 8 August 1868, p. 8, noting Thirlwall's concern about deacons being placed in sole charge of parishes, echoing an earlier call by "A Clergyman", *On Clerical Education*, 1st letter, pp. 5-8. J.D. Johnson argued that no vicar should be allowed to offer a title to a parish unless he able to continue his curate's training: *Report of the Church Congress, Swansea*, 1909, p. 200. Canon Hugh Jones asked that the diaconate be extended for training purposes: *Proceedings of the St Asaph Diocesan Conference*, 1881, pp. 20-1. A report of the Church in Wales in 1938 suggested bishops needed to limit the work that deacons could do: *Church in Wales: Report of the Revisory Sub-Committee*, pp.41-2 and note p. 39, and cf. *Report of the Llandaff Diocesan Conference*, 1920, pp. 39-40.

50 Brown, *John Griffith*, p. 212; John Griffith, *Welsh Church Congress*, pp. 14-15; *Proceedings of the St Asaph Diocesan Conference*, 1897, p. 6.

51 *Church Quarterly Review*, 20 (1885), 348-52; *Chronicles of Convocation*, 1865, pp. 1872-3. Thomas Walters made clear that incumbents wanted better pastoral training and sermon preparation during their ordination training: *Report of the Church Congress, Cardiff*, 1889, p. 166.

52 Brown, *David Howell*, pp. 16-17. Archdeacon Sandford of Coventry said he had gone straight from schools in Oxford to ordination two days later to find himself in sole charge of a parish of 7,000 to 8,000 people. He noted another cleric whose father had pushed him into ordination. Even after 30 years he felt unfit for office: *Chronicles of Convocation*, 1863, p. 1222.

53 Hughes, *Charge (St Asaph)*, 1871, pp.14-15.

54 Hughes, *Charge (St Asaph)*, 1871, p. 15; Edwards' Charge of 1898 in *CDH*, 28 October 1898, p. 3; John Gott, *The Parish Priest of the Town* (London, 1890), pp. 170-2; *Report of the Church Congress, Barrow-in-Furness*, 1906, pp. 345-6.

55 *An Appeal to the Lords Spiritual and Temporal upon the Necessity for Measures to Increase the Efficiency of the Established Church* (London, n.d.), pp. 3-5.

56 *Church Quarterly Review*, 20 (1885), 363-4; *Chronicles of Convocation*, 1863, pp. 1219-20; *Proceedings of the St Asaph Diocesan Conference*, 1881, p. 21; *Report of the Church Congress, Exeter*, 1894, pp. 562-3, 577. Miller called these men "raw novices": *The Defective Ministry Training of our Universities*, p. 29; cf. Henley Henson's remark that the clergy of the Church of England were the best educated ministry but also the most theologically ignorant in existence: in his *Church Problems* (London, 1900), p. 21.

57 *Report of the Church Congress, Swansea*, 1879, p. 536; *Report of the Llandaff Diocesan Conference*, 1886, p. 84.

58 *Report of the Church Congress, Leeds*, 1872, p. 462; Brown, *John Griffith*, p. 211.

59 *Report of the St Davids Diocesan Conference*, 1882, pp. 33-4; cf. *Proceedings of the St Asaph Diocesan Conference*, 1901, p. 27.

60 Lambeth Palace Library, Benson Papers 120, fol. 6.

61 *Report of the Church Congress, Swansea*, 1879, p. 261.

62 *Report of the Llandaff Diocesan Conference*, 1892, p. 67.

63 Campbell, *Charges (Bangor)*, 1872, pp. 38-40; 1878, pp. 9-10; *Report of the Church Congress, Swansea*, 1909, p. 218.

64 Edwards, *Wales and the Welsh Church*, p. 76.

65 *Report of the St Davids Diocesan Conference*, 1882, p. 41.

66 *Chronicles of Convocation*, 1863, p. 1220; Vincent, *The Church in the Diocese of Bangor*, pp. 10-11.

67 Lewis, *Charge (Llandaff)*, 1891, pp. 9-10.

68 Bullock, *Training for the Ministry 1875-1974*, p. 18. This was established by Bishop Jacobson in 1872. Lectures and parochial experience were given to Oxbridge graduates, who had gone there as lay helpers.

69 A Clergyman, *On Clerical Education, A Letter*, pp. 8-10. He suggested some men might discover before it was too late they had no taste for this work. Private training was endorsed by Convocation in 1865: *Chronicles of Convocation*, 1865, p. 1873.

70 *Report of the Church Congress, Bristol*, 1864, p. 202.

71 *Speeches at the Annual Meeting of the Llandaff Church Extension Society*, 1879, p. 21; Vincent, *The Church in the Diocese of Bangor* suggested the same in 1869: p. 10; as did W. Conybeare Bruce, archdeacon of Monmouth, in 1879, suggesting that others should follow Vaughan, though he didn't act on his own advice: *Report of the Church Congress, Swansea*, 1879, p. 553.

72 *Chronicles of Convocation*, 1900, p. 383. The bishop of Winchester said at this meeting that he had a scheme at Farnham where eight men were studying for whom a theological college was not ideal: p. 384.

73 Bullock, *Training for the Ministry 1875-1974*, p. 167.

74 Bullock, *Training for the Ministry 1800-1874*, p. 72.

75 *Chronicles of Convocation*, 1863, p. 1222.

76 *Report of the Church Congress, Bristol*, 1864, pp. 221-2. He said the late bishop of Durham (Montagu Villiers 1860-1) had been one of his students.

77 D.L. Edwards, *Leaders of the Church of England 1828-1978* (London, 1978), p. 226.

78 Alistair Mason, *History of the Society of the Sacred Mission* (Norwich, 1994), p. 90.

79 *Guardian*, 21 (1858-9), p. 219; and 21 March 1866, pp. 298-9. Knight, *The Nineteenth-Century Church*, notes others, and that it could be surprisingly lucrative: p. 111. Another scheme, for non-graduates, was at Stamford Hill, London, where young men trained for four years whilst continuing in their secular occupations: Leeming, *Church Scandals*, p. 82.

80 R.R. Williams, *The Word of Life* (sermons of Vaughan), pp. 6, 89-91; C.J. Vaughan, *Addresses to Young clergymen delivered at Salisbury* (London, 1875), pp. ix-xii; *Report of the Church Congress, Swansea*, 1879, p. 537; *Report of the Llandaff Diocesan Conference*, in which Vaughan described his work, 1886, pp. 59-60; Trevor Park, *"Volo Episcopari": A Life of C.J. Vaughan* (St Bees, 2013), pp. 246-51, 279-89: Chrystal Tilney, "Dean Vaughan and the Restored Cathedral 1879-1897", *38th Annual Report of the Friends of Llandaff Cathedral*, 1970-1, pp. 15-17; Lewis, *Charge (Llandaff)*, 1903, p. 4; "H.G.", A Nineteenth Century Ordinand at Llandaff', *Province*, 17 (1966), pp. 132-8; H.M. Butler, *He Served his Generation: A Sermon preached at Llandaff Cathedral on October 24th, 1897, being the Sunday after the Funeral of the Very. Rev. Charles John Vaughan*, pp. 14-15; *Recollections of the Ven. James Rice Buckley*, typescript at South Glamorgan Library, Cardiff; "Reminiscences of a Convert: R.H. Benson", *Llandaff Diocesan Magazine*, July 1913, pp. 54-6; Lambeth Palace Library, Davidson Papers 50, fol. 292.

81 *Report of the Church Congress, Nottingham*, 1897, pp. 408-10.

82 *Report of the Church Congress, Stoke on Trent*, 1875, p. 412.

83 *Report of the Church Congress, Folkestone*, 1892, p. 464.

84 *Report of the Church Congress, Nottingham*, 1897, pp. 409-10; Lord Hugh Cecil's speech in *Llandaff Diocesan Magazine*, July 1909, pp. 443-4.

85 *Report of the Church Congress, Northampton*, 1902, p. 399. According to Haig the percentage was the same in 1891: *Victorian Clergy*, p. 87. Walsham How was most unusual in that after his

degree at Oxford and being too young for ordination he took the theological course at Durham before his ordination in 1846: How, *Walsham How*, p. 26-7.

86 *First Report of the Cathedral Commissioners, Appendix* (London, 1854), pp. 815-6.
87 *CMG*, 1 September 1854, p. 2.
88 O.W. Jones, *Isaac Williams*, pp. 101, 104-5, 107-8.
89 *Report of the Church Congress, Leeds*, 1872, p. 460.
90 O.W. Jones, "Thomas Walters", p. 65 (he suggested it could be placed at St Davids); *Church and People [CPAS]*, 7 (1895), 57; Brown, *Parochial Lives*, p. 95; Brown, *David Howell*, p. 296.
91 *Report of the Llandaff Diocesan Conference*, 1907, p. 20. The *Report of the Royal Commission, 1911*, II-I, 257, noted that the warden did not speak Welsh and the sub-warden was not fluent in the language.
92 Watkin Williams to Ll. Wynne Jones, 7 June 1927, originally at the Dean's Library, St Asaph, but now mislaid. Earlier schemes to establish a college here were noted in 1873, utilising the canonries for the principal and vice-principal and linking it with both Lampeter and Bangor, and later in 1883 for a non-graduate college: SA/DR/53, fol. 32, and Price, *St David's University College*, I, 141. As early as 1851 there was a suggestion that such an institution was needed in north Wales: A North Wales Incumbent, *A Letter to the ... Bishops of St. Asaph and Bangor on matters relating to the well being of the Church in their Lordships' respective dioceses* (London, 1851), pp. 19-22.
93 *Report of the Llandaff Diocesan Conference*, 1886, pp. 64-5.
94 O.W. Jones, *St Michael's College, Llandaff*, pp. 7-14; Brown, *Llandaff Figures and Places*, pp. 67-75; E.S. Thomas, "St Michael's College, Llandaff", *Province*, 2/1 (1951), 58-9, 62. For a short period before the First World War the college hosted a hostel for undergraduate ordinands studying at the university college. Its students paid a subsidised £50 per annum: *Llandaff Diocesan Magazine*, April 1910, pp. 87-8; *St Michael's College, Llandaff, Report for 1909: appeal by Lord Hugh Cecil on behalf of the Building Fund*.
95 Emily Talbot to Davidson, 13 November 1907: Lambeth Palace Library, Davidson Papers 131, fol. 440; *St Michael's College, Llandaff, Report for 1909*.
96 O.W. Jones, *St Michael's College*, p. 10; Brown, *Llandaff Figures and Places*, pp. 69, 72-3. De Winton added that while a man might retain little of the college's theological stance, he would retain much of the higher motives learnt from the warden.
97 Knight, in Williams, *The Welsh Church*, pp. 351-2.
98 Bishop of Llandaff in *Chronicles of Convocation*, 1900, p. 362. Only 2 of the 20 students in 1902 paid fees: O.W. Jones, *St Michael's College*, p. 11.
99 Church in Wales: *Report of the Revisory Committee on Training for the ministry* (1938), p. 74.
100 O.W. Jones, *St Michael's College*, pp. 27-8.
101 Pritchard Hughes to Davidson, 1 July 1907: Lambeth Palace Library, Davidson Papers 131, fol. 428.
102 Lewis, *Is Disestablishment Just?* pp. 26-7.
103 O.W. Jones, *St Michael's College*, p. 37.
104 Brown, *Llandaff Figures and Places*, pp.70-5; O.W. Jones, *St Michael's College*, pp. 28-32; J.G. Hughes, *St Michael's College, Llandaff, 1907-1982* (1982), pp. 7-10.
105 *Report of the Llandaff Diocesan Conference*, 1910, pp. 87-8; *Llandaff Diocesan Magazine*, April 1910, pp. 147-8; *Report of the Royal Commission, 1911*, I-I, 44. Frances Knight notes that in 1899 only 3 of 40 graduating students of St David's College entered St Michael's College, forcing the warden to commence a vigorous recruitment campaign there and at Oxbridge: in Williams, *The Welsh Church*, p. 352.
106 Knight, in Williams, *The Welsh Church*, p. 351.
107 O.W. Jones, *St Michael's College*, pp. 39-40.

CHAPTER SIX: THE FINAL HURDLE

1 Bray, *The Anglican Canons*, p. 317.

2 John Lloyd, *Theosurus Ecclesiasticus* (London, 1788), pp. 383-8. These were further re-issued in 1770: *The Clergyman's Assistant*, (Oxford, 1808), pp. 308-10 (This includes the list of papers required for ordination, p. 111). Previous archiepiscopal requirements were issued by Sheldon in 1665, Sancroft in 1685 and Wake in 1716: Bullock, *Training for the Ministry 598-1799*, p. 101. William II also issued similar injunctions: Jacob, *Clerical Profession*, p. 31. All these were similar, and insisted that the canonical age was 23, that no man be made deacon and ordained priest on the same day, and that ordinations should take place only during the Ember seasons.

3 For specific notices in the press see, for example, *Guardian*, 21 November 1866, p. 1207, for Llandaff, and *Ecclesiastical Gazette*, 24 (1871), 1, for St. Davids. Detailed requirements are found in Warren, *The Duties of the Parochial Clergy* (1784), pp. 21-4; Burgess, *Charge (St Davids)*, 1807, p 43 (those attending schools were required to send a certificate from the master indicating regular attendance for four years and satisfactory moral conduct); Pinnock, *The Laws and Usages of the Church and the Clergy*, pp. 1-6,16-17, 22-4; Christopher Hodgson, *Instructions for the use of Candidates for Holy Orders* (9th. Edn., London, 1870, pp. 1-8); *Llandaff Church Calendar and Clergy List*, 1875, II, 123. Haig, *Victorian Clergy* (pp. 184-7) notes the arrangements required in the diocese of Ripon during the 1870s. In most cases the bishops' secretaries were London legal firms, such as Bunder and Dunning, of 27 Parliament Square, which acted for the Welsh dioceses. Oxbridge graduates were required to send certificates of attendance at the divinity lectures or of having passed the preliminary theological examination, and Lampeter men the certificates of the university examiners.

4 Bullock, *History of Ridley Hall*, I, 181.

5 Haig, *Victorian Clergy*, p. 192.

6 It was not unknown for men to advertise for a title, as did Joseph Brunskill, a St Bees man, whose 1850 advertisement in the *English Churchman* took him to a curacy in Tipton, Staffs.: Breay, *A Fellside Parson*, p. 16. See Haig, *Victorian Clergy*, pp. 187-8 for the difficulties occasioned in finding a title.

7 Burns, *Diocesan Revival*, p. 133; *Llandaff Diocesan Church Calendar and Clergy List*, 1875, II, 123.

8 *St Asaph Clerical Directory*, 1863, pp. 63-4; *St David's Diocesan Directory*, 1889, II, 1-2. Bishop Bull of St Davids (1705-10) required candidates to appear before him a month before the ordination when he conducted his examination: Sykes, "The Diocese of St. David's", p. 10. In the 1870s Bishop Bickersteth of Ripon kept a book in which he recorded the answers of candidates to fourteen questions. These were details about themselves, motives for ordination and "fundamental doctrines", depravity, atonement, justification, sanctification. It enabled the bishop to weed out unsuitable candidates straight away: Haig, *Victorian Clergy*, p. 184.

9 As noted by Bishop Kaye of Lincoln in his 1831 Charge (quoted Bullock, *Training for the Ministry 1800-1874*, p. 45), and by Canon Beavan at the St Davids diocesan conference of 1882; *Report*, p. 47.

10 Gregory and Chamberlain, *The National Church in its Local Perspective*, p. 132; Harford, *Thomas Burgess*, p. 442.

11 W. Basil Jones, *Some Ordination Addresses*, p. 45.

12 Welsh Freeholder, *Letter to the Bishop of St David's, on the Charge he lately Delivered*, p. 29.

13 E.T. Davies, "The Education of the Clergy in the Diocese of Llandaff", p. 61. It appears that three years sufficed in the diocese of Llandaff.

14 Brown, *Llandaff Figures and Places*, p. 4. Kaye of Lincoln (1827-53) did the same but in a more gentle spirit though his questions were deliberately contentious: Knight, *The Nineteenth-Century Church*, p. 112-3. Richard Warner in a published letter to the bishop of Gloucester, the evangelical Henry Ryder, protested about his ordination of like-minded men, "the scions of Whitfield or Wesley", suggesting he used a similar method of enquiry: *A Letter to the Lord*

Bishop of Gloucester on the Admission to Holy Orders of Young Men Holding Evangelical Principles (Bath, 1818).

15   Brown, *A History of the English Clergy*, p. 243; Johnson, *Bustling Intermeddler?* pp. 24-5. Varley, *Last of the Prince Bishops*, p. 119.

16   *Chronicles of Convocation*, 1872, pp. 196-8. This was in contrast to the Church of Ireland, whose bishops in 1790 agreed to ordain only those who had a certificate of attendance at specific theological lectures from Trinity College, Dublin, and prescribed the books required for the ordination examinations: Yates, *Eighteenth-Century Britain*, p. 160.

17   Basil Jones, *Charges (St Davids)*, 1880, pp. 29-31; 1883, pp. 27-9; 1886, p. 16. John Owen, his successor, noted that this policy had not diminished the number of candidates and had raised the quality of men ordained: *Church Reform and Church Progress*, p. 30.

18   Bullock, *Training for the Ministry 1875-1974*, pp. 49-53. A desire for this extra year was expressed at the 1892 Llandaff Diocesan Conference (*Report*, pp. 66-7), and by Bishop Richard Lewis in 1897 *(Charge, (Llandaff)*, 1897, p. 12), though regarded as impractical by the same diocese in 1911 (*Llandaff Diocesan Magazine*, April 1911, pp. 6-8). The principal of Cuddesdon, J.O. Johnson, in 1911, wished for this to be applied immediately for graduates, but hinted that the policy might not apply to mature candidates: *Report of the Church Congress, Swansea*, 1909, pp. 197-9.

19   Morgan, *A Study in Nationality*, pp. 274-5.

20   Short, *Sketch of the History of the Church of England*, p. lxviii; Hughes, *Charge (St Asaph)*, 1871, p. 14.

21   Rowland Williams, *An earnestly respectful Letter*, pp. 2-3n.

22   Pinnock, *The Laws of the Church and the Clergy*, p. 6; Leeming, *Church Scandals*, p. 83. The canonical age was set at 23 for deacons (enforced by statute law of 1804) and 24 for priests.

23   Knight, in Williams, *The Welsh Church*, pp. 344-5.

24   LL/CC/G/1237.

25   Carey to Roberts, 21 August 1833(?), NLW, Ms. 22754B, fol. 16.

26   *Chronicles of Convocation*, 1865, p. 1873.

27   Nelson, "Life of Bishop Bull", I, 361-6. Whether a further examination followed is not made clear.

28   Harford, *Thomas Burgess*, pp. 442-3; Hart, *The Curate's Lot*, pp. 170-1.

29   From a newspaper cutting of 1892, in SA/DR/46, fol. 48; *The St Asaph Clerical Directory*, 1863, pp. 63-4.

30   Glanely, *Church Reform*, pp. 100-3.

31   *Church in Wales: Report of the Revisory Sub-Committee*, pp. 3, 10, 47. Diocesan committees also awarded exhibitions: *St Asaph Diocesan Calendar*, 1936, p. 70.

32   R.W.D. Fenn, "Thomas Davies, Rector of Coity", *JHSCW*, 13 (1963), ftnt. 11 on p. 67.

33   Popkin, *Observations on the Nature of the House of God*, pp.12-15, quoting *The Cambrian*, 26 October 1811.

34   Jenkinson, *Charges* (St Davids), 1828, pp. 41-9; 1836, p. 43.

35   Basil Jones, *Charges (St Davids)*, 1877, pp. 28-9; 1889, p. 15-18, when he asked his incumbents to answer his queries about candidates without concealing what might be said against them; Campbell, *Charge (Bangor)*, 1875, p. 23 Lewis, *Charge (Llandaff)*, 1885, pp. 13-14. Archdeacon Sandford of Coventry feared in 1861 that as many testimonials were not honestly signed, many unfit men had been ordained who had no aptitude for spiritual things, and who might have loose habits and a damaged reputation: *The Mission and Extension of the Church at Home: Bampton Lectures* (London, 1861), pp. 118-9. J.C. Ryle echoed this concern in 1870: *Church Reform Papers*, pp. 135-7. The Si Quis could also be misused. Thomas Jones of Creaton, ordained in 1784, had a neighbour prefer unjust charges against him. The bishop wished him to prosecute him at his, the bishop's, expense: Owen, *Thomas Jones*, pp. 10-11.

36   *Report of the Church Congress, Swansea*, 1909, p. 214; cf. Campbell, *Charge (Bangor)*, 1872, p. 34. He expressed concern in his 1872 *Charge* (p. 34) that some clergy were bringing forward

candidates whose families were influential in their parishes, and canvassing support for them. An earlier example is provided by Griffith Jones of Llanddowror who suggested that sometimes these testimonials were signed on political grounds, so that some good men suffered and many unworthy ordained: *Welch Piety 1740-1*, pp.5-6.

37 Norman Sykes, *Church and State in England*, pp. 111-2.

38 *Quarterly Review* (1862), 435-6; Haig, *Victorian Clergy*, pp. 185-6; Knight, *The Nineteenth-Century Church*, pp. 109-10.

39 Lambeth Palace Library, Benson Papers 146, fols. 383, 387.

40 J.A. Bradney, *Llandaff Records* (London, 1914), V, 77-8, 158-9. Jacob, *Clerical Profession*, p. 36.

41 Jacob, *Clerical Profession*, pp. 68-9; H.W. Cripps, *The Law relating to the Church and Clergy* (5th. edn., London, 1869), pp. 181-9.

42 Nelson, *Life of Bishop Bull*, I, 362-3.

43 Fleetwood, *Charge (St Asaph)*, 1710, p. 61.

44 Quoted by Mather, *High Church Prophet*, p. 170. David Davies, ordained in 1801 was "granted a title for only £30" to serve as curate at Llandyssil, Monts., a statement which might indicate he paid for this title: *Twenty-One Practical and Familiar Sermons*, p. xviii.

45 Jenkinson, *Charge (St Davids)*, 1828, pp. 31-4.

46 Brown, *Letters of Edward Copleston*, pp. 137, 227, 229; Copleston to his father, 2 September 1828, NLW, Ms. 22721.

47 Conybeare, *Essays Ecclesiastical and Social*, p. 13.

48 Basil Jones, *Charges (St Davids)*, 1877, p. 27; 1880, pp. 27-31; *Report of the St Davids Diocesan Conference*, 1882, p. 61. However, Jones admitted in 1889 that this custom had been "virtually abandoned": *Charge*, 1889, p. 9, and note *Charge*, 1886, pp. 14-15.

49 Campbell, *Charge (Bangor)*, 1884, pp. 14-15.

50 *Chronicles of Convocation*, 1900, p. 366; cf. *Report of the St Davids Diocesan Conference*, 1882, p. 61, and Lewis, *Charge (Llandaff)*, 1885, p. 11, where they noted more would have been ordained if titles had been available. Roger Lloyd noted the difficulties of obtaining titles during the depression years of the 1930s due to the financial climate: *The Church of England*, p. 341.

51 Sumner, *Charles Richard Sumner*, p. 119, cf. p. 142 for his arrangements whilst bishop of Winchester.

52 Roberts, *Speculum Episcopi*, pp. 171-3. Walsham How stayed at the Star and Garter in Worcester when he was ordained 1846, and was not impressed by the way things were done: How, *Walsham How*, p. 29.

53 David Evans, *Adgofion gan 'Henafgwr'*, p. 147. Walsham How, when bishop of Wakefield, insisted on an episcopal house suitable for accommodating ordination candidates: Douglas Emmott, *Clergy Training in Victorian York* (Borthwick Papers 101, York, 2002), p. 10. Wilberforce did the same in the 1850s: Haig, *Victorian Clergy*, p. 188.

54 Philip Barrett, *Barchester* (London, 1993), pp. 247-8.

55 Williams, *Thomas Price, Carnhuanawc*, II, 44.

56 Brown, *Letters of Edward Copleston*, pp. 227-8.

57 Sumner, *Charles Richard Sumner*, p. 121.

58 Brown, *Letters of Edward Copleston*, p. 72; Llandaff Cathedral, Copleston Correspondence, Copleston to Bruce Knight, 16 September 1842, no. K108, and to Treharne, 4 September no year, no. T173.

59 Roberts, *Speculum Episcopi*, pp. 173-6.

60 Joseph Gilbert, *Memoir ... of the late Rev. Edward Williams, DD* (London, 1825), pp. 30-1. Bishop Bagot of Norwich suspended three candidates found intoxicated on the eve of ordination: Jacob, *Clerical Profession*, p. 37.

61 I.L.O. Morgan, *Memoirs of Henry Arthur Morgan, Master of Jesus College, Cambridge* (London, 1927), p. 123. Similarly, the only words addressed to Benson and the other candidates before their ordination by their bishop concerned the time of the dinner that evening. Several of

the candidates played billiards on the evening of their ordination: A.C. Benson, *Edwardian Excursions* (London, 1981), p. 28.

62   W.G. Wrenche, *Wrenche and Radcliffe of Cardiff* (privately published, 1956), p. 140.

63   Jenkinson, *Charge (St Davids)*, 1836, pp. 55-6. For English dioceses see, William Clewer [later bishop of St Asaph], *Books intended for the use of the younger Clergy ... within the Diocese of Chester* (Oxford, 1791), and R.W. Ambler, *Lincolnshire Parish Correspondence of John Kaye, Bishop of Lincoln 1827-53* (Lincolnshire Record Society 94 (2006), p. xxxvi.

64   *St Asaph Clerical Directory*, 1863, pp. 63-4.

65   *Llandaff Diocesan Church Calendar and Clergy List*, 1875, II, 123; *ibid*, 1911, p. 169; *Bangor Diocesan Directory*, 1896, pp. 249-60.

66   *Llandaff Diocesan Church Calendar and Clergy List*, 1911, p. 169.

67   *Chronicles of Convocation*, 1885, p. 315, and 1906, p. 262; Haig, *Victorian Clergy*, pp. 190-1.

68   Gott speaking at the Sheffield Church Congress 1878: *Report*, p. 526; Fraser to Davey, 11 September 1878, Lambeth Palace Library, Davey Papers, fol. 121. Davey was then vice-principal of Lampeter.

69   Brown, *Letters of Edward Copleston*, to Bruce Knight, pp. 103, 108.

70   Bullock, *Training for the Ministry 598-1799*, pp. 118-9.

71   Sykes, "The Diocese of St David's", p. 15; Mather, *High Church Prophet*, pp. 167-8. For a general survey see Sykes, *Church and State in England*, pp. 106-10. He notes that Burnet required candidates to be examined before the dean and chapter and examined them himself in doctrine and pastoral care.

72   Harford, *Thomas Burgess*, pp. 235-41. He notes that when Burgess was bishop of Salisbury he asked candidates what books they had read to qualify themselves for Holy Orders, how they were preparing themselves for ordination, and what were the characteristics of personal religion: *ibid*, pp. 443-4. Nigel Yates notes that Burgess gave men copies of Thomas Scott's *Force and Truth*, in which he pointed out Scott's then incompatibility with his position when he was made deacon, though warning them against its Calvinistic tones: *Bishop Burgess and his World*, p. 28.

73   Sumner, *Charles Richard Sumner*, pp. 119-21. At Winchester two examining chaplains took the written examinations and another the viva voce ones; the bishop later remarked upon their papers in a personal interview. Sumner also inspected the sermons prepared for him by those to be ordained priest and questioned them about their work in the diaconate: *ibid*, pp. 142-4.

74   Brown, *Letters of Edward Copleston*, pp. 139, 202.

75   Haig, *Victorian Clergy*, pp. 188-9.

76   W.H. Griffith Thomas, *Ministerial Life and Work* (Chicago, 1930s), p. 133.

77   Grey-Edwards, *Reminiscences of an Unknown Man*, p. 60.

78   Davies, *Life and Opinions of Robert Roberts*, pp. 376-7.

79   Gibson, *The Domestic Chaplain*, pp. 150-1.

80   John Beresford (ed.), *The Diary of a Country Parson* (London, 1924), I, 25.

81   Brown, "A Cardiganshire Incumbent writes to his London relatives", p. 22.

82   Varley, *Last of the Prince Bishops*, p. 93.

83   E.M. Sneyd-Kynnersley, *HMI's Notebook* (London, 1930), pp. 118-9. Another version has Benson failing some questions on the Old Testament: G. Palmer and N. Lloyd, *Father of the Bensons* (Harpenden, 1998), pp. 36-7.

84   John Vickers, *Thomas Coke: Apostle of Methodism* (London, 1969), p. 17n.

85   David Davies, *Twenty-One Practical and Familiar Sermons*, p. xx.

86   Quoted in Gibson, *The Domestic Chaplain*, pp. 152-3. Allan was examining chaplain to the bishop of Chichester and later of Lichfield, Grier, *John Allen*, pp. 65-6, and Haig, *Victorian Clergy*, p. 139. Allan claimed in his defence that he had rejected three men out of ten in 1865, two of whom were from St Bees and who had received the college testimonial: *Guardian*, 27 September, 4 and 18 October, 1865, pp. 952-3, 999, 1051.

87   G.C. Coulton, *Fourscore Years* (London, 1945), p. 182.

88   Morgan, *David James*, pp. 9-10.

89 Varley, *Last of the Prince Bishops*, pp. 93-4.
90 *Report of the Church Congress, Cardiff*, 1889, p. 551; Harford, *Thomas Burgess*, p. 245.
91 Hall, *A Letter to the Bishop of Llandaff*, p. 6. He was mainly criticising Lampeter for its lack of Welsh teaching.
92 *Report of the Llandaff Diocesan Conference,* 1910, pp. 80-1. This echoed a complaint by the Association of Welsh Clergy of the West Riding of Yorkshire in the 1850s, that the classics were seen as more important than the Welsh language: Brown, *'Welsh Patriotism' and 'Justice to Wales'*, p. 26. Nevertheless, candidates could be plucked for their lack of Welsh. For example, John Jones of Bangor, an examining chaplain, was obliged to "pluck" one candidate in 1838 as he knew little of Welsh beyond reading it: A.O. Evans, *Welsh Book of Common Prayer*, I, 238.
93 *Report of the Church Congress, Swansea,* 1879, p. 578.
94 *Report of the St Davids Diocesan Conference*, 1882, p. 62; cf. J.E. Southall, *Wales and her Language* (Newport, 1892), p. 226, who makes a similar comment.
95 SD/Misc B/80; Knight, in Williams, *The Church in Wales,* pp. 346-7, observes that Edwards' mother was English and the language of the home was probably English.
96 *Bangor Diocesan Directory*, 1896, p. 250;
97 "Draig Glas" (A. T. Johnson) in his *The Perfidious Welshman* (London, n.d.), p. 45, notes that the English duty of such a man was often lost through his Welsh accent.
98 Bevan, *The Case of the Church in Wales*, p. 40.
99 Roy Hattersley, *A Brand from the Burning* (London, 2002), pp. 366-7.
100 Beverley, *A Letter ... on the Present Corrupt State of the Church of England,* p. 29; *Welch Piety*, 1741, p. 6; Roberts, *Speculum Episcopi,* pp. 175-6.
101 *Report of the Church Congress, Oxford*, 1862, p. 12. Ffoulkes was speaking at the Stoke on Trent Church Congress: *Report*, 1875, pp. 427-8. John Griffith was writing in *The Star of Gwent*, 9 January 1880 (in South Glamorgan Library, Cardiff Ms. 5,157).
102 Bray, *The Anglican Canons*, pp. 582-3. Hastings Rashdall in the 1900s expressed concern that the bishops' examinations were more concerned with facts than interpretation, and candidates were never asked about social problems, Christian ethics or the philosophy of religion: June Garnett, in J. Garnett and C. Matthew (eds.), *Revival of Religion since 1700* (London, 1993), pp. 312-4.
103 Sandford, *Archbishop Temple*, I, 413-21; II, 341-2.
104 Owen, *Church Reform and Church Progress*, pp. 42-3.
105 Quoted by Margaret Pawley, *Faith and Family* (Norwich, 1993), pp. 48-9; Brown, *History of the English Clergy*, pp. 241-2. Stories were told of candidates being examined while the examining chaplain shaved or waited to bat in a cricket match: Bullock, *Training for the Ministry 1800-1874*, p. 47-8. Rowland Williams and others were told by the chaplain of Bishop Kaye of Lincoln in 1842 that the bishop was satisfied with the first day's work and would not keep them any longer: O.W. Jones, *Rowland Williams*, pp. 15-16. Virgin suggested if a man had a degree and title, and had subscribed to the 39 Articles, the bishops saw little point in being strict: *The Church in an Age of Negligence*, p. 138, while Mark Pattison in 1843 wrote that the examination hardly tested a man's ability and was not concerned with his general attainment, as this was supposed to have been done at the university: quoted by Kirk-Smith, *William Thomson*, pp. 52-3.
106 Richards, "The Diocese of Bangor during the Rise of Welsh Methodism", p. 201; G.N. Evans, *Religion and Politics in mid-Eighteenth Century Anglesey*, pp. 89-92. Richards states that Buckeley was not typical of Anglesey clergy at the time.
107 Saunders, *A View of the State of Religion*, pp. 59-60.
108 Ollivant, *Charges (Llandaff)*, 1857, pp. 11-12; 1860, pp. 64-7; 1863, pp. 14-17; and 1866, p. 10; Basil Jones, *Charge (St Davids)*, 1886, p. 17; *Report of the St Davids Diocesan Conference*, 1882, pp. 61-2.

109 *Report of the Church Congress, London*, 1899, p. 185; *Proceedings of the St Asaph Diocesan Conference*, 1899, p. 7, and 1897, p. 8; Gregory Smith, *Memoir of William Latham Bevan* (Hay, 1917), p. 5.
110 Lewis, *Visitation (Llandaff)*, 1897, p. 10.
111 Hughes, *Charge (Llandaff)*, 1907, pp. 28-9.
112 Basil Jones, *Charge (St Davids)*, 1877, p. 25.
113 F.D. How, *Lighter Moments from the Notebook of William Walsham How* (London, 1900), p. 71.
114 Harford, *Thomas Burgess*, pp. 225, 235; Jacob, *Clerical Profession*, p. 58.
115 Harford, *Thomas Burgess*, p. 385.
116 G.E. Evans, *Cardiganshire* (Aberystwyth, 1903), p. 85.
117 Llandaff Diocesan Memorandum Books, 1849-68 and 1868-89.
118 Ollivant to Gilbert Harries, 31 December 1866, in NLW, Church in Wales Records, John Morgan (Llandaff) Papers, Box 10.
119 R.K. Pugh (ed.), *The Letter-Books of Samuel Wilberforce* (Oxfordshire Record Society, xlvii, 1969), pp. 163, 215.
120 Basil Jones, *Charges (St Davids)*, 1877, p. 25; 1889, pp. 12-14.
121 *Report of the Llandaff Diocesan Conference* 1910, p. 79.
122 Llandaff Diocesan Memorandum Books.
123 Denning, *The Diary of William Thomas*, pp. 78-9.
124 Jacob, *Clerical Profession*, p. 37. One assumes the custom continued into the 19th century.
125 *Chronicles of Convocation*, 1870, pp. 504-5; Ollivant to Gilbert Harries, 25 February 1869, in NLW, Church in Wales Records, John Morgan (Llandaff) Papers, Box 10. Basil Jones declined to ordain such men (though when he came to his diocese he found many literates ordained to a five-year diaconate), and as a result he claimed he obtained a better quality of candidates: *Charge (St Davids)*, 1886, pp. 15-16.
126 Llandaff Diocesan Memorandum Books, 1849-68 and 1868-89. The St David's diocesan book of ordinands 1874-81 notes many such five-year men: SD/MiscB/80.
127 Knight, in Williams, *The Welsh Church*, pp. 344-5.
128 Short, *Sketch of the History of the Church of England*, pp. lxviii-lxix. Knight notes the reasons given for those men rejected by Bishop Hamilton of Salisbury in 1855: *The Nineteenth-Century Church*, p. 114.
129 S.C. Carpenter, *Church and People 1789-1886* (London, 1937), p. 256.
130 How, *Walsham How*, p. 29.
131 W. Basil Jones, *Some Ordination Addresses*, p. 26, cf. *Chronicles of Convocation*, 1900, pp. 353-5.
132 Quoted by Bullock, *Training for the Ministry 1875-1974*, p. 19.
133 *Report of the Church Congress, Bath*, 1873, pp. 131, 140.
134 *Report of the Church Congress, Sheffield*, 1878, pp. 538-9. He suggested the academic part of the examination should take place some time before the ordination, possibly at centres as was the case for pupil teachers. Members of the Newtown Clerical Association in 1877 argued that the ordination week should be more about spiritual preparation than examinations: Roger L. Brown, "The Newtown Clerical Association", *MC*, 104 (2016), 81.
135 This was the practice of Archbishop Temple when he was bishop of Exeter, 1869-85: E.G. Sandford, *Archbishop Temple*, I, 415-6. He split the examination into two sections, the first more academic, the second relating to ministry. Bullock notes that at Salisbury from 1864, and Lichfield from 1867, the examination concluded some two days before the ordination, allowing two days of spiritual preparation, while at Lincoln in the early 1870s, at the instance of E.W. Benson, then examining chaplain, a complete separation was made, later followed at Durham under Bishop Lightfoot in *c.* 1879: *Training for the Ministry 1800-74*, pp. 127-8, and ibid, *1875-1974*, p. 20. At Ely the examination was three months before the ordination: *Guardian*, 30 September 1874, pp. 1239-40.

136 *Report of the Church Congress, Folkestone*, 1892, p. 462, and p. 446 for a description of the practice at Salisbury under Bishop Wordsworth.
137 Campbell, *Charge (Bangor)*, 1881, p. 16.
138 *Proceedings of the St Asaph Diocesan Conference*, 1897, p. 6.
139 Gregory Smith, *Memoir of William Latham Bevan* (Hay, 1917), p. 6.
140 *Church in Wales: Report of the Revisory Sub-Committee*, p. 74.
141 Bullock, *Training for the Ministry 1875-1974*, p. 20.
142 W. Basil Jones, *Some Ordination Addresses*, esp. pp. 26, 40-2; Bishop Ollivant's ordination charge of 1850, commending the study of Scripture, is at Glamorgan Record Office, D/D l/DC E41. Robert Wilson Evans, who died in 1866 as archdeacon of Westmorland was a Montgomeryshire man who published his various addresses on these occasions under the title *The Bishopric of Souls*. It was said that Bishop Jebb of Limerick (1823-34) was the first to commence this practice: *Church Quarterly Review*, 20 (1885), 342-3.
143 E.G. Wright, "Humphrey Humphries, Bishop of Bangor and Hereford", *JHSCW*, 2 (1950), 75.
144 Knight, *The Nineteenth-Century Church*, p. 112.
145 Sykes, *Church and State in England*, pp. 99, 110.
146 Owen, *Thomas Jones*, p. 11.
147 E. Morgan, *Home Light: Brief Memoir of the Rev. R. Bassett, vicar of Colwinstone* (Carnarvon, 1860), p. 11.
148 Brown, *Letters of Edward Copleston*, pp. 112, 117, 153, 245, and Copleston to Bruce Knight, at Llandaff Cathedral, 8 January 1833, no K100.
149 Llandaff Memorandum Book 1868-89, entry for 20 Dec. 1868.
150 Roberts, *Speculum Episcopi*, pp. 166-9.
151 Eifion Evans, *Daniel Rowland and the Great Evangelical Awakening in Wales* (Edinburgh, 1985), p. 30.
152 Pryce, *The Diocese of Bangor*, p. lxiii.
153 E.J. Newell, *Llandaff* (SPCK series, London, 1902), pp. 211-12. He notes that Bishop Barrington 1769-82) ordained at Mongewell, Oxfordshire, in the 1770s.
154 Price, *Bishop Burgess and Lampeter College*, p. 35. Jenkinson regularly ordained at Lampeter: Price, *St David's University College*, I. 51.
155 David Evans, *Atgofion gan "Henafgwr"*, p. 141.
156 Brown, *Letters of Edward Copleston*, pp. 90-1, 202. John Griffith, later archdeacon of Neath, was also made deacon at St Paul's Cathedral by Copleston: Brown, *Ten Clerical Lives*, p. 105.
157 Brown, *Letters of Edward Copleston*, p. 264.
158 Brown, *Letters of Edward Copleston*, pp. 272, 278.
159 Basil Jones, *Charge (St Davids)*, 1880, pp. 26-7.
160 *CMG*, 21 June 1851, p. 3.
161 Edmondes to Lewis, 29 December 1887, in NLW, Church in Wales Records, John Morgan (Llandaff) papers, Box 10.
162 *Report of the Royal Commission, 1911*, IV, 538.
163 R. Tudur Jones, *Faith and the Crisis of a Nation*, p. 397.
164 A.O. Evans, *Welsh Book of Common Prayer*, I, 126.
165 John Jones (Bangor), *A Sermon Preached at the General Ordination holden at Bangor, September 1800* (Chester, 1800); Rowland Williams, *A Sermon Preached in the Cathedral Church of Bangor, September 23, 1804, at a General Ordination held by William, Lord Bishop of Bangor* (Oxford, 1804); A.O. Evans, *Minutes and Proceedings of an Old Tract Society of Bangor Diocese* (Bangor, 1918), p. 71 Other similar sermons are William Beveridge (Bishop of St Asaph, 1704-8), in his *Collected Works* (London, 1720), I, 22-8; Peter Williams, *Casgliad o Bregethau* (Dolgellau, 1814), II, 369-98; and John Jones of Llansilin, *A Sermon preached at the Cathedral Church of St Asaph at a General Ordination held by the Rt. Rev. the Lord Bishop of St. Asaph, July 19, 1812* (Wrexham, 1812). David Davies was ordained at the service at which

Rowland Williams preached, pronouncing it an excellent sermon. He was ordained on letters dimissory from the bishop of St Asaph: *Twenty-One Practical and Familiar Sermons*, p. xxiv.
166 Sumner, *Charles Richard Sumner*, p. 121.
167 Eryl Thomas, "Reflections on an Ordination Fifty Years Ago", *Welsh Churchman,* June 1984, pp.4-5.
168 Pinnock, *The Laws of the Church and the Clergy,* pp. 50c & d (in 1855); Conybeare criticised these fees, which in Gloucester came to £9.4s.6d, and in Hereford £7.10s.6d, amounting to around a tenth of the first year's stipend: *Essays Ecclesiastical and Social*, p. 202-3. Forged letters of orders were not unknown, particularly in the late 17th century: Hart, *William Lloyd*, p. 82.

A SOCIAL HISTORY OF THE WELSH CLERGY

SECTION TWO: THE INFERIOR CLERGY – THE CURATES

CHAPTERS

		TEXT	ENDNOTES
1	INTRODUCTION	187	*319*
2	THE PERPETUAL CURATE	198	*321*
3	THE STIPENDIARY CURATE: THE ISSUE OF NON-RESIDENCE	217	*326*
4	THE STIPENDIARY CURATE: THE CURATE OBSERVED	238	*331*
5	PERPETUAL AND STIPENDIARY CURATES: THE CONSEQUENCES	250	*334*
6	THE ASSISTANT CURATE: A NEW BREED	262	*338*
7	THE ASSISTANT CURATE: HIS DUTIES, CONCERNS AND DIFFICULTIES	296	*345*

CHAPTER ONE: INTRODUCTION

A story is told of William Paley, archdeacon of Carlisle from 1782-1805, and author of the celebrated *Evidences of Christianity.* Attending a clergy dinner, he was annoyed by a draught behind his back from an open window, but accepted some ventilation was required in a hot and stuffy room. Calling a waiter, he asked him to close that window but open one behind some of the inferior clergy, namely the curates. It is with these men, these inferior clergy, that this chapter deals.

The term "curate" is accepted today as being the title of an ordained assistant to an incumbent of a parish. This is a usage that only became common during the 1830s and 1840s, although there were assistant curates in parishes, especially large parishes, before that date. A pamphlet of 1866, quoted by Alan Haig, was not entirely correct in its suggestion that "[a]ssistant-Curates, holding the position and the performing the duties which they now do, are, as a class, the creation of the present century". It was correct, however, in its claim that these men replaced a body of some 5,000 clergymen who formerly had taken duty for non-resident incumbents. As James Obelkevich remarked, these assistant curates were akin to apprentices learning the craft of pastoral care. Until the 1840s those described as curates were almost immediately after ordination appointed as either stipendiary or resident curates, who looked after a parish for an absentee or non-resident incumbent; temporary curates who cared for a parish whose incumbent was incapacitated or had been sequestrated; or perpetual curates, who cared for parishes that were either impropriated to a layman, or appropriated to a cleric or an ecclesiastical body. Again, a distinction may be made regarding these perpetual curates, between those who shared the tithe income with the "rector", whether lay or ecclesiastical, and those who served in parishes where that income went entirely to the impropriator, and who received a small income from him as a stipend.[1] Yet another distinction has been drawn by W.T. Morgan who, writing of the diocese of St Davids, suggested "[c]urates were either young men starting their careers with good expectations of preferment or ill educated peasant clergy whose attainments did not entitle them to a high position in the Church."[2] However, it will be noted that many incumbents also acted as curates for other parishes, and research quoted by Peter Virgin for a number of English dioceses during the eighteenth century suggested that between fifteen and twenty-five per-cent of parishes were pastorally cared for by neighbouring incumbents.[3] This would be equally so for Wales.

THE STATE OF THE CLERGY

It is hardly surprising, considering Paley's remarks, that there were many disparaging comments made about these curates, especially the Welsh ones. A poem of 1743 relates to the Revd. Thomas Samuel, lately a servant to Bulkeley Phillips, Esq., "for thou thou'rt ordained, thou still smell'st of the stable".[4] Obviously many country clergy did smell of the stable, for in 1803 Bishop Horsley of St Asaph, speaking in the House of Lords, pictured some of the rural clergy foddering cattle and throwing dung on the land, thus mixing "in familiar habits with the inferior orders" of society,[5] and at a later date his successor in that diocese, Thomas Vowler Short, described his Welsh clergy as "cart-horses", an insult it was said they never forgave nor forgot.[6] In the 1750s Richard Bulkeley of Anglesey wrote of the curate of Llanfechell that he was ignorant of the Scriptures, unintelligible and confused in his preaching, even though he took his sermons from others.[7] Richard Edwards, curate of Trevethin, 1769-72, and tutor to the John Hanbury's children, referred to "the manner in which a *Welch Parson* is received and looked upon by some of the Esqrs of their parishes".[8] John Byng recalled how in 1787 the clergy of Brecon waited the coming forth of "my lord the bishop", and noted "with sorrow, and contempt, the misery and cringing of the lower clergy, and the pride and self-consequence of their superiors."[9] Thomas Pennant, some years later, described the curate of Bagillt, Thomas Hughes, as a "drudge in his profession," though an honest pauper and a man of good morals, decent and modest.[10]

In his 1795 tour of north Wales, Hucks writes of the curate of Llangynog, whose inability to reply to his queries in English indicated to the author a pride struggling with poverty. Meeting him at an inn he wondered if the lack of suitable company had driven him to pass his days with people far inferior to him, and so lose "that refinement of action as well as of thought, which properly distinguishes the gentleman from the honest but blunt peasant .." His experience bore credible testimony to "the shameful and scanty provision made for the Welsh clergy", and while Hucks accepted there was no disgrace in poverty, too often "the ignorant and uninstructed too frequently treat their teachers with a respect proportioned to their appearance .."[11] In 1799 the wardens of the parish of Brecon described their curate, Mr Jenkins, as having "no great talent in the discharge of his duties".[12]

It was such men as these who were depicted in the celebrated print of *The Welch Curate*, 1770. He is shown in his kitchen, listening to his son reading his lesson, rocking the cradle with his foot, peeling a turnip, and endeavouring to read a book, with clothes drying over the fire. Another print of the *Welsh Parson* by Woodward produced some twenty years later, had this inscription placed on it: "Best scene of all, with which I close this reverend description, is your Welch Parson, with his noble living, sans shoes, sans hose, sans breeches, sans everything."[13] As G.H. Jenkins notes, the common proverb, "as ragged as a Welsh curate", dates from the early eighteenth century, and became commonplace thereafter.[14] Bishop Copleston's comment of 1839 about one of his future curates described the man as possessing little refinement and manners, but his defects would not appear to be defects in the industrial areas where he would serve, for "[h]e is a Galilaean, about to preach in Galilee, where his speech will not betray him."[15] It was a tribute that might have done justice to George Eliot's Amos Barton, who was of the same breed.[16]

While the curate was seen as inferior by his superiors, ecclesiastically and socially, partly due to poverty, but in many cases to lack of education and breeding,[17] there were some who sympathised with his position and discovered many of them possessed a nobleness of character in spite of their circumstances. The anonymous writer of *A Letter from Snowdon* wrote about a curate, the only person in the parish capable of conversing with him. He was an elderly and venerable clergyman who wore his own natural grey locks, retained a ruddy bloom in his countenance, and had lived for forty years on a small estate he cultivated himself which, together with his curacy, produced £40 per annum, an income that exceeded his expenditure.[18] Mrs Morgan, in a published tour of Milford Haven in 1791, wrote that the ignorance, poverty and meanness of the Welsh clergy were frequent topics of conversation in England. She had heard that some fiddled at fairs and mended shoes to gain a better living. However, she found in that part of Pembrokeshire that the clergy were well-informed, well-bred and well-provided for, and on terms of familiarity with the "genteel people".[19] If Pembrokeshire was an excerption, there were plenty of other examples. Bingley, in his tour of north Wales, published in 1804, wrote of the curate of Llanberis, whose house was mean, his coat threadbare, his library meagre, and from its exterior one might suppose his cottage was the habitation of misery. Not so, for his smiles "would render even misery cheerful". With his stipend and a little farm, probably glebe land, his £40 enabled him not only to be perfectly contented and comfortable, but also permitted him to do "such good to his fellow creatures as his very slender circumstances would allow". As a result he was respected and beloved by all.[20]

Romilly, in his visits to Wales, met a Welsh curate at Brecon in 1827 and seemed surprised that he was sensible, and talked well about preaching and the classics.[21] Sir Watkin Williams Wyn, listening to as debate in the House of Commons during the early 1830s during which the Welsh clergy were disparaged, replied that he could say for himself that the curate of his parish, Thomas Thomas, later vicar of Caernarfon, was a gentleman and a scholar whom he was always proud to have at his table.[22] Such accounts were able to place the Welsh curate in perspective: though probably poor and lacking the educational and social advantages of the university-educated clergy, he was nevertheless one who was faithful to his calling and served as a true pastor to his flock. It was these men who kept alive the Welsh Church in the rural areas in which they served, and who were the mainstay of the circulating schools movement of Griffith Jones from the 1740s to the 1770s.[23] Sadly, Nonconformist hagiography, anxious to display Wales as a land of darkness before the Methodist revival, endeavoured to deny their work and minimise their spiritual contribution.

It may well be that these unfavourable accounts were occasioned by knowledge of those curates who misused their positions. Archdeacon Tenison's 1710 visitation of his archdeaconry of Carmarthen produced a number of rogue curates, including the curate of Kiffig and Marros who was dismissed as he had "got" a bastard and was notorious for clandestine marriages.[24] Some years earlier the curate of Manordeifi was reputed to be the father of several bastards and "a very ill-example … and a cause of great scoff" to the dissenters.[25] William Bulkeley wrote in 1737 of Robert Pugh, curate of Llanbadrig, describing him as one of the most immoral of men. Noting one of his sermons, during which "he very liberally threw about hell fire", he added that it was to the "great mirth" of several in his congregation who knew he could not believe what he said or "else he would not live in the manner he did".[26] Penry Bailey, curate of Llangamarch, Breconshire, was regarded by Edmund Jones as one who practised the magic arts, although he had the reputation of being a godly man.[27]

William Thomas, the mid-eighteenth century diarist of the vale of Glamorgan, noted a number of these dissolute curates. Amongst them was David Davis, a jolly man, who was ruined in debt by his drinking and carousing and had absconded to avoid his creditors.[28] Sadly, there were many like him. John Owen, curate of Llanllugan in the 1770s, was said to be addicted to drink, boarded in an alehouse for many years, and that no good could come of him.[29] William Jones, the schoolmaster of Llanbrynmair in 1791, once a decent, well-behaved clergyman, had formerly had several curacies but had lost them because of alcoholism, though in between them he had enlisted several times as a marine for a year or two.[30] Jack Roberts, curate of Llangwnnadl, was observed by Mrs Thrale, his patron, touring north Wales with Dr Johnson in 1774, as possessing a black eye, caused by fighting an excise man over a girl.[31] Thomas Williams, of the gentry family of Aberpergwm, was ordained in 1819 but had to pay £20 per annum maintenance for a bastard child. Thereafter, he resided on the family estate, and it was thought he had been forced into ordination by his family.[32] When William Evans went to inspect his new curacy at Gelligaer in 1850, he remembered going across to the local inn for a meal and seeing there a man he took to be a gamekeeper, dressed in a red velvet jacket and accompanied by dogs and a gun. He soon discovered it was his predecessor, whose interests lay more with outdoor pursuits than in parochial ministry.[33] Robert Roberts, schoolmaster at Amlwch in the 1850s, noted how the two curates of the parish, and their wives, lived in a state of petty war.[34] Such men, though a small minority of the whole, nevertheless brought the Church into disrepute and enabled Nonconformity to use such incidents as a means of self-defence.

THE UNLICENSED CURATES

It is difficult to know how many curates there were in the eighteenth and early nineteenth centuries. This is because many of them evaded the requirement that they should be licensed to their curacies by the diocesan bishop. This was often because of the expense of travelling to the cathedral or the bishop's palace, and the fees that had to be paid to the bishop's registrar. It took six years before one curate, Morgan David of Llangeinor, could afford the fees for his licence, which he obtained in 1724, while Roderick Lewis, curate of Trefeglwys from 1766-1802, was not licensed until June 1801.[35] As a result many curates remained unlicensed, a fact frequently noted in rural deans' reports and visitation returns. The rural deans' reports for the diocese of St Asaph in 1749 indicate that 8 of the 45 curates were unlicensed (17%) and in 1791 the figures were much higher, 31 out of 80 (38%).[36] Bishop Horsley of St Asaph in his

1806 visitation of his diocese discovered that over half of its 52 curates remained unlicensed.[37] As late as 1827 within the whole Church of England only 3,630 of the 4,250 curates were licensed, indicating that fourteen per cent were still unlicensed.[38]

This was a position the nineteenth century bishops endeavoured to rectify, though there had been many attempts beforehand.[39] Samuel Horsley regarded this requirement of licensing as a guard against the admission of improper persons, but in his charge to the clergy of Rochester of 1796 he expressed his concern that the provision of the 1713 Act, which regulated the stipends of curates serving for a non-resident incumbent as between £20 and £50 per annum, was now a hardship due to the increased cost of living. As such, he believed bishops connived at the non-licensing of curates to get around this restriction, even though the state had increased this sum to a maximum of £75. He would only allow a licence of non-residence if the resident curate was retained, approved and licensed by himself, and with a stipend that reflected the annual value of the benefice and which seemed adequate to himself. Those men who accepted a curacy without his licence would feel the weight of his displeasure.[40] He thus continued the policy he had adopted as bishop of St Davids when, in 1788, accepting the need to improve the position of curates, he insisted that each curate should exhibit his licence to his rural dean, well knowing that many were unlicensed. The rural deans were required to enter the details of the stipend, the value of the benefice, and the names of any other benefice served. As a result the unlicensed were required to appear before him, armed with a nomination from the incumbent of each of the parishes they served, a testimonial of their life and character signed by three clergymen, and their letters of orders. Twelve pages of his register indicated the result, with nearly one hundred licenses issued, and those curates who had been unlicensed and had a stipend of between £5 to £10 per annum, were licensed and their stipend increased to at least £15, though some were increased to £20 or £30.[41]

Horsley, in his 1806 Charge to the St Asaph Clergy, expressed deep concern at the number of unlicensed curates, which was a "a very high offence against ecclesiastical discipline; the continuance of which, I think it necessary to declare, I shall not endure". Without such licensing the door would be opened to the "greatest enormities" if the bishop was unable to make the proper enquiries into "the regularities of his orders, the godliness of his life and conduct, and his ability to instruct the people …" But even worse, an unlicensed curate was "a person unapproved by the bishop, and unknown to him, not bound by any oath of canonical obedience, nor by any declaration of conformity to the liturgy of the united Church of England and Ireland, nor otherwise amenable to the ecclesiastical jurisdiction but for offences of that enormity for which he would be amenable to the secular tribunals." Following his procedure in the diocese of St Davids by delegating the matter to his rural deans, he made it clear that no unlicensed curate would be allowed to officiate in his diocese, and no licence would be regarded as valid if it did not specify a stipend for the curate, though he allowed the incumbent and curate to come to an arrangement about the amount. Without a licence there was no more than a contract between incumbent and curate that could only be tried in the secular courts, but the bishop's licence would take any dispute wholly out of the hands of these courts, and this was the incumbent's best protection against "a litigious disposition in his curate".[42]

Bishop Sumner of Llandaff in his Charge of 1827 was a little more understanding. Though the practice of employing unlicensed curates "appears to have prevailed here to some extent", he accepted this was "with no intention of irregularity on the part of incumbents, or suspicion of the inconvenience which it occasions on the part of curates. Nevertheless, he would insist on this canonical requirement, for it was fitting that "for him who is responsible for the due administration of godly discipline, and the faithful delivery of God's word within his jurisdiction, to know who are the teachers of the people committed to his cure and charge." In every licence issued he had inserted a notice of his determination to refuse his signature to the testimonials of any curate who left his cure, or took the permanent duty of another, without his previous knowledge and sanction.[43] In the following year John Banks Jenkinson, bishop of St Davids, repeated this concern, and stated that any clergyman who offended or left his curacy without the mandatory three months notice to incumbent and bishop would have his licence revoked and he would refuse to countersign any testimonials presented to him, thus preventing him from obtaining any further position in the Church.[44] By the nineteenth century a licensed curate could only be dismissed after six months notice with the approval of the bishop.[45]

Though a curate needed to be licensed, the bishop could also withdraw that licence, leaving him without occupation, financial support and possibly a home for himself or his family. No other bishop would accept a man whose license had been withdrawn and without the bishop's counter signature on his testimonials, making it impossible for him to find a post in another diocese. Bishop Horsley, in his 1806 Charge, made this abundantly clear. Understanding that many incumbents had retained unlicensed curates for fear that, if licensed, they could not be easily removed, he endeavoured to check this fallacy. It was true, he stated, that a licensed curate could not be removed at the whim of an incumbent, who was unable "to dismiss his curate with as little ceremony as he might turn away his menial servant, at a month's warning or with a month's wages." Such a position would be a lowering of the clerical order in the eyes of the laity, while the relationship between incumbent and curate was not that of master and servant but of fellow labourers. A clergyman could not be removed from his cure save by the same authority that placed him in it, that is, the bishop, but "where a reasonable cause can be assigned for his removal, it cannot be supposed that the bishop would refuse to remove him." No bishop, he added, now granted a licence "but in such terms as to be revocable at any time by himself at pleasure." [46] A statute of 1838, The Pluralities Act, though allowing this right, regulated it, so that the curate was able to give "sufficient opportunity of showing reason to the contrary", and it allowed the curate to appeal to the archbishop which the latter was required to hear in person.[47]

Howell Howells, rector of Cellan in the diocese of St Davids wrote to his bishop in 1744 requesting that the licence of his curate, Mr Williams, be revoked. The terms of his appointment were that he should reside at Cellan and do the duty there, but to alternate with him, in his other parish, once a month. He had now removed from Cellan and was now serving in addition Lampeter and Bettws, "at a great distance", with the result he had neglected his duty at Cellan. As a consequence, on Christmas Day and some Sundays there was no service; a child had been buried without ceremony due to his carelessness; the time of the service had been altered for his convenience; he had neglected preaching and giving notice of celebrations of the Sacrament; refused to change with his rector according to their agreement which had been endorsed on his licence, and had told his angry parishioners, who had threatened to turn to dissent, he could do what he liked as he was secure with his licence. In all probability he soon discovered the case was otherwise.[48]

The Methodist clergy of the Church also found it difficult to obtain a licence from their bishops. Daniel Rowland, the revivalist, was ejected from his curacy of Llangeitho by Bishop Squire of St Davids in 1763, presumably by a letter that indicated his licence had been withdrawn, and the same bishop declined to licence him to the curacy of Nantcwmlle, in spite of the request to do so by its non-resident vicar, John Davies. Simon Lloyd, offered the curacy of Llanuwchllyn, was interviewed by his bishop, Horsley, then of St Asaph, who, having discovered he was a Methodist, declined to license him.[49] There are numerous other examples that could be cited.

Most examples come from the nineteenth century. Bishop Copleston of Llandaff, faced with the complaint of Isaacson, vicar of Newport, against his curate Beddington in 1831, withdrew his licence, and even though Beddington "begged hard" for itc continuance, he found his bishop "inexorable". Some years later, Copleston found it necessary to withdraw the licence of Jonathan Davis, curate of Cadoxton, knowing that as a result he would be a pauper, writing "how can such consequences he obviated if one regards the higher duty of serving the Church well."[50] Bishop Ollivant, in his memoranda books of the 1860s, notes the withdrawal of several licences. Lewis Roberts, in 1861, curate of Canton, was suspended for drunkenness, but as his bishop believed he had been led into temptation he was restored, though the promise was withdrawn as the result of another incident during a party given by Morgan Hughes, curate of St Mary's, Cardiff. Four years later John Alfred Morris, curate of Llanwynno, had his licence revoked having been found drunk on the GWR station at Mountain Ash on Christmas day.[51]

Bishop Lewis, Ollivant's successor, was more lenient, allowing curates to resign their posts rather than be deprived of their licences, though by now the archbishop's Lambeth List, circulated to the bishops, warning them of rogue clergy, was in being, and their names were probably placed upon it. In 1883 Llewelyn Jenkins resigned his curacy having been living in fornication, and having obtained a false certificate of marriage to deceive his vicar, and in the following year John James, curate of Ogmore Vale, resigned because of drunkenness.[52]

Robert Roberts, *Y Sgolor Mawr*, having been forced to resign a curacy in the diocese of St Asaph because of an alleged incident of drunkenness, emigrated to Australia, but on his return in 1870, in spite of testimonials from that continent, found that the bishop of Bangor refused to license him though he had been offered three curacies.[53] A newspaper reported in 1893 that Thomas Pugh, curate of Gwynfe, in Carmarthenshire, had been deprived having been drunk at the Holy Communion service on Easter day.[54] As Bishop Campbell of Bangor stated in his 1881 Charge (as noted before), the withdrawal of a curate's licence carried with it the "ruin of professional prospects."[55] And so it proved to be, although in some cases a bishop refused an incumbent's request that his curate's licence be withdrawn. This occurred in the case of the curate of Rhosymedre, R.D. Davies, when he refused to offer the chalice to R.W. Morgan, curate of Tregynon, who had become notorious for his attacks on Bishop Short. Though Davies' incumbent gave him the six months' notice of dismissal as required, and prohibited him from officiating in his church, Bishop Short said he alone had the right to withdraw a curate's licence, and that an admonition was sufficient, thus, in Morgan's words, making the vicar appear to be the offender.[56]

On an earlier occasion a Cardiganshire curate of unblemished life was summoned to meet his bishop at Abergwili in the 1820s and accused of being drunk. He replied he must have been drunk on buttermilk as he had never tasted anything stronger for years. Thankfully, the bishop realised it was a case of mistaken identity and apologised.[57]

Those who remained unlicensed were at the mercy of their incumbents and faced an even greater insecurity than their licensed brethren. An incumbent with an unlicensed curate could dismiss his curate with almost no notice at all and also avoid paying him the minimum stipend provided by the 1713 Act. In 1713, for example, the curate of St Issell, Pembrokeshire, Thomas Davies, serving as curate to two of the parishes of his near relation, Mr Griffiths, for £4 plus his diet, asked for a better bargain, and as a consequence was dismissed. His petition to the bishop claimed he had been pushed loose into the wide world, and he was likely to be reduced to great straits.[58]

The poet, Goronwy Owen, made deacon in 1746, received a title to care for the parish of Llanfair Mathafarn Eithaf, Anglesey, but three weeks later the bishop's chaplain wrote informing him that Bishop Hutton wished to oblige John Ellis of Caernarfon, a gentleman of great fortune, who wished to have a post in his diocese, and had offered him this curacy. Owen was forced to find another curacy at Oswestry instead.[59] Richard Edwards, curate of Trevethin, wrote a pamphlet in 1772 complaining he had been dismissed from his curacy for voting for Valentine Morris, who had unsuccessfully opposed John Morgan of Tredegar in the previous year during the general election, against the wishes of John Hanbury, his chief parishioner. Morris had been his patron for many years, so voting for him was a debt of honour. His vicar had told him to quit his curacy and added he could starve as he had given his vote against Hanbury. Presumably he had no licence, and his incumbent bowed to the pressure of his squire.[60]

Other cases arise in Copleston's correspondence. The bishop was warned not to license one Price of Neath, while William Thomas of Brithdir and "Little" Griffith of Eglwysilan remained unlicensed, probably quite deliberately, as all were regarded as infamous or inadequate. In another instance Edward Picton, vicar of St Bride's Major and Wick, dismissed his curate, Jonathan Evan Morgan, upon resigning his benefice in the favour of his nephew, Thomas Picton Jenkins. Morgan wrote to the bishop in a state of distress, but Copleston had to inform him there was no prospect of a curacy in his diocese and urged him to obtain one elsewhere, though he also asked Picton to do his best to assist him. This case of 1834 appears to be one where a new incumbent was able to dismiss his predecessor's curate.[61]

However, the dismissed curate was sometimes successful in winning his bishop's favour. This happened in the 1800s when John Collins, rector of Oxwich and Nicholaston and perpetual curate of Llanrhidian, decided to serve that curacy himself, and abruptly dismissed his curate Rogers, offering him a most inadequate amount of compensation. In the ensuing confrontation the parishioners sided with Rogers and the bishop took Rogers' side and eventually sequestrated the parish so he would remain as its curate.[62] One hopes too that Thomas Lewis, who described himself in 1814 as the oldest curate in the deanery of Brecon, aged 78, and having served for 53 years two neighbouring parishes of Llanfihangel Talyllyn and Llanywern, at stipends of £30 and £25 respectively, successfully appealed to Bishop Burgess against the incumbent of Llanywern's dismissal of him. It would deprive him of half his income, he pointed out in his defence, and he had to support himself, his blind son and his two children.[63]

CHAPTER TWO: THE PERPETUAL CURATE

A perpetual curate was a cleric nominated to a parish by a lay impropriator or ecclesiastical appropriator, who was paid a stipend by that nominator in lieu of the tithe, or the major part of it, which was reserved for the impropriator. These curacies had no glebe attached to them, with the result that their curates had no means of increasing their income. Because he had been nominated by his "patron" the perpetual curate was neither instituted nor inducted to that living as would be the case of a vicar or rector. This was a legacy of the Reformation, when parishes had been gifted to monastic houses and religious bodies as an act of piety. At the Reformation, when these monastic houses were dissolved, their estates, including their ecclesiastical revenues, fell into the hands of lay people or episcopal, capitular and collegiate bodies. A number of these curacies had been linked to ancient and large rural parishes and were described as chapelries, served by an assistant to an incumbent, though the majority of them were in the north of England. From 1714 onwards, provided the parish had been augmented by Queen Anne's Bounty (or at a later date by a diocesan society), its curate could not be arbitrarily dismissed and as such had a life interest in his curacy, and as a result was officially termed a perpetual curate. The Pluralities Act of 1838 made perpetual curacies into benefices, although the curates were still licensed rather than instituted and inducted, while the Clerical Subscriptions Act 1865 allowed perpetual curates to make the same oaths and declarations as were required of incumbents. Legislation of 1868 – The Incumbents Act - permitted the perpetual curate to be termed "vicar" if he was permitted to perform weddings and funerals, though if the full vicarial or rectorial tithes were restored to the parish he would be styled "vicar" or "rector" in any case. The number of perpetual curates was increased considerably by the various Church Building Acts of the early nineteenth century, by which, in order to protect the vested interests of the incumbent of the "mother" church, a new district carved out of it was regarded as a perpetual curacy rather than as a separate benefice. Yet it was not until the Pastoral Measure of 1868 that the Church of England abolished perpetual curacies, declaring them benefices pure and simple.[1]

One of the few advantages possessed by these perpetual curacies was that they did not count as a living under the laws of plurality. These laws did not permit more than two livings to be held by one person, except under certain circumstances, but as these curacies were not regarded as ecclesiastical benefices, they were exempt from this requirement. Consequently, a cleric could hold two livings and a number of perpetual curacies in both an official and an unofficial form of plurality.[2] *The Curate of Snowdon* also alleged another advantage, namely that as the tithes had fallen into lay hands, the rights of these perpetual curates could not be invaded without affecting the rights of their lay impropriators.[3] However, the disadvantages of these curacies were substantial, as we note later.

The number of these perpetual curacies was substantial, though it varied from diocese to diocese. Sir Thomas Phillips, quoting the first report of the Ecclesiastical Commission, 1831, stated that of the 132 livings in the diocese of St Asaph the tithes of 57 belonged to other bodies or persons than to the incumbent [43%], 30 to ecclesiastical bodies and 27 to lay owners. In Bangor, of 123 benefices, the figure was 52 [42%] (25/27), Llandaff with 192 benefices, 100 [52%] (53/47), and St Davids, with its 407 livings, 217 [53%] came into this category (91/126).[4] In total the tithe rent charges for the four dioceses amounted to £304,563, of which £81,639 went to ecclesiastical appropriators, and £67,457 to lay impropriators, leaving the parochial clergy with £155,456 [51%].[5] These figures were not dissimilar to those of the whole Church throughout England and Wales. In 1603, for example, 4,000 out of 9,284 livings were impropriate or appropriated.[6]

The diocese of St Davids was "riddled" with these impropriatorships. D.W. Howell notes that in Pembrokeshire nearly all the major landowners possessed them: the Philippses of Picton Castle had nine, the Campbells of Stackpole Court seven, the Owens of Orielton five, and the Barlows of Slebech four.[7] H.W. Clarke, estimating the amount of tithe income received by lay impropriators in 1890, offered a figure for this diocese of £22,211. In Radnorshire, where Clarke argued that the poverty of the clergy was notorious, £6,721 was taken from twenty-seven parishes by clerical appropriations.[8] Barker, in 1907, estimated that the total value of the commuted tithes for the archdeaconry of Carmarthen was £33,467, of which £7,505 went to ecclesiastical bodies as appropriators, £16,430 to lay impropriators, £161 to schools and colleges, and only £8,860 [26%] to the parochial incumbents for whose benefit it had been given in previous days. The archdeaconry of Cardigan was similar with a total value of commuted tithes of £26,681. Here the clerical appropriators received £3,488, lay £13,434, colleges £794, and the parochial clergy £8,961 [33%].[9] The Royal Commission of the 1900s clarified these figures. Of the total tithe rent charge for the diocese of St Davids, £111,159, lay impropriators claimed £35,909, ecclesiastical appropriators £28,479, leaving £46,778 for the parochial clergy [42%].[10] As Morgan points out, in the two counties of Cardiganshire and Carmarthenshire lay impropriators were actually in receipt of the majority of the tithes.[11]

Thomas Williams, archdeacon of Llandaff, writing in 1850 to his new bishop, pointed out that of the tithe rent charge in that diocese, amounting to £59,605, £25,624 was in other hands than those of the clergy for whom it was meant (including ecclesiastical corporations, colleges and schools), and of this £11,442 was in lay hands. The clergy were left with £33,981 of the total [57%], but this was an average, for in fifty-three parishes no tithe income was payable to the cleric, adding force to his remark that the provision originally intended for the remuneration of the clergy had been transferred to those who did no duties in return for this income and many had no connection with the diocese.[12] In fact, their only obligations were to pay the "historic" stipend to the curate in those benefices where no portion of the tithe had been reserved for them, and keep the chancel in repair.

The perpetual curate obtained none of this money, save for a fixed stipend paid out of the tithe income from the impropriator, though a few received the small tithes of a parish, as noted later. This, in most cases, was based on a settlement made during the Reformation, which might have been sufficient at that time, but which bore no resemblance to a living wage by the 1800s, and which ignored the fact that the clergy were now married rather than celibate. Glanmor Williams suggested that even by the seventeenth century clerical incomes were only a third to a half of their value in the previous century.[13] As Erasmus Saunders noted, few impropriators saw the necessity to increase this historic stipend, even though the value of their tithe income increased substantially over the years.[14] A.J. Johnes, in his celebrated but often inaccurate book on the causes of dissent in Wales, speculated that the grants made by Queen Anne's Bounty enabled these impropriators to ignore the just demands of their curates for an increase in their stipends.[15] Archbishop Tenison even suggested in 1713 that many impropriators chose the cheapest curates they could find, and it was these men, he suggested, who with their "poor and precarious maintenance", were "powerfully tempted to a kind of vagrant and dishonourable life".[16] In 1835 William Corbett considered the value of the tithe had increased twenty times since Tudor times, and castigated the impropriators for their meanness. In one example, that of Bentley, Hampshire, he considered that the value of the tithes at between £800 and £1000 should have allowed its perpetual curate, if paid according to the spirit of the Act, £560 rather than the £28 he actually received.[17] A parliamentary paper of 1832 indicated that, in spite of the work of Queen Anne's Bounty in augmenting parishes, there were still 1,631 curacies out of 4,254 with an income of less than £60 per annum.[18] While the diocese of Llandaff might have been an exception to the general trend, as John Guy suggested that impropriators generally paid between a quarter and a third of the tithe income to these perpetual curates,[19] the figures for other dioceses show a much greater variation. Even worse by some anomaly, probably due to vested interests, impropriators, being lay persons, were exempt from the various acts that empowered bishops to require a minimum stipend for curates.[20]

Many examples may be given. The Breconshire parish of Gwenddwr, in the hands of one Mr Macnamara in 1800, provided its perpetual curate with £6 per annum,[21] The Carmarthenshire parish of Egremont's impropriator, Rowleigh Mansel, paid £3 per annum to its curate, presumably the historic stipend. This is noted by Tenison in his visitation of the Archdeaconry in 1710, and was the same amount received by the curate of Llangynin, along with the £5 per annum paid to the curate of "Llanynio", although Tenison pointed out that Mr Rich, the impropriator, had an income of £60 to £70 from the tithes. Mr Bloodworth of Surrey allowed the curate of Eglwys Fair the sum of £4, and £5 or £6 to the curate of Llangain, though it was reputedly worth £80, while Mr Champion of the Inner Temple paid £10 to the "scandalous" Michael Jones, for serving the parishes of Llangynog and Llansteffan, though the value of the tithes was said to be £300. At Llanycrwys a salary of £4 to £5 was given, though the tithes had been let for £26 per annum by the impropriator. Mrs Cornwallis, impropriator of Talyllychau, with tithes valued at £100, gave the curate £8 per annum.[22] Erasmus Saunders recorded that while the tithes of Llanddewi Brefi, Cardiganshire, were valued at £400, the curate received only £8, and Sir John Philipps of Picton wrote in 1705 that the duke of Somerset had an income of £900 arising from the tithe income of six parishes, but the total sum he paid to his curates was £70.[23]

The curates of the parishes of Llanishen and Lisvane, near Cardiff, although later augmented by the Bounty, were still paid by the impropriators, the Lewis and Keymes families, the historic stipend of £10 each,[24] while the Mansel family, who were impropriators of Glyncorrwg in the same diocese, allowed its curate £10 per annum which he had been allowed "time out of mind".[25] The Revd. Charles Gore, living in London, was impropriator of four parishes, with a total of £350. These included Bedwellte and Mynyddislwyn, both centres of the industrial population, whose incumbents were hard pressed to find the resources required for their growing populations.[26] At Betws-y-Coed, in the diocese of Bangor, the historic stipend was a mere £3.13s.4d.,[27] and Beddgelert's curate in 1811 received £8 per annum from the Priestley family of Leeds though the tithes were valued at £80.[28] The curate of Llanuwchllyn, Merionethshire. had an income of £6 given him by the Price family, while the parish of Mold had two impropriators, the Knight family of Warwickshire who received in 1816 a tithe income of £1,691 and the Davies-Cooke family of Gwysaney received £487.[29] As late as 1851, as recorded in the returns of the religious census of that year, complaints were made against Sir R.W. Vaughan for his stewardship as impropriator of the parishes of Llanfachreth and Llanelltud, in Merionethshire. George Phillips, the perpetual curate of both, noted the tithes of the first were valued between £300-£400, out of which he received as his stipend the "paltry sum" of £7, "a sum at which sum his scullery maid would turn up her nose," and of the second, whose tithes were worth £80, he received "the munificent sum" of 4d. per day, "the average weekly allowance given to a pauper in this Union".[30]

The most extreme example of lay impropriator in Wales was that of the Chichester family of Devon. They had obtained the lay rectorships through Giles Chichester's marriage to a niece of Roger Palmer, earl of Castlemaine, the husband of Charles II's mistress Barbara Villiers, who had been granted the tithes by that king. As a result they possessed the tithe income of fifteen Cardiganshire parishes, including that of the large and scattered parish of Llanbadarn Fawr. By the nineteenth century this income amounted to £6,000 per annum, but only about a pittance of this sum was used for the historic stipends for the clergy who served these parishes. As E.G. Bowen remarks, the result was that the religious life of the area was impoverished, the clergy lived at subsistence level and the services they could offer were irregular and inadequate. In 1650 it was said that the cleric at Llanbadarn Fawr, with its population of 4,000 people, had a stipend paid at the will of the impropriator, and at late as 1851 it was stated that the vicar received £20 per annum from the impropriator, J.B. Brice Chichester, Esq. The tithes were then worth £2,404 per annum, while the perpetual curates of Llangwyryfon, Llangynfelyn and Llanychaearn received £6.13s.4d. each though the tithes of these parishes had been commuted at £225, £210 and £354 respectively.[31] At least this was better than the £6.13s.4d. recorded by Meyrick in 1810 for Llanafan, though he poignantly added that the family took the rest of the tithes for themselves.[32] Bishop Claggett (1732-43) remarked of this Chichester family that they had almost exhausted the whole revenue of the Church.[33] A comment made in the *Welshman* of 1843 stated that a much extravagated £1,500, out of the £6,000 income, given from the tithes to these perpetual curates had to support twenty-one parishes, and that the farmers who had to pay it looked upon it as a payment from which they obtained no return.[34] Writing of this family in 1910, J.T. Griffiths remarked about the parish of Llanilar that while the vicar had the small tithes commuted at £199, the great tithes of £300 were owned by a lady in Devonshire, who was never seen in the parish and no contribution was ever received from her.[35]

If it is assumed that the ecclesiastical bodies which possessed the appropriated livings were more generous than these lay impropriators with regard to their curates then, sadly, the evidence does not support this assumption. E.T. Davies suggested that the ecclesiastical income of the Principality, barring that which was retained by the parochial clergy or impropriated by laymen, went to four English bishops and the four Welsh bishops, six English deaneries and chapters and the four Welsh ones, and the quasi-ecclesiastical bodies such as Oxford University and several of its colleges, Eton College, Ruthin, Llanrwst and Abergavenny Schools, the Grocers' Company, and several local charitable bodies.[36]

At Llandyssul, the appropriator was Jesus College, Oxford, whose principal allowed the curate the sum of £26, plus the use of a small house and garden, from an estimated tithe income of £600.[37] In 1710 Tenison's visitation found that at Llanpumpsaint, Carmarthenshire, the curate's salary was £5 paid by the appropriators, the "Church of Windsor". The same body held the parish of Llanllawddog and paid the same salary. It is hardly surprising the same cleric held both livings.[38] In 1835 the archdeacon of Carmarthen obtained £439 as appropriator of the living of Llanfihangel Abercywyn, and £550 from the parish of Meidrim, but paid the cleric who served both a better sum than most, namely £116.[39] Edward Yardley in the 1730s noted the appropriations belonging to the chapter of St David's Cathedral. The curates of Jeffreyston and Uzmaston had £10 from the chapter, and the "old stipend" paid to the curate of St David's was £6.13s.4d.[40] At Llandudno, where the archdeacon of

Merioneth was appropriator, receiving an income of £32.10s., he allowed the poor curate a sum of £10, later increased to £20, but he, like so many others in his position, had to find his own accommodation. Llandegai in Anglesey belonged to the bishop of Bangor, who allowed his curate there the sum of £8 per annum, though it had been augmented by Queen Anne's Bounty, as had the parish of Llangystennin in the same county, whose appropriator was the bishop of St Asaph and who paid an annual stipend of £30.[41]

The dean and chapter of Gloucester were appropriators of some of the most important livings in the diocese of Llandaff, including Aberdare, the two churches of Cardiff, Llanblethian, Llantrisant, Llantwit Fardre, Llanwynno, Penmark, Roath and Ystradyfodwg, some of which were to be the centres of the nineteenth century industrial revolution.[42] The prebendary of Warthacwm in Llandaff Cathedral received the income of the parish of Llandevaud, but only paid its curate £4 a year in 1718, and was often in arrears. It was a similar tale with many other perpetual curacies attached to cathedral stalls.[43] The parish of Buttington near Welshpool had three quarters of its tithes owned by Christ Church, Oxford (who also partly owned the tithes of two other local parishes, Meifod and Guilsfield), and one quarter by the vicar of Welshpool. Their total value in 1800 was said to be £426, but the curate received £15 from the college and £2.10s. from the vicar.[44] The parishes of Holt and Iscoed were appropriated to the dean and chapter of Winchester. According to Johnes in 1832 the income from the tithes of these two parishes was £900, but the stipend paid from them to the perpetual curate of Holt was £20, and his colleague at Iscoed received nothing.[45]

Due to the difficulties of collecting the tithes in kind, and often because of endless disputes with the tithe payers, it was customary to lease out these tithes. Unfortunately, this was often done by allowing a lease for three lives, with the prospect of renewal at the end, and while the initial fine for the new lease or its renewal would benefit the office holder of the time, it would deprive his successors of the value of the estate, for the annual rent was generally far below the fair market value. The complaint was justified, therefore, that the ecclesiastical income of Wales which rightly belonged to its parochial clergy was not only denied them, but leased in such a way that its true income was lost even to those who possessed them. As Morgan comments, it was rare for any attempt to be made to charge an economic rent. Payment was made on the basis of a reserved rent, which if realistic before the increase in agricultural values, had become customary and bore no resemblance to the actual value of the tithes thereafter. In one instance, Lord Kensington in 1815 renewed his lease of the tithes of Llanwrda from the chapter of St Davids, but while the fine was now divided into seven parts, the term of the lease, paid annually, together with the reserved or historic rent, was only £56.8s.6d. per annum, for a property said to be worth £154.13s.4d. The chapter was receiving a third of its value due to accepting an historical rather than a current valuation.[46]

Half of the tithes of the Radnorshire parish of St Harmon's belonged to the prebendal stall of the same name in the collegiate church of Brecon. In 1830 the holder of this stall, William Alleyne Barker, leased his share to his son who then lived in Devon for three lives, the lease ending on the life of the last survivor. The lessee was required to keep that side of the chancel in good repair that belonged to the prebend, and to pay the annual sum of £14 to the prebendary of St Harmon, being one sixth of the rental, estimated in 1849 to be worth £90 per annum, although it had been commuted at £159. Barker's family thus were enriched at the expense of his successors in title, who had to wait for the lease to end before they could receive the stipend attached to their sinecure position.[47] Clarke estimated in 1890 that the chapter of Llandaff had a tithe income valued at £4,487. If the chapter collected the income itself it would receive, bar expenses, £3,814, rather than the £1,177 it received from the leases it had given, thus losing £2,637 per annum.[48]

At Old Radnor, admittedly in the diocese of Hereford, the dean and chapter of Worcester had leased its tithes to the Lewis family of Harpton Court for seventy years. It was estimated that the profits from the tithes over 30 years to 1841 amounted to £32,400 (shared between the two in some unknown division, even allowing for the stipend paid to the vicar of £70 per annum). When the parish endeavoured to restore these tithes to its rightful possessor, Sir Frankland Lewis stated that the dean and chapter regarded the parish as an estate and did not care "one straw" about the parish, while he and his family had enjoyed the tithes for seventy years and he intended to hand them over to his successor. If any attempt to restore these tithes took place then no property in the kingdom would be safe.[49] An even more glaring example was the new lease granted in 1824 to Sir John Owen of the prebend of Mathry in the cathedral. Bishop Burgess had granted this prebend to his brother-in-law, Thomas Stonehewer Bright in 1820, probably aware that the renewal of the lease of this so-called "golden prebend" was imminent. The tithes, commuted at £320 per annum were let on a reserved or historic rent of £26 per annum, but the fine for the new lease was £2,500. Bright had been rewarded at the expense of his successors in the prebend, who would probably be unable to obtain a renewal fine for several decades.[50]

These leases, and similar ones, could continue for centuries in one family through the use of renewals, which extended the lease for a further number of years. The prebend of Llanwrthwl, belonging to the collegiate church of Brecon, had been leased since 1559 to one family, represented in 1800 by the heir of Michael Cope Hopton, esq., of Pennant.[51] A chancellor of Llandaff Cathedral, who held the appropriated parish of Ystradowen in the right of his stall, had leased the tithes of that parish in 1632 to the Gwyn family of Llansannor at £30 per annum, with the stipulation they paid its curate £9 per annum. The lease and the historic stipend continued into the nineteenth century.[52] The tithe estate of Christ Church, Oxford, in Montgomeryshire, was leased for well over a century to the earls of Powis, but with both sides disputing its value, and with the college intimating that Lord Powis deliberately kept the tithe compositions low in order to retain his local popularity, it was not renewed in 1847, whereupon the celebrated Dr Pusey took over the lease.[53]

The parish of Kerry, then in the diocese of St Davids whose appropriator was its bishop, provides a case study of how these leases were renewed. The tithes were leased to Charles Walcot, Esq. in 1779 for a fine of £235 and an annual rent of £22 per annum. This was for a renewal of seven years, whereupon, in 1786, the same terms were repeated, while in 1800 the fine was set at £553 and in 1809 £2,873, reflecting, in part, the increased value of the land, but also indicating a more honest valuation of these tithes.[54]

John Griffith, vicar of Aberdare 1846-59, had a long and bitter controversy with the dean and chapter of Gloucester, which owned its rectorial and vicarial tithes in their right as impropriators of the parish of Llantrisant, whose vicar paid the incumbent of Aberdare the traditional stipend of £10. Their computed value was £352 per annum but from this they paid but £10 for a curate of a parish at the heart of the industrial revolution. They had leased the most valuable part of the glebe, which they owned, for a rental of £150 that Griffith claimed as building land and possessing mineral rights was worth an annual sum of ten times that amount. Furthermore, the chapter had almost neglected its responsibilities of maintaining the chancel of the small and inadequate parish church.[55]

These leases were ended when they came to their end of their term by the

Ecclesiastical Commission, which had taken over the estates of the episcopal and capitular bodies. Generally, the income, or a part of it, was restored to the parish, as an augmentation to the living. But this often involved a considerable dispute with the commissioners. In 1895 Basil M. Jones, the vicar of Llanfair near Ruthin made an appeal to the archbishop of Canterbury. His income, from one third of the tithes, was £291 in theory, but with the agricultural depression it had diminished to £150. The remaining two thirds belonged to the sinecure rector, the Revd. Percy Warren, who received £582. He had died the previous year, and his tithe rights were taken over by the Ecclesiastical Commission. As a result Jones was told by his bishop to apply to the commissioners for an augmentation to his stipend, for the payment of the curate's stipend, and for a grant to enlarge the parsonage house. The commissioners refused, only allowing a small grant to the local church school. Bishop, deanery chapter and conference, parish and vicar protested, especially as from his income Jones had to pay for help from neighbouring clergy to undertake the Church services in his parish. Surely, it was right, they argued, that these tithes belonged to the parish, and such a decision enabled the enemies of the Church to make capital of it. Eventually, after a long controversy, money was allocated for the improvement of the parsonage house and an annual grant of £60 allowed for a curate, but the living would not be augmented. One of the last letters on the file is from Basil M. Jones who said he was grateful for what they had given, but added there was great indignation in the village at their attitude.[56]

We need to note that there were other parishes where the incumbent had a share of the tithes, along with a lay or ecclesiastical impropriator. This was not infrequent, and meant that the other tithe owner had no need to pay a stipend to the incumbent, who was entitled to be termed vicar as he had a share of these tithes, generally the lesser vicarial ones. A report on the deaneries of Penllyn and Edeirnion in 1735 by the Revd. John Wynne notes the difficulties of the vicar of Gwyddelwern. The majority tithe holders were the vicar chorals of St Asaph Cathedral, who leased their share to "a knavish attorney", leaving a fifth share to the vicar which amounted to £40, if he could obtain it, as he had to gather it sheaf by sheaf throughout the parish. This was the vicarial tithe, the most difficult to collect, the smallest item in amount, and probably the subject of most disputes.[57]

At Gresford the tithes were divided between the vicar, who received £450, and the dean and chapter of Winchester, whose share amounted to £2,400 per annum, according to Johnes, who also stated that at Llanrhaeadr the rectorial tithes of £1,000 per annum were appropriated by an act of Parliament in 1680 to the repair of St Asaph Cathedral and the maintenance of its choir, while the vicar's share was £450.[58] Two thirds of the tithes of the Cardiganshire parishes of Llanwnnen and Lampeter went to the see of St Davids, and a third to their incumbents.[59] The parishes of Llanfihangel with Talyllyn in Merionethshire were appropriated to the bishopric of Lichfield, though the vicar received £40 as his share of the tithes.[60] Yardley notes in 1736 that the incumbents of the parishes of Llanhowel, Llandingat, Lywel, St Dogmaels and St Issell all had part of the tithes, generally the small tithes, and some had the use of the glebe, but the major tithes went elsewhere.[61] Griffith Jones, vicar of Aberdaron, 1785-1810, summed up the position in this way. He suggested to a visitor to imagine a stipend divided into eight parts. Four parts went to St John's College, Cambridge, three to the local squire, and the rest was his.[62]

We may conclude this section with the comment of W.T. Morgan that "[i]t was a monstrous abuse that tithes, which properly belonged to parish priests for the provision of means of grace in poor Welsh parishes, should be diverted from their original intention of the endowment to provide incomes for a large number of nepotists, pluralists, English prelates and wealthy ecclesiastical corporations".[63] Sadly, that is not the end of the story, for some of these impropriators abused their trust and endeavoured to rob the parishes "entrusted" to them.

THE RESPONSIBILITIES AND MALPRACTICES OF IMPROPRIATORS

A letter of 1610 written by Richard Parry, bishop of St Asaph, to Robert Cecil, expressed his concern that laymen were endeavouring to annex the vicarage of Henllan to its rectory, thus making it an impropriate curacy for their own advantage. There were other examples of the same practice too. Possibly, this is the origin of some of these perpetual curacies.[64] Tenison in his visitation discovered further malpractices. At Llanfair-y-Bryn one third of the tithes belonged to the minister, but the steward of Lady Campbell received it instead, while at Meidrim the lessee of the great tithes, Mrs Powel of Carmarthen, had taken possession of the parsonage house, claiming it as her prerequisite, though it had been built by a previous incumbent. At "Llacharn" the impropriator who received £250 per annum had forced the vicar, who had a small part of the tithe corn valued at £25 per annum but whose parish had been augmented by £65 a year, to pay £20 to a curate for serving Kiffig and Marros, whereas it was the impropriator's responsibility to do so.⁶⁵ A petition of 1703 to the bishop of St Asaph from the parishes of Llandysilio-yn-Ial, Bryneglwys and Llansanffraid, indicated that some new lay impropriators, including Sir John Wynne, had declined to supply the parishes with curates, as was their responsibility, and yet they were still required to pay the tithes. As a result there were neither services nor the occasional offices.⁶⁶ The same happened in 1672 at Egremont, Carmarthenshire, where the impropriator and the lessee were presented for refusing and neglecting to keep a curate. No prayers had been read for three months.⁶⁷

As impropriators were lay rectors, and had a responsibility for the repair of the chancel, they often insisted on some particular rights regarding seating or, in one case, the right to some pews therein or in a side aisle that they could rent out. This happened in St Mary's Church, Swansea, where the lay impropriator was Calvert Jones, a clergyman, who became known as a pioneer photographer. He claimed the north aisle as his own possession, and forced a monument placed there in 1869 to be removed. He rented the pews in this aisle for three times more than the churchwardens charged for equivalent seats in the south aisle. The vicar, Edward Squire, pointed out that though he derived an income of 60 guineas per year at least, and over the years of Squire's incumbency he must have received over 1,000 guineas from this source alone. Jones had made no contribution to the life and upkeep of the Church, though without these services his "rights" would be utterly worthless.⁶⁸ A few years earlier Miss Griffin, the lay rector of Dixton, near Monmouth, wanting more ventilation in the chancel where she sat and insisted on the chancel door being open during services. The vicar, fearful of draughts, put his own lock on this door. Though she went to court it was decided she had no right to the possession of the chancel as she had claimed, but only the right to one pew by prescription therein, as well as the duty of repair.⁶⁹ As Best rightly remarked, "many were the interferences to which an incumbent might be subjected by an uncongenial impropriator or his lessee, by virtue of the other rectorial rights accompanying the title to the great tithes," ⁷⁰ even though we might add most of these rights were assumed.

Yet it must be added, some impropriators were generous to their parishes. Some took great care over the appointments they made, as did Thomas Jones of Llandeilo in Radnorshire, the lessee of the tithes. In 1717 he wrote that it was his care as well as his duty to provide for the parishioners a curate who would "discharge himself to their satisfaction".⁷¹ Sir John Philipps of Picton, who died in 1737, gave generously towards the upkeep of those livings of which he was impropriator, including Haverfordwest and Pembroke, and insisted on the incumbents performing their duties.[72] Henry Vaughan of Cilcennin had a clause inserted into the lease of the rectory of Lledrod that the lessee should provide a literate man to take services in the parish church each Sunday.[73]

Meyrick records a "remarkable" wonder, namely that the vicar of Llanarth held the whole of the tithes, as the last impropriator had left his share to be annexed to the vicarage.[74] At Llanuwchllyn, Merionethshire, the impropriator William Price augmented the living in 1725 to £20 in his will on condition that the curate should reside in the parish. The rural dean, John Wynne, wrote in his 1730 report about this parish that had the impropriator not been encumbered with the debts of his uncle, he would have helped restore the church and make amends for the scandalous behaviour of his ancestors, though he had presented the church with "a handsome piece of plate" and had given £4 each year in charity to the poor. He had paid an annuity of £12 to the widow of a former incumbent, and directed that after her death it should be given to its curate.[75]

COMMENT AND CONCERN

It is hardly surprising that these impropriations led to much criticism and concern. The episcopal attempts to regulate them were almost ineffectual, though they tried their best to ensure that the men nominated by the impropriators were regularly ordained and competent.[76] Archbishop Laud endeavoured to try and reform the system, and much of the enmity against him, which led to his execution in 1645, was due to his attempt to restore to the Church its lost inheritance. In his report on the state of St David's Diocese of 1634 he wrote that its bishop complained grievously that the impropriators in those parts had pulled down chancels and suffered others to fall, with the result that churches were left open and cold so that people in those mountainous parts had to endure a good deal of hardship as they assembled for worship.[77] Bishop Bull of St Davids, who died in 1710, felt that Laud's attempt to end this "scandal of the reformation" should have been accomplished in 1660 at the Restoration, but, following Sir Henry Spelman, suggested that those impropriators who continued to commit sacrilege against the Church had God's curse against them, and would reap the rewards of their sin. He had applied to a number of the impropriators of the parishes in his diocese asking them to advance the salaries they paid according to the population of the parish and the value of their profits, but he had had little success. He believed, probably incorrectly, that as bishop he had the power to determine the stipends of curates, whether they were employed by a pluralist or an impropriator. His biographer suggested that had he lived he would have carried this further.[78] Bishop Warren of Bangor, replying to a petition from the parish of Pennal in 1799 asking him to provide a curate, wrote that because of the poor emoluments of the parish it was difficult to do so, and though Queen Anne's Bounty had recently augmented the parish it would take time to be effected. His expectation of an augmentation when the lease of the impropriation of Towyn was renewed had come to nothing, but he hoped that the impropriator would make a proper augmentation when he became aware of the disorder the church there had fallen into for want of its services being regularly performed.[79] Bishop Watson of Llandaff in his *Charge* of 1809 argued that lay and corporate impropriators should come forward out of a sense of duty and augment their parishes.[80] It is interesting he neglected to mention those who held ecclesiastical appropriations.

The meagre stipends allowed to these perpetual curates gave rise to considerable comment if not scandal. Christopher Hill in an apt phrase suggested they got the "leavings" not the "livings",[81] while Evan Evans wrote in 1767 that "the hand of sacrilege pressed sore on this county at the Reformation".[82] A writer describing himself as "A Pauper Clergyman" in 1857, described "a poor clergyman ... starving and shivering" but knowing that his poverty contributed to the living of a bishop. In addition, his parishioners, had had the tithes "wrung" out of them "by the agent of a stranger bishop, whose gracious countenance [had] never beamed upon them".[83]

Erasmus Saunders was eloquent in his criticisms. The allowance of a common sailor or a letter carrier in the penny post exceeded the stipends of most curates, he alleged, and asked how could such men give charity and hospitality, as their vows required, when they were in need of it themselves.[84] Jonathan Williams, writing about Old Radnor, stated that the small amount allowed its curate was "insufficient to maintain him in that degree of rank and estimation which he ought to hold in society", with the result that in this and other instances the ministerial office was disgraced, the stability of the Church establishment shaken, and an open door provided for schism and separatism.[85] At a later date the perpetual curate of Tregynon, R.W. Morgan, asked why the friends of the Church, who called themselves reformers, had failed to advocate "the claims of that ill-paid, ill-used, but laborious section of the clergy, the perpetual curates under lay rectors? Ecclesiastical rectors are obliged to pay their curates in a certain proportion to the value of the living; what reason can be assigned why lay rectors should not be obliged to do the same?"[86] He knew the answer well enough. Impropriatorships were seen as private property and thus untouchable.

An editorial in the *Welshman* argued much the same. Noting that in those areas disturbed by Rebecca in the 1840s were often of parishes where a substantial income was derived by an impropriator from the tithes, who gave a disproportionate sum to its curate, as at Llangendeirne with its £1,000 tithe income and £13.13s.4d. paid to its curate, asked how could such a person, a member of the Church, pocket such a large amount of money meant for the cure of souls, and grudgingly return to its curate a small part of it, and yet expect a blessing upon the remainder.[87] An anonymous writer in the *Edinburgh Review* of 1850, possibly Rowland Williams, referring in part to a visitation charge by Archdeacon Williams of Llandaff, asked why the impropriators, who had gained so much from the increased value of the tithe and from land enclosures, had not reflected this increase in the stipends they paid, bearing in mind that they had no arduous duties to undertake for this income.[88]

Many of the wealthier parishes should have supported an able and well-educated ministry, but as their income went elsewhere, the clergy who were appointed were generally ill-educated and pathetically poor.[89] Furthermore, those who paid the tithes of these parishes knew they were meant for the maintenance of a ministry, not the luxurious living of the privileged, a point made in a petition of 1703 by the parishioners of several Merionethshire parishes, and by Erasmus Saunders a little later, when he remarked that those people who struggled to pay their tithes were deprived of those benefits which that payment was intended to support.[90] At Nevern, Pembrokeshire, the lay impropriator was castigated in the 1851 religious census as contributing nothing for the spiritual wants of the parish save for a few bottles of wine at Easter.[91] The only remarkable thing about this remark is that it was publicly stated. This must have been the common experience of most impropriate parishes. Similarly, Christ Church, Oxford, was heavily criticised in the 1900s for not even offering a scholarship to the town of Welshpool in return for the large annual income they drew from its tithes.[92]

Such small salaries caused the curates to become pluralists, holding several cures at the same time, a situation we note later with respect to the stipendiary curates. Many held perpetual curacies with their other livings, with the result that many cared for four and more parishes. Erasmus Saunders thus noted that the stipend was so poor that the poor curate had to serve three or four churches for £10 to £12 per year, the parishes being almost as many miles from each other. As he wrote:

> Forc'd they are … to submit to any Terms; that is, they must Starve, or even be contented with the meanest Salaries, and yet Drudge and Labour for it as far as they are able; and having so little Time, and so many places to attend upon, how precipitately, and as if out of breath are they oblig'd to read the Prayers, or to shorten and abridge them? And what time have they or their Congregation to compose themselves for their Devotion, while thus forc'd to a kind of perpetual Motion, and like hasty Itinerants to hurry about from Place to Place? There is no time fix'd for going to Church, so it be on *Sunday*, so that the poor Man must begin at any time with as many as are at hand, sooner or later, so he can perform his Round. He then abruptly huddles over as many Prayers as may be in half an Hour's time, and then returns again to his Road fasting (for how earnestly soever his Appetite may call for it, it's seldom that he has time for, or that the Impropriators Farmer can afford to give him Dinner) till he has dispatch's his Circuit, and that Weariness or Darkness obliges him to Rest ….[93]

Amongst such men was John Rowland, brother of the revivalist Daniel Rowland, who in 1733 was rector of Llangeitho, vicar of Nantcwnlle, and perpetual curate of Llanbadarn Odwyn and Llanddewi Brefi. Each Sunday he would ride sixteen miles on horseback to take the four Sunday services required of him.[94] Presenting a petition in the House of Commons from the inhabitants of Chester, during 1833, Lord Robert Grosvenor spoke about the injustice of the curates of the southern dioceses whose stipends, derived from the episcopal appropriators in particular, were so poor they were forced to act as schoolmaster, rent farms for their subsistence or take a plurality of parishes, sometimes up to four in number.[95] Bishop Burgess, in his 1813 Visitation Charge, considered this "accumulation of duties, an evil, than which nothing has been more injurious to the credit of the established Church".[96]

As a result many claimed that parishioners were drawn to dissent, as suggested by the hints of Bishop Bull of St Davids in the 1700s and Archdeacon Tenison in 1710,[97] and more openly by that disappointed cleric, Evan Evans (Ieuan Fardd: died

1788). In his *Grievances of the Principality of Wales* Evans wrote that as the tithes of a parish, once appointed for the instruction of people in the true doctrine of Christ and the relief of the poor, had been transferred into lay hands, "so that the poor are deprived of their relief, the parishioners seduced from the true Religion of Christ embrace Superstition and old Women's tales, and rush headlong into all kinds of idolatrous Worship. For if the salary is taken away, the doctrine is taken away likewise, and by taking away the true doctrine ignorance is introduced".[98]

AUGUMENTATIONS AND PROPOSALS FOR RELIEF

It has been noted already that many of these former curacies became officially perpetual curacies when they were endowed by Queen Anne's Bounty. This charity commenced in 1704 and augmented livings under the value of £10 with a sum of £200 that had to be invested in land. This was by lot, and depended on the amount of monies available from its first fruit and tenths income. Alternatively, a benefactor could present an equivalent gift of money or of tithe income, and this would be met by a matching grant. These benefactions had first priority. It was not until 1715 that Parliament permitted these curacies to be included in these augmentations. The Act authorising this made clear that as these chapelries and curacies were not corporations with a legal succession, an impropriator could not only withdraw the stipend but also refuse to appoint a curate. The Act required that all the curacies in receipt of a Bounty grant would be termed perpetual curacies, their ministers would be in law "bodies politic and corporate" with an exclusive care of souls within their district; the succession would be permanent, and ministers of "mother churches" to which these chapelries were attached should not take this opportunity of reducing the stipends they paid to their curates. In 1736 a list prepared for the Bounty for the whole Church indicated that there were 5,638 livings under the value of £50, of which 1,678 were impropriations.[99]

Bishop Richard Smallbrooke was probably not alone in his hope that many impropriators would take advantage of this Act, by giving up their impropriations and allowing the tithe income to be restored to the parishes, and thus "gradually relieve many of those that suffer".[100] Sadly, it appears that few did so, as John Guy makes clear for the diocese of Llandaff, where some of its curacies, such as Llandevaud, had to wait until the 1770s to be augmented by lot, when its income was increased to £10, the wages of an agricultural labourer. Guy adds that the creation of these perpetual curacies caused more problems than they solved. Hitherto, the incumbent of a parish in which a chapelry lay could act as its curate, but he was not allowed to benefit from this augmentation and in theory had to appoint a curate for that chapelry, who would be dependent on the augmentation provided by the Bounty. In practice it is probable that a neighbouring curate took over the chapelry as an additional curacy. This procedure therefore added to the number of benefices unable to support a resident minister rather than reduced it as was the original intention and, in Guy's words, gave "further opportunity for the exploitation of an already far from satisfactory system".[101]

Yet not all applications for a Bounty augmentation were successful. Archdeacon John Jones, the appropriator of Llandudno, whose curate received £10 per annum, asked the Bounty to offer a return grant in exchange for a benefaction he had offered in 1818. It insisted on a sum of £15 per annum to ensure a capital grant of £200, but he could not afford this. The reason, he explained, was that he had allowed a new life to be inserted into the lease for a fine of £200 rather than the £400 it should have been with the condition that the lessee increased the traditional stipend from that £10 to £20. He believed this was a good bargain for the curate as the costs of investing in land and its maintenance could be substantial. His own income from the lease was £20. Disappointed, the archdeacon felt his measure was for the welfare of the Church and the comfort of the poor clergy, but rules were rules.[102]

In addition there were many calls for the secularization of these impropriate tithes. Appropriated tithes, belonging to bishops, cathedrals and colleges, could not be alienated from these bodies and returned to the original benefice without statutory authority. Acts of 1677 and 1831, however, facilitated this augmentation should these bodies wish it, which few did as their endowments were partly dependent on this source of income. But while there was no restriction on the part of lay impropriators to return their tithe income to the original owners, there was little inclination on their part to perform such a service to the Church.[103]

Equally, there were calls for parliamentary legislation to require the return of this money to the Church. The early Stuart parliament had endeavoured to regulate these concerns, without success.[104] Sir John Philipps had called for an act to buy in these impropriations in 1705,[105] while John Wade, in his infamous *Black Book* argued for this, though allowing for life interests to be commuted. He noted that in 1827 of 4,254 curates, 1,639 had less than £60 per annum (his figures would have included stipendiary curates), even though most of the work of the Church was done by

215

them.[106] William Corbett, by contrast, claimed that as the Reformation Parliament had enforced the payment of tithes and allowed lay people to possess them, it had sufficient power to end these impropriations.[107] But the eminent lawyer, Sir William Scott, speaking in 1802, said that the matter had become settled law, and the impropriations, "though originally perhaps mere trusts", were now lay fees. Such a ruling did not prevent many of the early Victorians requesting legislation to ensure that this tithe income should be restored to the Church, amongst them Bishop Phillipotts of Exeter, only to meet the assertion, that they were private property and their confiscation would "vitiate the constitution and subvert the establishment of the church". Others pressed the case that these impropriations were a kind of trust property, and could be interfered with in order to ensure that the purposes of the trust were being fulfilled.[108] However, nothing was accomplished, though the first breach in the case for the impropriators came with the disestablishment of the Welsh Church through the Welsh Church Act of 1914, though this only affected the tithes held by ecclesiastical bodies, including parishes, in Wales, whose tithes were confiscated and the income arising from them placed into funds for the social and educational benefit of the Principality. The tithes held by lay impropriators and ecclesiastical bodies in England remained intact until they were abolished, with compensation being paid to their owners, in 1936.[109]

CHAPTER THREE: THE STIPENDIARY CURATE: THE ISSUE OF NON-RESIDENCE

A stipendiary curate was one who cared for a parish in the absence of its incumbent, who generally, but not always, was a pluralist and non-resident and served his other parish or parishes. To all intents and purposes, on a daily basis, the stipendiary curate was the *de facto* incumbent, but his position was insecure as he could be removed if his incumbent chose to return or there was a change of incumbents.[1]

We need first to examine the position of non-residency, as the effect of this necessitated these stipendiary curates.

Non-residency meant, in strict legal terms, an incumbent not residing in his parsonage house, if there was one, though this required a licence of non-residence from the diocesan bishop. (If there was not, he was able to live within the boundaries of his parish without being classified as a non-resident). In reality, it meant an incumbent not living within his parish, but outside it, and this needed a licence as well.[2] Licences were issued for these reasons, provided they were justified, because of the illness of the incumbent or his family; the unfitness or lack of a parsonage house; or a poor income necessitating an additional income through another curacy or parish where there was an adequate residence. A number of clerics were exempted from the need for a licence, these being those performing duties in cathedrals, schools, universities, or as chaplains to the royal and noble families, but their number was limited. Without such a licence or a valid exemption the incumbent was subject to ecclesiastical and civil liabilities and could even be deprived of his living.[3]

In reality, there was a fair amount of what might be termed technical non-residence, where a cleric resided within or in a neighbouring parish but not in its parsonage house, should it possess one.[4] Often this was caused by the absence or the unsuitability of the parsonage house, John Wade considering this to be a common pretext for obtaining a licence of non-residence.[5] In south Wales it was hardly a pretext, as in the diocese of Llandaff in 1827 Bishop Sumner observed that out of 234 parishes 134 (57%) had no parsonage house, and those that possessed one were often inadequate, being small farm houses or even mere cottages. The same was true of the diocese of St Davids.⁶ There were other clerics who used the absence of a parsonage house to accept other responsibilities elsewhere, and so became pluralists and absentees. William Lucas Collins, rector of Cheriton, Gower, 1815-67, had a licence of non-residence due to this reason, but from 1853 served a number of curacies in Northamptonshire.⁷ Another reason cited was that the parish was too small to justify a resident minister and so was served from an adjacent parish,⁸ or that for various reasons, generally poverty, a neighbouring resident incumbent or curate served the parish in order to make up his income.⁹ Bishop Sumner of Llandaff (1826-8) thus observed, "it is true, that in many instances the population is so small, that the personal superintendence of two contiguous cures may, without impropriety, be undertaken by one individual, the parishes being considered, for all practical purposes, as one ecclesiastical district".¹⁰ This was true of many Carmarthenshire parishes in 1710, as it was equally true of the diocese of St Davids, mainly due to the poverty of the livings, but Nigel Yates argued there was little evidence of pastoral neglect in these parishes. He notes that Thomas Beynon, later archdeacon of Cardigan, personally served the neighbouring parishes of Llandyfeisant, Llanfihangel Aberbythych and Llanfihangel Cilfargen in the 1770s and later added Penboyr to this grouping, where he kept a curate.¹¹ The many complaints made by Lewis Evans and others in the 1830s that many of the Anglesey clergy cared for two, three or even four churches, failed to take into account that these parishes were small and most were adjacent to one another and provided natural groupings.¹² Bishop Bethell of Bangor noted in his Charge of 1834 there were four non-resident incumbents who lacked parsonage houses in their benefices, but who resided in neighbouring parishes, and yet performed all their parochial duties.¹³

There were those who made use of this position to bring actions against particular clergymen, when their offence was more technical than actual. At Llannon, Carmarthenshire, the minister was presented in a visitation return for non-residency in 1705, but his salary being so small it was not known how to redress the situation. In all probability he lived on a neighbouring cure.¹⁴ An even more disturbing case was that of John Williams, rector of Cheriton, in 1776. His parsonage house was in disrepair and he thus rented the Great House, Reynoldson, in a parish he held in plurality with his own. A neighbour, George Bevan, brought a vexatious action at law against him on the grounds that he was non-resident in the parsonage house. Lord Kenyon, consulted, argued that while the complaint was well founded on the strict interpretation of the law, he would have the sympathy of the court as the house he resided in was within one hundred yards of his other church, that he did the whole duty of the parish himself, and was well hospitable, charitable and respected. Thankfully, Bevan, probably apprised of this opinion, appears to have dropped his suit.[15] However, the 1803 Clergy Residence Act which regulated non-residence was enacted not so much as to enforce residence as to prevent clergy being persecuted by informers. It followed the conviction of a Durham incumbent who had taken lodgings in his parish while the parsonage house was being rebuilt. Lord Eldon recalled a case against the incumbent of Bow Church in London, William Van Mildert, later bishop of Llandaff and Durham, who lived outside his parish but performed its duty every day of the week. He and others were prosecuted by a group of lawyers. Van Mildert's case was heard at Guildhall by Lord Chief Justice Eldon, who was forced to fine him £110, but expressed the hope that the legislature would intervene and take these matters out of the hands of a common informer. Eldon wrote in his commonplace book that as the law stood, this excellent person was subject to the same penalties as a most negligent blameable incumbent. Two temporary Suspending Acts for the penalties for non-residence were passed, but Bishop Horsley deemed these insufficient and requested a revision of the law.[16]

The eventual Clergy Residences Act of 1803 required all spiritual persons to reside on their benefice, but if any absented themselves from that duty without a licence from the bishop, or had some special exemption, penalties were imposed varying from one third to three fourths of the annual value of that benefice, recoverable by action of debt by any person suing for the same. One Wright took advantage of this act. He had a clear advantage as having been secretary to four English bishops and was said to have been "basely treated" by them, and with the knowledge he had gained he commenced 200 different actions in 1811. He stood to gain £80,000, but regarded this as compensation for what he believed he had lost to episcopal perfidy. These clergy, and others who were in the same position, supported by their bishops, managed to bring in a parliamentary act to stay all legal proceedings against the clergy on account of the penalties they had incurred under this 1803 act.[17]

Wade considered that the majority of clerics who were non-resident were so because they resided on another benefice.[18] Some were so because of poverty. Reginald Heber, later bishop of Calcutta, wrote an unpublished defence of the Church against Wade's attacks. In it he considered that there were 1,566 benefices under the value of £80 within the whole Church of England, 15 per cent of the whole, and as these could not afford a maintenance for a clergymen, they had to be held with another parish.[19] One example was that of Walter Griffiths, vicar of Glyncorrwg 1850-62, which had an income of £100, who was also vicar of Resolven, whose income was £53. Even then he needed to provide a curate at the former parish. Resolven on its own could never have supported a cleric and his family unless he had a private income.[20]

Poverty was not always the case, however. Erasmus Saunders makes the surprising observation that the richer livings in the diocese of St Davids were no better served than the impropriate curacies, as their incumbents held "it with a Curates place" in London or with another benefice, and so left their Welsh livings to be cared for by inadequately paid curates.[21]

NON-RESIDENTS AND PLURALISTS

Non-residence was the term used for clergymen who left their parish in the care of an assistant and lived elsewhere, generally on another parish they held in plurality with the first.[22] The care of the parish might be left to a resident curate if the income allowed, or to another resident incumbent or curate in a neighbouring parish, utilising the time honoured method of working by deputy, a common matter amongst office holders during this time. Unfortunately, many made no distinction between actual or technical non-residence, nor did the statistics gathered by many reformers or parliamentary returns.

A few examples of this practice may be offered. Edward Davies, a Methodist cleric who was vicar of Coychurch in the Vale of Glamorgan 1768-1812 resided on his Bristol living, as his inability to speak Welsh was a liability in his Welsh parish.[23] Bishop Barrington's diocesan book for Llandaff, 1771, records many non-resident and pluralist clergy, and John Guy's study of it reveals that those who held the more valuable livings tended to be pluralists, not only of parishes reasonably adjacent to one another, but also of those at a considerable distance. If John Bassett held the livings of St Nicholas, Peterston-super-Ely and Bonvilston, reasonably close together, Robert Rickards held the substantial living of Llantrisant but resided on his other living in Gloucester. Gervase Powell, rector of Merthyr Tydfil, held the Breconshire parish of Llanfigan but was a non-resident on both; William Willis, rector of Gileston, held two Somersetshire parishes in addition, and Sir Combe Miller, Bart. was not only rector of Llansannor but also dean of Chichester.[24] John Webb, vicar of Cardiff 1822-64, an ever increasing industrial and port town, resided on his other living of Tretire, near Ross, leaving his substantial charge to curates, amongst them Thomas Stacey, the non-resident rector of Gelligaer.[25] George Foxton, rector of Newtown, Montgomeryshire, in the 1830s, was non-resident, his parish being served by a curate, as he possessed other livings in Gloucestershire and Leicestershire.[26] A rector of Halkyn, Hugh Williams 1799-1806, lived at Conwy, thirty miles away, though his predecessor, Thomas Clough, also a non-resident, lived at Denbigh but came to do duty eight times each year.[27] Daniel Nihill, vicar of Forden, Montgomeryshire, 1827-44, deprived of a parsonage house, took leave of his parish and acted as chaplain to Millbank Prison, London.[28] There was a precedent in that a former rector of Coety, Glamorgan, John Wilkinson, who also held parishes in Kent, was chaplain of the Savoy. He was sentenced to transportation for his involvement in clandestine marriages at that place in 1755.[29]

Some clerics, though they held benefices in English dioceses, remained in their native land as curates. One of these men was James Evans, whose death was noted by William Thomas in his diary entry of 1770. He was curate of St Fagans, Glamorgan, where he was buried, but rector of two English churches, who died of a "long, lingering melancholy", unmarried, and "not very much beloved with any sort".[30]

Taking these matters into consideration, it is not surprising that the number of non-residents was substantial. The deanery of Elwell, Radnorshire, in 1733 had 22 parishes and chapelries served by 15 incumbents and chapelry curates and four stipendiary curates, all of whom were technically non-resident in adjacent parishes, as were seven of the incumbents. Five incumbents were non-resident.[31] Figures for the diocese of Llandaff, extracted by Guy from the visitation returns of 1763, indicate that from the 145 returns only 37 parishes had a resident incumbent, and while four had a legal exemption, five were schoolmasters, three were naval or army chaplains, three claimed ill-health though another two in the same position resided on their benefices, five felt unable to minister to their parishioners in Welsh, while the others had no parsonage house or one inadequate for that purpose. He notes, however, how many incumbents endeavoured to reside on or near their parish while others employed resident curates, so that the number of permanent absentees from the diocese was comparatively small. Once again, the position was more of technical than actual non-residence, or rather keeping to the spirit rather than the letter of the law.[32] The rural deans' reports for the diocese of St Asaph of 1791 reveal many other instances. In the Montgomeryshire deanery of Cedewain eleven parishes are mentioned of whom at least four were non-resident incumbents. The incumbent of Aberhavesb lived ten miles away at Llanidloes; that of Bettws at Bridgenorth; that of Llanmerewig at Harborough, Leicestershire, with the incumbent of Llanwyddelan residing at St Asaph. In the deanery of Cyfeiliog (later in the diocese of Bangor) three of the eight incumbents were non-resident, two residing in Hertfordshire, and one, John Price of Llanwrin, at Freshwater, Hampshire. His rural dean wrote of him with disgust that he had been inducted in 1789 when he read the articles and preached, returned seven months later to do the "rest", and had not been seen since. Melvin Humphreys suggests that in the 1790s half the beneficed clergy of Montgomery were non-resident, compared to only a quarter in the 1730s and 1740s.[33] Archdeacon Bevan wrote that in the 1830s 15 incumbents in the archdeaconry of Brecon held 36 benefices between them, and 14 others resided in livings outside the archdeaconry.[34]

The 1828 visitation returns for St Davids indicate that of the 453 parishes and chapelries only 125 had a resident incumbent, and in 191 cases (58%) there was not a resident minister, incumbent or curate. Many of these would have been described as comprising technical non-residence, generally due to poverty, but all entered the statistics for non-residency.[35] Thus in the archdeaconry of Carmarthen between 1799 and 1842 there were four returns. In 1799 there were 36 non-resident incumbents out of 99 returns, with 25 resident curates, and in 1842 the non-resident incumbents had decreased to 32 out of 98 returns, with 14 resident curates, while between the two dates the number of resident incumbents increased from 38 to 52.[36] Johnes wrote of Radnorshire that in 1832 of sixteen livings held by absentees, six were in the hands of clergy residing in London, Portsmouth, Harrow, Lancastershire, and the remaining ten were shared between those living in Breconshire, Pembrokeshire and Glamorgan.[37] Conybeare, quoting the 1847 Education Report known as the Blue Books, wrote that of 56 parishes in north Pembrokeshire 33 were without a resident cleric.[38] As late as 1850 a parliamentary return indicated that more than half the curates in the two southern Welsh dioceses, 124 out of 194, served non-resident incumbents.[39]

Another way of assessing the amount of non-residence is from the returns made to Parliament under the 1803 legislation about non-residency in each diocese. A return of 1812 of resident licensed curates of non-resident incumbents indicated that Llandaff had 111 such curates of whom 18 were resident in the curacy they served, St

Asaph had 45 with 38 resident, and Bangor 51 with 27 resident. There was no return for St Davids.[40] A similar return of 1831 indicated that 34 per cent of the parishes had an incumbent either resident in the parsonage house or who lived within two miles of the church (315 out of 927), but this varied from 2 per cent for St Davids, 33 per cent Llandaff, 41 per cent Bangor and 55 per cent St Asaph, not surprisingly, as it was the wealthiest diocese of the four.[41]

These figures were slightly better than figures for the whole of the Established Church in England and Wales. In 1827 nearly a quarter of the incumbents were exempt from residence, but of these 82 per cent were pluralists and thus non-resident in one or more of their parishes, though 15 per cent of non-residents were still actively involved in their parishes.[42]

A further reason for non-residence was ill-health, although licences of non-residence obtained under this provision were sometimes obtained even though their circumstances were somewhat dubious. The consistory court of St Asaph at least attempted to regulate these issues in 1720, when it ordered William Meyrick to be paid £20 per annum for serving as curate to Thomas Williams of Denbigh, who was unable to perform his duty.[43] This was an unusual occurrence and most clergy in ill-health had to make their own arrangements. Thomas Bankes, appointed in 1770 to the living of Dixton, near Monmouth, claimed his right to non-residence on account of the lack of a parsonage house and of his health, and while he had livings at Oxford and Tunbridge Wells he remained in London as an assistant preacher of St George's, Middlesex. His claim that the climate of Dixton would kill him was true, for he caught a chill and died there after visiting it to sort out a problem about its tithes.[44] Another who claimed ill health as the reason for non-residency, along with his inability to speak Welsh, was George Martin Maber, rector of Merthyr Tydfil, one of the wealthiest livings in the Welsh Church. Rector from 1795-1844 he left the parish for Swansea in 1812, and is said to have returned but once thereafter, to vote for a church rate. This parish, by now a huge industrial district, was left in the care of ill-paid curates and thereby stagnated. There was little the bishops could do to remedy the situation save to condemn the perpetrator.[45] James Prince, rector of Llanfechain near Oswestry, obtained a licence of non-residence on medical grounds, and a certificate stating he needed sea air and bathing. He died aged 93 in 1850, after fifty years of non-residency.[46] Thomas Gronow, vicar of Cadoxton and rector of Cilybebyll, received such a licence from Bishop Copleston due to his wife's illness in

1831-4, although he over-extended his stay as his wife died in December 1832, but Copleston allowed him an annual licence for some time thereafter to get rid of him and because his parishes were reasonably served by curates.[47]

Thomas Stacey, rector of Gelligaer in the Glamorgan uplands, gave up residing on his parish after five years' residence in 1835, and became curate of Cardiff. The official reason was noted in his obituary: "his tender and delicate frame was sorely tried by the bleak climate of the inhospitable mountain regions." Nevertheless that delicate constitution survived for many years in the smoke and grime of a growing industrial town. The Welsh-speaking clergy, who regarded the aristocratic members of their profession like Stacey with disdain, not only noted that he retained his wealthy living as an absentee, and paid his curates there a pittance as opposed to his own income, but he had been sent to the hills as a cleric and magistrate at a time of national disturbance to keep order, and had fled in dismay.[48]

The bishops were not unwise about such excuses, and Mather notes that Bishop Horsley effected a marked reduction in the number of those who claimed this exemption between 1805-06, amongst them one of his leading clergy, H.W. Eyton, of Mold. The testimony of an "obscure apothecary" about Eyton's daughter's health was insufficient for Horsley, as he reminded the cleric, now residing at Bath, of the penalties he would incur should he continue his unlicensed non-residence.[49] There were, however, many more genuine cases, such as William Allen, vicar of Hay 1786-1831, which he served from 1824-7, having appointed curates beforehand, but became non-resident thereafter because his bad health "disabled" him from duty.[50] Similarly, William Powell, vicar of Abergavenny, had a certificate of non-residence in 1861 being in his ninety-first year.[51]

There are many other instances of a stipendiary curate being employed by an incumbent who was unable because of health issues to undertake the duty of the parish himself, but who remained within his parish.[52] The rector of Pentyrch, Charles Davis, who died in 1773 at the age of eighty, had been blind for some time "but kept the profits of the parish" by keeping a curate.[53] The rector of Hirnant, Montgomeryshire, William Edmund Williams, needed to retain a curate because of his ill-health from 1860-67.[54] The debt-ridden Richard Pendrill Llewelyn, vicar of Llangynwyd on the Glamorgan foothills, who found his share of the tithes almost uncollectible and as a result was sequestrated, died in 1891 after an incumbency of fifty years, though for his declining years he was an invalid and forced to employ two curates to do the duty of the parish.[55] A variation of this practice is noted with the example of John Williams, Ab Ithel, a controversial Welsh literary figure, who after a nervous breakdown received a licence of non-residence in 1852 from his remote parish of Llanymawddwy, and was allowed to take a curacy at Llangorwen, near Aberystwyth, where he regained his health before returning to his parish.[56]

There was one bitter complaint against some of those who acted as curates for disabled incumbents, namely that they insisted on the maximum stipend that often left little for the needs of the aged or sick incumbent, while "greedily" seizing his house, garden, "and every comfort which belongs to him; the quiet retreat of his declining years; the fruit from trees, which in better times his own hands have raised".[57] It was not without some substance. The elderly Richard Prichard, senior vicar choral of Llandaff Cathedral, conscious of his infirmities and inefficiency, knew that the only remedies, bar a retirement he could not afford and the death he expected, was to provide a substitute from his own pocket, but this he could not afford "without injury to the most unprotected part of my family".[58]

By the nineteenth century the bishops endeavoured to alleviate this position wherever they could. The vicar of Llanfair-is-gaer, Evan Williams, seems to have been placed in a lunatic asylum and Bishop Bethell in 1845 placed a curate, James Parry, in the parish with a stipend of £30 per annum. The living was worth three times as much, but no clerical charities would assist Williams and the expenses of his confinement were at least £40.[59] A list of curates' stipends for the diocese of St Davids shows further examples. Henry Miles was appointed curate of the Breconshire parishes of Llangammarch in 1869 whose rector was blind and elderly. In that same year Henry Simpson Blink became curate of Pembroke as once again its incumbent was blind. There would be great hardship if the full stipend was paid, the bishop wrote, and the curate was satisfied with what he would receive, possibly because this was his seventh successive curacy. David Davies, incumbent of Meline, incapacitated by old age and poor, received an allowance of £20 for his support, and the curate, David Jones, probably appointed by the bishop, was willing to accept a smaller sum as he had some private means, and Jonathan George, appointed to St Clears in 1890, was willing to accept a stipend of £120 instead of the £135 required as this would impose great hardship on its totally incapacitated vicar.[60]

Sequestration has already been noted. This happened when a cleric got into debt, with the danger that his creditors might endeavour to obtain for their relief his full ecclesiastical stipend and thus diminish or even foreclose the pastoral duty of the parish. The process meant placing the income of the living in the hands of trustees, who would ensure that from it the parish duty was fulfilled, generally by obtaining a curate (the bishop was able to assign the stipend), pay the incumbent something for his living expenses, and find other sums for the payment of his debts. In view of the poverty of many Welsh clergy it is surprising that so few were sequestrated, though those that were tended to face that procedure on more than one occasion. In the case of Leyson Jones of Glyncorrwg it was because he failed to pay the curate's stipend in the 1820s, being himself non-resident and acting as curate at Amersham.[61] But the position was also used when a pastoral breakdown had occurred. This happened in the Glamorgan parish of Cilybebyll in the 1890s, when its rector, David Walter Jones, faced sequestration after sequestration as he continually refused to pay the curates the bishop had appointed. Having a wide knowledge of ecclesiastical law he was able to cause immense difficulties for the bishop and the registrar, as well as interfering in the work of his curates.[62] John Williams Meyrick, rector of Beaumaris 1866-1900, was sequestrated for failing to pay the chancel repairs of his church, and when the bishop appointed a curate to the parish Meyrick refused to acknowledge his existence, claiming he could not afford £120 to pay him out of his £140 stipend. Meyrick even managed to padlock the doors of one of his churches against his curate. The churchwardens broke them open.[63]

The rector of Manafon, Montgomeryshire, Evan Jenkins, had his living sequestrated following his conviction for drunkenness in 1890. A long saga followed during which he made complaints to the archbishop that he had been forced to allow a curate at a stipend of £120 when the more customary £90 should have sufficed.[64] At Whitchurch, Cardiff, John Thomas Clarke, rector 1875-1903, was sequestrated in 1895 when, after months of evading the payment of his curate's stipend and his inability to pay the mortgage arrears to Queen Anne's Bounty, taken out for additions to the parsonage house, he had lost the sympathy of the diocesan registrar. Not only were the outstanding sums deducted from the income of the parish, so were the fees of over £11 due to registrar and sequestrators. A further sequestration occurred as well, and Clarke was only saved from permanent financial disgrace by the Bounty's revised rules that allowed the mortgage to be extended over a further period of time.[65] As a result of these and similar cases the Benefice Act of 1898 authorised a bishop to inhibit an incumbent from any participation in the duty of his cure when a curate had been imposed on him for neglect of duty.[66]

THE CONSEQUENCES OF NON-RESIDENCE

Non-residence caused pluralism, and pluralism meant that double duty, that is, the two services required by Canon Law in each parish per Sunday, had to be reduced to one service, and this sometimes at inconvenient or alternative times. It meant that the link between pastor and parish was lost, and if the parish was relegated to the care of a stipendiary curate, sometimes a man ordained to make up numbers,[67] effective leadership was equally lost. In addition, as Herbert Marsh suggested, non-residence often meant that the parsonage house, if there was one, was neglected and might fall into such decay that it was no longer suitable as a clerical residence, making it even more difficult to provide a resident pastor.[68] The State viewed this state of affairs with concern, as the pastor of each parish was meant to serve as a sort of moral policeman, instructing his flock in the discipline and doctrine of Christianity, which, to many, meant as the old Catechism put it, "to honour and obey the King, and all that are put in authority under him: to submit myself to all my governors, teachers, spiritual pastors and masters: To order myself lowly and reverently to all my betters," as well as to lead a moral life. Bishop Gibson commended residence as enabling:

> a daily oversight and inspection, and by that means, a constant check and restraint upon evil practices of all kinds, and upon the growth of corrupt customs and habits among the people: such are also a more intimate knowledge of their spiritual estate, and occasional exhortations and reproofs, and that which exhorts and reproves most effectively of all, the daily oversight and influence of good example: to which we must lead, the being always at hand, to observe and compose differences before they grow too strong; to assist the rich with counsel, the sick with comfort, and (according to your abilities) the poor and distressed with seasonable relief: and to perform among them all neighbourly and charitable offices of the like kind, which are not only excellent in themselves, but are the means of endearing ministers to their people, and of opening a passage into their hearts for spiritual instruction of all sorts.[69]

Johnes added to this assessment in relation to the Welsh Church. A resident clergyman, he wrote, "had the strongest interest in the good opinion of his flock; upon their good feeling will depend many of the every-day comforts of life, - and the degree of respect and kindness extended to him by the society of his neighbourhood, will generally be a mere echo of their report." He would collect his tithes according to claims of charity and right feeling. An absentee, however, would be little affected by the ill-feeling of his parishioners, and had to leave the care of his revenues to a middle man who would not act in a similar spirit to one who was resident.[70] As the "curate of Snowdon" suggested, a non-resident pastor would lose that intimate connection between incumbent and parishioners that was required and would be unable to offer the ministry his parish deserved, while the respect in which the Church was held would suffer. In addition, those who paid tithes did so to uphold a resident ministry, and would become disaffected to Church and State if they saw this tax upon their labours diverted to the pleasures of an individual or to the maintenance of an ecclesiastical corporation elsewhere, especially when the hospitality and pastoral and practical charitable care expected of the incumbent was lacking and the tithe income spent outside the parish.[71] Parishioners had a right to expect residence, maintained Archbishop Secker in 1758.[72]

Criticism of this system of non-residency was widespread throughout the Church and expressed not only by writers (such as Wade, Corbett and Johnes), but often by parishioners themselves. The parishioners of Manordeifi, Pembrokeshire, were loud in their protest to their bishop about their vicar, David Phillips, who declared himself a doctor of divinity. He had received the profits of the living for nineteen years, resided in London, "but had no manner of regard for the care of the precious souls committed to his charge nor any compassion for the wants of the indigent and poor of the parish". His curate was insufficient and immoral, he had wasted the glebe and allowing its buildings to fall into ruin making the place desolate, and had allowed his tenants to take down some valuable oak trees in the churchyard.[73] At a vestry meeting of the parish of Llansanffraid during 1782 it was ordered that the wardens should give the vicar notice that unless he provided a resident clergyman to do the duty of the parish within three months they would, at joint expense, pursue the proper methods to secure such duty. The vicar, Edward Williams, resigned the following year.[74]

This may have been known to the parishioners of Welshpool in the same county who some years later wrote to their vicar, John Pryce, who resided on his other living of Gunley. They claimed they had seen "for some time with great regret the melancholy consequences that have arisen to the morals and religious principles and conduct of many of our fellow parishioners, ... which are likely to increase to an alarming degree", if he did not return into residence. As it was the duty of a vicar to undertake not only the performance of the Church service, "but also to look over the morals of his people, to set a good example, to conciliate their temper, and bring about Christian charity and goodwill where wanted", and considering that "these necessary duties cannot be discharged without a constant residence", they were prepared to make a formal complaint at the forthcoming episcopal visitation unless he returned to his duties in their large and populous parish.[45] Another protest, from a dissenter, writing in 1841 about the non-residence of Heneage Horsley, son of the bishop of that name, at Gresford, who he claimed had not seen his parish for forty years, suggested that people were either taught by dissenters or were perishing for lack of knowledge.[76] It was untrue, for the parish was provided with curates, but the wider concern was there, namely that in many of these parishes only one Sunday service was provided, often at awkward times and taken hastily, as Archbishop Secker noted in 1758.[77] There was a fear that as a result people would change their allegiance to dissent, whose itinerant preachers, in the words of Bishop Porteus of Chester (1777-88), would look out for those parishes whose shepherds had deserted them.[78] A letter written to Bishop Horsley in 1803 made the same point. The non-residence of even one clergyman could put into jeopardy the eternal welfare of human souls, as the lack of residence was driving people into the "sects".[79] Even at the start of Victoria's reign the older bishops, such as Copleston, regarded dissent as schism against the established Church and as a danger to the State itself.[80] However, Thomas Arnold was probably not alone in realising that the real problem of the Church was not so much non-residence in the rural parishes, but the Church's inefficiency in the large towns where the resident minister was incapable of fulfilling the work required.[81]

PARLIAMENTARY ACTION

The legislature, determined to redress these issues, tackled the matter in rather a round-about route, and did so by a number of parliamentary acts over the course of many years. Royal Injunctions of 1610 allowed a bishop to sequester a benefice if a non-resident failed to supply a curate, and to appoint a curate to do the duty,[82] but it does not appear to have been widely implemented. By an act of 1713 (13 Anne, c. 11), the bishops were empowered before granting a licence to a curate and after enquiry into the value of a living "and other emoluments of the rector or vicar", to appoint a salary of not less than £20 per annum and not more than £50. It was discretionary, not mandatory, and hence not widely observed, and was out of the question in many parishes due to their poverty. Horsley, in the diocese of St Davids, found in 1788 that there were still stipends of £5 and £10 in value, and he laboured to increase them to £15.[83] When curates were competing for employment, was it possible, asked Sydney Smith, to prevent a curate from pledging himself to his rector, that he will accept only half the legal salary. The law was a dead letter.[84] The archbishop's directions to the bishops of his province, issued in 1759, reaffirmed the traditional requirement that no minister be allowed to serve more than one church or chapel in one day, unless the chapel be part of the same parish as the church or united with it, or one or both of them were unable to maintain a cleric by itself.[85] The last exemption rendered these instructions ineffectual in most of the Welsh dioceses.

An Act of 1796 empowered the bishop to offer a maximum stipend of £75 for curates of non-resident incumbents, though the official minimum remained at £20. Writing of this Act, Watson of Llandaff noted he had received several applications for the augmentation of the stipends of curates "ill provided for". He could pay little attention to some of these applications, for a stipend should not be regulated by the riches of an incumbent but by the value of the living and the nature of the duty it required. As the livings in his diocese were so small, if he used the full liberty the law allowed, he might benefit the curate but only by distressing and injuring his incumbent. While he would listen to the complaints, it would be more agreeable if the incumbents would leave their curates no grievances to complain of.[86]

The Clergy Residence Act of 1803 (43 George III, c. 84), noted already as an act more to prevent prosecutions than enforce residence, aimed to regulate non-residence, exempted certain classes of clergy from residence, including holders of second benefices, and empowered bishops to grant annual licences of non-residence to clergy on such grounds as ill-health or the lack of a suitable parsonage house. The act also gave statutory force to the episcopal power to enforce residence by monition. If this was not complied with, the living could be sequestrated, giving the remaining income after the parish had been cared for to Queen Anne's Bounty. If the benefice remained sequestrated for more than three years (reduced to two in 1817), it became void, and the patron was required to appoint another cleric to it. Horsley made it clear that he would not interfere between a resident incumbent and his curate in the matter of his stipend, letting them sort it out between themselves, but in the case of non-resident incumbents he would take care that "the hire of the labourer is duly proportioned to his service". But he would interfere no farther than necessary, but hoped that the "liberality of the beneficed clergy" would leave little occasion for "the interposition of my authority".[87] There was some concern that many curates would be displaced because of this act, and hence it allowed Queen Anne's Bounty to provide some relief for them. Few were affected, however, as the act was indifferently applied.[88] Sir William Scott endeavoured to follow up this act with a bill that would have required these non-residents to pay their curates a stipend that would have equated to a specific percentage of the benefice income. He was unsuccessful, for he was dealing with property rights, though Spencer Percival, a future prime minister, argued if incumbents were unhappy with this proposal, they should reside in the parishes and do the duty themselves. The income of a benefice was not to provide incomes for the clergy, but to provide religious instruction and pastoral care of the parishioners.[89]

In 1813 an act was passed for the augmenting of the stipends of stipendiary curates. A consolidation act of 1817 (57 George III, c. 99) was even more specific. While both these acts endeavoured to link the curate's stipend to the value of the living, the population of the parish and the amount of duty required, the acts only related to new incumbents and were not retrospective. They provided that no clergyman should officiate at more than two services or travel more than fifteen miles on the Lord's Day. Bishop Majendie of Bangor believed these provisions would lead to the more decent and orderly performance of divine service. The 1817 act was even more specific. It required the residence of a stipendiary curate for a non-resident incumbent when the value of the living was over £300 and the population was over 300, or when the population was over 1,000.

Though the 1817 act permitted the bishop to relax the requirement of residence to allow the curate to live in some nearby place, Bishop Marsh made it clear that he would consult the convenience of the flock as well as of the pastor, and felt that any relaxation would require exceptional circumstances. Incumbents who entered their benefice after 20 July 1813 (but not those before that date) were required to pay their stipendiary curates a salary in proportion to the gross annual value of their benefices: under 300 persons £80, £100 for 300, £120 for 500, and £150 when it was 1,000 and over. If the value was less than these figures, then the whole income of the benefice was to be paid to the curate. If the curate served more than one Church, then a sum of £30 could be deducted at the bishop's discretion but the lowest stipend for such a double charge was £50, however small the population. Curates were only permitted to serve two churches unless permitted otherwise by their bishop. It might be argued that the aim of these acts was to make non-residency less profitable to the incumbent and thus assist in reducing the number of non-residents.

Bishop Burgess, in his 1813 Charge to the clergy of St Davids, considered this act would be "likely to be productive of many beneficial consequences. Its probable operation will be to lessen the number of pluralities, to increase the number of resident incumbents, to provide a recompence worthy of the labourer; to raise the character of the Clergy employed in the inferior ministries of the Church, and, by promoting the improvement of parochial duties, to increase the usefulness, and personal influence of the Clergy; and so, to promote the credit, and to strengthen the hands, of the established Church". The act did not ensure, as he hoped it might have done, that each parish should have double duty each Sunday.[90]

As Bishop Marsh pointed out in his 1817 Charge to his Llandaff clergy, the residence of the parochial clergy on their respective livings was becoming more and more necessary day by day, and he could think of no measure more calculated to effect this than the augmentation in the value of the curates' stipends. "Where the Benefice is small, the Incumbent *must* do his duty; or it will be useless to *accept* it. Where the Benefice is of greater value, the Incumbent will at least be more *inclined* to do his duty, in proportion to the expence of providing a *Substitute*". Furthermore, he added, the curates of his diocese would be restored to that rank in society they ought to occupy, instead of receiving "the pittance of a day labourer". Those curates employed before this due date were equally entitled to a decent maintenance, and hence he would allow no licence to be issued with a stipend of under £40, which would be doubled on the assumption that two parishes were served, and he would increase the stipend according to the value of the benefice, the maximum being £90, the £75 stipend and £15 where the parsonage house was not assigned to the curate. No curate was to serve more than two parishes rather than the three or four at present, because they now had a sufficient income from the two. It could only be allowed in the case of pastoral necessity, but the churches were not to be more than four miles distance from each other.[91]

The acts were limited by two of their clauses. Bishop Burgess noted that it was impossible to define the minimum stipend in view of the poverty of many benefices, though the existence of this Parliamentary rule would serve as a means of raising the stipend as near to the rule as possible. At a later date Copleston held that while it needed the incumbent's consent for the stipends of curates appointed before the due date to be raised, he believed the incumbents were morally obliged to do so.[92]

The problem of the earlier legislation was that it was hard to enforce, generally because of the low level of benefice incomes. Sir William Scott, speaking in 1802 in a Commons debate, demanded to know how the public could insist on the residence of the clergy when "so large a proportion of the benefices of this kingdom do not pay more than what most of us in this House pay for our upper servants".[93] The Pluralities Act of 1838, discussed for many years beforehand, not only clarified the earlier legislation but also increased the minimum stipends for curates of non-resident incumbents. A curate in a parish with less than 300 population remained on £80, if over 300 £100, over 500 £120, if over 750 £135, and if over 1,000 £150. If a benefice had an income over £400 the bishop could assign a curate irrespective of the population, and if over £500, give an additional £50 to the stipend. However, this section of the act was often evaded. In addition, and of equal importance, the act provided that no cleric could hold more than two benefices, and the second could be no more than ten miles from the first, nor, save for emergencies, one could serve more than two cures in a day either as incumbent or curate. Pluralism was prohibited if the combined value of the benefices exceeded £1,000 or the population more than 3,000. The exemptions allowed to certain pluralists, such as chaplains and schoolmasters, were significantly reduced; licences for non-residence were still available for sickness or infirmity, but only for six months in the case of a family member, while penalties, ultimately sequestration and the voiding of a living, were imposed for those who continued as non-residents without licence or exemption. This act was significant for the Welsh dioceses as it gave power to their bishops to refuse institution to those who, after due examination, were found unable to speak Welsh in a living which required it, while within the wider Church it brought about a substantial increase in episcopal power.[94]

The bishops themselves took decisive action to ensure that these requirements were enforced, though until the later legislation mentioned above was available there was little they could do except privately admonish, as often non-residence was permissible even if destructive of parochial life. Even then their admonitions often fell on deaf ears, as Bishop Gilbert of Llandaff (1740-48) discovered.[95] However, when the law was flagrantly defied then bishops could be decisive. Thomas Sherlock, bishop of Bangor(1728-34) used his consistory court to enforce the duty of residence, and the eventual taking up of residence by the offenders was included as a marginal note in his register.[96] Bishop Warren of Bangor, made it clear that a licence of non-residence was not granted as a favour, but could only be justified when the service of the Church made it reasonable. Could a non-resident, holding two benefices, come within the spirit and intent of these laws, when constant residence is "rendered absolutely impossible on one?" He accepted that the poverty of benefices allowed an indulgence, especially to a married clergy, "but in the present state of so many of our parochial Cures, what else can be done?" Yet if neglect should take place, they would discover "the power and authority of the Diocesan".[97] John Randolph, bishop of Bangor, in his 1808 Charge, made it clear he was aware of a few instances of wilful non-residence, and he would act vigorously in this matter, advising his clergy to take out licences of non-residence for their own security.[98]

Bishop Copleston of Llandaff, using the new legislation available and thus having the right to assign a stipendiary curate's stipend, did so with a vengeance that must have upset many of his non-resident incumbents. For example, in 1834, Robert Paul, rector of Llantwit Major, was required to pay one of his curates £100 plus house rent and a further £50 for another (as he served another church), while the stipends for the curates at Glyncorrwg and Peterston were set at £60 and £80 respectively. John Richards, rector of St Bride's Minor and St Donats and lecturer or curate at Llantwit Major, was monitored to reside on one of his benefices, refused a licence of non-residence, and it was made clear that either he or a curate resided at St Brides.[99] Copleston thus acted on the principle he had expressed in his 1830 Charge that while he would relax the legal requirements in those cases where the poverty of the living or the needs of a disabled incumbent justified it, provided that the spiritual interests of the parish were not neglected, he would enforce the law with rigour in those cases where "the relief ... destined for the poor, ought not to be solicited, or even expected by the rich." [100]

The Llandaff diocesan memorandum books indicate that his successor, Ollivant, followed Copleston's example. In May 1850 Ollivant refused to allow the curate of Tredunnock to take an additional cure. Instead his stipend was to be advanced to £80 and he was required to reside on that parish and take double duty. The rector of

Llandow was allowed a licence of non-residence in December 1852 for one year only, but he was to build or rebuild the parsonage house and meanwhile reside at Lisworney within one and a half miles of the church.[101] Yet some clergy were able to continue as pluralists outside the terms of the 1838 legislation. One was Hugh Williams, chancellor of the diocese, who held the parishes of Llanarth and Radyr but served the perpetual curacy of Roath, When Ollivant offered him the living of Bassaleg it was on the condition he gave up Llanarth, but Williams continued holding Bassaleg and Radyr until his death in 1877.[102] Another was John Luxmoore who held the Montgomeryshire parishes of Berriew and Llanymynech until his death in 1877. Both of these had received their preferment before that act and so were exempt from its requirements.

THE GRADUAL DEMISE OF NON-RESIDENCE

This legislation and the episcopal pressure put on non-residence clergy brought the system of non-residence and the use of stipendiary curates to a slow but sure death. The reason for this slow death was that existing interests were respected, so that those incumbents in post before the passing of the 1838 act were exempt from its provisions.[103] A few lasted almost into the twentieth century, one being that of Joshua Evans, vicar of Llanover, Monmouthshire, 1862-91, when he was appointed to St James, Pontypool. His position was unusual, however, for he had come into some conflict with Lady Llanover, who allowed him £100 per annum from 1879 onwards on condition he absented himself from the parish, leaving it in the care of a clergyman of her choice.[104]

Between 1827-50 the number of non-residencies dropped from half the benefices to below ten per cent throughout the Church of England,[105] while in the diocese of Llandaff Copleston managed to increase the number of resident incumbents and stipendiary curates from 97 to 162 during the same period, whereas in 1827 there were 137 non-residents and by 1850 only 53. He had also managed to reduce the number of those who held more than three benefices to nine, and those who held two to twenty-seven, though he accepted that the real problem in his diocese was the pluralism amongst the curacies, which allowed only a single duty in many of the rural parishes.[106] In St Davids diocese the number of parishes held by an incumbent who had no other parochial responsibilities doubled between 1848-81, while the number of resident incumbents increased by one third during 1852-81.[107]

Yet in 1850 it was argued that over one half of the curates in the two southern dioceses of Wales, 124 out of 194, served as stipendiary curates for non-resident incumbents.[108] In an 1843 return it was stated that in St Asaph there were 23 stipendiary curates acting for non-residents, and 28 assistant clergy, while in Bangor the corresponding number was 19 and 35.[109] Within the wider Church of England in 1864 there were only 955 stipendiary curates, compared to 3,078 in 1838.[110] They were now a dying breed. Clearly, the assistant clergyman, working directly under an incumbent, was beginning to replace the older pattern. Unfortunately, the Church was hardly prepared for this phenomenon. It had little legislation to cover the existence of these assistant curates nor had it a minimum agreed stipend for them. The stipendiary curate was better protected and often had a higher stipend than these assistant curates, while Frances Knight also suggests that the incumbents fared far worse under the 1838 Act than the curates. Some were required to provide additional curates if they possessed a large urban or even a widespread rural parish, and this could soon eat into the resources of the living.[111]

Frances Knight points out that for the layman "perhaps the most obvious sign that the Church was changing was the disappearance of the band of transitory, sometimes non-resident curates – which had been so familiar a part of the ecclesiastical landscape in the first half of the century – and the arrival of the permanent, resident incumbent." While this brought many benefits to the parish, a higher standard of pastoral care, and the knowledge that the income of the parish from the tithes would be used for the benefit of the parish, both for charitable purposes and also benefiting local trade, it also had its disadvantages. A new man often set a new tone to the worship and ethos of the parish, and might ensure that his services were set at the same time as those of the local chapel, thus forcing parishioners, who had felt an allegiance to the two, to make a choice. She notes a hardening of attitudes between Church and Chapel, and wonders if this was one of the results of this new experience of residency.[112]

The bishops who had to administer these procedures found themselves in great difficulties, especially when facing recalcitrant clergymen. Bishop Ollivant of Llandaff, speaking to the Upper House of Convocation in 1878, explained the procedures for providing a curate in the case of non-resident benefices in this way:

One morning I received a letter from an Incumbent of two parishes in my diocese stating that he was going to leave for London, and that I might put in a Curate if I liked. Of course I could not do that unless I went to work in the legal way, for if I did, and I called upon the Incumbent to pay the Curate, he might have refused on the ground of illegality. Accordingly I made inquiries, and ascertained what was the course of proceeding. I was told that I must first issue a commission to inquire whether the duty of the parish was properly done or not. Then, if the commission reported that the duty was not properly done, I was to give three months notice to the Incumbent that if he did not provide for the proper discharge of the duty in the interval, I should exercise the power given me by law, and put in a Curate myself. Now, in the first place, the Incumbent was a poor man. He came to London, and dodged about from one Post-office to another, telling us that a letter would find him at one and then at another. Yet this notice had to be served three months before the Bishop could act. I think that all the machinery is exceedingly bad. Meanwhile, the two parishes were left at the mercy of anybody to serve them or not. That I think a very great evil.

Ollivant also related the story of an incumbent in his diocese with two churches who had absconded because of debt and his whereabouts were not known, but once again he would have to go through all this process before he could provide a curate. He had been told that if the creditors applied for a sequestration of the living, and obtained it, he could then appoint a curate who would be the first charge on the parish income. Surely, he asked, a bishop ought to have more discretion that this when he finds livings neglected by their incumbents.[113]

In all probability this long process of bringing non-residency to an end led to the union of parishes into a single benefice, for with the holding of more than two parishes forbidden or in any case severely restricted, many individual parishes must have become uneconomic as single entities unless an incumbent had his own private means. This was forecast by Thomas Williams, archdeacon of Llandaff, in 1852.[114]

CHAPTER FOUR: THE STIPENDIARY CURATE: THE CURATE OBSERVED

The *Hereford Journal* of 1806 contained an advertisement for a curate, though the parish, whether in that diocese or in one of the border parishes, is not recorded. It read:

> A comfortable and beneficial situation waits the acceptance of a person qualified to discharge the duties of it. He must be single, in orders, and disposed to bear confinement in a moderate degree; he will be required to assist in a school and may have the duties of one or two churches to perform. He will be treated as an equal.[1]

This particular position was clearly advertised in order to obtain a man to assist a pluralist, and it spells out the terms of servitude. Yet it was rare for such posts to be advertised in this way. Curates were generally found from within a diocese (often being local to the parish concerned if they could hold it in plurality), and sometimes through the good offices of the bishop, though some bishops were not averse to taking over the direction of the curates in their diocese.

One such was Bishop Copleston of Llandaff who took an active role in seeking stipendiary curates for his diocese. Isaacson, vicar of Newport, a town with a large radical and somewhat rebellious population, had had his living sequestrated because of debt, and a stipendiary curate was required to care for it. There was another issue as well, namely that the Roman Catholics were establishing a large church for the benefit of the many Irish people who had emigrated there, and as a means of evangelistic aggression. Writing to his successor as provost of Oriel College, Oxford, Edward Hawkins, Copleston asked if he could find a man of talent, energy, character and good judgment, possibly a fellow of a college, who would be an efficient curate and so counteract this menace, and live on a stipend of £100 out of which he had to find lodgings. He would thus need some resources of his own.[2] Lewis Jones, a Yorkshire incumbent, was also perpetual curate of the small Monmouthshire parish of

Llandevaud. In the 1840s its income had increased from £42 to £100 due to glebe land being sold for railway purposes, and rather than being served by a pluralist curate, Jones arranged with Copleston for him to appoint a curate and fix his salary.[3] Copleston's letters to his local agent, Bruce Knight, indicate he acted for many local clergy in finding them stipendiary curates, and generally expected them to allow him to do so. He thus made appointments of stipendiary curates to the parishes of Cadoxton, St Fagans, Peterston, Llantilio Crossenny and Undy (for which parish he had received a number of applications), though he felt it was small enough to be held with another parish. The bishop expressed dismay when the new incumbent of Llansoy, Richards, refused to accept his nomination of a curate as he would "derange a complicated plan", namely, Copleston's ordering of the diocesan stipendiary curates. He once described these arrangements as "a big move". Evan Morgan, who had become vicar of Llantwit Major, and was willing to reside, was persuaded to keep on the stipendiary curate, James, for some months, by which time Copleston was hopeful he would be able to provide for him. When clergy expressed diffidence about his arrangements, as did Dr Lisle, he told them if they did not comply with his wishes, he would threaten them with the letter of the law, and require them to reside themselves on their livings.[4]

Henry Payne, then rector of Llanbedr and Patrisio in Breconshire, and later archdeacon of Carmarthen, was asked in 1832 to find a curate for the parish of Llangenni in that same county. He discovered that Thomas Price, Carnhuanawc, was anxious to take on this parish instead of his existing curacies of Llanyre and Llanfihangel Helygen. It would be much to his advantage, for as he was caring for an aged mother any addition to his stipend would be welcome, and in this case it would be £50 plus the surplice fees. He needed episcopal permission for this, and Payne suggested as there was only one church in that parish he might well be able to obtain another curacy, but the bishop refused his consent to this arrangement.[5]

Other pluralists made more local arrangements. Speaking to the Leeds Church Congress of 1872, James Stewart Gamwell reminisced about his time as curate of Dolfor in Montgomeryshire in the mid-1850s. As a newly ordained deacon he had been given charge of a large rural parish, fourteen miles long, but a neighbouring incumbent, a non-resident, asked him to take over his parish in addition to his own at a stipend of twenty-five shillings a week. He declined, for he was aware that the previous curate had been unable to cope with the position and had given up.[6]

The stipendiary curate was by definition a much more responsible person than the assistant curate of later years. He had the full charge of a parish, and was to all intents and purposes its *de facto* incumbent, though without the security the freehold of a parish gave to the actual incumbent. However, in many instances he would be continued in office by a new incumbent, particularly if he was a pluralist, as happened in the case of William Williams, curate of Llanfynydd, Cardiganshire, who died in 1826, having been curate of that parish for forty years. During his lifetime the living had been presented to three different clergymen by its patron, the bishop of the diocese, but these, living at a distance and holding better and larger livings, retained his services. For many years Williams maintained a large family on an income of £30 per annum. It was later increased to £50 probably due to legislation.[7] This example must have been multiplied over and over again. Large pluralists had no wish to move into small and remote rural parishes, while a stipendiary curate, if he had a reasonable income and the use of the parsonage house and glebe, often had no wish to move.

On occasions, an incumbent might decide to reside, or wish to offer the curacy to a friend or relative, often newly ordained, and so give notice to his curate.[8] Thus in 1802 Hezekiah Jones, serving the parish of Sully, which he combined with Porthceri and possibly Cadoxton, found a new rector anxious to reside, but managed to obtain another group of curacies instead.[9] Roderick Lewis, curate of Machynlleth, found himself in the same position in 1812, for when he applied for the use of the parsonage house rent-free he was given notice by his incumbent to quit the curacy as he would serve it himself. He wondered about a small living, and had heard that Llandinam was vacant. It was a false rumour.[10] In 1798 the Johnes family of Hafod presented Lewis Evans to the perpetual curacy of Eglwys Newydd, Cardiganshire, but he replaced a stipendiary curate, D. Jones, who had expected the living for himself and had spent fourteen years in the parish. It was a difficult position for Evans, who feared the bishop's displeasure and Mr Johnes's wrath, and felt he would not be offered any other preferment if he declined the offer. The old and now displaced curate understood his predicament, and on his first Sunday there attended the service and later addressed the congregation outside the church, saying he bore Evans no ill-will, knowing it was not his choice he was supplanting him, and begging the parishioners to treat him as a friend and neighbour.[11] Another stipendiary curate, David Jones of Caldicot, "an honest, sincere & painstaking man – not very polished, but esteemed where he is known", was similarly "thrown out of employ" in 1834, and Copleston felt himself bound to provide for him, and made some suggestions to Bruce Knight about a possible curacy for him.[12]

It was often suggested that a good stipendiary curacy was often a far better prospect than a small living.[13] This was made clear by Bishop Copleston to his curate at Bedwas, a parish the bishop held in commendam, Watkin Williams, who felt hurt that the bishop had not offered him a living. "He is a poor creature – narrow minded and selfish – but harmless," wrote the bishop to Bruce Knight in 1832. "I have told him that as livings have declined in value his curacy has *in fact* advanced, but he seems hardly capable of understanding the thing." Williams received the full legal stipend of £120 together with the use of the parsonage house.[14] However, for some men, such as John Jones, curate to the absentee George Maber at Merthyr Tydfil in the 1820s, the position of a stipendiary curate was hardly a good prospect. Before legislation altered the position, Jones, a good man according to his bishop, had to continue on his own in that large and difficult parish, as Maber declined to appoint an assistant for him.[15] Bishop Watson of Llandaff, in his 1784 Charge, spoke about the unbeneficed and stipendiary curates of his diocese, accepting that for many their position was "peculiarly distressing". He asked them not to despair, for they were "the Servants of a Master who can and will reward them for their patient continuance in well-doing", and he asked their "superiors" to treat them with kindness and affability". Not only was this because "great preferment in the Church is no sure test of worth of Character", but also for the credit of the Order itself and for the general good of the Church and nation.[16] Such a sentiment was of little consolation to these men.

Many of those ordained were licensed to large parishes where they had the sole charge.[295] Jenkinson in his 1828 Charge offered a reason for this. It was cheaper to offer a title to a newly ordained man at £40 than to employ a curate whose stipend had been fixed by the Clergy Act at £80, or, if the incumbent had been in post before July 1813, the stipend required by the bishop of £75 plus £15 if the parsonage house was not included. He would insist on the full stipend being paid, and required his clergy to make use of those curates who were now unemployed rather than obtain a newly ordained man to serve their parishes.[18]

THE PROVISION OF A STIPEND

Before the legislation which stipulated the stipends of stipendiary curates, and in spite of the 1713 act which allowed bishops to assign a stipend of between £20 and £50 per annum, which was not mandatory, curates were paid a pittance, forcing many to take on other curacies.[19] We need to remember there was no legislation regarding the stipends of curates who served impropriate parishes and their position was often even worse than that of the stipendiary curate, bad though that might be. William Jones of Broxbourne wrote of the incumbent haggling with poor curates until they could obtain one who would "starve with the fewest symptoms of discontent."[20] Thus the curate of Cilymaenllwyd, in Carmarthenshire, Morris, had £10 per annum in 1710,[21] while the stipendiary curate of Penmon in Anglesey received thirty shillings a quarter in 1711, and one of his successors, William Jones, in 1788, received almost the same, £6.10s.2d. per annum, plus one shilling for announcing a notice in church warning against hunting rabbits during the night at Penmon Park.[22] The £10 stipend paid to the curate of Llanarth, Cardiganshire, in 1709 was made up of £2 in cash, the remainder in tithes, including a half quarter of tithe cheese at £1.4s., a tithe pig at 1s., and Easter offerings of 17s.[23] An agreement of 1791 between David Griffiths, perpetual curate of Llandilo Fach and John Williams, to serve this and another cure at £18 per annum, was unusual in that it allowed a further two pounds if he "engaged" in the married state.[24]

Guy, in his survey of the diocese of Llandaff in 1763, observes that apart from a few curacies at £30 the remainder were much less, down to the curate of Roath who received £9, though the average was around £16 per annum. Even at a slightly later date the curate of St Mary Hill had £8, though his other curacy of Penllyn brought him another £10, while the curate of Cilybebyll had but £16 for that curacy and seems to have had no other. Guy adds that this poor rate of remuneration, though almost inevitable because of the small income of the parishes, forced most of the curates to become pluralists, thus obtaining an income of between £30 and £50 per annum, equivalent to a small living. Thomas Edwards, for example, served Colwinston, Flemingston and Llanmihangel.[25] The curate of Llandrindod received £10 per annum in 1791,[26] while several years later the curate of Cheriton in Gower was rich on £15.[27] The same sum paid to the curate at Bishton brought forth a defence in 1814 from Griffith Richards, its incumbent, from his vicarage at Farlington, Hampshire, that his curate was obviously satisfied with this amount and he never enquired what he made of it.[28] It may be that many bishops allowed this, for as Archbishop Secker in his Charge of 1758 accepted that many parishes were so poor that the incumbents had to be excused if they tried to get help on easy terms, but if they made a hard bargain when they possessed a good income from the parish it would be a matter of severe reproach.[29]

Stipendiary curates in the diocese of St Asaph generally received a better stipend than those in the Welsh-speaking heartlands. The livings were generally better endowed. According to Virgin, in a visitation of 1738, the average curate's stipend was a little over £22, and had hardly increased by 1791.[30] At Selattyn, Humphrey Humphreys, the curate had a salary of 20 guineas, before dying of smallpox in 1749, while his successor bar one, Edward Maurice, had £30 plus the use of the parsonage house. He had been a curate in the diocese for fifteen years before his appointment in 1751.[31] The unlicensed curate of Halkyn, Thomas Hughes, from 1791 to 1806 and possibly beyond, received £30, the same as was received by the curate at Welshpool to the absentee vicar, John Pryce, in the 1790s.[32] This seems to have been a standard stipend, even in many parts of England, as William Combe describes his character, Dr Syntax, receiving the same from his incumbent, and commenting, "and while in wealth he cuts and carves, The worthy curate prays and starves."[33]

By the 1810s, even before the 1813 act, some stipendiary curates were receiving £70 and more, as was paid to the stipendiary curates of Rudbaxton and Letterston in Pembrokeshire.[34] Henry Hey Knight, for example, as curate of Neath received in 1824 £70 plus another £15 in lieu of the parsonage house, though in addition he received fees and offerings amounting to £65.[35] The minimum stipend under the 1813 act was £80, but it did not apply to all, for those incumbents who were in post on a due date were exempt from its provisions. This may be noted from a Parliamentary report of 1827 which found that out of 4,254 curates, 1,639 had less than £60 per annum (38.5%), six had between £10 and £20, and another 59 between £20 and £30. Some might have been assistant curates, but as 1,393 resided in the parsonage house the majority were probably stipendiary curates.[36] These figures for 1827 were somewhat better than a return of 1810. This showed that only 455 stipendiary curates acting for non-residents received more than £50 per year, whereas 1,290 received less, the median value being £37.[37] By comparison, Jacob quotes Arthur Young, the agriculturalist, who considered that a married labourer with three children needed at least £25 a year to survive.[38]

We can discover from Bishop Copleston's letters as to how he insisted on a better stipend for these curates. Robert Knight, rector of Newton Nottage was required to pay his curate £80, and that curate was admonished for allowing his rector to deduct £15 from that total, as being a deacon the rector had to celebrate the Sacrament four times in the year. The next year, 1834, Copleston fixed the stipends of the curate at Llantwit Major at £100 plus house rent; at Lisworney £50 as the curate had another curacy held in plurality; £60 at Glyncorrwg and £80 at Peterston.[39] By and large these were in line with the 1813 legislation, though adjusted in the case of pluralities. His colleague at St Davids, Jenkinson, had already told his clergy that even if they were exempt from the 1813 legislation, yet that of 1796 allowed a maximum stipend of £75 plus £15 if the parsonage house was not available. He would insist on this stipend, even though it might be a hardship to the incumbent, for ecclesiastical incomes were given on the condition of certain duties being performed.[40] One wonders what happened in those parishes where the income did not even reach this level. In fact there was little a bishop could do under such circumstances. Virgin offers figures about the effect of the 1813 legislation on the Church. In that year throughout the Church there were 868 curates whose stipends failed to reach the £40 mark, by 1838 this had declined to 161 out of 4,813 curates, a fall of four-fifths. But in St Davids there were still 32 such men, though one wonders how many held other curacies.[41] Copleston made it clear he would exercise his discretion to relax the requirements in favour of those incumbents who if the law was strictly enforced would be distressed by it, but this would not operate if the incumbent was not poor or resided elsewhere than in his parish.[42]

There were occasions when the non-resident incumbents neglected or were unable to pay the stipends of their curates. A letter from Thomas Edwards to the Revd. Mr Barker, a diocesan official of the diocese of St Davids, of 1796, states that his father in law, Richard Leach, had neglected to pay his curate's stipend at Manorbier. The aggravated curate had applied for a sequestration order, and though he would not blame the curate he felt he could have taken a more lenient course that would be less distressing to Mr Leach and his feelings.[43] Meanwhile, perhaps, the curate could starve.

Comments were frequently made about these low stipends given by non-residents to their stipendiary curates. In his book, *The Miseries and Great Hardships of the Inferior Clergy in and about London* of 1737, Thomas Stackhouse complained that their stipends of £20 to £30 could only offer them "the bread of affliction".[44] Wales was probably a cheaper place to live, but then Welsh stipends were hardly that high. In St Asaph in 1749 they ranged between £10 and £50, with most around £20 to £24, though in Llandaff by 1763 the average stipend was £16 and the highest £30.[45]. William Jones, the republican of Llangadfan, was disgusted with Matthew Worthington, rector of that parish from 1773 and a non-resident, who pocketed £100 of tithe money and paid but a quarter of it to his curate and "dogsbody".[46] Bishop Burgess accepted that the stipends of some of his clergy would "not satisfy the demands of the most ordinary manual labour", but accepted this was often due to the poverty of the livings "and the want of an established rule for the *minimum* of recompense" which he believed was the prevailing cause.[47] He was clearly stating that the £20 minimum under the 1713 legislation was no longer adequate. Benjamin Hall, speaking in a parliamentary debate on the Established Church bill of 1836, told of a curate who did the duty of two parishes with a large income for £100 per year, out of which he had to find £10 for a house, and "with as large a flock of children as curates are generally blessed with." Yet this man was fortunate for Hall claimed that many Welsh curates were eking out a miserable existence by working in the fields.[48] Stacey of Gelligaer was criticised in the press during 1850 for providing his curates with half of what he was receiving himself as curate of Cardiff (actually untrue), but it added as a barb about curates "whose wants are supplied by a leek and a Welsh rabbit".[49]

On the other hand, the bishop's right to fix the stipend of a curate caused some non-residents to complain they were left with little for themselves, as did William Watkins, curate to the bishop's parish at Bedwas but also perpetual curate of Merthyr Mawr in the vale of Glamorgan. This parish was served by a stipendiary curate paid at £40 plus fees, the living being valued at £69. But in 1832 Bishop Copleston insisted the stipends be increased to £50, receiving Watkins' complaint he was left with a mere £18.17s.6d.[50] Virgin notes the case of Henry Berkin, a multi-pluralist, with a living in the Forest of Dean and of two Monmouthshire parishes, Cilgwrrwg and Penteri. His English parish had been held since 1817, and therefore came under the 1813 legislation with the result that the curate was paid the full value of the living, £80. The two Monmouthshire parishes had been held since 1810 and were exempt, and the curates thereof received £30 each. But Berkin's own income, after these deductions, was a meagre £62. Pluralism hardly paid! He was one of many incumbents, four per cent of the total, who received less than their own curates as a result of this legislation.[51]

Copleston was one of many bishops who endeavoured to obtain the parsonage house for these stipendiary curates, rather than see it let out to a tenant to the detriment of the house itself and thus forcing the curate to seek other accommodation, often outside the parish.[52] Edward Maurice, curate of Selattyn in 1751, lived in the parsonage house,[53] as did David Jones, rector of Llangan, when he acted as stipendiary curate of Coychurch during the 1770s.[54] But by 1791 the parsonage house at Selattyn had been let, and the curate was forced to reside in Oswestry.[55]

Many of these stipendiary curates had to find their own home, or if they were unmarried, lodgings. The poor curate of Gwenddwr, Breconshire, Mr Price, about whom a malicious complaint was made in 1789, was said by his rural dean to have lived in lodgings in another parish at a price that exceeded his £15 salary. He asked how a clergyman could support himself with this sum. Presumably, he held another curacy for there was only single duty in that parish.[56] Thomas Wynne, curate of Llandrillo-yn-Rhos was forced to live in the next parish "for want of proper lodging" according to his rural dean in 1791.[57] Bishop Copleston was concerned to discover that the junior vicar of Llandaff Cathedral, in trouble for drunkenness, lodged at a public house.[58] It was not without precedent. The rural dean of Cedewain, Montgomeryshire, reported to his bishop in 1791 that the curate of Llanllugan was much addicted to drinking and lodged in an alehouse in that poor and obscure parish, but the keeper of the alehouse took good care of him and furnished him with clothes and all necessaries. As he was far advanced in years his habits would not easily be amended.[59]

John Guy notes that during the immediate post-Restoration period in Llandaff diocese many of the stipendiary curates were often natives of the parishes they served, and accordingly lived at home, and even might have worked the family farm. It seems this was a deliberate policy, thus neutralising the problems of poverty and the lack of accommodation.[60] John David Davies, later a distinguished rector of Llanmadoc, Gower, spend his earlier ministerial years after his ordination in 1855 as curate of several parishes in that area, but his father being rector of Reynoldston, meant he was able to live at home.[61] He did not neglect his parishes, nor did Thomas John Davies, curate of the Montgomeryshire parish of Llandysilio between 1803-33, then held by the bishop of St Asaph *in commendam*. Davies lived three and a half miles away at his ancestral home, Treveylan Hall, travelling back and forwards on horseback.[62]

SOME CASE STUDIES

As noted earlier, these stipendiary curates often were *de facto* incumbents of their parishes, and many did outstanding work within them. Many bore in mind, in service if not in recollection, Samuel Wesley's letter to a curate. He should undertake a house to house pastoral visitation, read prayers on Sundays and holy days and the liturgy on Wednesday and Friday, teach his congregation to sing the metrical psalms, catechise the young, preach and celebrate the Holy Communion monthly, encourage baptisms in the church rather than privately at the home, exact penances for breaking church discipline, and never enter a public house or dispute with dissenters.[63] Many parishioners might have preferred a young resident curate who was ambitious and pastorally minded to an aged rector who, if resident, might have given the parish the bare minimum he could get away with, and possibly quarrel with them about their payment of tithes. Let me offer some examples of exemplary service, though many gave the same sort of ministry without it being recorded.

As stipendiary curate of Llangenni, Breconshire, the evangelical Henry Vaughan, appointed as a deacon in 1829, exercised a pastoral ministry that reached out to the remote cottages of that widespread parish, cared for the poor and so proclaimed the Gospel that it was "impossible for anyone to despise his youth".[64]

John Blackwell, the Welsh literary figure, who became stipendiary curate of Holywell in 1829, is said to have entered upon his duties with a firm determination "to spend and be spent" for the temporal and spiritual welfare of his flock. His ministry was singularly successful, especially in his care of the poor and in his sympathy in the trials and sufferings of his parishioners, for he had faced them too in his life. A testimonial to him when leaving spoke of his active benevolence, his help to the poor in a severe winter, his commencement of a clothing club, and his assistance to the victims of a cholera epidemic. His sermons too were remembered: his thundering forth the terrors of the law, pouring the balm of consolation onto the wounded spirit of the penitent, and his unfolding of the glorious promises of the gospel.[65]

Henry Powell Ffoulkes, later archdeacon of Montgomery, was stipendiary curate of Buckley (then part of the parish of Hawarden) between 1840-57, commencing his ministry there a year after his priesting. There he established Tractarian practices, reordering the church, introducing a robed choir and daily services, making the service of the Church more attractive to his mainly working-class parishioners, and winning the hearts of his people by his "self denying labours", his concern and pastoral care for them and their children's education.[66] William Evans, later of Rhymney, was curate of Gelligaer in 1851, replacing a man he had mistaken for a gamekeeper. He visited and encouraged people to attend the services of the church, thus filling it once more, established an evening service in spite of the wardens' protests about the extra cost involved (he asked people to bring their own candles), and in spite of them, and with the bishop's backing, obtained new seating to replace ones almost unserviceable because of their condition. In all he revived the spiritual life of that parish.[67] In the early 1850s Robert Roberts recalled the newly ordained curate of Bethesda, acting for the non-resident dean of Bangor, whose Welsh was imperfect and his preaching indifferent. Nevertheless, as Roberts put it, you forgot the preacher in the man.[68] The curate of Presteigne in the 1860s, J.E. Cheese, is said to have won the admiration of the parish for his good works, especially among the street urchins, and building a ragged school for them.[69]

The diaries of John James Turner for the years 1857-8, provide an outstanding picture of the life of a stipendiary curate. Turner came from a minor gentry family, and became curate of Berriew, Montgomeryshire, in 1855, resigning in 1861 to become assistant curate to his vicar, John Luxmoore, who resided on his other cure of Llanymynech. Luxmoore was none too pleased that Turner elected, being unmarried, to go into lodgings, costing him £90 from his £150 stipend, rather than make use of the parsonage house, which had to be let. Turner found the cost of keeping a pony was too much for his pocket, so he hired a horse when required, but normally walked around the parish, to his home, twelve miles away, and even to Shrewsbury. As a Tractarian Turner endeavoured to introduce greater dignity into the worship of the church, but the choir resisted when he attempted to take control of the music, and when a harmonium was installed instead of a band, they revolted, choosing to sing a penitential psalm to the most lively tune they could find on the organ accompanied by "Hallelujahs". His first Harvest service was marred by the drunkenness of some of the labourers who attended, probably annoyed that their traditional rites had been supplanted, and his efforts to prevent private baptisms at homes was unavailing. Nonconformists rather disliked him, as he declined to accept that their ministers were "reverends".

There was conflict with the local squire who probably resented Turner's desire to supersede lay control in church affairs, while Turner was often annoyed by Mr

Lyon's demands and requirements and his attempted control of the offertory money. Even though he admitted he was not a good preacher, making use of published sermons at the last minute, he was clearly a good pastoral visitor, seems to have known most of the inhabitants of his parish, and acted with great kindness and charity towards the sick and poor. During his time in the parish he established two church-schools, which also doubled up on Sundays as mission stations. Yet his attempt to create a new "Jerusalem" in a remote Welsh village must have caused him much heartache, and after further rows with the village hierarchy, the imposition of an unsatisfactory scripture reader who took a too independent line, and the coming of an assistant curate who might have been more under the control of his vicar than himself, Turner departed into the new status of a resident assistant curate elsewhere. Clearly a man in too much of a hurry for a quiet and traditional community, he nevertheless planted the seeds of church growth and mission in that parish.[70]

Yet sometimes the task was overwhelming, and not only for Turner. The curate of Newtown for the non-resident and pluralist George Foxton, rector 1815-44, George Gardiner Williams, found it impossible to counteract the influence of dissent in that town. He lacked the authority to plant a much needed new church, and this had to await Foxton's resident successor. In 1833 the church congregation was about 300, compared to the Welsh Calvinists with their 800, the Baptists with 900, and the Wesleyans 700. Education was almost in the hands of the Nonconformists.[71]

There were many splendid stipendiary curates who did a noble job for little temporal reward. But in an age when hard decisions had to be made, church planting attempted, educational provision established, their hands were tied. As John Guy records of them, they managed to maintain church life rather than enhance it.[72]

CHAPTER FIVE: PERPETUAL AND STIPENDIARY CURATES: THE CONSEQUENCES

Those two classes of curates, the perpetual curates (and those who were curates of chapelries before they became such), and stipendiary curates, generally were ill-paid, often with less than that received by a labourer, and this meant they were forced to obtain other means of livelihood, often by taking on the care of further parishes. Yet it was not only these men who were forced to do so, for incumbents of poorly endowed livings found themselves obliged to do the same. There arose, therefore, almost historic groupings of parishes and perpetual curacies effectively served by a single priest, who might be incumbent of one parish and curate of some others. The grouping often contained two incumbents and one perpetual curacy, or in some other similar combination. The result was that many parishes had to be content with single duty, a clergyman who lived outside the parish, and a stipendiary curate possibly serving other parishes as well, whose ministry could not be as effective as an incumbent as he was unable to give the leadership that might be required.

We need to remind ourselves, briefly, about the poverty of these curacies, but we also need to remember that many livings were equally poor, as we note in a later chapter. The poverty of the Welsh curate was almost proverbial, and was based on fact, not hearsay. "As ragged as a Welsh curate" is mentioned in a pamphlet of 1744, and this was probably a quotation,[1] while as late as 1845 it was argued that the Welsh curate was entitled to pity, for his means of subsistence was limited and precarious. As in the history of "the church mouse" there are seasons when "some crumbs of comfort" fall into his path, "yet these seasons are, like angelic visits, few and far between".[2] A petition of 1670 to Bishop Lucy of St Davids by the inhabitants of the parish concerned John Griffiths, curate of the parish of Maenclochog. Though he was a conscientious minister, sober in life and conversation, and had eight children, he received but £5 from the church. The petition told the bishop he was now living without any subsistence or maintenance for himself or family, save for the bare revenue of this poor vicarage [which had been sequestrated and he placed in charge], and he was so destitute it was likely that he and his family would be evicted from their habitation during the cold of winter.[3]

Thomas Price, rector of Merthyr Tydfil, wrote in the 1720s that "many poor clergymen are not able to purchase more than bare food and raiment for their families".[4] John Jones, an Oxford tutor, called these men "hirelings" who, having spent their fortune on a college education, were forced to live a life of obscurity and indigence,[5] while John Wade suggested the Welsh curate was seldom able to eat meat, but lived instead on potatoes and bread.[6] This remained true for many of these curates. The *Annual Register* of 1788 notes a return to the House of Commons, that has not been traced, describing a poor Welsh curate, with nine children and one on the way, for whom he could not procure shoes or stockings, and only with difficulty could he provide them with food. His total income was £35 per annum and he cared for four parishes.[7] Two years later Bishop Horsley's half sister referred to these "patient, poor, plodding labourers of the vineyard", who were supporting a wife and large families upon a miserable pittance of between £10 to £15 a year with the care in some cases of up to six churches.[8] George Williams, curate of various parishes in the vale of Glamorgan, including Ystradowen 1763-86, possibly lived on a similar income, for he received from his parishes £30, plus some tithe money, though his account books indicate he was able to provide mutton and veal, tea and sugar, potatoes, oatmeal and bread, for his family, though possibly some came from land he cultivated. He bought fish and brewed his own ale. Two of his sons were later ordained.[9]

Sometimes, though not often, the position was redressed. A story is told of Bishop Shipley of St Asaph (1769-87) who received a complaint from a Welsh squire that the curate of his parish employed his leisure time in mending and repairing clocks for his parishioners. This, he declared, meant he was engaged in trade which the law prohibited. The bishop sent for him and asked for an explanation about why he was disgracing his calling. The answer was clear, namely to support his wife and children. Shipley said that would not do and he would inflict a punishment that would prevent him continuing this pitiful trade, and gave him the presentation to a living worth £150.[10]

It was even worse when such men became too old or incapacitated for active work and became dependent on charity. The Ladies of Llangollen recorded in the early 1800s how "a genteel serious-looking clergyman, very well dressed," presented them with a paper requesting them to read it. It was an account of his distresses. Owen Jones had been a curate for many years in the diocese of St Asaph but a violent asthma now prevented him from serving. He and his five children were now in great distress. On the other side of the paper was a list of the "most respectable names" in the county who had assisted him.[11]

The poverty of these men often made them contemptible in the eyes of their flock and perhaps nullified much of their work. A pamphlet relating to north Wales of 1701 defended them when a writer described them as "spiritual muckenders", "sow-gelders and alehouse-keepers", perhaps indicating some of their other activities.[12] John Jones, curate of Capel Garmon 1730-79, may have been one of those so-called, for he certainly felt his position sorely. A university graduate, living on £20 a year, he pleaded with his bishop, Drummond of St Asaph, in 1749-50 for a place where he could get "a wherewithal" to educate his six children, for they were at present not only without education but also without shoes. "May I presume to tell your lordship", he wrote, "that it is a general complaint that the revenues of the Church are very unequally divided amongst the inferior clergy ... These unhappy circumstances are enough to break the vigour of their parts and spirit and render their persons mean and their compositions equal to their condition and circumstances."[13]

There were certainly some clergy who took to menial jobs in order to eke out a livelihood for themselves and their families.[14] Some worked on the land, probably renting a smallholding or farming the glebe if that was available, so that like Henry Fielding's Mr Trulliber, being "a parson on Sundays but all the other six might more properly be called a farmer."[15] Wade mentions a curate in north Wales on £10 - £15 who acted as a boatman on a ferry, shaved as a barber, and taught children as well.[16] A story is told, possibly apocryphal, by *The Gamesters' Law* of 1710 of a Welsh curate, asked how he managed to maintain a wife and seven children on £9 per year, replied that his wife sold ale and he had a bear which he baited after each service, and they made "a very pretty business" of it.[17] These circumstances are confirmed by William Richards, writing in 1682, who described "rectors", probably curates, having "the perquisites of a drum and fiddle; which well managed on a Holy Day, make up a very pretty thing. Others have an Augmentation of a bull or a bear, which being solemnly baited about twice in a quarter, do pick up pretty comfortable tithe from the spectators' pockets, and makes the poor parson's purse to smile and mantle".[18] The keeping of an alehouse was certainly true of a curate of Capel Curig in 1819 when he married the widow of the landlord of a local inn, becoming the publican himself. One visitor was said to have remarked that it was a singular case of plurality, for though St

Matthew was originally a publican he forsook that occupation in order to be a teacher.[19]

A number became schoolmasters, generally of a parochial school set up by themselves or by a local magnate which they were easily able to combine with their curacy.[20] John Kenrick, later a leading supporter in north Wales of Griffith Jones's circulating schools, kept a private school during the time he was curate of Llaneilian 1719-26, later to become full-time master of Llanrwst School for some years.[21] In a study of education in eighteenth century Montgomeryshire Humphreys records schools kept by the local curates at Llanfihangel yng Ngwynfa in 1700, Llangynyw in 1749, Llanwnnog 1811, and Welshpool, during the second quarter of that century.[22] Thus Richard Edwards, curate of Trevethin, received £5 per annum in the 1770s for teaching some of Mr Hanbury's workmen's children, Hanbury being a local industrialist and squire.[23] Lewis Evans, perpetual curate of Eglwys Newydd from 1798-1812, had not only a number of curacies linked to that cure, but he became tutor to the Williams family of Castle Hill, Aberystwyth, where he lodged for a number of years, receiving his board and lodging free in return for his services. Later, with this family's help, he opened a successful private school in that town in the 1800s.[24] One wonders whether the Company of Mine Adventures of England in the first part of the eighteenth century used local clergy to act as a chaplain to their miners in Cardiganshire, to read prayers, preach and catechise the workmen and their children, at a stipend of £30, or whether this was a post held by a full-time cleric.[25]

A few curates obtained an additional income from acting as tutors to the children of local gentry, as did one Mr Morris, the curate of Wrexham, who in 1782 was paid 50 guineas per annum for teaching the two sons of Philip Yorke of Erthig. He gave eight hours a week, spread out over four afternoons. The boys later went to Ruthin School and from there to Eton.[26] In addition, there were also others, such as Lewis Anthony Nicholl, ordained in 1832, who appears to have freelanced, taking clerical duty as and when required in the Cardiff area.[27]

PLURALIST CURATES

The majority of stipendiary curates, and indeed many incumbents, if they wished to obtain a living wage, generally took on additional parishes and became pluralists, generally to non-resident incumbents.[28] Bishop Copleston of Llandaff maintained the real problem in his diocese was not the pluralities held by incumbents, but those held by curates, and he tried to ensure that no cleric had to take more than two services per Sunday. He was probably unsuccessful.[29] William Corbett in the 1830s wrote that it was common for one curate in parts of England (and he might have added Wales) to serve three parishes, even four, and nothing was so common as serving two.[30] The anonymous writer of a published letter to the bishop of St Davids in the 1790s argued that university men should not be condemned to take upon themselves the fatigue and trouble of serving three or four churches, for the trifling consideration of twenty or twenty-five pounds a year.[31] John Guy notes that many of these curates were content to remain as such, for their stipends as curacies combined were generally better than an incumbency. Thus John Evans, curate of Llanederyn, Roath and Rumney on the Glamorgan-Monmouthshire border, received a total income from them of £88. This was a better stipend than many incumbents received in that diocese.[32]

It is difficult to provide statistical evidence in many cases because many stipendiary curates remained unlicensed, and thus unnoticed, while the ministry of one man might consist of various combinations of incumbencies and curacies in order to make ends meet. Indeed, the parliamentary returns of the 1800s and beyond did not distinguish between *bona fide* curates and incumbents acting as curates.[33] The clerical life of Jonah Bowen Evans may serve as one example of this trend. Ordained in 1829 be became curate of Cwmiou, served Capel y ffin and Llanthony, and also Orcop, in the neighbouring diocese of Hereford. Five years later as perpetual curate of Talachddu, Breconshire, he also served the parishes of Llanfihangel Talyllyn and Llanddew as curate. Even while vicar of St Harmon's in Radnorshire he acted at various times as curate of Banhadlog and later of Llanwrthwl where he acted for an incapacitated incumbent, but he also farmed smallholdings to make ends meet.[34]

Numerous clerics served as pluralist curates. The 1710 visitation of the Archdeaconry of Carmarthen provides us with numerous examples of this practice. Samuel Morris, vicar of Llangan and also of Castelldwyran, was also curate for Mr Collins the incumbent of Kilymaenllwyd and Llangeler; George Thomas, curate of Llanddowror also served Pendine and Llandawke, and Morgan Williams served as resident curate of both Llansadwrn and Llanwrda. He received £12 for each.[35]

In the diocese of St Asaph John Jones was curate in 1784 of the adjoining parishes of Llangynog, Llangadfan and Garthbeibio, serving for a non-resident, William Worthington who allowed him for serving all three parishes £25 plus surplice fees.[36] In Llandaff diocese the diarist William Thomas recorded in 1762 that

Nathaniel Wells and his curate Powell were serving eight churches between them each Sunday: St Andrew's, Lavernock, Penarth, Cogan, Llandough, Leckwith, Llandaff and Whitchurch.[37] Some of these parishes seem to have been worked together in various ways, especially Sully, Barry and Porthceri. Hezekiah Jones was curate of these parishes in 1802 together with Bedwas and Rudry, possibly requiring some assistance in these two later Monmouthshire parishes.[38] In the 1760s again George Williams was acting as stipendiary curate to William Thomas, master of Abergavenny Grammar School, who was rector of Llansannor and curate of Ystradowen. He also acted as curate of St Donats for which he received an additional £10 in addition to the £14 he obtained from these other curacies.[39] Thomas Davies, rector of Coety, then non-resident and teaching at Trefecca College, the Countess of Huntington's training college for men in her connexion, pointed out in a letter to his bishop of 1776 that his curate at Coety, Mr Lewis, was also curate of St Bride's Minor ever since he had been ordained, and it was a great advantage to him as his salary from his own curacy was so small.[40] The curates of Tonyrefail, then a chapelry in the parish of Llantrisant, often doubled up as curates of Aberdare, Merthyr Tydfil and Llanwynno, although not all at the same time. John Davies, for example, curate 1790-5, also served Merthyr Tydfil.[41] One man, John Powell, served six churches in south Monmouthshire as a curate in 1798, replacing one resident and two non-resident clerics, and offering two of his churches a weekly service and three fortnightly ones.[42] David Griffiths was curate to the absentee Griffith Griffiths, a notable pluralist, who died in 1812, and served not only Llanharri on behalf of his rector, but also the neighbouring parishes of Llanilid and Llanharan, all for £32 per year.[43]

Thomas Price (Carnhuanawc), and his father, Rice Price, came into this category. His father served for a time the parishes of Llanlleonfel, Llanwrthwl, Llanganten and Llangynog, the first at least as perpetual curate, though the distances between them required him to keep a curate at Llanwrthwl. His gross income was £50 a year, less whatever he paid his curate. Unable to afford a horse, he walked sixteen miles each Sunday, "hastening from parish to parish all day long … so as to give to each, in regular rotation, … the advantage or disadvantage of a morning, an afternoon or an evening service; the service shortened by all possible omissions to enable the harrassed minister to complete his sum of Sunday labour". His parishioners were deprived of his weekly pastoral ministry, unless he was summoned to perform the occasional offices of the Church. As a result dissent increased in these parishes. His son in 1816 served as curate for five shilling a week at Llangatwg, Crickhowell, with the parochial chapelries of Llanelli and Llangenni, and lived in lodgings at Crickhowell, Breconshire. His incumbent was Lord William Somerset, a wealthy man in his own right.[44] A further example is that of Francis Taynton who was licensed to various curacies from 1828 onwards at Llancarfan, Eglwysbrewis, Porthceri, and later served Pendoylan and Ystradowen, though he then lived at Cowbridge,[45]

As already noted, it was quite common for a cleric to serve as the incumbent of one or two parishes and curate of another. In his study of the diocese of Llandaff in 1763 Guy suggests that only 25 of the curates were not incumbents or served another church, usually two or three parishes situated reasonably close together.[46] The remote perpetual curacy of Glyncorrwg, in the Upper Afan valley, was variously served by the incumbent of Ystradyfodwg, one of whom, the fiery Thomas Davies, was killed in 1754 when his horse lost its way in a fog and fell over some crag on the long mountainous journey between those two parishes, though his replacement, Thomas Morrice, was curate of the neighbouring parish of Michaelston, still seven or so miles away.[47] Thomas Williams, perpetual curate of Michaelston from 1762, became curate to William Thomas, an Oxford fellow, at Aberafan and Briton Ferry, neighbouring parishes, but lived at Aberafan parsonage house as he had not one of his own. Serving other cures at different times, such as St John's Swansea in 1781, he needed a curate for Michaelston, and in 1784 obtained the services of William Rees who doubled up as curate of St Bride's Minor, twelve miles away, and Llandyfodwg, seventeen miles away.[48] The rector of Llanmartin and Wilcrick in Monmouthshire, John Martin, from 1739-95, was ordered to live at Llanmartin by his bishop in 1742 when it was discovered he was also serving the curacies of Llanwenarth, Llanhillith and Aberystruth, though by the 1770s he was serving instead, from that parish, the curacies of Llanvaches, Rogiet and Langstone.[49]

Bishop Barrington's book of 1771 notes some further examples, such as John Walters, rector of Llandough who was also curate of St Mary Church.[50] Thomas Richards, vicar of Llanelen, in his will of 1770 noted a debt due to him from William Watkins for serving the curacies of Llanfihangel Crucorney and Llangatwg Lingoed. His widow also recalled the debt in her will of 1773.[51] A memorial in Llangatwg nigh Usk parish church commemorates William Charles, who died in 1819, who for forty years was curate of this parish but also rector of Llanddewi Rhydderch, thus both curate and an incumbent.[52] The Welsh scholar, Edward "Celtic" Davies, rector of

Bishopston 1805-31, who also held a parish in Breconshire and until required to reside in his parish acted as curate of Olveston, Gloucestershire, also served as curate of the neighbouring parish of Oxwich enabling him to live in its parsonage house as his own at Bishopston was in a state of total dilapidation.[53]

Other incumbents choose to be non-residents on their Welsh livings but took curacies in England, as did John Priest, vicar of Roath in 1771 who had a curacy in Bath; George Richards, vicar of Penarth in 1815, who was curate of a Worcestershire parish for 35 years; or Capel Blashfield, rector of Goetre, 1814, who was curate of Alresford, Hampshire.[54] Another example is William Lucas Collins, rector of Cheriton in Gower 1815-67, who in 1853 moved to Northamptonshire where he acquired a number of curacies.[55] The position of Stacey, rector of Gelligaer, and curate of Cardiff from 1835, has already been mentioned.

Many of these pluralities were more technical than actual, as noted beforehand. Serving parishes adjoining one another, or close to each other, meant some deprivation in ministry for the parishes concerned, especially in only having a single service each Sunday, but a pastoral ministry was still available, if only in a perfunctory form. Jacob, in his *Clerical Profession* suggests while there might have been irresponsible curates in these pluralities, attempts were made to correct and amend their mischief, but there was little evidence of real pastoral neglect.[56] Morgan, in his study of the nineteenth century diocese of St Davids disagrees. He argues that all that a man could do under those circumstances was to perform the minimal canonical duties, and parishioners were "deprived of those constant ministrations which were essential for effective pastoral work". The encouragement to a good life, the settling of disputes, the readiness to offer wise counsel, comfort the sick, give aid to the needy, was often lacking, and the difficulties of travelling, especially in winter, over rough mountain tracks or across swollen rivers, to reach the beside of one dying or to baptise a child not expected to live, could render the journey impossible. Many parishioners, he claims, as did Griffith Jones of the circulating school movement, hardly knew "the voice of the shepherd". Sunday services were rushed through as quickly as possible with the cleric's horse saddled and bridled for him to get off to his next assignment.[57] We need to remember that the traditional Sunday morning service consisted of Matins, Litany, Ante-Communion, and a Sermon. Thus Daniel Jeffreys, curate of Llangynog, admitted that sometimes he was in such a rush to travel the six miles to his other cure of Llanganten that he would omit the Litany on the occasion of a communion Sunday.[58]

It has been argued that an examination of deaneries and archdeaconries would indicate that these arrangements of livings served by one man were "an ingenious grouping of livings and inter-relation of benefices and curacies ... obviously designed to try and give as much service as possible to the parishes".[59] While this was true of many of these groupings, it was not true of all, mainly because of the widespread and scattered nature of parishes in the more mountainous areas of Cardiganshire, Glamorganshire and Gwynedd. A number of examples are noted below.

SOME CONSEQENCES OF THIS PLURALISM

The concern of both Church and State about non-residence and pluralism has been discussed before, as well as the attempt made by legislation to enforce residence by insisting on realistic and fair stipends for stipendiary curates. Here we look at some of the difficulties faced by these men, serving multiple parishes, and their parishioners, because of this system.

In many respects the position in Cardiganshire was more acute than in most other parts of Wales, or indeed of the whole Established Church. This was because of the poverty of its livings and the need for its clergy to take on numerous parishes in order to find the means to support themselves and their families. Although writing of a slightly larger area, Bishop Middleton of St Davids (1582-94) believed that they lived in such a "beggarly state" that they were forced to conclude poor bargains for another cure from the impropriators, thus being guilty of simony, and Bishop Richard Davies, his predecessor, wrote that some of these men had to come "galloping" from another parish to take the service in a ruinous building.[60]

Griffith Jones of Llanddowror in 1715 wrote of clergymen "pinched with poverty and forced to officiate in three or four parishes & therefore cannot pretend to do well in either, and thus are the children left uncatechised & the people in some places for months, yea for near (to say no more) twelve months together without a sermon".[61] It is a picture confirmed by Erasmus Saunders, who writing before 1721, argued (with perhaps a little extravagation):

> As the Christian Service is thus totally disus'd in some Places, there are other some that may be said to be but half serv'd; there being several Churches, where we are but rarely, if at all to meet with Preaching, Catechising, or Administring

> of the Holy Communion: In others the Services of the Prayers is but partly Read, and that perhaps but once a Month, or once in a quarter of a Year; nor is it indeed reasonable to expect that they should be better serv'd, while the Stipends allow'd for the Service of them are so small that a poor Curate must sometimes submit to serve three or four Churches for Ten to Twelve Pounds a Year, and that perhaps when they are almost as many Miles distant from each other.

He continued, in a quotation noted before, that these men had to hurry from place to place, and often had to shorten the service in order to accomplish their Sunday duty.[62]

A well-known example of this position is that of John Rowland, brother of the revivalist. He served between until his death in 1760 as rector of Llangeitho (where he resided), vicar of Nantcwnlle, and perpetual curate of Llanbadarn Odwyn and Llanddewi Brefi. On Sundays he would start a horse ride of 16 miles to arrive at Nancwnlle at 8.00, then Llangeitho at 10.00, and Llanddewi Brefi at noon, then commence a ten mile return journey to take an evening service at Llanddewi Brefi at four o'clock. He preached at each church on alternate Sundays, and the route varied in the same way. Llanddewi Brefi was valued at £8 per annum, though the impropriator, the Chichester family, obtained £400 from it, and in all he received £46 per annum.[63] Hughes of Eglwys Newydd, described as a diligent and sober man, in the 1760s travelled 27 miles each Sunday in order to serve his two chapelries, besides his main church,[64] while Lewis Evans, perpetual curate of Eglwys Newydd and curate of other parishes in that area, in the late 1790s claimed he had to travel up to 24 miles each Sunday on indifferent roads to take two services and visit the sick. In 1800 he wrote about the hardness of his lot. Each Sunday, acting as a "trotting curate" in "an extensive diocese" he had to travel ten to twelve miles and return cold and dreary between eight and nine o'clock.[65]

Morgan records a similar number of instances during the nineteenth century within the diocese of St Davids. Daniel Evans, who was the incumbent of a consolidated benefice of four parishes, including Llanafan Fawr, Breconshire, would take services at 9.00, 11.00 and at 3.00, reversing the order the next Sunday. In 1847 the Education Report – the famous *Blue Books* – described how in one of his churches, Llanafan Fechan, the service was only held if there were banns to be published or a wedding or funeral conducted; there was no service at Llanfihangel Abergwesyn for five out of six Sundays for want of a congregation, and at

Llanfihangel Brynpaduan Evans often rode by the church "but seldom had occasion to alight to do duty from the paucity of the congregation". Morgan notes, however, that in many similar cases, the two less populous parishes had a service every other Sunday.[66]

Besides those in Cardiganshire, there were many other similar parishes throughout Wales, though without the concentration of the former. A complaint was made in 1640 about a curate who served Mold, Tryddyn and Nerquis, in the diocese of St Asaph. As a result the morning service in one church did not finish until one o'clock, and the curate had to get a layman, a boy or even a ploughman to read evening prayer for him in one of his churches.[67] The rector of Llansannor, Glamorgan, William Cooke, had a number of outlying curacies, and it was said of him in 1718 "[h]ow he came to huddle up so many churches is not my business to inquire, but this I am assur'd, He is as poor as a church mouse". It was added that he seldom "troubles these cures", so perhaps the services were not so frequent as they should have been.[68]

The rural deans' reports of 1749 for the diocese of St Asaph offer other examples. Robert Conway, curate of the chapelry of Llangadwaladr was also vicar of Llansilin, and a complaint was made by the parishioners of the former that while service should take place between noon and 1.00 pm on the Sunday, he was often late.[69] Bingley, in his tour of north Wales, published in 1804, made a similar complaint. Noting that many clergy, to obtain a livelihood, had to serve several churches, he commented that the service had to be "hurried over with a carelessness that ill becomes the ambassador of God". He considered this had aided the cause of Methodism.[70]

With the profusion of churches in Anglesey served by one clergymen, the result in 1813 was that only ten per cent of the parishes on that island had double duty, 69 per cent had single duty and nearly twenty per cent had less than single duty, probably a service each alternative Sunday.[71] Yates records one example of a cleric's Sunday duty around this time. He notes how in 1801 the cleric who served the Anglesey parishes of Llechgynfarwy, Rhodogeidio, Llantrisant and Llanfair Gweredog, Richard Davies, had services at 8.00 without a sermon, or at 9.00 with a sermon, 11.00 at Llantrisant, a monthly service elsewhere in addition to occasional afternoon services, involving travelling, depending on the schedule, between seven and a half miles and up to eighteen miles per Sunday.[72]

In another instance the aged curate of Llanfihangel Talyllyn, Breconshire,

Thomas Lewis, who also served Llanywern, threatened with dismissal from the latter in 1814 because of his old age (he would soon be "in his long house"), having served these parishes for 53 years, wrote to his bishop asking for his intervention, and noting that he had three duties to perform, and a journey of four to five miles each Sunday.[73]

In 1853 Richard Williams Morgan, perpetual curate of Tregynon, Montgomeryshire, with its gross income of £83, and also curate of Mochdre, offering him an additional £50 wrote about his circumstances. The distance between the two churches was ten miles, with "roads of the roughest and most exposed description, presenting scarcely a mile of level or trotting ground in their whole extent". Over the previous eleven years he reckoned he had ridden between twenty and thirty thousand miles along this route, often through storms and floods which meant he had to officiate in wet clothes. His Mochdre stipend barely covered the expenses of a horse and groom. He had no family so that perhaps, and a housekeeper, was a luxury he could afford.[74]

The result of episcopal pressure allied with government legislation to end these pluralities was obvious. They had become an embarrassment, especially as it was believed that the lack of double duty and resident clergy had encouraged dissent and possibly allowed a revolutionary spirit to develop unchecked in many places. Furthermore, such parishes acted as a disincentive for men to come forward for ordination. Progress at redressing this position may have slow as vested interests were respected, but it was significant. In 1827, for example, only 26 parishes in the diocese of Llandaff had double duty, but 1849 there were 100, out of 216 benefices. In Monmouthshire the 137 cures that lacked a resident minister in 1827 had been reduced to 53 by 1850.[75] It may not be too surprising that many of these natural groupings, traditionally held together in a combination of incumbencies and curacies, often became the basis of consolidation, by which three or more parishes were linked into one benefice.[76]

By the 1840s the era of stipendiary curates was coming to an end, to be replaced by the assistant curate, a position almost unrecognised by legislation, and to this we now turn.

CHAPTER SIX: THE ASSISTANT CURATE: A NEW BREED

"Of late years an abundant show of curates has fallen upon the north of England; that lie very thick upon the hills; every parish has one or more of them", Charlotte Bronte famously wrote in her novel *Shirley*. These were assistant curates, those who acted for a resident incumbent, and these men were almost a new breed of clergyman. It was argued that assistant curates "holding the position and performing the duties which they now do, are, as a class, the creation of the present century". Though the stipendiary curates were protected and their stipends stipulated by legislation, the assistant curate had no legally stipulated stipends or any form of protection. In their case the 1838 Plurality Act, which had settled the stipends of those stipendiary curates, was a dead letter. Furthermore, many incumbents, especially of those newly created or industrial parishes where they were sorely needed, were unable to find or afford a reasonable stipend and paid a bare subsistence rate.[1]

Bishop Copleston believed he was empowered to license those who acted as lecturers in parishes, where they received a stipend to deliver a sermon at a stated period, as assistant curates to those parishes. This was mentioned by his archdeacon, Thomas Williams, in his Charge of 1845.[2] Bishop Wilberforce of Oxford from the late 1840s persuaded many incumbents to appoint resident assistant curates and through a diocesan society grants were available towards their stipends.[3] Other dioceses, included those in Wales, followed suit.

It took time, of course, for the old stipendiary curates to be replaced by the assistant curates. In a return of 1843 St Asaph had 23 stipendiary curates who did the whole duty of their parishes, and 28 assistant clergy, with the numbers in Bangor being 19 and 35 respectively.[4] Similarly, the 1851 religious census records both types of curacies. In the Bridgend district there were 8 assistant curates and 6 stipendiary curates; in Llandeilo Fawr three of each; in Monmouth one assistant and two stipendiary and in the Narberth district one assistant and four stipendiaries.[5] As late as 1881 there were still 14 stipendiary curates acting for non-residents in the four Welsh dioceses, compared to 353 assistant curates.[6]

Although these assistant curates were more a feature of the Victorian church than the Georgian Church, that church still possessed such men, even though their number was dwarfed by the overwhelming predominance of stipendiary curates. The resident incumbent of Llandeilo Fawr had an assistant curate living in the town in 1710,[7] and a number are noted as assisting stipendiary curates in the diocese of St Asaph in 1749.[8] Bishop Jenkinson of St Davids made it clear in 1828 that he refused to ordain a man to an assistant curacy for a resident incumbent while there were surplus clergy available.[9] A writer of 1832 suggested that as no practical training was given to ordinands only those who would serve as assistant curates to a resident incumbent should be ordained, for he could provide such training for them.[10] James Downes, assistant curate to William Bruce Knight, vicar of Margam, was one such man. In a letter of 1838 Knight wrote that he was an amiable person anxious to do his duty and had been well received by the farmers and kindly treated by the gentry.[11]

By 1867 it was alleged that over 5,000 assistant curacies had been created throughout the Established Church since the 1838 Act and this was an entirely new class of clergy.[12] In 1881 there was one assistant curate to every three clergymen in the predominantly rural diocese of St Davids and an average of one to two in the other Welsh dioceses.[13] The twenty assistant curates of that diocese in 1831 had become 148 by 1905.[14] By 1870 there were over 100 curates working in the coalfields of the diocese of Llandaff, and it was argued in 1886 that this diocese had more assistant clergy than any other diocese in England and Wales. There were some large industrial parishes in the diocese which required ten to eleven assistant curates.[15]

In order to sustain the number of curates required, especially for Welsh-speaking areas, the traditional standards demanded by many English dioceses had to be reduced, to the despair of the Welsh bishops. This, of course, was true of some of the English dioceses, such as Durham and Chester, though they did not have the issue of bilingualism to contend with, which made the position even more difficult.[16] Many of the assistant clergy working in the industrial areas were *gwerin* or native clergy, trained in the theological colleges, socially insecure and theologically deprived, as we have noted in the chapter on the route to ordination. Many were accused of being from a Welsh Methodist background, especially those from west Wales, and introducing Methodist practices within their parishes. These were the "bull-frog" clergy of John Griffith and in some years well over half those made deacon by Bishop Ollivant came from the diocese of St Davids, many with a Nonconformist background. Over one third of the clergy of the diocese of Llandaff were literates, that is, without a university education.[17] Complaints were made to the missioners to the Welsh dioceses appointed by Archbishop Benson in the 1880s by incumbents that the younger clergy neglected their pastoral work and seem to have considered that their work was completed when the services had ended. Clearly, they accepted the Methodist view that preaching was their predominant activity. It was also noted that many laymen considered there was a want of intelligence in the reading in church on the part of these clergy. The nine curates of William Morgan's incumbency of the large Rhondda parish of Ystradyfodwg, 1858-69, were all men of this ilk.[18] Yet these men were able to pastor those from the same background as themselves and speak to them in the language they understood. Slowly, their hard and often unappreciated labours helped build up the Church in those desolate parts and enabled it to hold its own against Nonconformity.

The shortage of such men was sufficiently acute for incumbents to try and lure curates away from other parishes, as John Griffith attempted to do in 1854, needing a Welsh-speaker for his parish of Aberdare. John Williams, the desired curate, was offered a purse of £30, subscribed by the congregation of Cadoxton, the parish he served, to remain in that parish, and a war of words and claims of deceit and of broken promises was heard on both sides. Bishop Ollivant, forced to intervene, told Griffith he needed another six Welsh curates in his diocese and that his parish was demanding five curates instead of the one it had had previously, and he would have to be satisfied with an English speaker. Alas, he concluded, his time was continually being taken up with the disputes among his clergy, but it was good that one of his clergy, namely Williams, had met with a substantial mark of respect.[19] Welsh-speaking curates were becoming increasingly difficult to recruit by the 1900s and beyond, a theme echoed by many incumbents, including Daniel Richards of Maesteg, who needed them for his bilingual population.[20]

Yet numbers were never sufficient, even where a bilingual man was not required. Even more so there was a lack of experienced curates who could with "safety" be placed in a difficult and important position, as Bishop Basil Jones stated in his Charge of 1880.[21] Vicar Hill of Welshpool told the St Asaph Diocesan Conference of 1887 that in 1865, when he offered £120 for a senior curate and £100 for another, a single advertisement in the *Guardian* had brought in sixteen applications, mostly university men. Lay munificence now enabled him to offer £180, but he had not a single response to a more recent advertisement.[22] In 1949 it was reported that forty per cent of the curacies were vacant, sometimes because of the drift of clergy to the better pastures of England. The number of deacons ordained was far below the number required to make good the losses due to the retirement and the deaths of clergy.[23] This was a position which would not go away.

Bishops continually informed the incumbents who had curates that they were responsible for their training. Canon A.S. Wilde, writing in *A Manual of Parochial Work* of 1888, suggested this training should be in the areas of preaching, especially in its preparation, school work and catechising children, pastoral visiting, habits of life at work and in play, such as early rising, attendance at daily Matins, studying the Greek Testament, and encouraging any particular aptitude a man might have, such as temperance work.[24] Basil Jones, in his 1892 Charge, suggested that clergy shrank from the task of training curates and so offered a vacant curacy to a man who had been ordained elsewhere and who was looking for a second curacy. But he believed they would obtain a better curate by training a man in their own ways than by importing one from outside.[25]

In his Primary Charge of 1890 Bishop Edwards of St Asaph asked how often a curate had the benefit of his incumbent's criticisms, helping to remove the peculiarities and mistakes of inexperience, and giving him directions as to his work and visiting. It was easy to forget that young men could be sensitive and enthusiasm easily chilled and they needed sympathy and consideration. "The influence of the first parish in moulding the character of a Curate is hardly less potent and permanent than the influence of the home in forming the character of a child". The lack of such assistance, especially in a first parish, claimed Bishop Lewis of Llandaff in his Charge of 1894, had caused men to be disheartened at the beginning of their ministry and even wrecked some clerical careers that might have proved a strength and a blessing to the Church.[26] In a paper delivered to the East Gower Clergy Chapter during 1886 W.E.T. Morgan possibly related something of his own experience when he described the haughty attitude of many incumbents to their curates. Instead, he asked for a spirit of fatherly and friendly direction and advice, which could comfort a wounded and struggling beginner.[27] In a parish with a large staff of curates the practical training was often left to the senior curates and often these men formed a fellowship of their own.

Not all did so. John Griffith suggested in 1870 that many men newly ordained to serve as assistant curates were being placed in sole charge of districts from the day of their ordination. "There they are the whole year through, from Sunday to Sunday", he added, "and never hear any voice but their own."[28] It was alleged at a Church Congress meeting of 1893 that few vicars helped their curates in their preaching.[29] D. Parry-Jones, curate of Pontypridd 1914-17, wrote that he only saw his incumbent at their weekly meetings on Monday mornings, but in a parish with two curates and three lay staff he relied on them for his training and for assistance. Some years later, as curate at Llansamlet he was placed in charge of the Glais Mission, and left to himself, save on the Monday mornings when he attended the chapter meetings with his vicar and two other curates, to be reminded he was "under authority".[30]

One reason for this lack of supervision was given by Bishop Basil Jones. Too often the curate was working and living at a distance from his incumbent, and so was in a semi-independent position. Equally, elderly incumbents might be too infirm to exercise the supervision required, or unable to teach what they had never learnt themselves. He lacked parishes with incumbents which could serve as efficient schools of pastoral work.[31]

There were occasions when a congregation demanded that an incumbent should provide a curate for their parish. This was often hard on the incumbent, as he was responsible for paying his stipend. This occurred in the Carmarthenshire parish of St Ishmael in 1870s. The incumbent was also responsible for St Thomas's Church, Ferryside, where he was obliged to give one Sunday service. This was difficult with his other responsibilities, especially as the chapelry wanted two services, one English, the other Welsh. Eventually the congregation promised to provide an offertory of £100, and the then vicar gave up a small endowment of £20 and the income from pew rents of £32. His successor, J.R. James, appointed 1885, said these sums belonged to him and the congregation must do without a curate or find that amount themselves. This they failed to do, nor could they obtain a curate willing to accept a £10 reduction in his stipend, while Jones was only willing to provide one service and that in the afternoon of 35 minutes duration, claiming he had two Welsh churches to serve plus one English chapel. Though James had a gross income of £300 the bishop argued that he could only act if neglect had been established, while his registrar said the case was not sufficient for proceedings to be started. The matter went before Archbishop Benson but the result is not known, though Bishop Jones wrote to him that it was a matter of a wrong-headed vicar and a female busybody.[32]

Parish petitions for the appointment of a particular man to a vacant curacy were not unknown. One hundred parishioners of Coychurch and Pencoed petitioned their rector, John Harding, in 1859, for the appointment of Thomas Evans. His ministry had been extremely prosperous during the short time he had been amongst them in the parish (as a locum?), and they claimed he was a good, active and evangelical minister of the Gospel.[33] In some cases, a local bigwig made the decision as to who should be appointed. The industrialist, Arthur Gilbertson of Pontardawe, who had built a daughter church there in 1895, appointed the curate, rather than the vicar of Llanguicke, and even arranged lodgings for him.[34]

STIPENDS AND FINANCES

It has already been noted that assistant curates did not have the benefit of a legally set scale of stipends. The Church lacked the means of regulating this matter and the State did not interfere. A stipendiary curate was paid out of the income of a living, and that position remained, in essence, for an assistant curate, even though the places where they were required, such as large towns and the new industrial areas, were areas whose livings were poorly endowed. By the 1830s various agencies had developed which gave grants to incumbents for assistant clergy; diocesan societies established for the Church's extension did the same, and later on the Ecclesiastical Commission, when its resources had become adequate, offered temporary grants for curates in populous and manufacturing areas. In many cases these supplemented rather than replaced the need for giving within the parish, and while many incumbents looked to their congregation for their financial support, the onus was on them to make up any difference between what was available and the stipend required.[35] Rural parishes, however, found it hard to obtain grants, and at a time of a shortage of curates and financial difficulties many were placed in the position of the new vicar of Llanelli, Breconshire, D. Parry-Jones, who in 1936 was told by his bishop that the parish could not afford a curate and took him away, moving him from one of the poorest parishes to one of the richest. But as Parry-Jones pointed out, it removed a financial burden from him.[36] On other occasions this decision had to be made by the unfortunate incumbent who then wondered how he would cope with the work-load required of him.[37]

It was claimed that over the years the stipends of curates had increased. An 1827 parliamentary report into the number and stipends of curates indicated that there were 1,006 assistant curates whose average stipend was £86. This compared favourably to the position of the 4,244 stipendiary curates whose average stipend was £79.[38] A study of advertisements for assistant curates indicated that in 1853 an average stipend was £79, by 1863 it was £97, and in 1873 £129, yet these were probably not net figures, rather they were baits to nibble prospective candidates.[39] Halcombe in 1874 suggested that the curate's stipend should be £130, but noted that if this was imposed many incumbents would not only find this a burden they could not sustain but might also mean they had to dismiss their assistant curates.[40] A study of these stipends in 1881 revealed that they ranged between £30 and £120, the majority being between £100 and £120; in the diocese of St Davids there were ten stipends below £60, nine between £70 and £90, while Bangor had 22 between £20 and £90, and St Asaph one at £40 and ten at £60.[41] The average stipend for a curate in the diocese of St Davids in 1888 was £111,[42] while in Llandaff they ranged between £100 and £120 by the early 1880s.[43] By 1890 in the diocese of Llandaff 184 curates had an average stipend of £130.[44]

The 1904 Llandaff Diocesan Conference heard that the vicar of Portsea in the diocese of Portsmouth had argued that £140 was an impossible sum to live on for a man having charge of a district, and it was suggested that the minimum stipend for a curate in the diocese should be £150. Lemuel James, then a curate, said that when the laity suggested the curate should have an increase, the reply was often, "Oh, no, we must have another man", to which James responded, "what can you expect on bread and butter and tea". A curate's stipend, the vicar of Grangetown stated, rarely exceeded £120, though the two grant-making bodies, The Church Pastoral-Aid Society [CPAS] and the Assistant Curates' Society [ACS] required, before a grant was made, that the stipend should be at that sum, and the diocesan societies should follow this policy. Parishioners forgot that the curates' fund depended on the mites of the people.[45] Yet some incumbents, such as Venables Williams of Llandrillo-yn-Rhos, Denbighshire, declined in the early 1890s the assistance of a curate, even when suggested by a bishop, because either they themselves could not afford the stipend or felt unable to press their parishioners to find the finances required.[46]

After disestablishment the Church in Wales established a uniform policy throughout its dioceses. It allowed each diocese a quota, and paid one third of the stipend by way of grant. The diocese and the parish also paid a third each. St Asaph, in 1936, had an allowance of 74 curacies, and the central grant was £66.13s.4d. per curate.[47]

All the grant-making bodies attached conditions to their grants. CPAS and ACS required a return grant (which made it difficult for clergy to collect subscriptions for their parochial curates' funds, as people felt they had already contributed by giving to these societies), the Ecclesiastical Commission (the commissioners) offered half a stipend on condition the other part was made up from other sources, while the diocesan grant was regarded as a means to an end, rather than being sufficient in itself. The other sources required by the commissioners could be from collections made at services or subscriptions to a parochial curate's fund, from the incumbent's own pocket, or from the grants given by the agencies mentioned above. But problems might arise when a grant was suddenly withdrawn or was not renewed. This may be illustrated from a letter written by Richard Pendrill Llewellyn, vicar of Llangynwyd, a parish which included Maesteg, a growing industrial town, in the hill country of Glamorgan. In appealing for a curate's grant from the commissioners, he stated his parish needed four curates, three at £105 and his English curate at £150, £465 in all. He requested £232 in all, stating that he had subscriptions from the Llynvi Vale Iron Company of £190, £2 from a Mrs Turberville, and £40 from the Llandaff society. But, he added, without warning this society had reduced its grant from £60 to this lower sum. Had he not been without a curate at that time he would have been utterly ruined as a curate could have insisted on his full salary, and he would have been expected to make it good out of his own limited pocket.[48]

A few illustrations can indicate how this system worked, before we look at these agencies and the more local or parochial sources themselves. David Howell, when vicar of Cardiff, had two curates in 1866, at £130 and £100. Not being a mining area he was unable to obtain grants from the commissioners, but he received £100 from CPAS and £50 from diocesan funds, which meant he had to pay £80 from his own stipend of £302. In 1866, to ease the pressure on him, the vestry agreed to find £50 from an offertory on the third Sunday of each month. When he left in 1875 he had five curates, supported by CPAS, diocesan funds and increased parochial giving.[49] William Lewis of Ystradyfodwg had a staff of ten and more curates for his vast parish. It has been estimated by Prichard that between 1887-1920, 55 per cent of his grant income came from the commissioners, 11 per cent from CPAS, 3.6 per cent from ACS, 19 per cent from diocesan sources, and the remainder from individuals, including Mrs Llewelyn of Baglan, a local landowner, who provided the stipend for one curate. At one stage the parish only needed to find £40 from its own resources, reflecting Lewis's abilities in obtaining assistance from non-parochial sources. The grants from CPAS and ACS went to different curates, as neither society was prepared to jointly grant-aid the same person.[50] John Daniel James, vicar of Cadoxton, a large parish with two chapelries in the Neath valley, reported to a royal commission of the 1900s that he had three curates costing in all £380. He had two grants from the commissioners of £60 each, £40 from the Llandaff fund though he was required to return £20 of this as a return grant, £20 from ACS, and the remainder came from subscriptions and offertories.[51] Not surprisingly, Bishop Ollivant of Llandaff spoke in 1869 of his great obligation to the Ecclesiastical Commission, CPAS and ACS and the diocesan society for providing 60-70 additional curates in his diocese, while his successor, Bishop Lewis, maintained that without these grants many parishes in his diocese would never be able to afford curates, as their populations comprised mainly working men.[52] It must be remembered that this grant income was often insecure. The Ecclesiastical Commission gave only temporary one-year grants for most of the nineteenth century, and application had to be made for their renewal, which was not always certain, while the other societies often withdrew grants if cutbacks were required because of the state of their finances.[53]

THE ROLE OF THE INCUMBENT

It was the incumbent who was responsible for finding the stipend of his curate. Some incumbents, however, were able to attract men who had a private income and who required no stipend. Puller, vicar of Roath, Cardiff, in 1872, had seven curates three of whom worked without a stipend.[54] This was not unusual amongst some of the larger Anglo-Catholic parishes, but such incumbents were fortunate. In an 1894 book about the effects of disestablishment on the Church of England it was pointed out that 18,000 of its 21,000 clergy had incomes of less than £180, out of which many had to pay stipends for their curates.[55] A speaker at the Swansea Church Congress of 1909 recalled hearing an incumbent announce that the offertory was for the curate's fund. He added that if they did not find the money he would have to pay it out of his own pocket. He got the money, recalled the speaker.[56]

We may quote several examples. Charles Butler Clough, who became vicar of Mold in 1825, paid the stipends of two curates out of his stipend of £322.[57] Bishop Lewis of Llandaff told his fellow bishops that he had an incumbent in his diocese who was £400 out of pocket through being required to pay the major part of his curates' stipends, and another who had to pay £250 each year out of a living whose gross value was £700.[58] John Lewis Cloughor, who followed the wealthy Archdeacon Edmondes in the parish of Coety (Bridgend) in 1901, discovered that his curate's stipend of £130 made him £26 better off than himself. This was because he was expected to make up from his own stipend the £120 required for his two curates after the grant money had been deducted from the total required. He found it appalling that his parishioners should decline to allow him to have the benefit of the income of the parish for himself. While he did not blame his predecessor for subsidising the parish, he now saw his mistake in following a succession of rich and generous incumbents, while his own income and the private income of his wife meant they were only able to pay their way with strict economy.[59]

At Hawarden, a large parish with many daughter churches and thus a large staff of five or six curates, previous rectors had been members of the Glynne and Gladstone families, besides which the living was wealthy. Nevertheless, they had found that in paying their curates they had overspent their stipend. When F.S.M. Bennett was appointed rector in 1910 he was unable to afford the £800 required for these curates, and thus a free will offering scheme was introduced.[60] Similarly, when the parishioners of Welshpool during a vacancy in 1916-17 suggested that part of the incumbent's stipend could be used to pay for its two curates, Lord Powis, who contributed £75 to the curates' fund, protested, stating that the endowment of the benefice belonged to the vicar. If assistant clergy were required then the parishioners should provide the monies required so that the burden would not rest upon the incumbent.[61]

The 1907 Bangor Diocesan Directory indicated that two years earlier the incumbents of the diocese had paid £2,274 towards their curates' stipends; £4,341 came from other parochial sources, and £1,142 from church collections and offerings. These are in a list of voluntary contributions given for the work of the church and take no account of grant assistance; and while it is impossible to quantify this further, there were 76 assistant clergy, suggesting that on average the incumbents paid around £30 towards their curates' stipends.[62] As late as 1920 some of the incumbents in the diocese of Bangor were still making a contribution towards the stipends of their curates from their own pockets.[63]

The incumbent might well have to pay a penalty for such enforced generosity.

Evan Lewis, vicar of Aberdare, claimed in 1863 that while he was required to find £50 out of his income as vicar of £182 net towards the stipends of his assistant curates, the commissioners would not take this into account when calculating the income of the parish, so that his chance of an augmentation from that source towards his own stipend, dependent on the net income of a benefice, was lost.[64] Archdeacon D.R. Thomas, in his visitation address to the archdeaconry of Montgomery in 1897, expressed surprise that no allowance was given to an incumbent on the rateable assessment on his tithe income for any amount he contributed to his curate's stipend. Clergy, he continued, were the only people who were rated on their whole professional income, and while most of it came from agricultural produce, they were unable to take advantage of the Agricultural Relief Rate Act.[65] Halcombe argued that "of the many causes of the unsatisfactory position of curates none is more fruitful of evil as the over generosity of incumbents taking upon themselves a burden which they cannot bear, and a removing of all sense of responsibility from those [the laity] to whom it would be no burden at all."[66]

This enforced giving was not a position which commended itself to these incumbents. John Griffith of Merthyr Tydfil's outburst in 1867 might well have been echoed by many. He was responsible for the stipends of his curates, expected to contribute to the various charities of the Church and make up deficiencies in the accounts of churches and church schools. The parson, he declared, was looked upon as a sort of public property whom everybody had the right to fleece. What he possesses, it was said, was given him for the common good, and no account is made of his family or his own needs. Compared to Nonconformity whose ministers had no such responsibilities, there was no wonder that the Church did not thrive, since there was only one back to support her.[67] The fall in the value of the tithe from the 1870s meant that clerical incomes had dropped, and there was often a similar fall in the private incomes of clergy due to the economic climate of that day. As a consequence incumbents found it more difficult to obtain the money required for their curates' stipends, and became more reliant on contributions from their parishioners. This was especially true of urban parishes, though less true of rural ones where voluntarism had yet to develop.[68]

THE PARISHIONERS

The ways in which parishioners assisted in finding the monies required for a curate ranged from a specific fund for the stipend to collections made in the churches on designated Sundays, In a few instances the whole stipend might be found by a wealthy parishioner. Mrs Gwyn of Duffryn seems to have paid the stipend for a curate at Alltwyn in the parish of Cilybebyll, above Neath,[69] and the Vivian family of Swansea did so in respect of a curate at Hafod, where their copper works was situated.[70] The Beaufort Ironworks paid for a curate at Sirhowy, Monmouthshire, who also acted as a schoolmaster,[71] as did the proprietor of the local copper works, probably Grenfell, for the two assistant curates of the parish of Llansamlet, Swansea, who looked after the areas of Kilvey and Foxhole.[72]

In an introduction to a pamphlet published by the Curates' Augmentation Society, the bishop of Llandaff, Ollivant, wrote that his initial suggestion about augmenting curates' stipends was to enable the laity to accept their responsibilities. Where one pastor was once required in the pre-industrial parishes, now six and more were needed, and for an incumbent to give up £60 to £100 out of his income for these stipends was a grievous burden, but if this sum was made up of shillings, half-crowns, or sovereigns of a congregation, no one would feel poorer for what they had given. John Morgan, its writer, noted how one parish in south Wales had established a parochial collection towards this end with notable success.[73]

The parish of Welshpool was one of many where there was a separate curates' fund. It had been started by a new vicar, John Edward Hill, in 1865, when he made it clear two curates were required and that his income as vicar was insufficient to pay their stipends (his predecessor, William Clive, was a wealthy man and probably paid his curate's stipend himself). In 1874 a sum of £150 was collected with subscriptions ranging from two guineas to five shillings, and probably others of a smaller amount. This money supported one curate, while the lay rector of the parish, Christ Church, Oxford, which had the great tithes, paid £50 towards the other, and it seems a diocesan grant of £50 was also given. In the previous year, as the parish boundaries had been altered to include another area, a third curate was required, as there were now six Sunday services. Claiming that the first charge on the tithe income was the requirement to support the spiritual needs of the parish, the parishioners petitioned the College to provide a grant of £20 to £30 towards this end. A third curate was provided, which suggests this appeal was successful.[74]

More information is derived from the Royal Commission's Report on the Church of England and other Religious Bodies in Wales and Monmouthshire, published in 1911. During the 1900s the Rhondda parish of Cymmer paid the cost of the curate's stipend less whatever its incumbent could obtain in grants, while the parish of Aberdare, under the redoubtable C.A.H. Green, had commenced a Clergy Maintenance Fund. As he explained to the Royal Commission all wage-earning church persons in his large parish were given a quarterly letter and envelope and asked to give proportionally to their income. In 1905 there were 426 subscribers, and 274 amounts of ten shillings or below. Christ Church, Newport, obtained £110 from contributions for its curate, though £30 came from an unspecified grant. At Roath parishioners found £260 and with a commissioners' grant of £120 the parish was able to support three curates. At Brecon, where no grant aid was forthcoming, Edward Bevan had three curates, costing in all £410. He himself gave £145, being a wealthy man, but the rest was found from offertories and subscriptions.[75] There must have been many appeals in parish magazines for contributions to these funds. The vicar of Berriew thus pleaded with his parishioners in 1898 for further donations to the Assistant Clergy Fund as its 1897 total fell short of the sum required by almost £17. He promised to include a list of donations in the next issue but it did not appear.[76] The Swansea parish magazine of the 1900s also made strong hints about the position of its clergy fund. Mr David Glasbrook, a churchwarden, was praised for offering a subscription of £25, and it was hoped that the congregation would respond to the quarterly envelopes that were being provided. In 1908 a sum of nearly £16 had been collected during one quarter, in sums ranging from a pound to twopence.[77]

Many landowners were generous subscribers to the parochial funds for curates. Some will be noted later. A number of letters in the Bute Papers indicate that Lord Bute, the patron of the parish of Merthyr Tydfil, was often for solicited his assistance. In 1834 Bishop Copleston wrote to him asking if he could help provide the parish with a second curate, for its non-resident rector, Maber, had made it clear that while he gave £10 more than the £90 required for a curate's stipend, he could do no more without personal distress to himself. If it was in his power he would insist that Maber paid for this second curate, whose salary would be £100. However, he requested £50 from Bute as the assistant curate could also be employed in a classical school at £20. He himself would offer £20 and the stipendiary curate had promised £10, though the bishop did not want to take this as his stipend was already low. It was important to have two resident curates in such a populous place, and while he was aware of the claims made upon his lordship, he hoped he would oblige for the sake of this large parish.[78] A decade later, Thomas Williams, curate of Merthyr Tydfil, wrote to Lord Bute in 1844 about his distress that his lordship was discontinuing his "liberal" subscription towards the Welsh weekly lecture. The new rector, Campbell, had come into residence and from being the stipendiary curate on £300 he had been reduced to being assistant curate on £120, but this lecture added another £30 to his stipend. The loss of his subscription would involve him in difficulties from which he could not be extricated.[79] Evan Jones, who became curate of Radyr in 1853, had £10 added to his £80 stipend by the owner of the Pentyrch Ironworks for taking a Welsh service for his workers.[80] When the vicar of Llangurig approached A.O. Humphreys Owen of Glansevern, a prominent Montgomeryshire landowner, for a subscription for his curate at Belan in 1877, where there were two chapels, he insisted on a guarantee there would be no proselytism to which the vicar's reply seems to have been that if Owen knew the feelings of the people in respect of property he would see how sound teaching was necessary.[81]

THE DIOCESE

Most dioceses possessed their own society for church extension and as part of their brief they offered grants for assistant curates. The first such society was the Llandaff Church Extension Society founded in 1850 after a series of public meetings and an influential published letter to the new bishop, Alfred Ollivant, from his archdeacon, Thomas Williams, setting out the difficulties and needs of the diocese. It not only gave grants for building churches and parsonage houses, but also for "additional pastors". By 1879 over 70 per cent of its grants were given for the provision of stipends for curates. In 1852 it found £673 for this purpose, and in its 1858 Report it claimed to have raised since its foundation £5,147 towards curates' stipends, with grants of between £30 and £80 each. Four years later it gave ten grants amounting to £680 in all. On average, it was said, the grants enabled three additional services in each grant-aided parish. By the 1870s its outlay in this direction hovered between £1,065 and £1,342 each year, but this tapered off towards the end of the period. Indeed, its 1874 Report advised that the Society was unable to assist many incumbents even though they were struggling single-handed amongst populations ten to twenty times larger than the old parochial endowments had contemplated. This was regrettable as their grants would be met with great liberality by the Ecclesiastical Commission for those parishes in industrial areas. In 1879-80 various public meetings were held to raise interest, as a result of which the Society was able to offer more grants. These, with the grants they attracted from the commissioners and other agencies, meant the Society was able to supply the diocese with 40 additional pastors who were responsible for 120 additional services. By 1898 there were 90 grants given, 48 at £40, 29 at £30, and others between £10 and £35. The total cost was £3,105.[82] It was later augmented by the Bishop of Llandaff's Fund of 1883, which offered grants of between £10 and £50 towards the stipends of curates, and in 1907 by a New Diocesan Fund, whose purpose was to increase the grants available for these stipends.[83]

The St Asaph Church Extension Society, established in 1870, gave 18 such grants in 1878 at a cost of £970, mainly in bilingual parishes, such as Flint and Mold, though Welshpool and Berriew were also included, the first because of its population, the second because of its extent. It was claimed that through these grants others were obtained, £420 from the commissioners, £375 from local gifts, and £90 through CPAS and ACS. In 1885 the Society made ten grants at a cost of £875 on condition that £229 be returned in subscriptions to it from these parishes.[84] The Bangor diocesan society is mentioned in a Charge of Bishop Campbell in 1881. No grant would be given of more than half the stipend, and he believed that in every instance there should be some readiness by the parish to contribute to these stipends. The quarrying parishes of the diocese were able to benefit from the commissioners' grants, but in the poor rural areas its emphasis on industrial parishes was seen by the bishop as equivalent to a denial of help on its part.[85]

THE SOCIETIES

The Church Pastoral-Aid Society [CPAS] was founded in 1836 as a Church auxiliary to forward the mission of the Church, especially in industrial areas. Its grants for curates and layworkers (a subject of much controversy at the time) tended to be given to these areas. It was an evangelical society and insisted for many years on a north end celebration of the Holy Communion, and it would decline to assist or even end a grant if more "catholic" trends appeared in the worship of a grant-aided parish. A severe critic of this Society, J. Pugsley, of Swansea, said that the ACS did not require an applicant to face catechetical questions about the details of the way his services were conducted, what hymnbook was used, or whether the eastward position was adopted or if an altar cross was placed on the communion table.[86] The Assistant

Curates' Society [ACS], formed two years later by a group who found themselves at variance with the policy of CPAS, was Anglo-Catholic in tone but gave curates' grants without distinction of churchmanship, and was available to rural as well as urban and industrial parishes.[87] Both societies encouraged the development of auxiliary societies in the parishes they grant-aided, whose remit was to raise money for the society and to support it in other spiritual ways. Whether there was an auxiliary society or not these parishes were required to give a return grant to the main Society – a return of half the grant was encouraged – so as to enable them to practise generosity at a time when there was no Quota, when the income of the incumbent was found from the tithe or other sources, and the church rate paid for the maintenance of the building and its worship. In addition, there was probably the unspoken assumption that this policy would allow a parish to draw upon its own resources if a grant was withdrawn, and would not be over-dependent on the assistance of these societies.[88] But both these societies received far more requests than they could accept. The ACS secretary in the 1870s said the society received 20 to 30 requests each month, many of them from parishes with a population of 9,000 plus, whose incumbents could not even afford a servant, and yet were expected to give £30 themselves towards their curate's stipend out of an income of £150 - £200. As their applications had to be declined year after year many wrote to say that they thought it better not to trouble the Society any further.[89] Both societies discovered by the 1900s that between 10 – 19 per cent of the parishes they had been awarded grants were unable to take them up because they could not afford their share of the cost.[90]

The Church Pastoral Aid Society

The Church Pastoral-Aid Society was founded in 1836 as a home missionary society. For many years it had its own Welsh secretary, and it appears that it acted on the assumption that a bilingual parish with a population of three thousand was equivalent to an English parish of five thousand. While its financial contribution was immense, especially in the diocese of Llandaff, its beneficiaries found the encouragement the Society provided to them in their often isolated parishes was of equal importance. The Society provided a "hand of sympathy" to such men, in Archdeacon John Griffith's phrase, and he added that it had "fanned the well-nigh dying embers on the Church on the hills and in the crowded valleys of the southern portion of the Principality".[91]

In 1855 the CPAS requested each parish which received a grant to hold an annual sermon on behalf of the society in order to promote subscriptions to its work. Soon after, it appears, local associations were formed to assist this process, while parishes were asked to make a return grant to the society. In 1880 it was said that in Wales few parishes returned even half of the grant, sometimes a third or a tenth, and in that year for the £5,000 of grant aid given only £1,600 had been returned. A year later it was stated that in 44 years Wales had received £140,000 in grants but had only managed to return £29,500; but many parishes made it clear it was not unwillingness on their part that prevented more being given, but rather poverty.[92]

The Cardiff auxiliary or local CPAS association, which actually related to St John's Church, raised through giving, subscriptions and probably collections, a sum of £65 in 1869. David Howell as vicar considered this extremely poor as the parish received £250 in grants for its curates and a Scripture reader, and managed to increase this to £101 as against grants of £280 five years later.[93] It seems this local association was a branch of the Diocesan Auxiliary. It reported in 1858 that the diocese received from the society 29 grants for clergy and five for lay assistants, and that the total population of these parishes was 193,062. The total amount received from the Society was £1,920, and for this sum seven churches and twelve licensed rooms were opened or kept open, with 37 Sunday services, 26 weekday services, 12 cottage lectures and 19 Bible classes each week. In return the auxiliary had contributed a sum of £600 to the parent body.[94]

Those incumbents who received grants from the Society were encouraged to sing its praises. A description was given of the work of such a grant-aided curate in 1846, probably in the parish of Eglwysilan in the diocese of Llandaff. He held cottage lectures, a private weekly meeting with communicants, was able to visit frequently the poor and the sick, and preach impressively and persuasively. As a result the pastoral ministry of the Church had benefited, the congregations had grown, and the glory of God advanced in the salvation of souls.[95] Edward Jones, vicar of Tredegar, wrote in the Society's quarterly paper of 1878 that if it had not been established, he and incumbents of other parishes would feel weakened, crippled and disheartened. They would have to resort to the old standard: two services, one English, the other Welsh, on Sundays, with the result they would starve both congregations and drive them to other pastures. But now they had six services in both languages and three weekly services.[96] David Howell argued that without the work of the Society in his parishes of Cardiff and Wrexham the work of church extension, humanly speaking, would have been impossible. In Wrexham, for example, he could argue that without their grants one third of his large parish would have remained "unprovided for". Without the Society's aid he would be helpless, as these grants had enabled the former five Sunday services to be extended to sixteen, and the three Sunday Schools to ten.[97]

The existence of a grant was precarious, and the grant might be lost if part of a parish became a separate district. Consequently, when Lord Cawdor wished to make Ystradffin into a district chapelry he was prevented by the then vicar of Llandovery who feared he would lose his curate's grant from CPAS.[98] The parish of Llanycil, which covered the town of Bala, was refused the renewal of its grant in 1897 on the grounds that its population was too small. This refusal caused great annoyance in the diocese because the Society had not referred to the bishop or archdeacon as was consistent with the Church's discipline and order. It was argued that if the population was small the acreage was great; Bala was the centre of Calvinistic Methodist work and the Church needed a strong presence there, while evangelicals such as David Howell had supported the application. Bishop Edwards was greatly embarrassed as he had persuaded its new vicar, Lewis Daniel Jenkins, to accept this parish rather than a more valuable one.[99] It may have been that this new vicar was not believed to be a suitable grantee incumbent because of his churchmanship. This actually occurred when Eli Clark, vicar of Christ Church, Swansea, a CPAS grantee incumbent, invited Fr. Benson of the Anglo-Catholic Society of St John the Evangelist, a monastic order, to preach at his church during the 1878 Church Congress held in that town. He had local connections and the service was said to be fully evangelical as was his sermon, but the CPAS grant was withdrawn.[100]

The Assistant Curates' Society

Founded in 1838, its aim was to support clergymen for work amongst the poor. Its original name was the Society for Promoting the Employment of Additional Curates in Populous Places. In an advertisement of 1863, which appeared in the St Asaph Clergy Directory, the Society stated that it took into account, when making grants, the wants of a parish, its population and income. There were no party considerations. The curate was to be appointed by the incumbent, licensed by the bishop, and if a grant was made, additional services and sermons should be provided, together with a house-to-house visitation of the parish.[101]

Two of the first grants given by this Society were to the Cardiganshire parishes of Llanfihangel Genau'r Glyn and Llanbadarn (whose incumbent was the evangelical John Hughes), and by 1849 both parishes had auxiliary societies that forwarded the work of ACS by fund raising and spiritual assistance.[102] Another early grant was in 1843 to the parishes of Llanidloes and Llansamlet, each receiving £80.[103] In 1863, according to the St Asaph Clergy Directory of that year, it gave four grants to the parishes of Brymbo, Llangollen, Mold and Rhyl, totalling £240 in all, while the various local associations returned £220, including amounts from parishes that did not receive grants, such as £33 from the rural parish of Castle Caereinion.

A letter from William Lewis of Ystradyfodwg to ACS in 1885 is representative of many such applications for assistance. In it he requested a grant for the isolated and bilingual village of Maerdy on the borders of his parish, in another valley and miles from the parish church. A service was held on a Sunday afternoon in a hired hall. It was a promising field for church work and two good congregations had been gathered for each language. A curate was needed to superintend this work, but he had not obtained a penny towards his stipend.[104]

It seems clear that ACS was prepared to act according to the spirit rather than the letter of its rules. This emerges in a letter of 1893 from its Welsh secretary, A.T. Fryer, stating that it would help Aberdare Junction even if it meant straining a point. It appears that it was part of the parish of Llanwynno, but in an area far away from the parish church.[105] Nevertheless, there were times when the Society had to withdraw grants because of its own financial difficulties. This occurred in 1870 when John Griffith, rector of Merthyr Tydfil, was told by its secretary, Edward E. Cutts, that having 250 good cases pending, the most rigorous economy was being practised, and as his parish had large claims upon the commissioners, he was reducing his grant to £50 from £80 (though a return grant of £30 was required, and this had recently been increased from £20 to Griffith's disgust). With a population of 30,000, Griffith asserted he needed at least four curates, three of whom were supported from 1866 by the commissioners' grants, but he could not expect the commissioners to do any more. "Though it is a heavy pull, yet such are the spiritual wants of the parish I must submit to it."[106]

Much appreciation was shown to the ACS by bishops for their grants to their dioceses. In 1878 the diocese of St Davids received from it a total sum of £1,354,[107] in 1883 Bangor had six grants amounting to £400, St Asaph the same, at £390, St Davids 19, at £1,200 and Llandaff 22, at £1,230.[108] By 1907 Bangor had £625 allocated to it shared between fifteen parishes, and in the previous year the diocese had contributed £173 to the society, down on its 1903 figure of £218. The 1906 report indicated that in the previous year 91 out of 144 parishes had contributed to the Society, and the diocese owed the Society a great debt through its help with "the bilingual difficulty", by which it meant the double round of services required and the additional clergy needed to take them.[109]

THE ECCLESIASTICAL COMMISSION

It was not until the 1860s that the commissioners had sufficient funds to offer "temporary" grants for assistant curates working in mining areas, while it was only in 1888 that there were sufficient funds to extend this provision to populous parishes. These grants generally amounted to half the stipend, the parish having to find the other half (sometimes described as a benefaction) from its own sources or from other agencies. For example, the parish of Nantyglo used a CPAS grant as its benefaction for one of these grants.[110] The grants were for one year, and each year incumbents had to apply for their renewal, which was not automatic. They were paid half-yearly at first but from 1871 quarterly. Those incumbents who forgot to apply for their renewal had to write forceful apologies for their lapse, though some pleaded that as new incumbents they were uncertain of the procedures, and all made clear the difficulties they would face if the grant was not renewed.[111] Ollivant in his Llandaff visitation charge of 1863 drew attention to the act of 1860 that allowed the commissioners to make such grants for the provision of the cure of souls in mining districts. Already, the diocese had obtained twenty grants collectively valued at £960, which was equal to what the diocesan society was able to give.[112]

One of these early grants was obtained by the parish of Ystradyfodwg which covered a large area of the Rhondda valley. This was in 1862 and such was the acceptance of its need that by 1867 it received five separate grants. Though the commissioners required the parish to find an equivalent share of the stipend, it appears that at times this was not rigorously enforced. Thus, at a time when these stipends amounted to £570 the commissioners gave £300, £65 came from the diocesan society, £120 from the Home Mission Society (a branch of the diocesan fund) and the remaining £85 came from other landowners and employers of labour. William Lewis, its vicar, managed to obtain further grants, which he matched with those given by other agencies and individuals, such as the diocesan funds, CPAS and

ACS, the Crawshay Bailey estate and the Dunraven family. Yet the commissioners declined to give grants for two further areas of his parish, both of which had growing and substantial populations.[113]

The commissioners also refused an application in 1864 from David Griffiths, vicar of Glyncorrwg. He resided on his other parish, Resolven, which was a necessity in his case and permitted by his bishop. Though he had received promises from CPAS and the diocesan society towards his half share of the total stipend of a curate, he was turned down on the grounds that a population of 606 was not within the commissioners' remit. However, two years later, his population having increased in this new mining area to 1,200, he was successful, and was able to offer a stipend of £100.[114]

Another early grant went to the parish of Ffestiniog for a curate at the emerging quarrying district of Manod which had become a separate district in 1851. A first grant had been obtained in 1868 of £40 towards a stipend, and a CPAS grant and parochial contributions supplied the other half share. The following year a new incumbent, Richard Killin, applied for a second grant. His application, (stating he was paying £50 for this curate from his own income, that there were nine Sunday services in the parish, of which he took four, travelling nine to eleven miles on horseback, and that the remainder were taken by his curates, walking ten miles,) secured the grant.[115]

The Ecclesiastical Commission was generous to the diocese of Llandaff, which was arguably the fastest growing diocese, in terms of population, within the Established Church. Ollivant managed to obtain funds by 1870 that would support 100 curates, mainly from the commissioners though with assistance from other bodies.[116] By 1890 the commissioners supplied 45 per cent of the monies required for the 100 out of the 184 curates of the diocese, (£5940 as against £12,944), while CPAS gave £1,826, ACS £2,520, the diocese and other societies £925, and £1,753 was locally raised.[117] It seems, however, that not all its incumbents were honest about their intentions in applying for these grants. For in that same year, 1870, Bishop Ollivant had to send a letter about the commissioners' grants to his rural deans for circulation amongst the clergy. At the end of each six months the curate was required to certify to the commissioners that he had been paid the parish share of the grant for that period, that is its half share, and then request the payment of the other share from the commissioners. The normal amount of the parish share on these occasions was £30, but Ollivant had discovered that some incumbents had lent £10 of that money, requiring its return when the other half had been received. This was fraudulent, as was another practice, that of telling a curate that his stipend was £100 but if his friends could find another £10 it would be made up to £120.[118] An alert bishop noted in 1897 that Daniel Lewis, rector of Merthyr Tydfil, had paid only one of his curates £100 instead of the stipulated stipend of £120. Lewis's excuse, that the missing £20 was for board and lodging at the rectory, was disallowed. That was a private arrangement, and the full amount had to be shown to be paid on the certificate sent to the commissioners.[119]

A curate's grant might be continued even when that curate became vicar of a new parish formed out of his curacy, provided he had no other income and was probably awaiting an augmentation from the commissioners for the provision of a stipend. This happened to Thomas Richards who became vicar of the mining parish of Bargoed, in the Rhymney Valley, formed out of the parish of Gelligaer in 1904. Two years later he received an augmentation of £150, with the result that the bishop arranged for the curate's grant to be used for his parish, though he admitted that the parish share of £60, less some grants, came from his own pocket. In the following year Richards applied for a second grant, claiming that the parish was poor and the claims already put on its people were heavy. ACS had promised £40 and he hoped for a diocesan grant. It was hard to obtain curates because of the disadvantages they were labouring under, and a higher stipend was required to obtain a better class of men. It appears the commissioners were not persuaded by these arguments.[120]

There was another method of obtaining curate's grants from the Ecclesiastical Commission, provided one was able to establish a local claim. The commissioners had taken over the episcopal and capitular estates, and when the various leases that had been taken out on these properties had expired, they were ready to consider assisting those parishes in which they owned property. Thus when the lease of the rectorial tithes of the parish of Llansilin expired, formerly held by the dean and chapter of St Asaph Cathedral, the parish was provided in 1876 with a permanent stipend for a curate of £120. Even better, no parochial contribution was required for this grant.[121] This was one of the few ways in which a rural parish could benefit from the work of the Ecclesiastical Commission. Yet these grants were not always easy to obtain. In 1895 the vicar of Llanfair, near Ruthin, Basil Jones, appealed to Archbishop Benson about the refusal of the commissioners to augment his parish now that its sinecure rector had died. The rector had received two thirds of the tithes, about £388, and these had now reverted to the commissioners. His bishop, A.G. Edwards, had told him to apply to the commissioners to augment the living, pay for a curate's stipend, and enlarge the parsonage house. But on the grounds they had given a grant of £29 to the benefice in 1862 the commissioners declined his request. His large parish of 9,000 acres and population of 962 needed a curate, and he was paying for help for one Sunday service already, being unable to afford a curate due to the agricultural depression and the loss of half his tithe income. It was hard that this dedicated and devoted man should suffer because of the lapse of these tithes, his bishop wrote; the local rural deanery chapter protested as did the deanery conference, wondering what the enemies of the Church would make of these circumstances, and Jones himself, in a printed address that had been delivered at St Asaph Cathedral, compared the Ecclesiastical Commission with the Pharaoh who knew not Joseph. Eventually he was awarded £500 towards improving the parsonage house and given a grant of £60 for a curate. In expressing his gratitude to this new Pharaoh, he made it clear there was still great indignation in the village as to the way he had been treated.[122] Denbighshire was sufficiently far from London for the commissioners to be worried about such trifles.

Applications to the Ecclesiastical Commission were not always successful, especially as its funds were limited and its grants were awarded to the most needy parishes. Kidwelly was hardly one of these, even though Gruffydd Evans in 1910 put up a strong case for a grant. The parish had raised £40 towards its curate's stipend of £100, the ACS gave £60, but the going rate was now £120 and it was impossible to get a man for less. Although the deficiency was £20, even finding the £40 previously required was hard enough but to find £60 would mean much strain and the neglect of more important work on his part. The reply he received was that funds would not permit the commissioners' assistance.[123]

Issues and Difficulties with the Ecclesiastical Commission

There were many problems connected with these grants, with many incumbents believing that the commissioners' rules were petty and exasperating. We may quote several examples. Rice Jones, rector of Eglwysilan, a vast parish that stretched into the Taff Valley above Cardiff, obtained a temporary grant of £40 for a curate at Nantgarw on the usual condition that he found an equivalent sum – for which he used an existing grant from CPAS. The curate had been taken ill and had to go to his family home, when it was discovered he had never been licensed by the bishop, which was a condition of the grant. The bishop refused to certify him as the curate of the parish for the previous six months, with the result that the balance of the grant for that period was disallowed, and Jones had to find the money from his own pocket. It was a hard price to pay for his oversight. The grant was later reinstated with an increase to £60. A school church built at Taffs Well was opened in 1869, and Jones managed to obtain a further grant of £40, an equivalent sum being found by the Llandaff diocesan society. In 1873 Jones asked for the first grant to be increased to £70, as he could not afford to pay more than £50 for his curate, who as a married man could not afford to live on £100 at a time when prices were rising. The commissioners declined to assist, and in difficulties itself, withdrew this second grant in 1874, in spite of repeated pleas that one curate could not manage two churches and that the church was growing in spite of the disestablishment controversy. A new rector managed to have this grant restored and another one granted for a different part of his parish, only to discover in 1897 that one grant had to be withdrawn because of the commissioners' other commitments, while the parish was unable to pay its share of another. Henry Morgan was forced to work his parish with two stipendiary lay readers instead. By the 1910s the Taffs Well curate, on £140, had his stipend made up of a £60 grant from the commissioners, £30 from CPAS and £30 from church collections, and his Nantgarw colleague on a sum of £80 received a diocesan grant of £35 and £45 obtained from giving within the parish.[124]

Another early problem concerned the parish of Glyncorrwg, whose first grant from the commissioners of £100 was given in 1866. David Griffiths, its vicar, had received grants towards his half share of the stipend from the Llandaff society of £10 and £20 from ACS, both given on the condition he was able to retain the commissioners' grant. His anxiety in this respect emerges in his application for its renewal in 1868. His population had trebled over the past three years, his income from his three churches was but £160, and he requested the commissioners if they declined to renew the grant that he would be allowed sufficient notice as he had to give his curate three months' notice, or else, as he insinuated, he would have to pay him that quarter's stipend from his own pocket. The next year he received the notice he dreaded. The reason given for the withdrawal was that the population was small and he held another benefice. His reply, as well as the bishop's letter of protest, stated that the two other societies which supported him were anxious to continue their grants and had given them being fully aware of his circumstances, of the large extent of the parish and the smallness of its stipend. Were the grants to be lost he would have to give up "a work so successfully commenced amongst colliers and miners and in a district *lately developed* to be without again a resident clergyman". Bishop Ollivant considered the fact that Griffiths held another benefice could "be left out of consideration", for without that other parish (Resolven) he would have no parsonage house, would still need to find a curate for part of his parish, as its two churches were separated by a mountain almost impassable in winter, and from an income of £110 find the stipend for that curate. The bishop's strong letter and plea forced the commissioners to change their minds, and the grant was restored. It was increased to £60 in 1874, indicating that its curate received the full recommended stipend of £120.[125]

Griffiths was not alone in deploring the requirement of an annual application for the renewal of these grants. David Howell when at Wrexham argued it was hard on the clergy to face the worry of losing a grant year by year. He had two grants of £60 each for two of his many curates, and had to find himself £200 for these stipends out of an income of £665. When a new district was created in 1880, that of Esclusham, one of these grants was withdrawn. Howell protested as he still needed another curate and would have to find a further £60 from his own pocket for otherwise "I shall thus be seriously crippled in my efforts to extend the influence of the Church in a parish deplorably neglected during many years ..."[126] It is hardly surprising that incumbents' letters requesting a renewal of their grant stressed the importance of retaining it, often entering into considerable detail, and were followed by letters of almost absurd appreciation when the renewal letter was acknowledged.

In 1884 the commissioners declined to renew their temporary grant to the Monmouthshire parish of Llanhilleth, another colliery area, because of their own financial difficulties. The parish drew in many people from other parishes as their own parish churches were five miles away, and it had a parish church and two licensed schoolrooms. As a result of this refusal one of these schoolrooms had had to be closed for Sunday worship and only one service held at the other, it being at some distance from the parish church. The voluntary contributions for the curate's stipend were already inadequate. Writing to ask for Archbishop Benson's intervention, James Hughes as rector said the bishop had visited the parish and told them there was hardly another parish where the grant had been more appropriately bestowed. Surely, he argued, rather than withdraw the grant, it would have been better to have reduced it by

£10 to £50.[127]

A number of issues were faced by the various incumbents of Aberdare, a parish that needed eight curates by 1883. In the early days of these grants it appears that the incumbents had to forward their half yearly share of the stipend to the commissioners, who then made it up and sent it to the curate concerned. But in 1864 Evan Lewis, then vicar, pointed out that the Llandaff society had through some misunderstanding failed to pay its share of one of its grants. He had been unable to forward the £50 required, and as a result his curate had not been paid for two months. As the commissioners did not meet for another two months he pleaded that his curate's share be sent directly to him as it was hard on him to be kept so long without his stipend. Thankfully, they were merciful. Another request, that a grant be continued during a vacancy in a curacy, the work being undertaken by other curates not grant-aided by the commissioners, was declined. H.T. Edwards, then incumbent, wrote in 1866 informing the commissioners that CPAS had had to decline continuing its grant towards Hirwaun, where there was a school-church three and a half miles distance from the parish church and a population of three to four thousand. If they were unable to help, this work would have to cease. If he offered £40, could the commissioners meet him with £60? In the end he was offered £50 as a fourth grant, but the commissioners were also willing to increase the other three grants by £10 if the parish could raise its share by £30. Edwards had to reply that though loath to lose such an opportunity he could not afford that expense as the contributions of his parishioners would not stretch that far.[128]

The parish of Pontypridd also faced similar difficulties when curates left. In 1893 one of the grant-aided curates left the parish in November but his replacement, a deacon, would not be ordained until 21 December. The commissioners were asked if the grant could be used to employ a *locum tenens* for that short period of time, who was needed not just for Sunday duty but for a full week's work each week. But such a person could not be found. Instead, the vicar asked if another curate, who was not grant-aided, could step into the vacant place, so that the vicar would not lose two months of grant income. The answer appears to have been negative. A similar situation arose in 1912. The commissioners deducted £3.10s. from their quarterly cheque as there had been a vacancy in one of the grant-aided curacies. An indignant vicar pointed out he had to pay the deficiency from his own pocket, as he had employed a *locum tenens* for that period of time, since it was impossible to work the parish without that additional assistance. His protests were in vain. The commissioners made clear that their rules stated that the grant was applicable to a full-time curate and could not be transferred.[129]

When John Griffith of Merthyr's son, who acted as one of his curates, was taken ill and ordered a three month rest, Griffith's alternative proposal of using local clergy to take his place on a temporary basis was rejected by the commissioners, and fearing he might lose all his grants if he did not retain this one, he recalled his son. Thankfully, the matter was re-considered, and although the commissioners argued that he had misread their letter, it seems probable that they had found this a convenient excuse after episcopal pressure had been placed on them.[130]

The parish of Ffestiniog had a similar problem, but almost got away with it, though by then the rules appear to have changed and allowed a grant to continue if assistance was found during a vacancy. A vacancy occurred in one of the curacies during the mid-1900s and Gwilym Rees, curate of Eglwysilan, assisted for three weeks. A sharp-eyed clerk noted he had also been mentioned in the return for his own parish, and an explanation was requested. The answer was given that he was undertaking a holiday locum, and that many incumbents allowed their curates two or three Sundays as a holiday entitlement, and this locum meant that a hard-working curate and his family were enabled to have a much needed holiday they would otherwise be unable to afford. The commissioners' reply stated that they could not pay a double grant for the same person, and accordingly reduced that quarter's cheque by a third. The rector, Cadwgan Price, had the final word: "I always dread a vacancy, under the most favourable circumstances it involves me in a pecuniary loss".[131]

It paid, sometimes, to refuse to accept the commissioners' refusal to offer a curate's grant. This was the attitude of the fiery Thomas Walters when he was rector of Ystradgynlais, an industrial town at the top end of the Swansea valley. He had already obtained one grant in 1865, but he wished for another grant to enable a curate to serve some of the more outlying parts of his parish, such as Abercrave, where a school-church had been built to counteract the influence of five dissenting chapels. The commissioners were prepared to increase their first grant to £60 from £50, provided the parish increased its own share, but this Walters refused with some indignation. Instead, he reiterated his claim for a grant, specifying once again the needs of his parish and making clear that any additional grant would not relieve him of any part of his own duty. He even appears to have persuaded the commissioners to act against their own rules, by allowing him to use the grant for temporary assistance while he searched for a Welsh-speaking curate, arguing if he did not do so then people would feel neglected, leave the Church, and the work of many years would be lost in a few weeks.[132] But not every incumbent had Walters' verve and persuasive powers, or his acidity in letter writing.

Daniel Lewis, rector of Merthyr, had requested a fourth curate's grant for his parish from the commissioners, and applied year after year from 1885 without success, being informed each time that the financial circumstances of the commission were such they could offer no new grants nor increase existing ones. In vain he pleaded his plight, though he was careful to avoid informing them that his was one of the richest livings in the Church itself through the leasing of the glebe land for building purposes. In 1892 he suggested that one of the grants given to Pentrebach parish, whose incumbent had just died, could be transferred to him. That parish had half his population and half the number of churches, with one curate paid by an endowment and the other two supported by the commissioners' grants. This was declined, but in 1900 he was answered back in his own coin when the new district of Treharris was created from his parish, and one of his grants was transferred to that parish at the bishop's suggestion. By now the commissioners were obviously deeply annoyed with him, for they had to send out constant reminders for him to renew his grant applications, and he was sending back to them outdated cheques for re-signing which he had failed to bank in time. Further pay-back time came in 1905, when the vicar of Llantrisant requested the renewal of his three grants plus an additional one. This could only be granted by the transfer of an existing grant. The commissioners noted that Lewis had made no request for the renewal of his grants since November 1902 and had failed to return the certificates of employment from the following year. One has the impression that the clerks had given up reminding him although he was still receiving two grants. Llantrisant had eight places of worship compared to Merthyr's five, and though its population was only half that of the other, it was in public patronage whereas Merthyr was in the patronage of the marquis of Bute. By this time the commissioners had taken the view that private patrons ought to be more responsible for the parishes in their patronage, and Lewis had been a disastrous appointment. And thus Lewis lost one of his grants, leaving him with only one.[133] He had no one to blame but himself.

POVERTY AND RELIEF

As we have noted, there was no legislative scale of stipends for these assistant curates, and though the various grant-making societies and the commissioners required a set stipend, in the case of CPAS and ACS £120 by 1904 before a grant would be awarded,[134] there was considerable concern within the Church that these stipends were inadequate considering the duties demanded of a curate, his need to be seen as a gentleman, the responsibilities imposed upon him and the requirement for an extensive and expensive education. It was accepted that the position had changed drastically over the previous fifty years, to the disadvantage of the assistant curate.[135] Some maintained, however, that if these stipends were increased then clergy would not accept the lower-paid incumbencies, as the difference in stipends between the two was little and an incumbency involved far greater responsibility.[136] On the other hand it was constantly argued that a stipend of £120 was less than that of most colliers, whose minimum wages amounted to the same figure, or on average £2 per week without overtime, and while the working hours of the collier were diminishing and his pay increasing, the poor curate's work was becoming more demanding without any increase in his stipend.[135]

Joseph Leach in the 1840s suggested that a wealthy man who gave a subscription of 20s. for a curate spent more on his claret bill than the curate had as a stipend.[138] Of 22 advertisements for curates in 1858 noted by Hart only two offered £100 and fourteen were between £20 and £70, at a time when a butler or cook could earn £70 to £80 all found and an elementary schoolmaster £150.[139] A writer of 1866 maintained that curates with a family on £100 were living in "real and hopeless misery, arising from straitness of means, such as none but those who have looked into the matter can form any idea of."[140] In 1869 it was alleged that a curate on £100, and there were 68 of them in the diocese of Exeter who had given 15 to 50 years service to the Church, had less than a bank clerk, and that it was impossible for a married man to live on this sum, particularly when a rented house might cost almost half his stipend, and he would need to live on one pound a week "for clothing, maintenance, medical attendance, personal expenses, books, parochial and other claims". A skilled artisan had 6s.6d. to 8s.6d. per day, but a curate 5s.6d., and it was impossible on this sum to dress well or give liberally to charity as was expected.[141]

Clergy too often submitted to this regime rather than complain. A few did complain, however. Speaking to the Llandaff Diocesan Conference of 1904 Lemuel

James, a curate himself, said he knew diocesan clergymen who had to exist on bread and butter and tea from Monday to Saturday and argued they should have an adequate stipend for their needs without having to resort to charity.[142] This was a point raised earlier at one of the Church Congresses. Clergy, it was argued, were sick to death of charitable doles and humiliating charitable agencies.[143]

The incumbents themselves felt responsible for being unable to afford better stipends. D. Llewelyn Jones, a Newport incumbent, said he could not sleep when his curate with a family of five and no private means received a stipend of £130.[144] At least one clergyman came to an arrangement about such matters. Henry Eldridge Curtis, curate of St Mary, Monmouth, ordained in 1868 on a stipend of £135, agreed with his vicar (and with Bishop Ollivant's permission), that if the vicar, who claimed he could not afford more than £75, was unable to make up the difference he would give him three months notice.[145]

Partly because of economic reasons, T.E. Espin maintained, many curates whose title parish was a populous and laborious district, having served the two years required by their bishops, sought employment in country parishes that offered them not only social advantages but also made less exhausting demands on their strength and their pocket.[146] A similar picture was presented by J. Vyrnwy Morgan, perhaps not such a detached observer as he liked to make out. He alleged in 1908 that many Welsh curates migrated to England where conditions were more favourable, there was more assistance from the laity, pleasanter surroundings and a higher remuneration.[147]

A married curate cost no more than a bachelor, but his financial needs were much higher, and the difficulties that might result were often so embarrassing that incumbents preferred single men.[148] Besides, unmarried men could live in lodgings, sometimes with their incumbents.[149] Clericus, a frequent letter writer to the press, was not impressed by this arrangement. While delicate ladies were holding bazaars to erect new churches, he wrote in 1874, the curates who were required to serve them had to eke out a miserable existence in humble lodgings for £100 a year.[150] Isaac J. Williams, curate of Rhymney, rather bravely related to the Llandaff Diocesan Conference of 1905 his own experiences. When ordained he had to live in three small and "pokey" rooms because he refused to pay the exorbitant demands of "a blood-sucking Shylock of a landlord", and had to leave his house.[151]

Married curates, one senses, were almost an embarrassment to the Church. In a letter of 1891, written to Archbishop Benson, the secretary of the Corporation of the

Sons of the Clergy, an ecclesiastical charity for the relief of poor clergy, wrote about Philip Morgan of Trehafod. In it he declared that he society discouraged applications from those under ten years in Orders and those who incurred the responsibility of matrimony upon nothing but a curate's stipend.[152] The advice given by an "old stager" in 1881 to his "younger brethren in the Church" was this: "never marry as a curate unless you or the lady have a sufficiency to live upon in the married state, independently of the stipend of the curacy. This act of prudence would save us from a multitude of sorrows and disappointments".[153] A London curate, M.R. Neligan, later bishop of Auckland, argued in 1893 that assistant curates lowered their social status through tea parties and imprudent marriages. Too often the laity were apt to throw their unmarried daughters at clergymen with the result that their children had to find jobs as clerks or as schoolmistresses and lady-helps.[154]

T. Jesse Jones, rector of Gelligaer, suggested that "home" and therefore marriage for a curate could only come with his own living for no curate could be really settled as the tenure of his curacy was at the "will" of the incumbent. He added rather maliciously that "if sometimes these marriages [of curates] are improvident and poverty ensures, a more certain purity in the ministry will the more likely be secured."[155] Furthermore, curates were not a good commodity on a marriage market, and fathers were not prepared to allow their daughters to marry unbeneficed men whose prospects of a living of their own and thus independence might not be considered good. This, of course, happened to Francis Kilvert in 1871 when Daisy Thomas' father, a cleric himself, told him to give up all his hopes of marriage with her and he felt totally humiliated.[156] There were contrary views, however. A man can do his work so much better with a wife "at his back" claimed A.E.H. Hyslop, vicar of All Saints', Cardiff, in 1904. He suggested that the reason why so many curates left important districts after a year or so was because they wished to marry and needed a house. He thus argued that parishes needed to provide houses for their curates.[157]

Though charities were disliked, they were needed. It was said there were over 200 clerical charities in the 1870s.[158] A number of these societies came into existence in order to augment the stipends of the older curates, who often found that the older they became, the less stipend they received. The younger men, especially the unmarried, had the pick of the market as incumbents wanted fresh blood rather than older and possibly embittered men, or men more experienced than they were who might show up their limitations, and might even prove to be a rival.[159] The older ones had to take what was available. James H. Jenkins, ordained in 1892 and by 1910 curate of St Mark's, Newport, was one of those who thought this position despicable. Describing the older curates as part of the "dead-line", being displaced by younger men and offered no provision for the future, he asked what other profession discarded twenty years of experience (he was nearly there himself) in favour of those with none? He was one of many who asked for remuneration according to length of service.[160]

The Curates Augmentation Fund, founded in 1866, was one such organisation. It was meant to replicate Queen Victoria's Clergy Fund which assisted poor incumbents, but was unable to include curates in its remit because of its own financial restraints. Arguing that on average a curate of 25 years standing would receive 30 to 40 per cent less than the stipend of those newly ordained, and it would decrease £5 over every five years, it offered by the 1900s a grant of £50 not as a charitable offering but as a right, to a curate who had been more than fifteen years in Orders and was in full and active work. It later had to reduce its grant to £20. On average a grant ran for seven or eight years, possibly because the grantee had obtained a benefice, had found a better curacy, or because grants were only given to older men. At first it was hoped to provide an additional stipend of £100 for those who had less than £100 or £80 with a house, but financial circumstances prevented this and the capital base it hoped to achieve never materialised, though the Fund had started with subscriptions and donations of £12,000.

The organisation argued that many curates were forced to move frequently, and if a man was married this was an expensive business, especially as there were no grants available for this purpose. The Ordinal presupposed a married clergy and the Church expected it, but as children grew up they needed to be educated while the expenses of life became larger as the years moved on. Such provision as this Fund offered, even on a limited scale, "would cheer many an anxious heart even in prospect, and eventually fill many a poverty-stricken home with thankful gladness...". In 1909 it argued that the average stipend of its recipients was less than £3 per week, the average length of service 29 years, and that the Church was multiplying curacies at a rate three times greater than benefices, so that many men would never have the chance of their own benefice. In 1908 it voted £10,000 in grants, but throughout its history it was clear it could only assist the most needy so that many applications had to be turned down. Though it was calculated in 1866 that only 537 men were eligible for assistance, by 1874, when £14,000 had been distributed in 200 grants, some of £20 each, 70 claims had had to be rejected. By 1882 there were 1,000 applicants, but the Fund could only offer this £50 grant to 250 of them, while by 1900 there were 1,300 applications for its aid, and within seven years this had increased by another hundred.[161]

Another society that seems to have a brief existence was one publicised by Richard Davies, archdeacon of Brecon, in the 1810s. He had raised £704 to establish a diocesan society to relieve superannuated curates who were unable to do duty, or to provide substitutes for incumbents in a similar position. One he mentioned was an elderly curate, aged 77, totally deaf, and quite unequal to his ministerial duties.[162] Another early society was that of the Society for the Relief of Poor Pious Clergymen, founded in the 1790s by Thomas Jones of Creaton, a Welsh curate of that Leicestershire parish whose stipend was £25. The plight of his friend, Thomas Richards of Llanymawddwy, who brought up eight children on £30 per annum, caused him to establish this society.[163] There was also a charity administered by the Sons of the Clergy, known as Mr Stock's Donation, that offered £10 to ten poor curates of the Church of England whose income was less than £40. In 1795 out of 40 applicants, six of the ten elected were from Wales, including Maurice Anwyl, curate of Pennal, with four children and £20 income; William Jenkins of Reynoldston, with the same number of children but only £15, and John Jones, curate of Roath, whose twelve children had to be supported from an income of £33.[164]

A more local society was the Llandaff Association for Improving the Status of the Unbeneficed Clergy which reported its activities in the diocesan magazine. In 1913 it expressed not only a desire that stipends be paid through diocesan funds, but also its concern that the unbeneficed were given no life interest, as were incumbents, in the bill to disestablish the Welsh Church.[165]

Various suggestions were made about ensuring that assistant curates had a better income, though few were practical. One suggestion was that one third of the value of a benefice should be assigned for the assistant curate, another was for a sliding scale with an income adjusted in proportion to the population of the parish,[166] but these were impractical as few benefices were wealthy enough to sustain such schemes. A further suggestion was that if the patronage system was reformed and bestowed on a fixed method, thus allowing a man to know he had a reasonable prospect of a benefice after a few years, serving some years as a curate on £100 a year might be acceptable.¹⁶⁷ But this would mean interfering with property rights and could not be considered. Sadly, it had to be concluded, it was the Church's poverty rather than her will which allowed this state of affairs.¹⁶⁸

CHAPTER SEVEN: THE ASSISTANT CURATE: THEIR DUTIES, CONCERNS AND DIFFICULTIES

The duties of an assistant curate were never stipulated in ecclesiastical law, save that he was to assist the incumbent in his parochial duties.[1] This lack of definition caused frequent disputes and friction between incumbent and curate, especially when the curate was more experienced than his incumbent.

In the larger towns curates generally cared for a district, visiting and encouraging its inhabitants to attend the church services, and involved themselves in teaching the Catechism in church schools, running clothing clubs and other similar organisations.[2] John James Turner, curate of Welshpool from 1873-9, and a relative of its vicar, had his own district, which he cared for with the aid of lay district visitors, making sick visits and giving house communion, as well as obtaining subscriptions for church organisations, including the curates' fund. He was also responsible for the Belan mission church, its school, choir and services; the weekly cottage lectures at Pwll, held in a private house; various confirmation classes, and assisted with the preparation for two missions to the parish. There were the monthly clerical meetings as well as considerable school work, and with the other clergy he helped administer the parochial charities. In addition, as a member of a local gentry family, Turner took part in society events, attended sporting occasions and concerts, and had day excursions and walking holidays with friends.[3]

John Melbourne Perry, curate of Swansea from 1913-17 under Talbot Rice, apart from assisting with the Sunday services, was superintendent of the Sunday Schools; promoted overseas missions; held a Bible class for women; Scripture Union meetings and evangelistic services for children, and devoted himself to pastoral care and visiting. During the First World War he acted as correspondent to the men of the parish serving in the forces. It was said his work was heavy and his stipend small, though he had private resources of his own.[4]

It is hardly surprising that many curates in these town and industrial areas found their work difficult and demanding. David Edmondes Owen, who died in 1922 as vicar of Llandovery, started his clerical career as curate of Rhymney under Canon

William Evans. His biographer wrote that he had to battle with a sea of new experiences, having just left St David's College, and that he often confessed the struggle was an unequal one, but he went forth to his task with buoyant cheerfulness even for the least congenial tasks.[5]

Curates were worked hard. After his more leisurely time at Cwm, where he received much help from an older curate in a neighbouring parish, Robert Roberts moved to Bala where his vicar, Richard Pughe, was said to be a terrible taskmaster. There were four Sunday services with three sermons and a demanding weekday schedule, made worse as his vicar was too ill to do much himself.[6] Roberts also noted, as schoolmaster of Castle Caereinion in 1852, that the poor curate of that parish had to go each day to the Rectory to receive his orders with respect to visits and general parochial work "and woe betide him if any of the work cut out for him was neglected". He even had to go over his Sunday sermon the evening before, and it was rumoured the "Rectoress" was present too.[7] John Morgan, later archbishop of Wales, when vicar of Caernarfon in 1919 had four curates. Each was required to present himself on Monday mornings to receive their orders for the week and a list of people to visit. They were required to attend the daily offices when any irregularity was corrected, and one was even turfed out of bed when he overslept. While this was not an unusual position in those and even later days, his fierce and quick temper and his martinet ways made him feared by his junior colleagues who would probably never have referred to themselves by that description in his presence.[8]

Joseph Leach in his *Rural Rides of the Bristol Churchgoer* wrote about his dread of the watering place curates. These were those men who served an idle population of old and young ladies who spoilt them and as a result they contracted "a kind of fashionable religious effeminacy" and "frittered away their time on classes, morning calls and "coteries of lady theologians".[9] Such men were not unknown in Wales, where there was an even more subtle temptation. Bishop How, in his lectures on pastoral work of 1883, noted the rural parishes whose curates had little to do. This was especially so in Wales where so many people were dissenters and there was little sympathy with the Church and scarcely any society. His remedy against the dangers of excessive leisure was to read and read and read, and even to establish a weekly class of clergy to read the Greek Testament together.[10] Ellis Griffith, then vicar of Welshpool, publicly told his curate, E. H. Saunders, when he left that parish in 1917 to become curate of the more rural parish of Llandrinio, that he hoped he would use his time to read and study rather than play tennis and drink afternoon tea.[11]

By way of contrast, there are the reminiscences of a curate of Pentyrch, Lundy Richards, who served that parish between 1919-21. Though he visited throughout the parish, including nonconformist families, gave lantern slide lectures supplied by the Church Army, and had to walk between the three churches of his parish, he appears to have spent much of his time receiving hospitality from the wealthier parishioners and playing tennis, having formed a tennis club. This may be the reason why he and his vicar had an uneasy relationship.[12]

Rural parishes were not often a soft option compared with town parishes. A Welsh country curate, wrote Glendower in the 1910s during the disestablishment campaign, who had probably had to struggle hard to obtain his education and be ordained. "Behold him in his dingy lodging with his few books, his small stipend – gladly turning out, as few ministers do, to a sick call! Loyally and in spite of unpopularity upholding the discipline of the Church; patiently instructing stolid children how to chant and sing; conscientiously explaining the mysteries of Septuagesima and the Quicunque vult; a friend to the poor and suffering, in fastings often, in storm and cold, in good repute, and in evil repute, teaching, warning and helping his little flock."[13]

As Owen Nares, rector of Llandysilio, publicly said to his curate, E. Ellis Williams, who was leaving him to take another curacy in the parish of Oswestry, he would have more work to do in a town than a country parish, and his claims for preferment would be much better. Yet in describing Williams' work in that parish he indicated a wide range of activities that, with his other duties, had taxed his time: helping with the choir, introducing a full choral service into the church; forming church guilds successfully; organising entertainments, and running two Bible classes for men and women in the winter months.[14]

In some cases there was a good working relationship between incumbent and curate. Francis Kilvert, the diarist, curate of Clyro, and his vicar, Richard Lister Venables, offer one example. Venables had an estate at Llysdinam, twenty miles away, was an active magistrate, and spent time at his London home during the season, and so needed a curate who was sufficiently experienced to be left on his own to run the parish during his absence. Kilvert spent seven and a half years with him, and his stipend was increased several times, and when he felt it right to assist his father in his parish Venables offered him a stipend his father could never afford, of £160.[15]

Sometimes curates were employed in order to redress the deficiencies of their incumbents. Robert Roberts, when curate of Cwm, found his vicar was not so generous or kind hearted as he could have wished, but as his standard of excellence was low, he was far from being exacting to his curate, who found he had little to do, and so found time for visiting the parishioners. But as his vicar seldom preached Roberts had to prepare two weekly sermons, and found this a hard task.[16] At Criccieth it was said that the rector employed a curate to take the English duty. This consisted on a Sunday service for the rector's wife and servants.[17] An obituary of Lewis Price, vicar of Llandeilo Fawr, who died in 1906, said he didn't visit his parishioners much, but ensured they were not neglected by requiring his curates to do so.[18]

In an age when few clergy were able to provide a retirement pension for themselves, many clergy continued in their parishes till death intervened. Many were incapacitated and consequently employed a curate, forcing them to exist on a smaller income but enabling them to remain in the parsonage house. Often these curates had full responsibility for the parish.[19] This occurred, for example, in 1873 when M. Rice Morgan of Llansamlet was in a state of "imbecility",[20] while John Owen, rector of Eryrys, who died in 1886, had left his parish in charge of a curate while he went to reside by the sea for reasons of health.[21] In another instance Evan Jones, rector of Trefdraeth, 1875-90, obtained a curate to assist him in his closing years, Evan Davies, declaring it was a pleasure to work with him.[22]

On those occasions when an incumbent was found to be inadequately performing his duties, or the living was sequestrated, a bishop could impose a resident curate to serve the parish. The problem was, in the first case, the curate's stipend had to come out of that incumbent's parochial income, and even though the bishop could allocate a stipend up to £150 without restriction the eventual sum had to bear some relation to the income of the parish. In all probability few men were prepared to take on such responsibilities in what must have been an awkward position in any case, especially when, until legislation of 1898 prevented it, the incumbent could still continue to work in his parish.[23] One example of the difficulties that might occur happened in the parish of Cilybebyll, which was sequestrated in the 1890s and a curate placed in the parish. One curate, D.J. Davies, found that his rector, David Walter Jones, required all communications to be in writing, was forbidden to call at the Rectory, and was told they would only see each other in church. His successor, John Alfred Rees, introduced some elements of ritual in a daughter church, including vestments, with the result that his rector turned up at that church, insisted on taking the service, only to be escorted out of the church by a policeman. Jones even took the matter to court, demanding that the curate be dismissed for his great insult to him, but lost the case, the magistrate informing him that even a servant was entitled to a month's notice.[24]

The devotion and care of some assistant curates was long remembered in parishes, even when their incumbents had been almost forgotten. Constable Ellis, later of Llanfairfechan, started his ministerial life as assistant curate of Holyhead in 1846. It is said that his courage and faithfulness during a cholera epidemic, even placing bodies in coffins when undertakers refused to do so, was remembered in that parish for years thereafter.[25]

THE DIFFICULT CURATES

If some curates were models of propriety and clerical behaviour, others could be difficult and troublesome. As David Parry of Defynnog wrote to John Griffith of Merthyr in 1870, curates were scarce and were becoming difficult to manage.[26] In a large parish with many curates, jealousies between them might disrupt its good working. A dispute between the curates of Rhyl is recorded in 1882, when one of the curates, John Thomas, claimed to be the senior curate, a matter disputed by his colleague E. Tudor Owen, who claimed his licence for the parish was dated from 1866, six years before Thomas was ordained. Owen, who seems to have worked for a time as a non-stipendiary minister in the parish (possibly giving Thomas some credibility to his claim for seniority as a stipendiary curate) claimed that Thomas had appropriated the degree of B.A. Lampeter to which he was not entitled, while another said that Owen had sought the vicarage of Rhyl for himself but the bishop had refused to place a ritualist in such a prominent position.[27] The three curates of Wrexham were described in the early 1870s as lazy and indifferent. One was of dull mediocrity, and another had disgusted many with his ritualistic tendencies. Their vicar, Cunliffe, was said to be aristocratic, no preacher and isolated from his parishioners.[28]

Archbishop Benson's missioners in the diocese of Llandaff during the late 1880s frequently described some of the curates they had met as being of an inferior stamp; one was so objectionable that it was stated he would do far more harm than good in any parish, and that his vicar was trying to get rid of him. Another curate was one who would be hardly likely to be of any use in a parish, and yet another had little idea of his calling. The incumbents complained that their curates neglected pastoral work and seemed to regard their work as complete when the services had ended, while superior laymen complained of a want of intelligence in these men as they conducted these services. Canon Lewis of Ystradyfodwg complained that his curates were not "up to the mark", and saw themselves more as ministers of a sect than of the Church. They behaved more like chapel people than church folk by failing to kneel for prayer and being defective in the doctrines of the Church. At Blaina vicar and curate were at loggerheads and church life was feeble. The vicar, with tears, promised amendment if only he could be freed from his curate. The bishop found another sphere for that man, and an excellent young man was sent to replace him with beneficial results.[29] Yet these raw men, ill-educated, were able to speak to their congregations drawn from the same strata of society as themselves and thus win them for the Church.

The curate of Penarth parish church, Playter, was known as a good preacher but preached, it seems, Unitarian doctrines. Asked to resign, he did so, only to establish his own tin church in the parish, taking with him some of its wealthier ship-owning families. He later became a Unitarian minister before returning to the Church of England.[30] In an appeal to Archbishop Temple, in 1900, Hugh Thomas Owen, curate of Trevor in the diocese of St Asaph wrote that after 35 years on an inadequate stipend with an invalid wife and several children he had been driven into bankruptcy and had been deserted by his patron and bishop. His bishop disputed this. He only did Sunday duty and lived five miles from his curacy at Valle Crucis Abbey, which he showed to visitors for a fee. The income of his chaplaincy was £100, and he had allowed his parsonage house to get into such a state that the local authorities were taking action regarding its unsanitary condition. In the last ten years he had received more in charity than any other clergyman of the diocese.[31]

A number of curates found themselves in debt, sometimes because they refused to live within their income. Amongst them was G.H. Garrett, a former curate of St Mary's Cardiff. In 1860 he was imprisoned under the Insolvency Act at Derby for eight months, having accumulated debts of £100 for wine and spirits at Chesterfield on an income of £150, and it was said he owed £700 to trades people at Cardiff.[32] The curate of Clydach in the Swansea valley, S.E. Cornish, was in debt in 1897 and appears to have defrauded some of the church funds. His curacy terminated, and notice given to leave the house provided for him, he was asked to do his best while he worked out his notice, and if he did so he would be allowed to resign. If he did not, an enquiry would have to be held. A further note states he was a "sad shuffler and utterly without conscience" and had defrauded others as well.[33]

The vicar choral of St David's Cathedral, Philemon Appleby, was one of many accused of drunkenness. In his case, of 1858, the offence was aggravated by using abusive language. Though he described these statements as "Liverpool truths", he remained in office but by 1877 is noted as not having any charge.[34]

Yet it may not have been all the curate's fault. As a writer to the *Carnarvon and Denbigh Herald* claimed in 1846, "the haughtiness with which the rectors and vicars treat generally the curates of their parishes is greater, and more insufferable, than that of the esquire or baronet to his butler." But, he added, when these curates became incumbents they treated their curates in the same way, thus allowing their parishioners to see the curate in the same relation to the incumbent as that of a valet to his master.[35] The faults were clearly not all on one side.

DIFFICULTIES BETWEEN INCUMBENT AND CURATE

It is hardly surprising that there was often friction between incumbent and curate, bearing the uncertain nature of the latter's responsibilities, or the desire of a curate to make his own decisions in those areas assigned to him. This appears to have been the background to several disputes in the diocese of Llandaff that were referred to Archbishop Benson.

In 1883 Jonathan William Dunk, curate of Maindee, Newport, appealed to the archbishop about a threatened withdrawal of his licence, for this meant for himself and his family little else than disgrace and ruin. He had rented a house whose agreement could not be broken for five months, and had spent £60 in moving to this curacy. The lot of a curate on £150 per annum with a young and increasing family was hard enough without incurring fresh expenses through another move. He was curate in charge, as he called it, of a mission church in that parish, and clearly believed that this gave him a sort of independence. The charges made against him were that he was late for services and had refused to take a service at St Andrew's Mission Church; had started the 8.00 service at Easter half an hour late as he had other services; had refused to take charge of the boys in the Sunday School unless he also had oversight of the girls and infants, intending his wife to be the superintendent of the girls; had changed the time of the Bible Class by half an hour without the consent of the vicar; told people how badly the vicar was treating him; allowed a novice to play a valuable American organ, even at night time, so that candle grease had spilt on the floor and organ, and permitted her to hold a key; had carved up his district for lady visitors without informing his vicar; held a choral communion without his vicar's permission and had a communion hymn at the distribution of the elements, and even worse, had claimed his vicar had no power to interfere with him as he was curate in charge of a conventional district.

In his reply Duck said that the original agreement was that he was placed in charge of a mission church, and had been introduced to the parish as such. He believed the whole work of that district was in his charge, including the choir, Sunday School and district visitors, and he had made it clear he was not to be regarded as an assistant curate required to work between the various churches of the parish. The vicar's wife had suggested his wife should act as superintendent of the girls, but this the vicar had forbidden and he had killed a successful Sunday School, and had then closed the mission church, to the indignation of its members. He had worked hard in the parish, covered for the vicar on his holidays, had established bright and cheerful services at St Matthews, though the vicar had so arranged things that he would only be there for two Sundays in each month. The bishop had told Dunk that these charges would have to be investigated, and if he could not answer them he would either have to resign or he would revoke his licence. The archbishop advised Dunk that he should give his notice to his vicar as it was clear there was a conflict between them which was not in the best interests of the church "that you have at heart", while he advised his bishop to accept the resignation as the revocation of a licence was too great a bar to future work. A final letter from Dunk to the archbishop expresses his gratitude, but quoted a letter he had sent to his vicar that if peace and goodwill could be secured by any concession and apology on his part he would gladly make it. It clearly did not, and one has the impression of a vicar over-insistent on his rights and acting in a dictatorial manner, but also of a curate who was a little insensitive to the reality of his position. Dunk had to serve numerous other curacies before he had a living of his own, Awre, Newnham, Gloucestershire, in 1907. He had been a curate for 37 years.[36]

A further dispute was between the vicar of Pentrebach, William Green, and his curate, John Jones, in 1886, during which controversy the parishioners memorialised the archbishop in favour of the curate. Jones claimed that Green had misappropriated monies given to the church he served towards the cost of his stipend, and argued if he had to leave, so would the congregation of his mission church. Bishop Lewis told Archbishop Benson that Jones was one of three curates in the parish, had not worked cordially with his colleagues, having accused one of them of intemperance, and had caused division. As a result, and with the agreement of the rural dean, he had been given three months' notice. Green added that the monies had been paid, but that Jones had refused to meet his vicar and fellow curates on their Monday morning chapters, and persisted in officiating at funerals for non-church people. His churchwardens argued that at the root of the problem were people who had left a dissenting chapel after some dispute and had become members of Pentrebach Welsh Church. It seems it was a clear dispute between church and chapelry, the chapelry people, led by or leading their curate, to seek an independence that the vicar could not allow, and making accusations about matters they did not understand.[37]

Archdeacon Griffiths of Neath was also involved in a confrontation with one of his curates, J.R. Hosbons, who cared for one of the daughter churches of that parish, St Catherine's. What began as a simple incident in 1895 soon escalated into a major incident that brought in a host of issues arising from that church's feeling itself to be a poor relation to the parish church. Griffiths who, hitherto, had allowed this church to make its own Harvest arrangements, subject to his approval, had gone ahead and made his own arrangements, making the congregation feel they had been treated arbitrarily with Hosbons arguing that his authority had been questioned. The curate was suspended by Griffiths, and having broken down in a service, found an even greater degree of support than he might have received otherwise. There were further complications, and at one service the choir walked out with other members of the congregation. Griffiths, in writing to the bishop, probably identified the root of the problem, namely that St Catherine's wished to be an independent chapel and its members were resentful of the restraints imposed upon them by a distant authority. Though he accepted that under Hosbons much work had been accomplished, it was a question of authority in the parish. Eventually matters were patched up and Hosbons was allowed to remain in the parish, but Griffiths' comment that he was a man deficient in certain qualities might have been true, for he remained a curate for most of his life.[38]

The case of Hosbons, in which Griffiths probably felt he was obtaining a power-base in his church that was detrimental to his position as incumbent, had a parallel at Llandrillo. Here a new church had been built at Colwyn Bay, and a curate appointed for it. By 1884 the vicar, W. Venables Williams, was demanding the resignation of his curate, Richard Jennings, on the grounds that he was permitting nonconformists to enter and teach at his Sunday School and refusing to dismiss four of its teachers for failing to attend the parish church. In a significant phrase Williams demanded that he be master in his own parish, and while the bishop made it clear there were no grounds for his curate's dismissal and urged common sense, especially as the Colwyn Bay congregation supported their curate, Williams made matters worse by refusing to speak to his curate or acknowledge him in the street. Eventually the situation became so intolerable that, having received a handsome testimonial, Jennings left the parish for another curacy, arranged by the bishop, only for the bishop to receive a missive from Williams complaining that as the bishop had not given him the statutory three months notice, he would have to work the parish on his own for that period of time.[39]

As already noted the ritualism of a curate was often a source of offence to many incumbents. At Maesteg the curate preferred "mummery and outward display" but though the vicar wished to dismiss him he felt diffident as his stipend was paid by the Llynfi Vale Iron Company.[40] The curate of St Woolos, Newport, looking after the mission church of St John the Baptist, H.M. Bannister, was high church in a low church parish, and obviously allowed his beliefs to be expressed in its worship. In 1884 he was forced to resign, probably a better way for him as the alternative might be the withdrawal of his licence.[41] Six years later the situation repeated itself, and Archdeacon Bruce, the same vicar, required his curate at the mission church, Henry Burdett, to resign as he had introduced a choral weekly celebration in that church, even though it was well attended.[42]

THE LACK OF SECURITY

In 1867 a group of East London curates sent a memorial to the first Lambeth Conference, though it was not considered by it. They noted their insecurity, for the possibility of the revocation of a licence gave them little protection; their stipends were inadequate; length of service and individual merit was not taken into account when preferment was given; they were not represented in Convocation, and they were often treated as deacons rather than as priests, that is, they did not celebrate the Communion.[43] A pamphlet of the same year, possibly related to the above, made the same points, and asked pertinently whether the curate was to have no opinion, no zeal, no capacity, no desire to be anybody but a living machine, set in motion by the rector.

The National schoolmaster had more liberty of discretion and independence of action than the curate, yet both he and his incumbent were responsible to God, and the curate's ministerial power came from ordination, not from his incumbent.[44] In addition, though a married curate's expenses were greater, and a house was required, or if provided, the rent deducted from his stipend, there would be little or no increase in his stipend.[45] We note some of these concerns below.

This lack of security was a major concern. If a man quit the curacy on his own volition he had to give three months' notice and secure the permission of the bishop, but if the incumbent wished to dismiss his curate he had also to secure the bishop's permission and give the same notice, unless the parting was mutual. Corbett claimed that the Pluralities Act of 1813 was a pretence and "gave no protection to these poor creatures". He also noted that a bishop could also refuse to sign the testimonials of a curate to enable him to move to another diocese, so dooming him either to certain ruin or an absolute submission to the will of his master-parson.[46]

In most disputes bishops took the side of the incumbents. Curates were expendable. It was popularly believed that Bishop Thirlwall had trained his dogs to bite the legs of the Welsh-speaking curates.[47] This rumour, false as it was, indicated the general concern of curates that bishops were hardly ever on their side. Speaking at a Church Congress in 1908 a headmaster stated that curates were in theory the bishop's curates, "but when friction arises, it is the exception for the curate to be supported."[48] Equally, the bishop was not only able to withdraw a curate's licence, thus ensuring that his clerical career was at a close, a new incumbent had the right to dismiss the curates he found *in situ* within his first six months in the parish by giving them six weeks notice, but if he failed to do so the curates could continue in office.[49] Such insecurity meant, it was claimed in 1867, that often a curate had no initiative to carry out plans or projects, and a move meant finding another curacy, accommodation, and a break in his children's education.[50]

Having to leave a curacy, due to the appointment of a new vicar, was not infrequent. If this meant a desperate search for a new appointment by the curate, it also meant that the good work he had done might be lost as well as the continuity of that work.[51] One reason alleged for these dismissals was that a younger curate could be had at a cheaper stipend than an older one. The fear of such a dismissal was always there. Thomas Williams, curate of Merthyr Tydfil, noting in 1844 that his incumbent, Maber, was dying, asked Lord Bute if he could use his influence with his successor so he could retain his curacy. He had served the parish for eight years and hoped he had done so faithfully, for he desired to "spend and be spent in the service of our common Lord and Redeemer."[52] Copleston in one of his letters of 1843 notes the concern of the curate of Malpas, one Harris. It appears his new incumbent had claimed as he did not live in the parish he was not entitled to any length of notice, but his bishop told him that in common courtesy he might be sure that fair notice would be given him before his services were dispensed with.[53]

Further cases of the dismissal of a curate by his incumbent may be recorded. An unknown curate in the diocese of Llandaff, probably in Monmouthshire, in the 1840s disputed the stipend allowed him by his incumbent when his vicar was required to leave his rented house and live outside the parish. It meant the curate assumed he was a stipendiary curate rather than an assistant curate, and thus entitled to a stipend of £120 rather than £80. But his incumbent was only technically non-resident and continued with the work of the parish. Matters became heated, the curate was dismissed, and thereafter claimed that this dispute was a matter of non-residence, pluralism (it was a united benefice of three parishes), of ill-treating curates and even brought in Copleston's residence at St Paul's Deanery as a matter of reproach.[54]

Llewelyn Wynne Jones, when given a presentation upon leaving Chirk to become rector of Llanymynech in 1890, regretted that he was unable to take his curate, Hugh Jones, with him, as he did not require an assistant there, but he hoped that with the many livings available in the diocese, the bishop would not forget Mr Jones, who had proved a faithful, earnest and devoted minister of the Gospel over the seven years he had been in the parish. It seems that he neither received a living in the diocese nor was he able to continue at Chirk with his vicar's successor, for by 1891 he was curate of an Edinburgh Church.[55]

A further Welsh case concerned John Morgan, curate in charge of the daughter church of Tongwynlais in the parish of Whitchurch. He was dismissed by his vicar, John Thomas Clarke, in 1894, on the ground that he had given great dissatisfaction to the local squire and his wife, Henry Lewis of Greenmeadow, who were the major contributors to that church. It is probable that Morgan took an independent line and introduced ritual displeasing to that squire, who wreaked his revenge by refusing to pay his contribution to the curate's stipend.[56] In another episode, Humphrey Lloyd, curate of Llanarmon-yn-Ial in the diocese of St Asaph lost that curacy in 1906 when his incumbent moved, and for the next three years, unable to find another curacy, existed on a licence to officiate in that diocese.[57]

Frances Knight notices several cases, albeit from English parishes, where curates had to resign, one because his vicar had lost a CPAS grant and could no longer afford to pay his stipend, others because parishioners objected to a man due to his accent, or was unpopular, or because a want of "cordiality" between vicar and curate meant that the spiritual interests of the parishioners would suffer. At least one curate pointed out the incompatibility of the wording of his licence, that he should remain in his curacy "until otherwise provided with some ecclesiastical preferment, or lawfully deprived for a crime", with his actual position disposed of at the whim of his incumbent.[58]

Licences to officiate were withdrawn by a bishop for many reasons, such as marrying a woman in an advanced state of pregnancy, as did Evan William, curate of Beaufort, in 1853, who had no "sense of culpability" about his offence, or when the curate of Gwynfe, Carmarthenshire, Thomas Pugh, was discovered to be in a state of intoxication at the Easter communion service of 1893.[59] As late as 1932 Archbishop Edwards of St Asaph suspended Lewis Roberts, curate of Chirk, for preaching socialism and pacifism. It took him six years before he could obtain another curacy, this time in England.[60]

The withdrawal of a licence was a serious affair, as Archdeacon Thomas Williams of Llandaff maintained, for it meant that a man's worldly prospects were almost totally lost, and he felt that curates needed to be protected from caprice of power and some provision made for their defence.[61] Without a licence, or a bishop's counter signature on testimonials, a man was unable to obtain any other clerical post, and he was debarred from entering a trade to earn his livelihood, and as a consequence would probably be driven into the ranks of the unemployed.[62] A speaker at the Wolverhampton Church Congress of 1867 alleged that this power of revoking licences was often used if there was a dispute between the bishop or an incumbent and a curate and was sometimes a matter of personal prejudice. For the curate there was "no regular process of law, no trial by jury; the veriest trifle is accepted against him – a newspaper report, an anonymous letter, may be enough to stop his ministrations; for he is presumed guilty, and mercifully permitted, in certain cases, to show reason to the contrary. He may be separated from the people who respect him, from the incumbent who values him, and at a moment's warning be deprived of the means of earning his daily bread". He added that the bishops had an unlimited power here, and that its use was preventing many university men from going forward for ordination.[63]

There was thus a real concern about the insecurity of a curate's position, but there were also concerns about the insufficient prospects for promotion (which will be dealt with in the following chapter) and the absence of any progressive increase in the stipend. Yet as J.J. Halcombe suggested, it was easier to find fault with the present system than to propose something better, especially when one bore in mind there were two different sets of curates, those who were "apprentices" and those who had passed beyond that stage.[64]

FURTHER CONCERNS

A further complaint was that curates were not represented in the official bodies of the church, such as Convocation, so that the legitimate concerns of the curates were never heard or only given second-hand.[65] Maurice Jones, then a curate at Welshpool but later principal of St David's College, Lampeter, made this complaint at the St Asaph diocesan conference of 1890 respecting membership of its standing committee on which they were unrepresented. In many parishes of the diocese curates did most of the arduous duties and cared for far more people than some incumbents in parishes of 100 to 150 souls.[66] It is not surprising that some dioceses had an association of unbeneficed clergy, as had Llandaff, though it seems this association was for mutual support and learning, rather than for campaigning on particular issues.[67]

Concern was also expressed about the lack of pastoral case for curates and their families. James H. Jenkins, curate of Taffs Well, near Cardiff, told the 1908 Llandaff diocesan conference that one curate who was paralysed discovered there was no provision for him. In sixteen years of Orders he himself had only a fortnight's holiday, and when he had to bury his seven-year old child he had to preach the following day, and when his father drowned he had to go and preach at a neighbouring church at some distance away.[68] Another concern was expressed by his former bishop, Richard Lewis, in 1903, when he felt that clerical poverty, especially amongst the curates, demanded the attention of the diocesan conference. When a curate died, he asserted, his family became dependent on clerical charities or were driven to the workhouse.[69] Sadly, nothing seems to have been done to alleviate this position.

As there were more curacies than incumbencies, a man might have to wait many years for a living of his own and some never achieved that position, as we note later.

This position meant in turn that many curates had to move frequently: Haig suggesting that on average a man might move every three or four years, though Halcombe suggested every two years. Halcombe considered that many curates were forced to move because of the difficulties of obtaining an adequate house, especially in very poor districts. Yet there was no provision for removal expenses, and neither the Ecclesiastical Commission nor Queen Anne's Bounty were able to assist with these heavy and draining costs.[70]

Various reforms were suggested. Many desired that curates should be placed on the strength of a diocese (and paid through the diocese) and given a permanent status, rather than being attached to individual incumbents.[71] Another suggestion was that the various daughter churches served by curates should become independent districts, and yet another that no bishop should licence an assistant curate to a town parish unless a stipend of £250 was available for him.[72] A session of the Wolverhampton Church Congress of 1867, possibly connected to the curates' petition sent to the Lambeth Conference, heard a number of suggestions. Three thousand of the smaller livings could be augmented up to £300, on condition that the next appointment was a curate who had served for at least seven years; the laity should augment the older curates' stipends so that the competition between them and the cheaper and younger curates might not be decided in the latter's favour; and that the various societies which gave grants for curates should offer a larger one to an established curate than to one just ordained.[73] A group of unbeneficed clergy petitioned Lord Salisbury, the prime minister, in 1898, requesting they should have greater security of tenure, for they were not in the position of other employees in so far as legislation prevented them starting in business on their own account. In addition they asked for a fixed limit of five years as the period of service before a man could be appointed to a benefice, thus ensuring a fairer distribution of livings.[74] The Association for Improving the Status of the Unbeneficed Clergy, in its fourth annual report of 1913, had sent a deputation to the Home Secretary about the plight of unbeneficed Welsh clergy who were given no life interest in the Disestablishment Act, but it also made clear its desire that the diocesan bishop alone should have power to remove a curate from his post and that their stipends should be paid from a diocesan fund.[75] Few of the bishops who heard these concerns had been curates, or had only served short curacies in fashionable parishes, and consequently they seem to have fallen on deaf ears.

THE HOPE OF PREFERMENT

The vast majority of clergy anticipated having their own parish, though the reality could be quite different for many of them. Those who came from wealthy families might eventually be pushed into a family living, often with indecent haste, or had an interest with a patron or sufficient wealth to enable a living or a next presentation to be purchased on their behalf.[76] Those with university connections, especially those who had served as fellows of colleges, could expect a college living to come their way. Chaplains to peers and bishops, and those who served as minor canons in cathedrals, were in an equally advantageous position. While a diocesan bishop was regarded as a source of patronage for his clergy, many bishops had only sufficient patronage to assist a small number of their clergy.[77] Independence was so much desired that many curates were willing to accept livings whose net income was far less than their stipends as curates,[78] though the archdeacon of Exeter suggested in 1866 that many, especially those who obtained benefices late in life, were not bettered by the exchange.[79] Even if a benefice of £300 was obtained, there would be a "multitude of new expenses" which would "make the poor man wish himself back again in his less dignified position". The claims of charity, the upkeep of the parsonage house, the maintenance of the parish school, would haunt him, and make his heart "heavy with anxiety".[80] Yet in spite of these fears, T. Jesse Jones, then rector of Gelligaer, perhaps spoke for many curates when he asserted in 1893 the following:

> We may say what we will, and treat them [the curates] as fellow-labourers and brother priests, but the fact remains that the curates hold a subordinate position, and that the incumbent is the *persona* after all. There are, of course, instances where this subordination is a delight and a privilege, and to be associated with the incumbent's work, even in a relatively inferior position, the greatest joy, but it is often otherwise. The subordination is not rarely emphasized, and often rendered intolerable by the thoughtless wicked bearing of incumbents, who allow jealousy and a false notion of the means whereby to shew their superiority to sway them, "Only a curate," what a vista does not that expression reveal of inconsiderate treatment and inferiority of importance! The position may not always prove unpalatable, but it often does and becomes the more so as years roll by. Who can wonder, therefore, that emancipation from such a state is longed for, and that the curate stage of clerical life is spoken of as "Egypt"? For

man as man to seek advancement and an escape from a subordinate position is what we see all around us, and this is true of the curate also; and for him there is but one escape, which offers only when the gate of preferment opens and admits him to the realm of the beneficed.[81]

The number of men ordained by the 1850s and beyond far exceeded the number of benefices available to them, even if their patronage had been fairly distributed instead of being reserved for the family and friends of their patrons. A.M. Deane, a contributor to Halcombe's book argued in 1874 that if bishops refrained from nepotism and private patrons from simony then the position would be altered for the better. He also suggested that if livings were given according to years of seniority, a man would receive a benefice within eleven years, though for eight years the income of it would be less than a curacy, while at the age of 44 he might obtain a better living valued at £150 to £300, and by the age of 54 one worth £300 to £600.[82] Curates were ordained for the rapidly growing industrial parishes in such numbers that the clerical profession was over-crowded,[83] and even though new parishes were created, the number was never sufficient to go around all those who were ordained. Bishop Edwards of St Asaph, speaking at the London Church Congress in 1899, said that while the number of beneficed clergy had increased by less than five per cent, the number of unbeneficed clergy had increased by seventy per cent, adding that this would lead to the "bitter cry of disappointments, discouragements, and grinding poverties". The issue needed to be faced.[84] Around the same time T. Jesse Jones claimed that the number of the unbeneficed was multiplied at every Ember season, but the number of livings remained almost stationary.[85]

Another writer estimated in the 1860s that only one third of the incumbencies within the wider Church could afford clergy a decent maintenance, that is providing an income of £200, so that without private means many were beyond the reach of assistant clergy, even if offered them.[86] Bishop Wilberforce accepted this position, writing it was "arithmetically impossible that the existing incumbencies can afford maintenance within a reasonable time for more than one-third of the clergy ordained".[87]

It was a situation which meant that many men had to wait for many years before they had a living of their own, and in some cases never attained one. Thus John Morgan in a pamphlet of 1873, addressing the position in Llandaff diocese, argued that some curates had to wait twenty to thirty years before they could obtain a benefice, and by then a number were too old to be promoted.[88] In 1894 it was estimated there were 515 curates of more than twenty years standing in Wales alone, and eight-tenths of them had little prospect before them "beyond a life of hard work" with £100 to £170 per year; the inference being this would be the same whether they remained as curates or became incumbents.[89] In 1902 Bishop Lewis of Llandaff stated that of 7,500 curates, over 1,400 had been more than 15 years in orders.[90]

Comparisons were often made with the old stipendiary curate whose position was quite different. He might serve for life in one parish or, if required to move, would soon find another sphere of ministry. In those days, it was argued rather unjustly, one remained as one was ordained, either as an incumbent or as a curate. Unlike the assistant curate, there was no suggestion that if the stipendiary curate failed to obtain a living it was because he was inadequate, inefficient or indolent.[91] As Archbishop Longley of Canterbury made clear: "the position and prospects of the curates are much worse than they were fifty years ago, must be patent to every one that has had an opportunity of examining the question".[92] Indeed, the stigma still remained. Those who could not obtain preferment were often thought of as "failures" as the Rev. E.G. O'Donaghue complained at the Derby Church Congress during a session devoted to the unbeneficed clergy.[93]

Some assistant curates were fortunate to obtain parishes of their own within a reasonable amount of time. Other men were not so fortunate. Jonah Bowen Evans, became vicar of the small rural parish of St Harmon's, in Radnorshire, in 1845, having been ordained in 1829 and having served curacies in Carmarthenshire, Monmouthshire and Breconshire.[94] William H. Whitworth, ordained in 1834, held nine curacies in 23 years, including Llanbedr in Breconshire, though his stay was short here as he had no Welsh. An unfair testimonial from a non-resident incumbent who hardly knew him damned him for years, and he was sixty-six before he obtained his first and only living.[95] John James Turner, in spite of being a Cambridge graduate and of a gentry family, only obtained a living, that of Buttington, after four curacies and twenty-five years in Orders, in 1879, and this was given him by his cousin who was vicar of Welshpool, in whose patronage it lay. Sadly, he died before he could be instituted.[96] John Thomas Clarke, an Oxford man, waited twenty three years for his first living, that of the industrial parish of Brynmawr, having served four curacies and possibly some time as a schoolmaster.[97] Robert John Oliver, curate of Castle

Caereinion in 1911, was fortunate in being appointed to the parish of Llawrybettws, having been ordained in 1895 and having served six curacies in the dioceses of Llandaff and St Asaph.[98] Rice Price Hughes, a year younger in Orders than Oliver, had fourteen curacies in thirty-three years, staying about two years on average in each one, and serving in the four Welsh dioceses and three English ones. He was sixty-one when he received his first living, that of Llangynog, Montgomeryshire, where he remained for ten years.[99] Howard Morton, a Cambridge man, remained as curate of Penarth for thirty years, only having his first incumbency at Bargoed in 1924. To mark his twentieth year in his curacy he was given a presentation, when it was observed he had served under four rectors and had nine curates as his colleagues.[100]

By the 1850s those curates who were leaving their parishes for livings of their own, or even another curacy, were given testimonials by their parishioners. The first reference I have found is one to John Morgan, curate of Michaelston near Port Talbot who was moving to another curacy in the diocese. This was in 1852 and he was presented with a silk gown. The dissenting bodies had closed their meetings in order to attend, possibly because he claimed he preached the whole counsel of God, and was thus an evangelical man.[101] Other presentations of the same period consisted of a purse of sovereigns, a gold watch or a pocket communion set, indicating that their work had been appreciated.[102] When Timson Wrenford left his curacy at St Mary's, Cardiff, for the new parish of St Paul's, Newport, he was presented with a silver pocket communion set, a silver inkstand and a gold pencil and pen case, while his farewell sermon is said to have reduced the congregation to tears.[103] Another presentation was made to Cyril Stacey, assistant curate of Cardiff, in 1860, upon his removal to a parish near Wellington, Somerset, consequent of his marriage. As his father was stipendiary curate of Cardiff he might have arranged the testimonial for his son.[104]

Cockayne Frith, who left the curacy of Welshpool in 1876 to become vicar of Market Lavington, Devizes, was presented with a clock, a purse of money and a silver goblet subscribed by 360 of the working class of the parish. In all £100 had been collected.[105] A lengthy newspaper account reported the presentation made to T.C.V. Bastow, curate of St Oswald's Church, Oswestry, who was leaving in 1885 to become incumbent of Little Peatling, Lutterworth. Presented with a cheque from the congregation and a chair by some of the ladies, he asked them to pray for him serving a parish with a population of 120, that he should neither rule nor be slothful, and in working the glebe to remember he was a priest and not a farmer.[106] After John Griffith of Merthyr's death in 1885, his son, Charles, left the curacy in that parish and accepted the living of Blaenafon, though the parish had petitioned that he might succeed his father. The Farewell Meeting, reported in the *Merthyr Express*, was reprinted as a separate pamphlet, and indicated that, after long speeches, he was presented with a silver tray, coffee service and spoons, salt cellars, a clock and other items from the parish and various groups within it. He later became dean of Llandaff.

THE ELDERLY CURATE

It must have been galling for men of experience, who remained as curates, to see men who were young and inexperienced placed over them as incumbents or given parishes of their own. An incumbent of an English parish noted that there was no pecuniary recognition for years of service, and many men with thirty or forty years of service discovered men who had been three years in orders receiving the prizes of their profession.[107] Thomas Walters offered a reason for this in his claim that there was no fair system of patronage, for too often curates "who had borne the heat and burden of the day" were displaced by men without their experience but with "connections".[108] Concern was also expressed that men who had never served in a diocese were being appointed to its better livings, especially when they knew little or nothing of parochial work. This occurred, for example, in the parish of Cowbridge in 1883, when the patronage lay with the dean and chapter of Gloucester.[109] "Clericus", describing himself as a curate of thirty years standing, said much the same in a letter to the *Western Mail* of 1875. The plight of the "half-starved curate" was never discussed in ruridecanal meetings or Convocation, and men in their forties and fifties deserved a better stipend than one newly ordained. He instanced a man to whom a short time ago he was teaching the alphabet of Greek and Latin who was twenty-two years of age. He had been promoted to a living of £300 while his tutor remained a curate on £80. The injustice was so palpable and so glaring that even an old woman could see through it.[110]

Bishop Lewis of Llandaff not only noted the difficulties facing a curate who wished for his own benefice, but also the fact that the older a curate was the greater difficulty he would find in obtaining another curacy, as younger incumbents did not want older men as their curates.[111] One reason for this was such men might become a threat to them because of their experience or, alternately, had become weary with their years of service and thus lost any sense of initiative.[112] Incumbents were well aware than at unmarried curate was far cheaper than a married man with a family.[113] One newspaper correspondent complained that he had been seeking a curacy of £150 for six months without success. He needed that amount in order to rent a house for his family. Leave out the words that you are married with a family and you will get plenty of answers, but insert them and you will get none. Incumbents, he argued, preferred single men or married men "without incumbrances".[114] What other profession, asked James H. Jenkins of the Llandaff Diocesan Conference of 1910 (in a quotation already cited), would discard men of twenty years' experience in favour of those with none.[115] As a result many older curates found themselves frequently changing posts with an ever-diminishing income, and many, it was alleged, were beyond hope. Though proposals for a pension for such men had been suggested, it meant they would need to start paying premiums from an early age, and this was not feasible.[116]

There were many men who remained curates for life.[117] David Howell, later dean of St Davids, was warned by his father when he ventured to think about ordination in the 1850s that he might be a curate for life and be not much better than a beggar.[118] John Davies, a Lampeter man who was ordained in the diocese of Llandaff in 1865, a noted antiquary, nevertheless served fifteen curacies in south and north Wales, and died in 1933, still unbeneficed, and was buried at Mydroilyn, Cardiganshire.[119] A former Nonconformist and literate, Walter Brown Corfield, who had been ordained in 1869, served nine curacies before his death in 1910.[120] Others will be noted in the following section as they desperately but unsuccessfully tried to find a benefice of their own.

The plight of the elderly curate was often pitiful. Such men, wrote T. Jesse Jones, would become disappointed and embittered, who while they might still work on in their declining years, had to look forward "to the emancipation and home and kingship above, but for ever deprived of the possibility of them on earth".[121] Many eked out an existence on clerical charities, thankful for cast-off clothing, having no prospect of a better income and knowing that they would reach an age when it would be difficult to find employment at all, and after death would be bequeathing their wives and children as a legacy to the clerical charities.[122] Anthony Trollope perhaps spoke for some of these men when he described one of them "as a man whom from time to time his friends are asked to lift from unutterable depths by donations which no gentleman can take without a crushed spirit – as a pauper whom the poor around him know to be a pauper and will not, therefore respect as a minister of their religion".[123] Some were even more unfortunate. An elderly curate, Francis John Bleasby, entered Tiverton Workhouse in 1902 after making 470 unsuccessful applications for a curacy.[124] Howell Thomas died aged fifty at Newport Workhouse in 1897, where "he had lived a life of placid contentment". Thomas had served curacies at Ystradgynlais and Mynyddislwyn, but had become mentally deranged, though this was denied by another paper. He had declined to go into lodgings, and the diocese had kept up his insurance policy to enable him to have a decent funeral, and he left the remainder of his small estate to the board of guardians.[125]

There were other men who simply dropped out of the system. Some entered the teaching profession, probably the only alternative legally available to them, while others vanished into obscurity. Virgin estimated that in the early nineteenth century such men accounted for twenty to twenty-five per cent of those ordained.[126] It was suggested in 1882 that for every man ordained another was compelled to seek other means of maintenance outside the Church, and that the number of unattached clergy, some of whom might take occasional duty, nearly equalled the number of curates on active service.[127] Another asserted in 1896 that there were six thousand experienced clergy unaccounted for in the clergy lists and wondered how many of these were unemployed.[128] Two men may be mentioned, whose entries are found in the 1911 *Clergy List* without addresses, John Jones and William Evan Lloyd, ordained in 1868 and 1870 respectively, who after two curacies, had no further responsibilities. By 1911 Jones had had no clerical employment for 22 years, and Lloyd for over 35 years.[129]

****

Though the Church was aware of the conditions under which many assistant curates laboured, it found it difficult to remedy them, even though there was a continuing fear that these conditions prevented good men from coming forward for ordination and requiring bishops to ordain men not quite up to the mark socially or educationally.[130] Yet, those who were ordained, especially those from the *gwerin* class, and served as curates in the industrial valleys of south Wales, enabled the Church to retain a parochial ministry and serve a bilingual community. It was these men, unappreciated and unrecognised, who ensured the Church remained a viable entity in these areas, and who were, in the words of a CPAS local secretary, "a power of God unto salvation".[131] Strangely, by the 1920s it was claimed that curates were becoming a dying breed, and Archdeacon A.O. Evans of Bangor warned that a motorbike or horse was no substitute for a curate.[132] Assistant curates remain, even though many of them today are non-stipendiary ministers.

ENDNOTES TO SECTION TWO
THE INFERIOR CLERGY – THE CURATES

CHAPTER ONE: INTRODUCTION

1. Pinnock, *The Law of the Church and the Clergy*, pp. 83-4; Best, *Temporal Pillars*, pp. 16-17; Obelkevich, *Religion and Rural Society*, pp. 117-18; Haig, *The Victorian Clergy*, p. 219; Jacob, *Clerical Profession*, pp. 64-5; Knight, *The Nineteenth-Century Church*, p. 116.
2. W.T. Morgan, "The Diocese of St David's", Part A, pp. 29-30. Haig, quotes J.J. Halcombe who, writing in 1874, argued that the clergy were divided into two classes, incumbents and curates, at the time of their ordination. Due to the difficulties of preferment, the latter remained as they began for the remainder of their lives: *The Victorian Clergy*, p. 222.
3. Virgin, *The Church in an Age of Negligence*, pp. 218-19.
4. Quoted by H. Holdefast, *Haverfordwest and its Story* (Haverfordwest, 1882), p. 150. Evan Lloyd noted that curates were expected to clean the cutlery, black the shoes and run errands for their incumbents: Cecil J.L. Price, *A Man of Genius and a Welsh Man* (Swansea, 1963), p. 14. Another disparaging story about a clergyman assumed to be a beggar is given by Shôn Gwialan in his letter to the Rt. Revd. Dr Warren: *A Letter to the Rt. Rev. Dr. Warren on his Conduct as Bishop of Bangor* (n.d.), pp. 26-7.
5. Quoted by Bax, *The English Parsonage*, p. 132.
6. Edwards, *Wales and the Welsh Church*, p. 325n.
7. Evans, *Religion and Politics in Mid-Eighteenth Century Anglesey*, p. 82.
8. Quoted by Bradney, *Monmouthshire*, I-2b, 442-3, cf. Jane Austen's comments in her novels as noted by Galbraith, *The Established Church as depicted on English Prose Fiction*, p. 106-8.
9. John Byng, *The Torrington Diaries* (ed. C.B. Andrews: London, 1934), I, 309-10.
10. Thomas Pennant, *The History of the Parishes of Whiteford, and Holywell* (London, 1796), pp. 272-3. He adds that the reason for his poverty was because of his care of his two sisters.
11. J. Hucks (ed. A.R. Jones and W. Tydeman), *A Pedestrian Tour through North Wales in a Series of Letters, 1795* (Cardiff, 1979), pp. 12-13.
12. Margaret Walker, "The Priory Church of St John the Evangelist, Brecon, 1782-1808", *Brycheiniog*, 28 (1995-6), 120.
13. Peter Lord, *Words with Pictures* (Aberystwyth, 1995), pp. 17, 69-70, and M.G. George, "Some Caricatures on the Clergy of Wales", *NLW.Jnl.*, 4 (1945), 53-4. The earlier print was probably based on Richard Graves's description in his *The Spiritual Quixote*: see Galbraith, *The Established Church as depicted in English Prose Fiction*, p. 70. One also wonders if this print inspired Sydney Smith's comment about the curate being "a learned man in a hovel, with sermons and saucepans, lexicons and bacon, Hebrew book and ragged children ... the first and purest pauper of the hamlet", as quoted by Simon Goodenough, *The Country Parson* (Newton Abbot, 1983), p. 53.
14. Jenkins, *Literature, Religion and Society in Wales*, p. 6.
15. Copleston, *Edward Copleston*, pp. 165-6.
16. See, for example, Hart, *The Curate's Lot*, pp. 132-3.
17. Sykes, *Church and State in England*, p. 209. Jacob, in his *Clerical Profession* (p. 72) argues there is little evidence to support Sykes' contention, but it was certainly true for many Welsh curates. W.J. Conybeare, though writing of Westmorland, noted a squire who said he could not invite his curate to his home as his sister was a maid in a friend's house: *Essays Ecclesiastical and Social* (London, 1855), p. 27.
18. *A Letter from Snowdon* (London, 1770), p. 53.

19 H. Holdefast, *Haverfordwest and its Story* (Haverfordwest, 1882), pp. 112-13.
20 W. Bingley, *North Wales* (London, 1804), I, 238-9.
21 Morris, *Romilly's Visits to Wales*, p. 8.
22 Harriet Thomas (ed.), *A Memoir: Llewelyn Thomas* (London, 1897), p. 7.
23 Brown, *Evangelicals in the Church in Wales*, pp. 33-44; David Jones, *The Welsh Church and Welsh Nationality*, p. 114.
24 Griffiths, "A Visitation of the Archdeaconry of Carmarthen, 1710", p. 314. Performing clandestine marriages was not uncommon, see Roger L. Brown, "Clandestine Marriages in Wales", *THSC,* 1982, pp. 74-85, and Sykes, *Church and State in England*, p. 221.
25 R.J. Colyer, *The Teifi* (Llandysul, 1987), p. 61; and see Guy, *Thesis*, pp. 784-6, for the case of Thomas Rinbron in 1775.
26 Evans, *Religion and Politics in mid-Eighteenth Century Anglesey*, pp. 88-9.
27 Edmund Jones (ed. John Harvey), *The Appearance of Evil* (Cardiff, 2003), p. 48.
28 Denning, *The Diary of William Thomas*, p. 45.
29 G.M. Griffiths, "Montgomeryshire in the Records of the Church in Wales", *MC*, 58 (1963-4), 133. He also notes William Edwards, curate of Llanwyddelan, who was said to be unable to produce any testimonials as to his good behaviour.
30 Humphreys, "A Conspectus of Schools in Eighteenth-Century Montgomeryshire", pp. 101-2, quoting SA/RD/28. The schoolmaster's brother was churchwarden and had appointed him to this post.
31 T.J. Prichard, *Eglwys S. Gwynhoedl* (2004), p. 23.
32 T.G. Davies, *Neath's Wicked World* (Swansea, 2000), pp. 191-2.
33 Brown, "The Parish of Gelligaer in the Nineteenth Century", p. 26.
34 Davies, *The Life and Opinions of Robert Roberts*, p. 315.
35 Guy, *Thesis*, p. 1 (this was in 1724); C.E. Vaughan Owen, "The Vicars of Trefeglwys", *MC*, 54 (1955-6), 45; Best, *Temporal Pillars*, pp. 20-1. Richard Watson in his 1788 Charge to the Clergy of Llandaff said he would not permit any curate to officiate without a licence now that the chief obstacle attending their licensing had been removed. This related to the removal of stamp duties imposed upon the licences: *Charge*, 1788, pp. 33-4.
36 SA/RD/26 and 28, but the figures refer to the number of curacies rather than curates, some of whom may have held curacies in plurality, as did Hezekiah Jones who had a number of curacies in the vale of Glamorgan in 1788: Luxton, "Hezekiah Jones", pp. 17-18. In instance, of 1749, the bishop of St Asaph allowed a licence granted by the bishop of St Davids "to be sufficient to save the expense": SA/RD/26, Llanfyllin.
37 Mather, *High Church Prophet*, p. 196.
38 Brown, *A History of the English Clergy*, p. 16.
39 Edward Stillingfleet, *Ecclesiastical Cases relating to the Duties and Rights of the Parochial Clergy* (London, 1698), I, 160-1, and Secker, *Eight Charges*, pp. 219-22, to give but two examples. John Warren, bishop of Bangor, also pointed out that it was the duty of the bishop to judge if the stipend was sufficient for the cure he was about to enter: *The Duties of the Parochial Clergy*, p. 24. As late as 1856 Bishop Wilberforce of Oxford took an incumbent to task for not informing him about his appointment of a curate so he could ascertain his fitness: Pugh, *The Letter Books of Samuel Wilberforce, 1843-1868*, pp. 359-60.
40 Horsley, *Charges*, pp. 84-115. He rejected the case for allowing curates higher stipends than those stipulated in legislation.
41 Mather, *High Church Prophet*, pp. 172-3; O.W. Jones, "The Mountain Clergy", in Jones and Walker, *Links with the Past*, pp. 171-2.
42 Horsley, *Charges,* pp. 178-92; Yates, in Williams, *The Welsh Church*, p. 239.
43 Sunmer, *Charge* (Llandaff), 1827, pp. 24-5.
44 Jenkinson, *Charge* (St Davids), 1828, pp. 13-17, 25-6.
45 Hart, *The Curate's Lot*, p. 181.This was as a result of the 1838 Pluralities Act, though it was restricted to the case of a new incumbent who wished to dismiss his predecessor's man. The act

also required that any dispute over the stipend should be heard by the bishop and not taken to court, for it was believed that if a man had agreed to take less than the law allowed then he should be required to stand by that agreement: Rodes, *Law and Modernization*, pp. 175-6. It was thus argued in 1911 that a curate was contracted to an incumbent and this was enforceable by the bishop but could not be taken to a secular court : *Report of the Royal Commission, 1911*, IV, 86.

46 Horsley, *Charges*, pp. 186-8. Rodes notes an incumbent who told his bishop he preferred his curate to remain unlicensed as it would be easier to dismiss him if required: *Law and Modernization*, p. 61. We note later the concerns of the assistant clergy at the arbitrary power this gave to the bishops.

47 Rodes, *Law and Modernization*, p. 176. The *St Asaph Directory and Clergy List* of 1911 notes that if an incumbent wished to dispossess his curate, he needed the bishop's sanction and was required to give six month's notice, unless it was by mutual consent: *ibid.*, p. 117.

48 SD/LET/1808. Howells claimed he had advanced the curate's salary by £5 to £10, and had given him a furnished room, with a feather bed, in the parsonage house.

49 Eifion Evans, *David Rowland* (Edinburgh, 1985), pp. 325-6; Mather, *High Church Prophet*, pp. 196-7.

50 Brown, *The Letters of Edward Copleston*, pp. 81-2, 150.

51 Llandaff Diocesan Memoranda Book, volume 1.

52 Llandaff Diocesan Memoranda Book, volume 2.

53 Phillips, *Robert Roberts*, pp. 68, 84.

54 *News of the Week*, 5 August 1893, p. 7.

55 Campbell, *Charge* (Bangor), 1881, p. 27.

56 *The Letter of the Rev. R.W. Morgan ... on the Welsh Church, to Lord Palmerston* (London, 1857), pp. 16-20.

57 *Yr Haul*, 1874, p. 245.

58 SD/MISC/1198.

59 W.D. Williams, *Goronwy Owen*, pp. 21-3. In theory Owen should have been protected as being in his first or "title" parish. One John Ellis became incumbent of this parish in 1770: Pryce, *The Diocese of Bangor*, p. 35.

60 Richard Edwards, *A Letter to John Hanbury, Esq.* (Bristol, 1772). He hints that Bishop Barrington had dismissed him, having had an unfavourable and biased report from Hanbury. See also Bradney, *Monmouthshire*, I.2b, 442-3. In 1832 the curate of St Woolos, Newport, was ejected by his vicar for supporting Benjamin Hall in the election of that year: Arthur Clark, *The Story of Monmouthshire* (Monmouth, nd.), II, 170.

61 Brown, *The Letters of Edward Copleston*, pp. 12, 180-1. In those cases where a curate was dismissed because his non-resident incumbent decided to reside and dismissed his curate, Copleston endeavoured to provide them with another curacy (*ibid.*, p. 16). Copleston was defended by his archdeacon, William Crawley, in respect of another curate who claimed he had been dismissed because he endeavoured to obtain the stipend he believed was his due: *CMG*, 25 November 1848, p. 4. For an English example of the 1830s see Breary, *A Fell-Side Parson*, pp. 66-7.

62 Robert Lucas, "John Collins of Oxwich", *Gower*, 38 (1987), 55.

63 Noted by Yates, in Williams, *The Welsh Church*, pp. 252-3.

CHAPTER TWO: THE PERPETUAL CURATE

1 Rodes, *Law and Modernization*, p. 169; Best, *Temporal Pillars*, pp. 16-17. For the historical background see *Report of the Royal Commission, 1911*, V, 222-3; E.J. Newell, *A History of the Welsh Church* (London, 1895), pp. 410-12 (quoting John Ecton); D.W.V. Weston, "The Origins, Development and Demise of Perpetual Curacy", *Ecclesiastical Law Journal*, 5 (1998), 89-103. Queen Anne's Bounty, established by the Queen of that name, restored to the Church the clerical taxes of first fruits and tenths that had been reserved for the Papacy and had passed into

Crown hands during the Reformation, and was used to offer augmentations to the poorer parishes. To give one illustration of this process: Llanfabon parish in Glamorgan was an appropriation of the dean and chapter of Gloucester. This body had leased it to laymen, but when the lease ran out in the 1870s the minor tithes were returned to the parish, allowing the curate to be styled "vicar". Later, the major tithes were returned and the incumbent became "rector": Thomas Evans, *The History of Miskin Higher* (Abercynon, 1970s), p. 51.

2 Guy, "Perpetual Curacies in Eighteenth Century South Wales", 332.
3 "The Curate of Snowdon" (Dr Charles Symmons?), *Religion in Danger* (London, 1795), p. 55.
4 Phillips, *Wales*, pp. 194-6. Comparison with the *Clergy List* of 1844 indicates that the figures for the diocesan benefices included parochial curacies, but probably listed parishes in united benefices as a single rather than a multiple unit. The percentages I give are similar to those presented by Philip Jenkins in Gregory and Chamberlain, *The National Church in Local Perspective*, p. 268. In the 1710s Bishop Bull estimated the number of impropriatorships in the diocese of St Davids as 120 out of 308 parishes [38%]: Nelson, *The Life of Bishop Bull*, p. 351; Jenkins and Jones estimated these at one third of the total: *Cardiganshire County History*, III, 456; and Conybeare in the early 1850s estimated that in the diocese of Bangor one third of livings came into this category, St Asaph and Llandaff, one half, and St Davids, four sevenths: *Essays, Ecclesiastical and Social*, pp. 6-7. An estimate based on the 1851 religious census, suggests that in the registration districts of Bridgend, 14 out of 41 parishes were impropriate, 23 out of 39 in Narberth, 6 out of 10 in Tregynon: Jones and Williams, *The Religious Census of 1851*, volume 1.
5 Davies, *Religion and Society in the Nineteenth Century*, p. 52.
6 Russell, *Clerical Profession*, p. 29.
7 Howell, *Patriarchs and Parasites*, p. 204.
8 Clarke, *The Revenues of the Church in England in Wales*, pp. 48-9. He quotes the figure of £20,565 for the tithe rent charge that was received by lay impropriators in the diocese of St Asaph, or 21.2% of the whole amount.
9 Barker, *Diocese of St David's: Particulars relating to Endowments &c. of Livings* (Carmarthen, 1907), for Carmarthen, I, liv; cf. Cardigan, III, l; Brecon, IV, lv.
10 *Report of the Royal Commission, 1911*, V, 223. The figures are derived from the 1887 Tithe Commutation Returns: see Morgan, "The Diocese of St David's", Part A, p. 6.
11 Morgan, "Diocese of St Davids", Part A, p. 25. His figures for Carmarthenshire are £14,706 to lay impropriators, £6,640 to clerical, and £7,419 to the clergy. He also notes that the Corporation of Haverfordwest possessed the rectorial tithes of St Mary's Church, and that of Tewkesbury the greater part of the tithes of St. Ishmael's, Pembrokeshire.
12 Thomas Williams, *A Letter to the Lord Bishop of Llandaff*, pp. 6-7.
13 Glanmor Williams in *ibid.*, *The Welsh Church*, p. 13.
14 Saunders, *A View of the State of Religion*, p. 9. A similar sentiment is given by the anonymous author of *The Clergy-Man's Advocate: A Historical Account of the Ill-treatment of the Church and Clergy from the beginning of the Reformation to this Time* (London, 1711), pp.23, 49, 61-2.
15 Johnes, *Causes of Dissent*, p. 191. The first edition was in 1832.
16 Quoted by Sykes, *Church and State in England*, p. 207.
17 *Corbett's Legacy to Parsons*, pp. 93-6.
18 Hart, *The Curate's Lot*, p. 109. The reference must be to stipendiary curacies.
19 Guy, "Perpetual Curacies in Eighteenth Century South Wales", p. 328.
20 *The Substance of a Speech by Sir William Scott in the House of Commons upon a Motion to bring in a Bill relative to the Non-Residence of Clergy* (London, 1802), pp. 30-1.
21 Theophilus Jones, *Brecknockshire*, III. 14.
22 Griffiths, "A Visitation of the Archdeaconry of Carmarthen, 1710", I, 299, 303-4, II, 313-15, 319, 321; *Report of the Royal Commission, 1911*, V, 222, cf. Jacob, in Williams, *The Welsh Church*, p. 107, for other examples.
23 Saunders, *View of the State of Religion*, p. 15; Clement, *The S.P.C.K. and Wales*, pp. 90-1.

24 L. Dowse, *Llanishen and Lisvane* (Cardiff, 1972), pp. 31-2.
25 Prichard, *Representative Bodies*, p. 94; LL/LB/5, fol. 331 (Llandaff Diocesan Book), states that in the 1860s Lord Jersey paid £16.14s.2d., but it was thought some of this money was for arrears.
26 W.J. Probert, "Monmouthshire Parishes and the Tithe Commutation Act, 1836", *Gwent Local History*, 73 (1992), 39-40.
27 Richards, "The Diocese of Bangor during the Rise of Welsh Methodism", p. 202.
28 A. Bott and M. Dunn, *The Priory and Parish Church of St Mary, Beddgelert*, (c. 2000), pp. 94-5. In 1830 the stipend was increased to £18 though the commuted tithes were valued in 1839 at £130.
29 Thomas, *St Asaph*, III, 114; M.J. Seaborne, "Charles Butler Clough", *NLW.Jnl.*, 29 (1996), 283. The stipend of the curate of Mold is not recorded.
30 Jones and Williams, *The Religious Census of 1851*, II, 270-1. Both parishes had been augmented by Queen Anne's Bounty and he had some glebe land in the former and £7 of the tithe in the later parish.
31 E.G. Bowen, *A History of Llanbadarn Fawr* (Llanbadarn Fawr, 1979), pp. 67-8; Enoch notes that in 1742 curate and impropriator rebuilt the chancel: *Llanfihangel Genau'r Glyn*, p. 26; Morgan states that the family had the impropriatorships of only nine parishes, though he gives the same figure of £6,000 as its joint income: "The Diocese of St David's", Part A, p. 26.
32 Meyrick, *Cardigan*, p. 317. J. Baber, "'A Fair and Just Demand.' Tithe Unrest in Cardiganshire, 1796-1823", *WHR*, 16 (1992-3), 183-206 in passim, describes the difficulties of the family during the 1800s, when they endeavoured to lease their tithe estate at a time of economic hardship (at £2,000 per annum), but whose agent defaulted being unable to obtain such a sum, or even to pay the clerical stipends.
33 Quoted by Jenkins and Jones, *Cardiganshire County History*, III, 456.
34 *The Welshman*, 27 October 1843, p. 1. I suspect that the total incomes of these parishes was recorded, rather than the amounts allowed by the Chichester family.
35 J.T, Griffiths, *Origin of Tithe* (Lampeter, 1910), p. 12. His concern was that under the disestablishment bill for the Church in Wales the clerical tithes would be confiscated, but the lay impropriators would retain their tithe income and rights. Mrs Chichester later claimed compensation from the Welsh Church Commissioners for the loss of the patronage of two parishes under the Welsh Church Act of 1914, but her solicitors made clear she would return whatever she was awarded to the church authorities: SD/LET/581.
36 Davies, *Religion and Society in the Nineteenth Century*, pp. 52-3.
37 Meyrick, *Cardigan*, p. 147.
38 Griffiths, "A Visitation of the Archdeaconry of Carmarthen, 1710", I, 296; J.T. Evans, *The Church Plate of Carmarthenshire* (London, 1907), p. 80.
39 Conrad Evans, *The Story of the Parish of Llanfihangel Abercywyn* (1975), p. 38.
40 Yardley, *Menevia Sacra*, p. 334.
41 Brown, "The Nineteenth Century Parish of Llandudno", pp. 7-8; Johnes, *Causes of Dissent*, p. 192. He said elsewhere that the tithes were worth £250 but had been leased for a pittance: *Correspondence on the subject of the Church in Wales in reference to "A Letter" from A.J. Johnes to Lord John Russell* (London, 1837), pp. 16-17.
42 Davies, *The Story of the Church in Glamorgan*, pp. 71-2. Guy notes that in 1718 the curates of Aberdare and Llantwit Fardre received £6 each, and Ystradyfodwg £10, from the appropriator. They later received augmentations from Queen Anne's Bounty: "Church and Churchmen in Llantrisant Parish", p. 88.
43 Jacob, in Williams, *The Welsh Church*, pp. 107-9. This dean and chapter possessed the tithe income of twenty parishes in Monmouthshire: W.J. Probert, "Monmouthshire Parishes and the Tithe Commutation Act 1836", *Gwent Local History*, 73 (1992), 38.
44 Roger L. Brown, "A Poor Parish and a Rich College", *Severnside*, Dec. 1994. In the 1850s Christ Church raised the stipend to £65 but said this was voluntary and could be withdrawn at

any time. The value of the tithe income from these parishes was said to be £2,500 per annum: Johnes, *Causes of Dissent*, pp. 127-8.

45 Johnes, *Causes of Dissent*, p. 201. Queen Anne's Bounty made up the stipends to £120 each.
46 Morgan, "The Diocese of St David's", Part A, pp. 7-8.
47 Roger L. Brown, "St Harmon: before and after Kilvert", *T.Radns.S.*, 43 (1993), 62-3.
48 Clarke, *The Revenues of the Church of England in Wales*, p. 24. In fact the Ecclesiastical Commission had taken these over, and its policy was not to renew them when the leases fell in.
49 Howse, *Radnorshire*, p. 76; Jonathan Williams, *Radnor*, pp. 194-5.
50 Morgan, "The Diocese of St David's", Part A, p. 8. He offers further examples.
51 Theophilus Jones, *Brecknockshire*, II, 224. He suggests there was some fraudulent dealings in the past. Morgan suggests that in the 1820s the lease of St Twynnell from the chapter of St Davids to the Owen family of Orielton had commenced in 1554, and that of St Dogwells to the Edwards family of Sealyham dated from 1580. The result was that these lessees believed that had a prescriptive right to their renewal: "The Diocese of St Davids", Part A, pp. 9-10. See also Jonathan Williams, *Radnor*, p. 228.
52 Thomas, *Ystradowen*, pp. 8-9. Many of these leases are in the Church in Wales records at the NLW, for example, LL/MISC/DEEDS/100, is a lease from the archdeacon of Llandaff to Griffith Lloyd of the parish of Biston, including its glebe and tithes, for 21 years, with a fine of £100 and an annual rent of £4, with £6 per annum to be paid to the curate.
53 Roger L. Brown, "Christ Church, Oxford, and the Lease of the Welshpool Tithes", *Sayce Papers*, 10 (2004), 1-29.
54 E. Rowley Morris, "History of the Parish of Kerry", *MC*, 26 (1892), 268-9.
55 Brown, *John Griffith*, pp. 27, 74-5, 78-80, 82-3. The Chapter declined to give a grant for the cost of a much needed new church in the parish, as it had spent large sums on the cathedral.
56 Lambeth Palace Library, Benson MS. 137, fols. 177-216.
57 Griffiths, *Deanery of Penllyn and Edeirnion*, pp. 45-7.
58 Johnes, *Causes of Dissent*, pp. 125, 200. The vicar of Guilsfield's share of the tithes of this parish, mainly held by Christ Church, Oxford, was one fortieth part of the product over 16,000 acres, and amounted to £380: Brown, "Some Montgomeryshire Parishes", p. 99.
59 Meyrick, *Cardigan*, pp. 197, 201.
60 Lewis Lloyd, *A Real Little Seaport* (Caernarfon, 1996), II. 256.
61 Yardley, *Menevia Sacra*, p. 334.
62 Quoted by Christopher Armstrong in J.M. Wooding (ed.), *Studies in the Religious History of Bardsey Island* (Trivium, vol. 39, 2010), p. 51.
63 Morgan, "Diocese of St David's", Part A, p. 24.
64 J.G. Jones, "Richard Parry", p. 178.
65 Griffiths, "A Visitation of the Archdeaconry of Carmarthen, 1710", I, 293, 298, 306-7.
66 Edwards, *Landmarks in the History of the Welsh Church*, p. 171.
67 E.T. Lewis, *Local Heritage from Efailwen to Whitland* (Carmarthen, 1975), I, 158.
68 Brown, *Parochial Lives*, pp. 189-92; R. Buckman, *The Photographic Work of Calvert Richard Jones* (London, 1990), pp. 16-17. Counsel's opinion of 1874 argued that the lay rector had a right to a principal seat for himself and his family in the chancel of the church, but no right of objection to the placing of choir seats in that chancel: Church in Wales records, SA/MISC/94. A faculty for the rebuilding of the church in 1895 reserved the lay rector's right to his own pews and porch in the north aisle.
69 K.E. Kissack, "Lay Influence on Religious Life in Monmouth since the Reformation", *JHSCW*, 19 (1969), 72-5. John Evans in his visitation charge to the clergy of the Archdeaconry of Carmarthen, of 1864 mentioned this, suggesting there were similar problems in that area: *Charge*, pp. 9-10.
70 Best, *Temporal Pillars*, pp. 52-3.
71 Jacob, in Williams, *The Welsh Church*, p. 109. He notes an ulterior motive, as a satisfactory curate would prevent dissatisfaction amongst the tithe payers.

72 Howell, *Patriarchs and Parasites*, p. 205. He also insisted that George Thomas, the curate of Llandawc (and also of Llanddrowor) should serve that parish "carefully": Griffiths, "A Visitation of the Archdeaconry of Carmarthen, 1710", I, 305.

73 Lloyd, *The Gentry of South-West Wales*, p. 185.

74 Meyrick, *Cardigan*, pp. 233-4. Its value as a result increased to £500. This also occurred at Bonvilston, Glamorgan, in 1764, when the vicarial tithes were given as a benefaction towards an augmentation by Queen Anne's Bounty: Orrin, *Medieval Churches of the Vale of Glamorgan*, p. 109.

75 Griffiths, *Deanery of Penllyn and Edeirnion*, pp. 13-14; Thomas, *St Asaph*, III, 114; E.D. Evans, "A Llanuwchllyn Ecclesiastical Dispute", *J.Mer.HS.*, 11 (1993), 427-8. These accounts do not entirely agree.

76 Hart, *William Lloyd*, pp. 57-9. An earlier example from the 1620s relates to Bishop Bayley of Bangor and his difficulties regarding the parish of Beddgelert is noted in *The Calendar of the Wynn (of Gwydir) Papers*, nos. 991 and 1094, and by A.H. Dodd, "Bishop Lewes Bayly", *T.Caerns.HS.*, 28 (1967), 33.

77 *The Works of William Laud* (1853, repr. New York, 1977), V, 328-9, and see Christopher Hill, *Economic Problems of the Church* (Oxford, 1956), pp. 317-20.

78 Nelson, *Life of Bishop Bull*, pp. 367-70. Spelman's book, *The History and Fate of Sacrilege*, was written in 1632 and gave illustrations of God's revenge against those who committed sacrilege. Bull may have mentioned the year 1660 as it was in that year that Charles II instructed his bishops not to lease the impropriate rectories they held *in commendam* until they ensured that a stipend of at least £80 was given to their curates: Snape, *The Church of England in Industrialising Society*, p. 137.

79 Henry Thomas, "Some Pennal Documents", *J.Mer.HS.*, 6 (1972), 415-6.

80 Watson, *Miscellaneous Tracts*, I, 229-30 (his 1809 Charge); Watson, *Anecdotes of the Life of Richard Watson*, I, 363; Richard. A writer of 1832 said much the same: A Clergyman, *On Clerical Education: A Letter*, letter III, pp. 9-10.

81 Quoted by Lloyd, *Gentry of South-West Wales*, p. 184.

82 Quoted Jenkins and Jones, *Cardiganshire County History*, III, 456.

83 A Pauper Clergyman, *How to Make Better Provision for the Cure of Souls*, pp. 29-30. From its context, including an attack on Bishop Short, this may well be a work of R.W. Morgan.

84 Saunders, *View of the State of Religion*, pp. 7-9, 83-5; cf. R.W. Morgan, *Maynooth and St Asaph* (London, 1845), p. 41, who wrote that the Welsh curate was unable to offer any relief in kind to the sick and poor, save for words, as the tithes of his parish, meant to provide such relief, were spent in England.

85 Jonathan Williams, *Radnor*, p. 195.

86 R.W. Morgan, *Notes on Various Distinctive Verities of the Christian Church* (London, 1849), p. 287. Cf. Best, *Temporal Pillars*, pp. 233-6, for the 19th century concern that the government should compel impropriators to increase these stipends. Those who leased tithes from an ecclesiastical body were probably exempt from this requirement.

87 *Welshman*, 13 October 1843, p. 1.

88 "The Church and Education in Wales", *Edinburgh Review*, lxxvii (1850), 350, 365.

89 Williams, *Glamorgan County History*, IV, 227-8.

90 Edwards, *Landmarks in the History of the Welsh Church*, p. 171; Saunders, *View of the State of Religion*, p. 26.

91 Jones and Williams, *The Religious Census of 1851*, I, 464.

92 A cutting, "Yr Hen Eglwys", signed by "M.N.O.", from a Montgomeryshire paper, contained in Robert Owen's scrapbook at the Powysland Club Library, Welshpool.

93 Saunders, *View of the State of Religion*, pp. 24-5. Often, he continued, the pastor would meet his congregation in the local hostelry when his duty had been completed. A similar picture of the curate's travels is presented by Evan Evans in his unpublished manuscript, *The Grievances of*

the Principality of Wales, pp. 5 and 31 in a transcript provided by Gerald Morgan and used by kind permission. These groupings often became historic and later merged into united benefices.

94   Quoted Jenkins and Jones, *Cardiganshire County History*, III, 456. The parishioners of Pendine complained in 1710 that their curate George Thomas sometimes left them without Sunday prayers as he had so many cures to attend to and lived in another parish: Griffith, "A Visitation of the Archdeaconry of Carmarthen, 1710", I, 306.

95   *Hansard's Parliamentary Debates*, XVI, 3rd series, 1833, pp. 105-6.

96   Burgess, *Charge* (St Davids), 1813, pp. 16n (quoting Burnet), 18.

97   Nelson, *The Life of Bishop Bull*, p. 368; Howell, *Patriarchs and Parasites*, p. 204.

98   Evan Evans (transcript by Gerald Morgan), *The Grievances of the Principality*, p. 33

99   D.W.V. Weston, "The Origins, Development and Demise of Perpetual Curacy", *Ecclesiastical Law Journal*, 5 (1998), pp. 97-9; Best, *Temporal Pillars*, p. 90; Savidge, *Queen Anne's Bounty*, pp. 61-2; Anthea Jones, *A Thousand Years of the English Parish*, pp. 156-9; Hodgson, *Queen Anne's Bounty*, p. 40. Many complaints were made that these augmentations increased the value of these curacies at no expense to the impropriators, and discouraged them from augmenting the curacies themselves: Virgin, *The Church in an Age of Negligence*, p. 69; Best, *Temporal Pillars*, pp. 234, 236.

100 Richard Smallbrooke, *Primary Charge* (St Davids), 1725, p. 38.

101 J.R. Guy, "Perpetual Curacies in Eighteenth Century South Wales", pp. 328-9, 333. In his Thesis Guy notes from the records of Queen Anne's Bounty that many of these perpetual curacies needed several augmentations to give their curates a living stipend. Llantwit Fardre, for example, received five between 1727-93, with a total capital sum of £1,000: *Thesis*, pp. 674-5.

102 Brown, "The Nineteenth Century Parish of Llandudno", pp. 10-12.

103 Best, *Temporal Pillars*, p.232. A proposal to restore to their parishes the great tithes belonging to the episcopal and capitular bodies was made in 1791, and seems to have some support from Bishop Horsley: Mather, *High Church Prophet*, pp. 141-2.

104 Christopher Hill, *Economic Problems of the Church* (Oxford, 1956), p. 251.

105 Clement, *The S.P.C.K. and Wales*, pp. 90-1.

106 Wade, *The Black Book*, pp. 57, 91.

107 *Corbett's Legacy to Parsons*, p. 29.

108 Best, *Temporal Pillars*, pp. 233-6.

109 John Owen, *Welsh Disestablishment and Political Tactics* (Carmarthen, 1911), p. 7. He noted that half of the parochial endowments of the Welsh parishes, £110,737, came from tithe. See also Griffiths, *Origin of Tithe* (Lampeter, 1910), pp. 11-13, noted earlier, for the unfairness of this Act.

CHAPTER THREE: THE STIPENDIARY CURATE: THE ISSUE OF NON-RESIDENCE

1   See Knight, *The Nineteenth-Century Church*, pp. 116-18 and Johnes, *A Letter to Lord John Russell*, pp. 10-11.

2   Rodes, *Law and Modernization*, pp. 203-4. For a general survey see Virgin, *The Church in an Age of Negligence*, pp. 192-5. Jacob notes an understanding held by many parishioners that in return for the payment of their tithes, clergy were obliged to reside in their parishes: *Clerical Profession*, p. 101.

3   Rodes, *Law and Modernization*, pp. 199-200. The difficulties of proceeding against non-residents made the bishops reluctant to take legal action: Brown, *A History of the English Clergy*, pp. 21-2. In 1850 Benjamin Hall stated that throughout the Established Church there were 937 non-resident clergy who remained unlicensed, and demanded that the bishops be sent down to their dioceses in order to compel residence: Maxwell Fraser, "Sir Benjamin Hall in Parliament", part 1, *NLW.Jnl.*, 15 (1967), 74-5.

4   Copleston, *Charge* (Llandaff), 1833, p. 18; Jacob, *Clerical Profession*, pp. 104-5.

5 Wade, *Black Book*, p. 37. For details from English dioceses see Gregory and Chamberlain, *The National Church in Local Perspective*, p. 193 and Jacob, *Clerical Profession*, pp. 102-3.

6 Sumner, *Charge* (Llandaff), 1827, p. 21. Of 23 licences for non-residence granted by Bishop Majendie of Bangor, 1812-14, 20 were because of the lack or unfitness of a parsonage house: Yates, in Williams, *The Welsh Church*, pp. 257-8. Morgan states of the diocese of St Davids in the early 19th century that 221 livings had no parsonage house and 78 had ones that were unfit: "The Diocese of St David's", Part B, p. 18.

7 F.G. Cowley, *Llanmadoc and Cheriton*, p. 15.

8 As stated by Bishop Phillpotts of Exeter: G.C.B. Davies, *Henry Phillpotts*, p. 148.

9 Griffiths, "A Visitation of the Archdeaconry of Carmarthen, 1710", notes many such instances, I, 300, 303, 306; II, 311-12. Yates notes that of the 142 parishes where a non-resident was incumbent in the diocese of Salisbury, 119 were served by clergy who lived within five miles of the church: Yates, *Eighteenth-Century Britain*, p. 137, but cf. Mary Ransome (ed.), *Wiltshire Returns to the Bishop's Visitation Queries, 1783* (Wiltshire Record Society, XXVII, 1971), p. 9.

10 Sumner, *Charge* (Llandaff), 1827, p. 22. Jacob writes of natural groupings of parishes: *Clerical Profession*, p. 105, and note p. 101 regarding the poverty of livings.

11 Yates, *Eighteenth-Century Britain*, pp. 146, 137; Griffiths, "A Visitation of the Archdeaconry of Carmarthen, 1710", I, 296-7, 303.

12 Evan Evans, *The Claims of the Church of North Wales to the Enjoyment of its own Revenues* (Chester, 1843), pp. 10-11; Yates, in Williams, *The Welsh Church*, p. 256. Johnes alleged that Anglesey had 75 parishes and chapelries, but 62 were held by non-resident incumbents and 55 had no resident minister; of the 40 incumbents 22 were non-resident and 19 parishes were served by six ministers. He later accepted that many benefices had four or six parishes within them: Johnes, *Causes of Dissent*, p. 184. It was said that at a meeting called by the bishop of Bangor in 1869 a speaker alleged that Anglesey had 79 parishes held by 40 incumbents, two of them had two parishes each, and three of them held three parishes, but in probability most of these were small parishes adjacent to one another, and were unable to support a resident incumbent. Fifty-two of these parishes had no parsonage house: Thomas, *The Church in Wales, Past and Present: Facts and Suggestions*, p. 22n.

13 Bethell, *Charge* (Bangor), 1834, p. 29.

14 Clement, *The S.P.C.K. and Wales*, p. 52.

15 Robert Lucas, *A Gower Family* (Lewes, 1986), pp. 16-17. Evan Lloyd, absentee rector of Llanfair Dyffryn Clwyd, threatened by Squire Price of Rhiwlas with prosecution for non-residence, wrote asking John Wilkes to arrange a chaplaincy to a nobleman for him, thus giving him a valid exemption: E. Alfred Jones, "Two Welsh Correspondents of John Wilkes", *Y Cymmrodor*, 29 (1919), 124.

16 *Lord Eldon's Anecdote Book* (ed. A.L.J. Lincoln and R. McEwen, London, n.d.), p. 68; McClatchey, *Oxfordshire Clergy*, pp. 31-2; Varley, *The Last of the Prince Bishops*, pp. 34-5; *Corbett's Legacy for Parsons*, pp. 83-6; Mather, *High Church Prophet*, pp. 153-5 (he argued that the St Davids consistory court had heard an action for absenteeism, but it had floundered because of its inefficiency and as the ecclesiastical judge was himself a non-resident cleric). See also, A Magistrate, *Thoughts on Non-Residence and Farming in a Letter to the Bishop of St Asaph* (London, 1803).

17 Wade, *Black Book*, pp. 33-40; *Corbett's Legacy to Parsons*, pp. 86-7 (he claimed that 700-800 informations had been squashed by that "infamous Act"); *Hansard*, 16 (1833), 111-12.

18 Wade, *Black Book*, p. 37.

19 *The Life of Reginald Heber*, II, 85-6. He noted of 10,421 benefices that 4,809 had no parsonage house or one unfit for use.

20 Brown, *Through Cloud and Sunshine*, pp. 91-2. His brother succeeded him in both, 1862-91.

21 Saunders, *View of the State of Religion*, pp. 51-2, 58.

22 A dispensation from the archbishop was required to hold livings in plurality: Rodes, *Law and Modernization*, p. 197.

23 Higham, *David Jones, Llan-gan*, pp. 37-8. An inability to speak the language of the parish was also responsible for non-residence: Lewis Beddo, minister of Llanglydwen, was one, though he also held the English-speaking parish of Carew: Griffiths, "A Visitation of the Archdeaconry of Carmarthen, 1710", I, 302.

24 Guy, "Bishop Barrington's Book", 115-16; cf. Davies, *The Church in Glamorgan*, p. 72.

25 Brown, *David Howell*, pp. 43-4.

26 M. Richards, *A History of Newtown* (Welshpool, 1993), p. 65.

27 Ellis, *The History of Halkyn Mountain*, p. 157. These are probably examples of clergymen who preferred to live in the cultural climate of a small town rather than in rural back waters: Yates, in Williams, *The Welsh Church*, p. 257. See also Guy, *Thesis*, pp. 753-62, and McClatchey, *Oxfordshire Clergy*, pp. 35-6.

28 Brown, "Some Montgomeryshire Parishes", p. 113.

29 R.L. Brown, *The Fleet Marriages* (Welshpool, 2007), pp. 190-3.

30 Denning, *The Diary of William Thomas*, p. 242.

31 E.D. Jones, "Ecclesiastical Visitation Returns of the Deaneries of Elvell and Melineth", *T.Radns.S.*, 8 (1938), 59-76.

32 Guy, *The Diocese of Llandaff in 1763*, pp. 181-4.

33 SA/RD/28; Humphreys, *The Crisis of Community*, p. 43. Unfortunately many details are missing from the 1791 returns, 36 out of 128 parishes have incomplete entries regarding residence, and of the remainder 20 incumbents were non-resident and another 8 were technically non-resident but did the duty of their parishes. In 1749 there were 21 non-resident clergy and 11 technically non-resident in the returns of 121 parishes: SA/RD/26. Figures for 1807 are given by Yates, in Williams, *The Welsh Church*, pp. 239-40.

34 Howse, *Radnorshire*, p. 72.

35 Morgan, "The Diocese of St David's", Part B, p. 17. In 1809, 308 benefices out of 424 lacked a resident incumbent (28%), but probably many of the non-residents were still undertaking the duty of their parishes: Mather, *High Church Prophet*, pp. 168-9.

36 Yates in Williams, *The Welsh Church*, p. 257.

37 Johnes, *Causes of Dissent*, p. 117.

38 Conybeare, *Essays Ecclesiastical and Social*, p. 9n. A similar complaint about this county was made in 1873, but some of the non-residence was probably technical rather than actual: *WM*, 2 June 1873, p. 4.

39 Jones and Williams, *The Religious Census of 1851*, I, xxxi.

40 PP 1812, X (257), 157.

41 PP 1833, XXVII (329-33), 35: on Clergy Residence, p. 2. Of 408 curates throughout the Principality, St Davids diocese had over half; 68 resided in the parsonage house and 113 in the parish, thus indicating much non-residence and probable pluralism amongst curates as well as incumbents.

42 Brown, *A History of the English Clergy*, pp. 15, 36-8; cf. Sykes, *Church and State in England*, p. 217.

43 Trevor Parkin, *The Consistory Court of St Asaph* (n.d.), p. 4.

44 K.E. Kissack, "Lay Influences on Religious Life in Monmouth since the Reformation", *JHSCW*, 19 (1969), 70-1.

45 Brown, "George Martin Maber, pp. 63-70.

46 John Price, *Llandudno* (London, 1875?), pp. 69-70.

47 Brown, "The Captain's Brother: Thomas Gronow, pp. 44-9. He eventually resigned in 1834.

48 Brown, "The Parish of Gelligaer", pp. 23-4. Llandaff Diocesan Memorandum Book (I) for 8 January 1850 states he had "a strong medical certificate", indicating some disbelief.

49 Mather, *High Church Prophet*, pp. 194-5. Wade's *Black Book*, pp. 34-5, gives numerous examples of abuse regarding claims of ill-health.

50 G.L. Fairs, "Annals of a Parish", *JHSCW*, 23 (1973), 78-9.

51 Llandaff Diocesan Memorandum Book, I, for May 1861.

52 Jacob, *Clerical Profession*, p. 70.
53 Denning, *The Diary of William Thomas*, p. 254.
54 *MC*, 13 (1880), 68.
55 Jones, *Richard and Mary Pendrill Llewelyn*, pp. 23-4.
56 James Kenward, *Ab Ithel* (Tenby, 1871), p. 78.
57 *The Curate's Appeal Examined* (of 1820), pp. 186-7. The poor incumbent might even find himself in the parish workhouse.
58 Brown, *Llandaff Figures and Places*, p. 23. Bishop Ollivant eventually persuaded the cathedral chapter to provide a substitute for him from their own funds.
59 B/LET/3079-80.
60 SA/MISC B/ 79.
61 Brown, *Through Cloud and Sunshine*, pp. 80-1.
62 Brown, "The Cilybebyll Commission".
63 Fairlamb, *The Clergy of the Beaumaris Parishes*, pp. 9-11; *Guardian*, 9 March 1881, p. 348.
64 Brown, "Sad, Mad or Bad: the Case of Evan Jenkins, Rector of Manafon", p. 183.
65 Brown, *Llandaff Figures and Places*, pp. 47-51.
66 Rodes, *Law and Modernization*, pp. 176-7.
67 Saunders, *A View of the State of Religion*, p. 59. Non residency, he wrote, required the necessity of ordaining those who might be worse qualified in their place.
68 Marsh, *Charge* (Llandaff), 1817, pp. 7-8. The 1813 Act required that a non-resident should keep the parsonage house in proper repair to the satisfaction of the bishop, and if not, to be liable to the penalties of non-residence, notwithstanding any exemption to the contrary.
69 Jacob, *Clerical Profession*, pp. 100-101, quoting Gibson's 1724 *Directions to the Clergy of the Diocese of London*.
70 Johnes, *Causes of Dissent*, p. 68; cf. Mather, *High Church Prophet*, p. 149.
71 The Curate of Snowdon, *Religion in Danger* (London, 1795), pp. 52-3, notes some of these issues. Copleston suggested that non-residents should compensate for their absence not only in providing the Sunday duty, but also in the provision of schools, assisting the sick, and making the church building decent and warm: *Charge (Llandaff)*, 1830, pp. 26-7.
72 Secker, *Eight Charges*, p. 209.
73 SA/MISC/120. The hand is of the 18th century.
74 *MC*, 4 (1871), 123.
75 Brown, *The Clergy and People of Welshpool*, pp. 20-1.
76 A Dissenter, *The Consistency of Dissent* (Wrexham, 1841), p. 10.
77 Secker, *Eight Charges*, pp. 207-8.
78 William Gibson, *The Church of England, 1688-1832* (London, 2001), p. 126; noted by Jacob, *Clerical Profession*, in the diocese of York, p. 108.
79 A Magistrate, *Thoughts on Non-Residence and Farming in a Letter to the Bishop of St Asaph* (London, 1803). pp. 6-8; Bishop Marsh believed that the inconvenience of the church service times in these pluralities would mean that parishioners would "desert the Church for some other place of worship, in which their convenience is better consulted": Marsh, *Charge (Llandaff)*, 1817, p. 23.
80 Brown, *The Letters of Edward Copleston*, pp. 29-31.
81 Thomas Arnold, *Principles of Church Reform* (4th ed., London, 1832), pp. 72-3.
82 K. Fincham (ed.), *Visitation Articles and Injunctions of the Early Stuart Church, I* (CERS, I, Woodbridge, 1994), p. 94.
83 Sykes, *Church and State in England*, pp. 206-7; Jacob, *Clerical Profession*, pp. 64-5.
84 Quoted by Best, *Temporal Pillars*, pp. 207-8.
85 John Lloyd, *Thesaurus Ecclesiasticus* (London, 1788), p. 384.
86 Watson, *Charge* (Llandaff), 1798, pp. 32-3.
87 Horsley's 1806 Charge to the diocese of St Asaph, in Horsley, *Charges*, p. 185. For Horsley's concern about non-residence see Mather, *High Church Prophet*, pp. 149-55. See also Jacob,

Clerical Profession, p. 110, and Rodes, *Law and Modernization*, p. 200. The act also required the bishop to submit annual returns regarding non-residency to the Privy Council, together with the income of the parish, and to satisfy themselves that the duty was adequately performed in such parishes. See also *The Substance of a Speech by Sir William Scott in the House of Commons upon a Motion for Leave to bring in a Bill relative to the Non-Residence of the Clergy* (London, 1802).

88 Best, *Temporal Pillars*, p. 222; Hart, *The Curate's Lot*, pp. 127-8. £8,000 was set aside for this purpose.

89 Yates, *Eighteenth-Century Britain*, p. 172; Mather notes Horsley's "grudging support" of this bill: *High Church Prophet*, p. 156. Pitt's plan to augment livings and thus make better provision for curates as well as to establish a system of episcopal jurisdiction over residence failed for the same reason: G.M. Ditchfield, in J.P. Parry and Stephen Taylor, *Parliament and the Church 1529-1960* (Edinburgh, 2000), p. 71.

90 Majendie, *Charge* (Bangor), 1814, pp. 13-14, notes the 1813 legislation. Herbert Marsh, *Charge* (Llandaff), 1817, where pp. 1-30 are devoted to an analysis of this act, the quotation is on pp. 20-1; Marsh noted that under the Act a bishop could also require the appointment of a curate if the duty was not adequately performed, due to the number of its churches, the distances between them and between the church and the residence of the curate. He endeavoured to alleviate the clergy from their fear of the arbitrary powers given to the bishop under this act, but made it clear that he would enforce the performance of double duty where it was possible, for in many churches it had been dropped to enable the church to be served at a lower price. This act also allowed any house in the parish to be a legal residence when there was no parsonage house, revised the rules of non-residence but applied them more strictly, and required incumbents who did not reside in the parsonage house to keep it in repair.

91 Burgess, *Charge* (St Davids), 1813, pp. 15-19.

92 Burgess, *Charge* (St Davids), 1813, p. 18; Copleston, *Charge* (Llandaff), 1836, pp. 9-10.

93 Quoted, Jacob, *Clerical Profession*, p. 110.

94 Jacob, *Clerical Profession*, pp. 68-9; Knight, *The Nineteenth-Century Church*, pp. 119-22; C. Hodgson, *Instructions for the Use of the Clergy*, pp. 20-2, 75-97; Rodes, *Law and Modernization*, pp. 175-6, 196-7, 200. See Virgin for a discussion regarding the effect of this act: *The Church in an Age of Negligence*, pp. 231-41. The preliminary bills were noted by Bethell (with many reservations), *Charge* (Bangor), 1834, pp. 12-16, and William Bruce Knight, *Charge to the Archdeaconry of Llandaff*, 1833, pp. 43-4. The act allowed the bishop, after a commission of enquiry, to impose a curate on a resident incumbent if there was evidence of the duty not being performed, but he could not assign more than half of the total income of the benefice for his stipend, which rather defeated the object. It allowed a new incumbent to give six months notice to his predecessor's curate, but in other cases the bishop's permission was required. The curate's licence had to specify the stipend, and both parties had to agree to give or receive it. If the population of a parish was over 2,000 the bishop could assign two curates, but the stipends, taken together, were not to exceed the higher rate allowed for one. In some cases the incumbent was left with very little for himself. If the stipend was equal to the value of the living then that curate would be responsible for all its outgoings rather than the incumbent. A further Pluralities Act of 1885 reinforced these requirements, allowing the bishop to issue a commission to investigate the pastoral care of a parish in the case of complaints, put in a curate if required, and forbade the incumbent to return to his parish, if sequestrated, without the bishop's permission: "New Pluralities Act", *Church Quarterly Review*, 21 (1885-6), 148-66.

95 Guy, *Thesis*, pp. 658-60.

96 Edward Carpenter, *Thomas Sherlock, 1678-1766* (London, 1936), pp. 129-30.

97 Warren, *The Duties of the Parochial Clergymen*, pp. 14-17.

98 Randolph, *Charge* (Bangor), 1808, pp. 29-30; see also Jenkinson, *Charge* (St Davids), 1828, pp. 18-19.

99   Brown, *The Letters of Edward Copleston*, pp. 15-16, 152, 175-6; and see Brown, "The Parish of Gelligaer", p. 25.
100 Copleston, *Charge* (Llandaff), 1830, pp. 21-4. Bishop Phillpotts of Exeter advised those who could not reside to resign their benefices: Davies, *Henry Phillpotts,* p. 124.
101 Llandaff Diocesan Memoranda Book, volume 1.
102 Brown, *Ten Clerical Lives*, pp. 31-6.
103 Knight, *The Nineteenth-Century Church*, p. 121. She notes a return for Lincolnshire of 1853 that whereas 3% of incumbents instituted after the 1838 act became operative were non-resident, 25% of those instituted before came into this category.
104 Bradney, *Monmouthshire*, I-2b, 392; Llandaff Diocesan Memorandum Book, II, for 31 December 1879.
105 Russell, *The Country Parish*, p. 221, but *cf.* Gilbert, who, quoting parliamentary reports, states that in 1810 46.9% of incumbents were non-resident and not taking duty, in 1835 it was 31.5%, 1841, 24.4%, 1846, 19.2%, and in 1850, 15.5%.: *Religion and Society in Industrial England*, pp. 131-2.
106 Copleston, *Edward Copleston*, pp. 233-5. Ollivant stated that in 1838 there were 23 assistant clergy in the diocese, but by 1848 the number had risen to 45, while in that year the number of resident incumbents was 124 along with 19 resident stipendiary curates: Ollivant, *Charge (Llandaff),* 1851, pp. 15, 18.
107 Cragoe, *Anglican Aristocracy*, p. 214.
108 Jones and Williams, *The Religious Census of 1851*, I, xxxi. In the registration districts of Bridgend there were 6 non-resident incumbents for 41 parishes, 4 out of 39 in Narberth, and 3 out of 10 for Tregynon, while in north Wales, in the Bangor district, 2 out of 12, 1 out of 9 in Montgomery, none in the Holywell district where there were 16 parishes and 7 assistant clergy: Jones and Williams, *The Religious Census of 1851*, volume II.
109 PP 1843, xl (189) 113, a return of benefices in the dioceses of St Asaph and Bangor.
110 Halcombe, *The Church and her Curates*, p. 148.
111 Knight, *The Nineteenth-Century Church*, pp. 126-7.
112 Knight, *The Nineteenth-Century Church*, pp. 34-5.
113 *Chronicles of Convocation: Upper House*, 14 May 1878, pp. 168-9.
114 Thomas Williams, *Charge to the Archdeaconry of Llandaff*, 1852, pp. 10-11.

CHAPTER FOUR: THE STIPENDIARY CURATE: THE CURATE OBSERVED

1 Quoted by Howse, *Radnorshire*, p. 75.
2 Copleston, *Edward Copleston*, pp. 174-6.
3 *Report of the Association of Welsh Clergy*, 1852, p. 23. Thomas Stacey of Gelligaer placed the nomination of his curates to that parish in the hands of his patron, Lord Bute: National Library of Wales, L80/13, 46, 78.
4 Brown, *Letters of Edward Copleston*, p. 16, 153, 188, 193 and 228. He insisted on the new incumbent of Llanmihangel and Flemingston, the non-resident Biedeman, who wanted to reduce his curate's stipend, continuing his employment on the same terms as his predecessor. Copleston felt unable to place Lister at Cadoxton for "how can we expect to bring a man of superior qualifications there, on a small salary – no house – a turbulent people – and the dissenting interest predominant": *ibid.*, p. 157. See also Brown, "The Captain's Brother: Thomas Gronow", pp. 50-4.
5 SD/LET/1264, Henry Payne to Bishop Burgess, 20 Nov. 1822.
6 *Report of the Church Congress, Leeds*, 1872, p. 466.
7 D. Simon Evans, *O Fancy Spite* (Llanbedr Pont Steffan, 1996), p. 234.
8 *The Curates' Appeal Examined*, p. 187. This was part of the plot in George Eliot's *Amos Barton*.
9 Luxton, "Hezekiah Jones, pp. 18-19. At the same time he held the curacies of Bedwas and Rudry, but probably had a local curate to serve them for him. Jacob notes that the Welshman and

diarist, William Jones, stipendiary curate of Broxbourne, Hertfordshire, 1781-1801, was in continuous fear of losing his curacy when his incumbents died, but he actually succeeded to the living in 1801: *Clerical Profession*, p. 71.

10   B/LET/905: Roderick Lewis to John Roberts of Bangor, 16 October 1812.
11   Brown, "A Cardiganshire Incumbent", p. 23. Evan Evans in 1767 wrote about an attempt by parishioners to deprive an elderly curate after sixty years service, "which persons of common humanity would hardly do to an old horse that had in his time been of service to them".: D.S. Evans, *Gwaith y Parchedig Evan Evans* (Caernarfon, 1876), pp. 213.
12   Brown, *Letters of Edward Copleston*, pp. 16, 189.
13   *The Curates' Appeal Examined*, p. 187, cf. S. Brewer (ed.), *The Early Letters of Bishop Richard Hurd, 1739-1762* (Church of England Record Society 3, Woodbridge, 1995), p. 125. Curates did not have to pay the land tax or the poor rate based on the tithe of the parish. The writer of *The Curates Appeal Examined* argued that recent legislation had shown a bias towards the curates' position.
14   Brown, *Letters of Edward Copleston*, p. 107.
15   Brown, "George Martin Maber", p. 64.
16   The 1784 Charge is contained in Watson, *Miscellaneous Tracts*, I, 312-5.
17   Evan Jones wrote that he was placed in sole change of the parish of Radyr after his ordination in 1883: *Atgofion am Ddeugain Mlynedd o'm Gweinidogaeth*, pp. 15-16. Heeney notes Archdeacon John Sandford's 1863 comment that on the Sunday he was ordained he was placed in sole charge of a parish of 7000 – 8000 souls: *A Different Kind of Gentleman*, pp. 107-8,
18   Jenkinson, *Charge* (St Davids), 1828, pp. 31-41.
19   Virgin, *The Church in an Age of Negligence*, p. 223. He notes there were 3,826 livings, one third of the total throughout the Church of England, worth less than £50, indicating the impossibility of reaching this standard in many parishes. The legislation was flawed. Some incumbents required their curates to accept half the stipulated stipend, especially if there were a number of candidates for the post, as Sydney Smith alleged: quoted by Best, *Temporal Pillars*, pp. 207-8.
20   Hart, *The Curates' Lot*, p. 114.
21   Griffiths, *A Visitation of the Archdeaconry of Carmarthen, 1710*, I, 302. In 1684 in the diocese of Worcester out of 25 such curates 3 were under £10 per annum, 9 between £10 and £20, 11 between £20 and £30, and only two £30 to £40: Paul Morgan (ed.), *Inspection of Churches and Parsonage Houses in the Diocese of Worcester* (Worcestershire Historical Society, NS 12, 1986), p. 14.
22   Helen Ramage, *Portrait of an Island* (Llangefni, 1987), pp. 304-5.
23   G.E. Evans, "Llanarth cum Llanina", *Old Wales*, 2 (1906), 100.
24   SD/MISC/687.
25   Guy, *The Diocese of Llandaff in 1763*, p. 186, and his "Bishop Barrington's Book", p. 120. Sykes suggests that in the 1800s Llandaff curates had an average stipend of at least £25 to £30: *Church and State in England*, p. 209.
26   Howse, *Radnorshire*, p. 74.
27   Cowley, *Llanmadoc and Cheriton*, p. 14.
28   Quoted Guy, *Thesis*, p. 779. Possibly he had other curacies, for John Powell's six curacies in 1798 brought him £44 and Ezra Powell's four £40: *ibid.*, p. 778.
29   Secker, *Eight Charges*, p. 231. Some, he suggested, tried to obtain a man for the smallest price rather than choose the worthiest person.
30   Virgin, *The Church in an Age of Negligence*, p. 224. Thus in 1749 in the deanery of Penllyn and Edeirnion there were three curacies at £20 each, but in 1791 two at £30, one at £3 and two others at £12 and £20; in the deanery of Rhos in 1749 curacies were between £15 and £24, averaging around £20, by 1791 they ranged between £20 and £25, averaging about £23; while in the deanery of Marcia, on the borders, the average in 1749 was £20, and in 1791 there were three curacies at £25, £40 and £62 respectively: information compiled from SA/RD/26 and 28.
31   Mrs Bulkeley Owen, *History of Selattyn Parish* (Oswestry, n.d.), pp. 423-4.

32 Ellis, *The History of Halkyn Mountain*, p. 157; Humphreys, *The Crisis of Community*, p. 44.
33 William Combe, *Dr Syntax's Three Tours: in Search of the Picturesque* (London, 1842), pp. 3, 5-6, 20. Gregory and Chamberlain suggest in the diocese of Norwich in 1806 most of the curates had stipends of between £31 and £40 per annum: *The National Church in Local Perspective*, p. 193. See also Hart, *The Curates' Lot*, p. 127. Knight estimates that in Lincolnshire during 1832, 62% of the stipendiary curates received under £80, though in 1835 only 13% of the livings were valued at under this sum, suggesting that the legislation was not being applied, or that some incumbents were exempt from its provisions: *The Nineteenth-Century Church*, p. 129-30.
34 Brian Howell in *Pembrokeshire County History*, (Haverfordwest, 1987), III, 240.
35 B.M. Lodwick, *Henry Hey Knight* (Neath, 2012), p. 31. He had been offered the curacy previously but had declined it as it meant replacing an existing curate: *ibid.*, pp. 28-9.
36 Wade, *Black Book*, p. 57. He argued the average was £75, and collectively these curates received £319,050, and yet they did most of the work of the Church. Brown suggests the average stipend for stipendiary curates was £79 in 1831: *A History of the English Clergy*, p. 16.
37 Virgin, *The Church in an Age of Negligence*, p. 229.
38 Jacob, *Clerical Profession*, p. 67. Hart notes a comment that a bricklayer at 2s. a day was better off than most curates, as was a footman at £7 per annum plus board wages: *The Curates' Lot*, p. 112.
39 Brown, *Letters of Edward Copleston*, pp. 15-16, 134-6, 152.
40 Jenkinson, *Charge* (St Davids), 1828, p. 40.
41 Virgin, *The Church in an Age of Negligence,* p. 239. By 1838 the median figure was £83 per annum (*ibid.*, p. 260).
41 Copleston, *Charge* (Llandaff), 1830, pp. 22-3. In 1833 Copleston he hoped he had given his incumbents the hint that they should provide a proper salary for their curates and so be spared his interference: *Charge (Llandaff)*, 1833, p. 20.
43 SD/LET/1841. Later a son in law of the rector made arrangements to prevent the sequestration.
44 Thomas Stackhouse, *The Miseries and Great Hardships of the Inferior Clergy in and around London* (London, 1737), pp. 85, 91.
45 Jacob, in Williams, *The Welsh Church*, p. 115.
46 G.H. Jenkins, "'A Rank Republican [and] a Leveller': William Jones, Llangadfan", *WHR*, 17 (1995), 375. John Jones wrote about the rector living luxuriously upon his tithes while the poor underling curate starved or the sorry pittance of £20 per annum: *Considerations on the Illegality and Impropriety of preferring Clergymen*, p. 39.
47 Burgess, *Charge* (St Davids), 1813, pp. 17-18.
48 *Hansard's Parliamentary Debates,* xxxv, 1836, p. 1134.
49 Quoted by Brown, *Ten Clerical Lives*, p. 16. Copleston required Stacey to upgrade his curates' stipends from £40 to £70, plus fees, and Ollivant went further and insisted on £120 plus the use of the parsonage house for the senior curate: Brown, "Parish of Gelligaer", pp. 25-6.
50 Brown, *Reclaiming the Wilderness*, p. 170.
51 Virgin, *The Church in an Age of Negligence,* pp. 230-1, 237, 260. Some English incumbents found themselves paying anything from half to the whole of their parish income to their stipendiary curates: Jacob, *Clerical Profession*, p. 66.
52 Brown, *Letters of Edward Copleston*, p. 15. Henry Jones Williams, curate of Castle Caereinion 1804-12, had a stipend of £63 plus the use of the parsonage house, but he was also rector of Hirnant: Brown, *Church and Clergy at Castle Caereinion*, p. 22. Wade in his *Black Book* quotes the 1827 figures (p. 57), that out of 4,254 curates, 1,393 had the use of the parsonage house (32%). Bishop Wilberforce of Oxford arranged in 1855 for a curate to have the use of the parsonage house and enquired if he wished to make use of the furniture at 10% of the valuation: Pugh, *The Letter Books of Samuel Wilberforce*, p. 333; while in Lincolnshire a curate allowed £120 a year plus the use of the house was required to pay £50 for using his incumbent's furniture: Ambler, *Correspondence of Bishop Kaye*, p. 51.
53 Mrs Bulkeley Owen, *History of Selattyn Parish* (Oswestry, n.d.), p. 423.

54 Higham, *David Jones, Llan-gan*, p. 37.
55 SA/RD/28.
56 SA/MISC/1204. George Griffiths, curate of Llangower in 1749, also lived in a rented house: SA/RD/26.
57 SA/RD/28.
58 Brown, *Letters of Edward Copleston*, p. 110.
59 SA/RD/28.
60 J.R. Guy, "The Significance of Indigenous Clergymen in the Welsh Church at the Restoration", *Studies in Church History*, 18 (1982), 340-2. The 1749 and 1791 rural deans' reports on the state of the diocese of St Asaph reveal many similar instances: in 1749 William Conway, curate of Northop, lived on his own estate; David Lloyd of Bettws, a native of the parish, lived at his brother's house; Thomas Edwards, Llanarmon Mynydd Mawr, another native of his parish, probably lived in a family home, as would John Roberts of Llanuwchllyn, another native, while David Lewis of Castle Caereinion lived a mile away in his wife's home. In 1791 Thomas Hughes of Llansanffraid Glan Conwy lived in his own home, as probably did the curate of Welshpool, Francis Bromley, who was a native of the town: SA/RD/26 & 28.
61 F.G. Cowley, "Revd. John David Davies", *Morgannwg*, 38 (1994), 12.
62 Pryce, *History of the Parish of Llandysilio*, pp. 69-70.
63 Quoted by Hart, *The Curates' Lot*, pp. 125-6. By contrast a writer of 1732 wrote about the curate's position as being imposed upon by idle parishioners, such as to pray for an old woman sick from tooth ache at night for she could not sleep, or to baptise at midnight. If he wanted a fine reputation in the parish he must listen with patience to the idle tittle tattle and broad tales of his parishioners and kiss every toothless dame: *A Dissuasive from Entry into Holy Orders, in a Letter to a Young Clergyman* (London, 1732), p. 26.
64 Vaughan, *Memoir and Remains*, pp. 27-8.
65 Blackwell, *The Beauties of Alun*, pp. 35-6, 43-4.
66 T.W. Pritchard, *The Making of Buckley and District* (Wrexham, 2006), p. 201; Brown, "Henry Powell Ffoulkes", pp. 132-3.
67 Brown, *Parochial Lives*, pp. 34-5.
68 Davies, *Life and Opinions of Robert Roberts*, pp. 286-7.
69 Howse, *Radnorshire*, p. 74. William Cathrall notes with much satisfaction the work of George Cuthbert, stipendiary curate of Oswestry 1853-73 and of his colleague, Llewelyn Wynne Jones: *History of Oswestry* (Oswestry, 1855), p. 152.
70 R.L. Brown, "The Curate of Berriew", pp. 109-52, in passim.
71 Maurice Richards, *A History of Newtown* (Welshpool, 1993), p. 65.
72 Guy, *Thesis*, p. 781.

CHAPTER FIVE: PERPETUAL AND STIPENDIARY CURATES: THE CONSEQUENCES

1 Quoted in *A Dialogue between the Rev. Mr Jenkin Evans ... and Mr Peter Dobson ... concerning ... Bishops in the Principality of Wales* (London, 1744), p. 54.
2 *Church and State: A Controversy: by a representative of the Anti-State Society and the Curate of Dolgellau* (Evan Andrews: Dolgellau, 1845), p. 23.
3 B.E. and K.A. Howells, *Pembrokeshire Life: 1572-1843* (Pembrokeshire Record Society, 1972), pp. 47-8.
4 Quoted in Williams, *Glamorgan County History*, IV, 438. Goronwy Owen complained that while he was curate of Donnington, in England, his boys were clothed in rags and "tatters": W.D. Williams, *Goronwy Owen*, p. 33.
5 John Jones, *Considerations on the Illegality and Impropriety of Preferring Clergymen*, p. 55.
6 Wade, *Black Book*, p. 54n.
7 Quoted by M.D. George, "Some Caricatures on the Clergy of Wales", *NLW.Jnl.*, 4 (1945), 53n.

8   Quoted by Mather, *High Church Prophet*, p. 171.
9   Thomas, *Ystradowen*, pp. 45-9. Thomas Jones of Creaton, while he was curate of Eglwysbach in Cardiganshire in 1779 had £20 per annum, and spent £6 of this on his board and lodging, £6 on clothes, £3 for the run of the mountain for his horse, £1 for charity, and saved £3, but he was unmarried: Owen, *Thomas Jones*, p. 342.
10 *Bye-Gones*, 21 June 1893, p. 104.
11 Mrs G.H. Bell (ed.), *The Hamwood Papers of the Ladies of Llangollen* (London, 1930), p. 108.
12 Quoted by Jenkins, *Literature, Religion and Society*, p. 8.
13 Edwards, *Memories*, pp. 52-3.
14 Jenkins and Jones, *Cardiganshire County History*, III, 457.
15 Quoted by Jenkins, *Literature, Religion and Society*, p. 202, though he refers to incumbents. We have already noted beforehand Bishop Horsley's comment about clergy acting as farm labourers and thus demeaning their professional status: quoted by Bax, *The English Parsonage*, p. 132. See also John Griffith's comment: Brown, *John Griffith*, pp. 20-2.
16 Wade, *Black Book*, pp. 54n-55n.
17 Quoted in *Bye-Gones*, 14 October 1896, p. 451.
18 Quoted by Jenkins, *Literature, Religion and Society*, p. 6.
19 Dafydd Tomas, *Michael Faraday in Wales* (Denbigh, 1975), p. 139.
20 As such noted by Jenkins and Jones, *Cardiganshire County History*, III, 457. I make a distinction between these curates who looked after a school as an additional means of income or ministry, and those schoolmasters who were primarily that but also served parishes as curates to augment their income. Such men were schoolmasters at Ruabon School (T.W. Pritchard, *Remembering Ruabon* [Wrexham, 2000], pp. 92-3); Monmouth School (Warlow, *A History of the Charity of William Jones*, p. 197); Abergavenny (Orrin, *Medieval Churches in the Vale of Glamorgan*, p. 231); Swansea Grammar School (F.G. Cowley, "St Mary's Church, Swansea, in 1790", *Gower*, 25 [1974], 69); Berriew School (Humphreys, "A Conspectus of Schools in Eighteenth-Century Montgomeryshire", pp. 95-7); and see S.C. Passmore, "The Rev. John Pugh, Motygido, Llanarth, and his School", *Ceredigion* 12/4 [1996] 34-7, while Phillips mentions a Radnorshire schoolmaster who neglected his school for his two parishes with a circuit of 20 miles each Sunday: *Wales*, p. 218.
21 Teague and Brown, "Griffith Jones' 'Pious Minister'", pp. 27-9. In 1761 John Lloyd, the curate of Caerwys, kept a school in the town to augment his income: Paul Evans, "Reverend John Lloyd of Caerwys (1733-93), *Flint Historical Society Publications*, 31 (1983-4), 111.
22 Humphreys, "A Conspectus of Schools in Eighteenth-Century Montgomeryshire", pp. 104, 106, 109, 114; R.L. Brown, in *Sayce Papers*, I (1995), 4.
23 Bradney, *Monmouthshire*, I-2b, 442-3.
24 Enoch, *Llanfihangel Genau'r Glyn*, pp. 36-7; Brown, "A Cardiganshire Incumbent", pp. 21-5. He was offered a curacy at Llanfair Caereinion in 1796 worth £40 and an additional £30 for taking a school.
25 Noted by Clement, *Correspondence and Minutes of the S.P.C.K.*, p. 255.
26 Eric Griffiths, *Philip Yorke I: Squire of Erthig* (Wrexham, 1995), pp. 34-5. Once again, I exclude those men who were ordained into curacies but whose principal means of employment were tutorships to families. John Griffith, later of Merthyr Tydfil, commenced his ministry as curate of Astbury, Cheshire, in 1842, without stipend, as he acted as tutor to the Antrobus family of Eaton Hall: Brown, *John Griffith*, pp. 13-14. See also A.T. Hart, *Clergy and Society, 1600-1800* (London, 1968), p. 64. See also Gibson, *The Domestic Chaplain*, pp. 48-9.
27 A.O. Evans, *The Welsh Book of Common Prayer*, III, 315. Joseph Leach described such men as supernumeraries, and believed they were those who suffered from the Church ordaining more men than there were posts available: *Rural Rides*, pp. 172-3.
28 Jacob suggests that using a deputy was a frequent practice at the time, especially in the government service: *Clerical Profession*, p. 108.

29 Copleston, *Edward Copleston*, pp. 235-6. Copleston's predecessor, Sumner, in his 1827 *Charge*, said much the same, and after his protest about this practice made it clear he would not allow any curate to care for more than two churches on a Sunday, or travel beyond a certain unspecified distance: *Charge (Llandaff)*, 1827, pp. 23-4. Bishop Jenkinson of St Davids also endeavoured to prevent curates serving three churches per Sunday: *Charge (St Davids)*, 1828, pp. 26-7.

30 *Corbett's Legacy to Parsons*, p. 106. In Devon during 1779 16.7% of parishes were looked after by neighbouring clergy, and in north-east Norfolk 21 out of 72 parishes were in a similar position. In Oxford during 1778 24% of parishes had incumbents who were curates of other parishes, and in Worcestershire the figure was 23%: Virgin, *Church in an Age of Negligence*, pp. 152-3, 218. In 1827 Bishop Kaye discovered that many curates in Lincolnshire served three curacies: Obelkevich, *Religion and Rural Society*, p. 117. See also Jacob, *Clerical Profession*, p. 67; Mather, *High Church Prophet*, pp. 151-2.

31 *A Letter ... concerning the Admission of Unqualified Persons into Holy Orders* (London, 1790s), pp. 6-7.

32 Guy, *Thesis*, p. 283. Leyson Morgan is another example of the 1750s. He was vicar of Penllyn and curate of Caerau and Glyncorrwg, a scattered group. His total income of £75 gross was reduced by £20 as he had to pay £10 to his curates on these two curacies (ibid., p. 282). See also Guy: "Bishop Barrington's Book", p. 120, and his "Perpetual Curacies in Eighteenth Century South Wales", pp. 332-3.

33 A point made by Virgin, *The Church in an Age of Negligence*, p. 218. He tentatively suggests that there were far less stipendiary curates than hitherto thought: *ibid.*, p. 222.

34 D.H. Williams, Jonah Bowen Evans", pp. 106-13, 115-8.

35 Griffiths, "A Visitation of the Archdeaconry of Carmarthen, 1710", I, 300, 305, 311; II, 323-4.

36 T. Elwyn Jones, *About Llangynog and Neighbouring Villages* (1999), p. 110.

37 Denning, *The Diary of William Thomas*, p. 52.

38 Luxton, "Hezekiah Jones", pp. 18-19. In 1815 he became vicar of St Bride's Wentlloog, having been curate there for many years. As there was no parsonage house he lived at Cadoxton and probably had to lodge overnight in his own parish.

39 Thomas, *Ystradowen*, p. 18.

40 Eifion Evans, "Gleanings from the Thomas Davies, Coety, MSS", *JHSPCW*, 46 (1961), 39-40. It appears he acted with David Jones of Llangan in this capacity.

41 Guy, "Church and Churchmen in Llantrisant Parish", pp. 87-8.

42 Guy, *Thesis*, p. 780. One church appears to have remained unserved.

43 David Francis, *A History of St Illtyd's Church, Llanharry* (2004), p. 9. Griffith Griffiths held the Worcestershire living of Eckington and that of Shadwell, London, but lived in Wiltshire.

44 Williams, *Thomas Price, Carnhuanawc*, II, 5, 15-16, 61-2; Bevan, *The Past and Present of a Welsh Diocese*, pp. 24-5.

45 Morris, *Romilly's Visits to Wales*, p. 15; Walter Vile, *A History and Description of the Parish Church of St Michael, Michaelston-super-Ely* (1981), p. 17. Other examples will be found in Guy, *Thesis*, p. 280; Guy, *The Diocese of Llandaff in 1763*, pp. 188-90; Guy, "Bishop Barrington's Book", p. 120, and Eryn M. White in Jenkins, *The Welsh Language before the Industrial Revolution*, p. 242.

46 Guy, *The Diocese of Llandaff in 1763*, pp. 186-88. The same pattern was seen in Bishop Clavering's Visitation of 1726: Jacob in Williams, *The Welsh Church*, p. 116. Shute Barrington, when bishop of Salisbury (1782-91) discovered that 25 of his incumbents served a second parish as curate, while in the diocese of Norwich in 1784, 65 incumbents cared for a neighbouring parish and nearly all the 220 unbeneficed curates served more than one parish: Gregory and Chamberlain, *The National Church in Local Perspective*, pp. 126-7, 193.

47 Brown, *Through Cloud and Sunshine*, pp. 44, 47-8.

48 R.L. Brown, "The Parishes of the Aberafan Area", pp. 103-4; D.R.L. Jones, "An Eighteenth-Century Clerical Life: William Thomas of Baglan", *Morgannwg*, 44 (2000), 38-9. William

Thomas in 1764 held, besides his fellowship, two benefices, a chapelry and two perpetual curacies. He was able to do so as he was chaplain to the earl of Northampton.

49 Guy, *The Diocese of Llandaff in 1763*, p. 167.
50 Guy, "Bishop Barrington's Book", pp. 117. For other examples see Guy, *Thesis*, pp. 2, 245, 280; Knight, *Nineteenth-Century Church*, p. 119.
51 Bradney, *Monmouthshire*, I-2b, 375.
52 Bradney, *Monmouthshire*, I-2b, 346-7.
53 G.R. Orrin, *A History of Bishopston* (Llandysul, 1982), pp. 56-7; Brown, "The Revd Edward Davies v. the Men of Gower", *Morgannwg*, 57 (2013), pp. 34-53.
54 Guy, *Thesis*, pp. 652-3. He notes this also applied to Wales: *ibid.*, pp. 773-4.
55 Cowley, *Llanmadoc and Cheriton*, p. 15.
56 Jacob, *Clerical Profession*, pp. 311-2. He adds that they were tolerated as an economic necessity.
57 Morgan, "The Diocese of St David's, Part B, pp. 17-20.
58 Morgan, "The Diocese of St David's", Part B, p. 22. He suggests the service was the communion service, which may have meant that the whole of that service was added onto the morning service. It probably took at least two hours, especially if a sermon was preached.
59 Joan Varley writing of Stow Archdeaconry, quoted by Jacob, *Clerical Profession*, p. 105.
60 Lloyd, *The Gentry of South-West Wales*, pp. 178-9. Saunders also noted how curates were forced to agree on terms with impropriators, to their disadvantage: *A View of the State of Religion*, pp. 24-5.
61 The quotation is from the Ottley Papers at the NLW, no. 100, quoted by Jenkins, *Literature, Religion and Society*, p. 7. Ambler notes how in the early 1830s a Lincolnshire curate cum rector undertook two services, and how a parish clerk would watch to see him at a distance before ringing the church bell and allow him to rush through the service before galloping back: *Correspondence of John Kaye*, p. xxxii.
62 Saunders, *A View of the State of Religion*, pp. 24-5.
63 E.D. Jones, "Some Aspects of the History of the Church in North Cardiganshire in the Eighteenth Century", *JHSCW*, 3 (1953), 103; Jacob, *Clerical Profession*, pp. 176-7; Philip Jenkins in Gregory and Chamberlain, *The National Church in Local Perspective*, pp. 268-9.
64 Meyrick, *Cardigan*, p. 362.
65 Brown, "A Cardiganshire Incumbent", pp. 23-4.
66 Morgan, "The Diocese of St Davids", Part B, pp. 20-3.
67 T.W. Pritchard (ed.), *Our Village: Nercwys* (Wrexham, 2000), p. 110.
68 O.J. Francis, *The Border Vale of Glamorgan* (Barry, 1976), p. 35.
69 SA/RD/26.
70 W. Bingley, *North Wales* (London, 1804), I, 212.
71 Yates, in Williams, *The Welsh Church*, p. 256. By comparison the archdeaconry of Carmarthen was even worse. In 1813 only 7.4% of its parishes had double duty, 88.3% had single duty, and 4.3% less than single. However, the number of churches with a monthly communion was 73.5% compared to Anglesey's 10.5%. The number of Anglesey parishes with two Sunday services diminished from 20 in 1801 to 6 in 1837, though the number with a single service increased from 35 to 59: *ibid.*, p. 259.
72 Yates, in Williams, *The Welsh Church*, p. 256, 258-9. He notes that afternoon services were not popular with congregations when there had been a morning service with the result that double duty in some parishes had been abandoned.
73 SD/LET/1240.
74 Brown, *Parochial Lives*, pp. 134-5. Copleston received a request from James, curate to Gronow, asking that he might live at Cadoxton, as the hardships of having to ride to Aberpergwm and Crynant were proving too much for him: Brown, *Letters of Edward Copleston*, p. 154.
75 Copleston, *Edward Copleston*, pp. 233-5. Copleston endeavoured to end these traditional groupings, and though he was forced to allow them on some occasions he insisted that on

adjacent pluralities held by a non-resident incumbent curates should be employed for both parishes: Brown, *Letters of Edward Copleston*, p. 19.

76   Philip Jenkins in Gregory and Chamberlain, *The National Church in Local Perspective*, p. 269.

CHAPTER SIX: THE ASSISTANT CURATE: A NEW BREED

1   *The Position and Prospects of Stipendiary Curates*, p. 4.
2   Halcombe, *The Church and her Curates*, pp. 6-7, 17, 92-4; Hart, *The Curate's Lot*, p. 135.
3   Thomas Williams, *Visitation Charge to the Archdeaconry of Llandaff*, 1845, p. 6. This is from a newspaper cutting pasted into a volume containing his other Charges formerly in the Llandaff Cathedral Library.
4   Hart, *The Curate's Lot*, p. 131.
5   PP 1843, xl (189) 113, of 1841. The 1851 figures are abstracted from Jones and Williams, *The Religious Census of 1851*, I. In north Wales Montgomery District had 1 stipendiary and 5 assistant curates, Ruthin 2 and 6, and Flintshire nil and 7, respectively: Jones and Williams, *The Religious Census of 1851,* II. Virgin suggests that in 1813 there were about 1,300 assistant curates: *The Church in an Age of Negligence*, p. 222.
6   *Guardian*, 23 March 1881, p. 425, and 6 April 1881, pp. 481-2, which states that out of 5,000 curates only 387 were stipendiary, and some of these acted for incapacitated incumbents. The diocesan figures are as follows: Bangor, stipendiary curates 0, assistant 73; St Asaph, 1 and 78; St Davids 10 and 99; Llandaff, 3 and 103, respectively, making the total 14 stipendiary curates and 353 assistant curates.
7   Griffiths, "A Visitation of the Archdeaconry of Carmarthen, 1710", II, 322. See also Guy, *Thesis*, pp. 769-70.
8   SA/RD/26 and 28. In the deanery of Pool there were six assistant clergy in 1749, in that of Bromfield and Yale four in 1749 and one in 1791, and in Marcia one in 1749 and two in 1791. Guy suggests in 1763 the diocese of Llandaff had 25 assistant curates, several of whom were deacons: *The Diocese of Llandaff in 1763*, p. 186. However, these figures may be misleading, as some might have assisted an incapacitated or non-active incumbent, served an extra-parochial district, or were recorded under the wrong category.
9   Jenkinson, *Charge* (St Davids), 1828, pp. 34-6. He noted that a title or first curacy post was cheaper than a more experienced man.
10   A Clergyman, *On Clerical Education: A Letter*, letter I, pp. 5-6, and letter II, pp, 7, 10.
11   Evans, *The Welsh Book of Common Prayer* , II, 22, and see I. 243 for another example see Brown who notes that Thomas Hancorne, resident incumbent of Newcastle, Glamorgan, with its three chapelries, though also a pluralist, had two resident curates who cared for these chapelries: *Reclaiming the Wilderness*, p. 172.
12   *Report of the Church Congress, Wolverhampton*, 1867, p. 88.
13   Cragoe, *Anglican Aristocracy*, p. 214. In the 1900s the diocese had 369 incumbents and 148 curates (28% of its total clerical strength): *Report of the Royal Commission, 1911*, IV, 407.
14   W.L. Bevan, *Notes on the Church in Wales* (London, 1905), pp. 19-20.
15   Wills, "The Established Church in the Diocese of Llandaff", p. 249; *Report of the Llandaff Diocesan Conference*, 1886, pp. 133-4. Ollivant stated that between 60 and 70 of the assistant clergy of his diocese were supported by grant-making bodies: *Charge (Llandaff)*, 1869, p. 10.
16   Lee, *The Church of England in the Durham Coalfield*, pp. 58, 63, 77.
17   *CMG*, 28 January 1854, p. 4, letter of Cadvan of Towyn; Brown, *Evangelicals in the Church in Wales*, pp. 166-9; Brown, *Reclaiming the Wilderness*, pp. 28-30; Brown, *John Griffith*, pp. 22-4, 120-1 (noting some of the lame ducks he was forced to employ); Brown, *Reviving the Clergy, Renewing the Laity*, pp. 4-5.
18   Report of November 1889: Lambeth Palace Library, Benson MS, 170, fol. 236; Prichard, *Representative Bodies*, p. 121. Morgan's successor, William Lewis, was said to be good at obtaining curates, and out of 39 during his incumbency 1869-1918, 13 were theological college

trained, eight were literates, ten non-graduates and three graduates from Lampeter, three Oxbridge graduates and one London graduate: *ibid.*, 171-2.

19 Brown, *John Griffith*, pp. 89-90. He claimed to have had 20 curates over 23 years, many of whom stayed with him for many years: *ibid.*, p. 123.
20 Richards, *Honest to Self*, p. 227.
21 Basil Jones, *Charge* (St Davids), 1880, p. 31.
22 *Proceedings at the St Asaph Diocesan Conference*, 1887, pp. 13-14. There were various registry offices for curates. One in Whitehall claimed it had the sanction of the two archbishops: *Ecclesiastical Gazette*, vol. 41, 17 Jan. 1879, p. 104.
23 The Church in Wales, *Report of the Nation and Prayer Book Commission*, 1949, p. 33.
24 John Ellerton (ed.), *A Manual of Parochial Work* (London, 1888), pp. 308-18.
25 Basil Jones, *Charge (St Davids)*, 1892, p. 57.
26 Lewis, *Charge* (Llandaff), 1894, pp. 12-13; Edwards, *Charge* (St Asaph), 1890, pp. 22-3. See also Campbell, *Charge* (Bangor), 1875, p. 24; Basil Jones, *Charge* (St Davids), 1886, pp. 70-1 (he noted that often a man might be two or three miles distant from his incumbent); and a plea from a layman, *Report of the Llandaff Diocesan Conference*, 1886, p. 72.
27 Morgan, *Church Reform and Church Defence*, p. 6.
28 Brown, *John Griffith*, p. 212.
29 *Report of the Church Congress, Birmingham*, 1893, p. 210. Some incumbents would not allow their curates to celebrate the Holy Communion.
30 Parry-Jones, *A Welsh Country Parson*, pp. 13-16, 87. By contrast in the late 1940s John Charles Jones, later bishop of Bangor, then vicar of Llanelli, required his curates to read the Greek Testament with him, criticised their sermons, and encouraged them to explore new ways of commending the Gospel: Edward Lewis, *John Bangor* (London, 1962), pp. 90-2.
31 Basil Jones, *Charge* (St Davids), 1880, pp. 31-2.
32 Lambeth Palace Library, Benson MS, 85, fols. 209-21.
33 *CMG*, 14 May 1859, p. 5.
34 F.W. Jackson (ed.), *The Letter Books of W. Gilbertson and Co. Ltd., Pontardawe* (South Wales Record Society, Cardiff, 2001), p. 369.
35 The responsibility of the incumbent to pay his assistant curate's stipend appears to have been customary, but I have failed to find any reference to this in such works on ecclesiastical law as Stephens, 1848, Phillimore, 1895, or Cripps, 1869 and 1921 editions. The form for a nomination to a title, thus enabling a person to be made deacon, required a stipend to be stipulated, and from 1838 both incumbent and curate were required to sign a declaration that this stipend would be paid by the first and received by the second: Pinnock, *The Laws of the Church and the Clergy*, pp. 27-8, and see p. 19, suggesting the amount of the stipend was a matter of agreement, and pp. 177-8 which ignores the stipends of assistant curates. It was unjust that incumbents were called upon to pay for their curates, especially when the income of the parish was hardly sufficient for one, wrote the author of *The Position and Prospects of Stipendiary Curates*, p. 5, while a paper entitled "The Church and her Curates", argued that it was only a conscientious feeling on the part of the incumbent that induced him to pay any part of his curate's stipend, "supposing, of course, that is able and willing to perform the duties himself for which the endowment was originally intended to provide": *Church Quarterly Review*, 123 (1867), 236).
36 Parry-Jones, *A Welsh Country Parson*, p. 133:
37 For an English example see Parsons, *Religion in Victorian Britain*, II, 277.
38 Brown, *A History of the English Clergy*, p. 16.
39 Morgan, *Curates and Colliers*, p. 9. The Llandaff Diocesan Memoranda Books, vols. I & II, record the stipends offered the newly ordained. In December 1851 they ranged between £40 and £90, though most were of £80: By 1869 they ranged from £80 to £100, the lowest being received by a St Bees man.
40 Halcombe, *The Church and her Curates*, p. 60.

41 *Guardian*, 23 March 1881, p. 425; Haig notes that in 1848, 51% of assistant curates had less than £100 and only 15 over £120, by 1879 the proportion was 10-74: *Victorian Clergy*, p. 223.The *Guardian* of 1865 argued that the stipend had been raised to £120: 7 June 1865, p. 596.
42 Cragoe, *Anglican Aristocracy*, p. 213.
43 Wills, "The Established Church in the Diocese of Llandaff", p. 249. He doubts if all received this amount.
44 Clarke, *The Revenues of the Church of England in Wales*, p. 29.
45 *Report of the Llandaff Diocesan Conference*, 1904, pp. 45-59, esp. pp. 47-8, 53.
46 As a result a new parish was created instead, much to his indignation: Brown, *Ten Clerical Lives*, pp. 246-7.
47 *St Asaph Diocesan Calendar*, 1936, pp. 70-1. It was noted that some parishes were finding difficulties in obtaining their share of the £200 stipend required, and were using lay help instead. It had been agreed in 1933 to allow a minimum stipend of £150 instead: A.O. Evans, *A Survey of the Clerical Staffing of Bangor Diocese*, p. 3.
48 Ecclesiastical Commission Records, Church in Wales Office, Llangynwyd file, letter of 13 August 1866 of Llewelyn to the EC.
49 Brown, *David Howell*, pp. 102-3.
50 Brown, *Reclaiming the Wilderness*, p. 28. In 1898 the parish of Pontypridd had 3 curates, one on £150 and two at £120. The EC gave £120, the diocesan funds £70, ACS £90 and local collections and subscriptions raised £340: *ibid.*, p. 131.
51 *Report of the Royal Commission, 1911*, II, 282-3.
52 Ollivant, *Charge* (Llandaff), 1869, p. 10; *Report of the Llandaff Diocesan Conference*, 1886, p. 133.
53 Knight suggests that when a curate left the parish the grant was terminated. This was not always the case, especially with the EC, though incumbents were always anxious to fill a vacancy immediately to ensure its continuation: *The Nineteenth-Century Church*, p. 123.
54 Ralph Holtham, *The Parish of Roath* (Cardiff, 1970), pp. 23-4. Timothy Rees, later bishop of Llandaff, shared one stipend with a colleague as curate of Mountain Ash to ensure the parish had the two curates it needed: J.L. Rees, *Timothy Rees of Mirfield and Llandaff* (London, 1945), p. 17.
55 H.C. Shuttleworth (ed.), *Some Aspects of Disestablishment* (London, 1894), pp. 44-5. Conybeare estimated in 1855 that 282 Welsh livings were under £100 (167 of them in St Davids diocese), 527 below £150: *Essays Ecclesiastical and Social*, p. 7.
56 *Report of the Church Congress, Swansea*, 1909, p. 248.
57 M.V.J. Seaborne, "Charles Butler Clough", *NLW.Jnl.*, 29 (1996), 283.
58 *Chronicles of Convocation*, Upper House, 17 May 1881, p. 213.
59 Brown, *Reclaiming the Wilderness*, p. 178.
60 T.W. Pritchard, *A History of the Old Parish of Hawarden* (Wrexham, 2002), p. 114; *Report of the Royal Commission, 1911*, records the evidence of Canon Drew of Hawarden, who stated his gross income from the parish as £2,324, but net £1,187. He paid £865 himself towards the cost of his curates' stipends and stated it needed a private income to run the parish. He was a son-in-law of W.G. Gladstone: *ibid.*, III, 50.
61 NLW, Powysland Club Deposit, Box 28. It seems that the wardens wished to take over the EC augmentation of £60 per annum given to the incumbent towards one of his curates' stipends.
62 *Bangor Diocesan Calendar and Clergy List*, 1907, pp. 181, 71. Figures suggest the total cost of these curates was £9,120, but only £1,360 came from grant-making bodies. A paper of 1867, "The Church and her Curates", suggested that the sum contributed by the clergy of the Established Church to these stipends was £500,000, often out of private income: *Church Quarterly Review*, 123 (1867), 236. This was repeated in the *Church Quarterly Review* of 1882. "The Position and Prospects of Curates" (vol. 14, p. 205). See also *Guardian*, 11 July 1866, pp. 734-5.
63 Evans, *A Survey of the Clerical Staffing of Bangor Diocese*, pp. 4-5.

64 Brown, *Reclaiming the Wilderness*, pp. 53-5. Lewis based his case on a local claim that the Ecclesiastical Commission had taken over the capitular estate in his parish. He was told he needed to obtain an equivalent benefaction of £27 per annum before it would make up his living to £300 as the living was in private patronage. The sum required was based on the gross income of £255 and not its net income.

65 SA/DR/49, fol. 127, p. 3. .

66 *Report of the Church Congress, Leicester*, 1880, p. 475. A.M. Deane endorsed this, but appears to assume that the legislation regarding stipendiary curates' stipends still had a moral force for assistant curates: Halcombe, *The Church and her Curates*, pp. 92-4.

67 Brown, *Reclaiming the Wilderness*, pp. 21-2. As he put it, the church people had nothing to pay save for the seats on which they sat in church. The new church at Merthyr charged pew rents.

68 Haig, *Victorian Clergy*, pp. 239-40.

69 Brown, "The Cilybebyll Commission".

70 E.G. Williams, *Move On!* p. 10.

71 *Famous People of Blaenau Gwent* (1989), I, 74.

72 Brown, *Parochial Lives*, p. 121.

73 Morgan, *Curates & Colliers,* pp. 3-4, 13-16.

74 Brown, *The Clergy and People of Welshpool*, p. 56; *Report of the Offertories in the Parish of Welshpool for 1874*, p. 5; Christ Church, Oxford, MSS. Estates 50, fols. 1741, 1743. Lord Powis's contribution of £75 was probably included within the subscriptions.

75 *Report of the Royal Commission, 1911*, II, 207, 251, 344, 431, 479. C.A.H. Green, then vicar of Aberdare, stated in a letter to J.A. Lewis of 1914 that for the sake of his successors he declined to pay any part of his curates' stipends from his own resources, arguing that with careful working the parish could supply the deficiency: Glamorgan Record Office, P/61/CW/10/15i. The EC papers for the parish of Aberdare contain its printed accounts for 1912. £346 came from the parish fund, £240 from the EC, ACS £19 and other bodies £37, leaving a deficiency of £13.

76 *Pool Deanery Magazine*, March 1898.

77 *Swansea Parish Magazine*, November 1906, p. 173; August 1908, p. 113. In 1890 the parish clergy fund received £224 in subscriptions from 259 people, ranging from £10 to 2s.6d., the EC gave £360, for stipends totalling £1,350. Sir John Llewelyn had given £300 to this fund over a number of years: *Report of the St David's Diocesan Conference*, 1890, p. 20.

78 NLW, Bute Papers, L77/70, 75.

79 NLW, Bute Papers, L89/229.

80 *Haul*, March 1897, p. 129.

81 NLW, Glansevern Papers, 4899: A.D. Humphreys Owen to Rob (?), 13 July 1877.

82 Wills, "The Established Church in the Diocese of Llandaff", pp. 245-8; *CMG*, 24 April 1852, p. 4; Brown, *Reclaiming the Wilderness*, pp. 27-8; *Reports of the Llandaff Diocesan Church Extension Society*, 1858, p. 8; 1874, p. 7; 1881, pp. 7-8, and the 1898 Report, p. 8.

83 Lewis, *Charge* (Llandaff), 1894, pp. 34-8; *Report of the Llandaff Diocesan Conference*, 1910, p. 22.

84 SA/DR/53, fol. 15; *Proceedings of the St Asaph Diocesan Conference*, 1885, p. 6; Hughes, *Charge* (St Asaph), 1871, pp. 12-13.

85 Campbell, *Charge* (Bangor), 1881, pp. 12-13.

86 Pugsley, *Reminiscences*, p. 12.

87 Solway, *Prelates and People*, pp. 328-9.

88 Brown, *Evangelicals in the Church in Wales*, pp. 160-1.

89 Quoted by Morgan, *Curates & Colliers*, p. 11.

90 Hart, *The Curate's Lot*, p. 175.

91 Brown, *Reclaiming the Wilderness*, p. 27.

92 Brown, *Evangelicals in the Church in Wales*, p. 161.

93 Brown, *David Howell*, p. 96, 102-3.

94 *CMG*, 25 September 1858, p. 8. By 1891 it was estimated that 29 churches and 22 mission rooms owed their origin to or had been kept open through these grants: Brown, *Evangelicals in the Church in Wales*, p. 164.
95 Brown, *Evangelicals in the Church in Wales*, pp. 165-6.
96 *Church Pastoral-Aid Society Quarterly Paper*, cxiii, April 1878, p. 11.
97 Brown, *David Howell*, pp. 130-1; Brown, *Evangelicals in the Church in Wales*, pp. 164-5.
98 Cragoe, *Anglican Aristocracy*, pp. 214-5.
99 SA/DR/54, fol. 303: printed correspondence from Archdeacon Watkin H. Williams.
100 Pugsley, *Reminiscences*, p. 12. ACS gave a grant to replace the one lost.
101 In the *St Asaph Clergy Directory*, 1863, no pagination. See also *Guardian*, 7 June 1865, p. 596, for a lengthy account of its work and importance. Knight suggests the society only assisted parishes with a population of over 3,000. This was certainly not true at its beginning, nor does it appear true for Wales itself: *The Nineteenth-Century Church*, p. 123.
102 Jane Ross, *A Light upon the Road* (Aberystwyth, 1989), p. 35.
103 *Ecclesiastical Gazette*, September 1843, pp. 46-7.
104 LL/MISC/496.
105 In a file of miscellaneous correspondence contained in Llandaff Diocesan Memoranda Book, volume 1.
106 Brown, *John Griffith*, pp. 119-20. Griffith's first application to the EC had been turned down as he offered too much information, allowing the commissioners to believe that his curates were already provided for. His four curates cost £420 and he had to find £190 in subscriptions or from his own pocket towards this cost.
107 Cragoe, *Anglican Aristocracy*, p. 213.
108 *Haul*, 1885, pp. 265-5. The 1887 ACS report for the diocese of Llandaff indicated 35 grants were given to parishes in that diocese where the Church's influence would be severely crippled without the Society's aid. It also regretted that few rural parishes contributed to the work of the society: LL/MISC/501 and 494.
109 *Bangor Diocesan Calendar and Clergy List*, 1907, pp. 235-6; *ACS Report for the Diocese of Bangor*, 1906, p. 5.
110 Brown, *Reclaiming the Wilderness*, pp. 114-6.
111 As occurred when Pritchard Hughes was appointed vicar of Newcastle in 1877, though his letter is dated February 1879. In it he noted the loss of £10 from the diocesan society because of its lack of funds, and of £15 - £20 from subscriptions to the parochial fund due to the then trade depression: Brown, *Reclaiming the Wilderness*, p. 183.
112 Ollivant, *Charge* (Llandaff), 1863, pp. 52-3.
113 Prichard, *Representative Bodies*, pp. 120-3, 153-4, 172. He estimates that between 1887-1920 74% of the grant aid came from the EC, 17.5% from CPAS, and 4.84% from ACS whose grant was discontinued in 1901. In 1897 the cost of the curates' stipends was £720: *ibid.*, p. 172. For similar appeals from parishes see that for Neath in Brown, "The Parish of Llantwit with Neath", pp. 37-40.
114 Brown, *The Tribulations of a Mountain Parish*, pp. 14-15.
115 Brown, "The Parish of Ffestiniog with Maentwrog", p. 243.
116 Wills, "The Established Church in the Diocese of Llandaff", p. 249; and W.D. Wills, "Ecclesiastical Reorganisation and Church Extension in the Diocese of Llandaff, 1830-1870", MA thesis, University of Wales, May 1965, p. 193. He calculates that in 1870 the curates' grants for the diocese was made up of £3,780 from the EC, £2,487 from CPAS, £365 from ACS, and £1,215 from the Llandaff Church Extension Society.
117 Clarke, *The Revenues of the Church of England in Wales*, p. 29.
118 Church in Wales Records, John Morgan (Llandaff) Papers, Box 10, File of miscellaneous correspondence: letter of 11 February 1870.
119 Brown, "The Wealthiest Place and the Poorest Ministry", p. 75.

120 Brown, "The Parish of Gelligaer", pp. 45-6. This also applied to the parish of Pontypridd when it was taken out of the parish of Glyntaff in 1884, and to the new parish of St Matthew, Pontypridd, taken out of Pontypridd in 1909. The procedure had the disadvantage of keeping the former curate under the bondage of his previous incumbent, and preventing the latter from obtaining a further grant from the commissioners: Brown, *Reclaiming the Wilderness*, pp. 127, 131.

121 *MC*, 41 (1930), 144.

122 Lambeth Palace Library, Benson Papers 137, fols. 177-215.

123 Brown, "Aspects of the Nineteenth-Century Parish of Kidwelly", p. 70.

124 R.L. Brown, *The Churches in the Parish of Tongwynlais* (Tongwynlais, 1986), pp. 27-34. The rector in the 1930s was so financially handicapped that he required his curates to go round the parish and beg parishioners for contributions to their stipends.

125 Brown, *The Tribulations of a Mountain Parish*, pp. 15-17.

126 Brown, *David Howell*, p. 129.

127 Lambeth Palace Library, Benson Papers 14, fols. 326-31.

128 Brown, *Reclaiming the Wilderness*, pp. 79-80.

129 Brown, *Reclaiming the Wilderness*, pp. 131-2. Similar problems occurred at Coety: *ibid.*, pp. 182-3; Merthyr: Brown, *John Griffith*, p. 121; and Neath: Brown, "The Parish of Llantwit with Neath", p. 38.

130 Brown, *John Griffith*, pp. 121-2.

131 Brown, "The Parish of Ffestiniog with Maentwrog", pp. 244-6. A previous vacancy of 1898 of four months, though spread over two quarters, had caused him acute embarrassment, and unable to find a locum tenens he sought help from the two curates of the neighbouring parish of Blaenau Ffestiniog, with its incumbent's permission. The EC refused to pay the grant for that period of time as these men were already in receipt of grants and duplication was not permitted. Thus Price had to pay for their services from his own pocket. Another vacancy was supplied by the diocesan curate, whose job was to fill in on these occasions and so prevent the loss of grant-aid. Holiday locums were rare and I suspect this was a case of special pleading. J.H. Jenkins, a curate in the diocese of Llandaff, claimed that in sixteen years as a curate he had only had a fortnight's holiday: *Report of the Llandaff Diocesan Conference*, 1908, p. 23.

132 Brown, *Ten Clerical Lives*, pp. 190-1.

133 Brown, "The Wealthiest Place and the Poorest Ministry", pp. 73-6.

134 *Report of the Llandaff Diocesan Conference*, 1904, p. 53.

135 Haig, *Victorian Clergy*, p. 224. .

136 Brown, *Clergy and People of Welshpool*, p. 100.

137 John Morgan, *Curates & Colliers*, pp. 9-10; Wills, "The Established Church in the Diocese of Llandaff", p. 249.

138 Leach, *Rural Rides*, p. 101.

139 Hart, *Curate's Lot*, pp. 136-7.

140 *Guardian*, 24 February 1866, p. 217.

141 *The Position and Prospects of Stipendiary Curates*, pp. 10-11. It argued that as a result parents would not allow their sons to be ordained. See also "The Church and her Curates", p. 232, and *Substance of Speeches at the Meeting of the Llandaff Diocesan Church Extension Society*, 1863, p. 28.

142 *Report of the Llandaff Diocesan Conference*, 1904, pp. 47-8.

143 *Report of the Church Congress, London*, 1899, p. 249. Hugh Williams argued that curates did not want to be mendicants, living off charity with their children wearing cast-off clothes: *Report of the Llandaff Diocesan Conference*, 1910, p. 70.

144 *Report of the Llandaff Diocesan Conference*, 1910, p. 73.

145 Llandaff Diocesan Memoranda Book, vol. I, for 23 December 1868.

146 Espin, *Our Want of Clergy*, p. 25.

147 Morgan, *Welsh Political and Educational Leaders*, pp. 37-8. He suggests this was one of the reasons for the dearth of curates.

148 This occurred as late as the 1930s as R.S. Thomas the clerical-poet relates in his *Autobiographies* (London, 1997), p. 10. See Brown, *Clergy and People of Welshpool*, p. 112. Copleston wondered why such poor men married, proclaiming in one particular case of married misfortune, "What a sad thing to have such a poor creature saddled upon us": Brown, *Letters of Edward Copleston*, p. 236.

149 Few curates could afford to rent a house from their meagre stipends, and even if a house was provided by a parish its rent might be deducted from the stipend: "The Church and her Curates", pp. 224-5. One who did acquire a house was John James Turner at Welshpool in the mid-1870s, but his sisters lived with him. Previously Turner had had lodgings at 15s. a week though he bought his own food which was cooked by a servant of the house, and paid 4s. a week for coal: R.L. Brown, "The Curate of Welshpool", p. 35. Most had to find lodgings. Evan Jones, as curate of Radyr in 1853, lodged with a nonconformist family, as he did during his second curacy at Llandysilio Gogo, though the family turned "church" and two sons were ordained, Daniel and Owen Evans, one becoming vicar of Caernarfon and the other warden of Llandovery College. During his third curacy at Llandysul he had lodgings for himself and for his horse: Evan Jones, *Atgofion am Ddeugain Mlynedd o'm Gweinidogaeth* (Carmarthen, 1894), pp. 17, 27-8, 38. The curates of Llanblethian seem to have lodged in the 1870s at Stallscourt Farm: G. Alden (ed.), *Llanblethian Buildings and People* (Cowbridge, 2001), p. 22. A story is told of a curate of Whittington, Shropshire, then in the diocese of St Asaph, whose landlady passed him on to her successor as tenant for a goodwill price of £10, which in the end he paid himself: F.D. How, *Lighter Moments from the Notebook of Bishop Walsham How* (London, 1900), pp. 28-9. Many appear to have lodged with their incumbents, as did the curates of Aberdare before Vicar Green was married: Edwards, *Archbishop Green*, pp. 40-1. Robert Roberts, in his first curacy of Cwm, 1859, stayed with the family of his vicar, receiving £30 and his board: Davies, *Life and Opinions of Robert Roberts*, pp. 382-3. Kilvert records that Tom Williams, vicar of Llowes, 1870, had his curate boarding with him: Dafydd Ifans (ed.), *The Diary of Francis Kilvert, June – July 1870* (Aberystwyth, 1989), p. 104n. A curate of Leeds in the 1850s had £60 of his £80 stipend deducted for this reason: John Breary, *A Fellside Parson* (Norwich, 1995), p. 60. Bishop Lewis' *faux pas* was long remembered when he suggested that the curate he was placing in that parish to assist the bachelor vicar of Cilybebyll could be "his bedfellow" in his large Vicarage: Brown, "The Cilybebyll Commission".

150 *WM*, 29 July 1874, p. 6.

151 *Report of the Llandaff Diocesan Conference*, 1905, p. 39.

152 Lambeth Palace Library, Benson Papers, 98, fol. 289.

153 *Guardian*, 13 April 1881, p. 519, letter of "Z". Halcombe argued that those curates who married recklessly would be no better off in ten years time: *The Church and her Curates*, p. 95. D.J. Davies, curate of Cilybebyll in 1895 found himself in such difficulties with a son in public school that his wife returned to her parents' home in Swansea until he obtained a better post: Brown, "The Cilybebyll Commission".

154 *Report of the Church Congress, Birmingham*, 1893, pp. 211-2.

155 T.J. Jones, *How to Improve the Condition of the Welsh Church*, p. 16.

156 William Plomer (ed.), *Kilvert's Diary* (London, 1961), II, 30-3; John Toman, *Kilvert: the Homeless Heart* (Logaston, 2001), pp. 169-71, 177-8, 344. Many men were forced to wait until they had livings on their own before they could afford to marry, as did Howell Jenkins, vicar of Glyncorrwg 1901-26: Brown, *Tribulations of a Mountain Parish*, p. 29, and see Brush, *Thesis*, p. 42. The story of one curate of Presteigne who eloped with his intended after he had been turned down by her father is related in K. Parker, *A History of Presteigne* (Logaston, 1997), pp. 161-2.

157 *Report of the Llandaff Diocesan Conference*, 1904, pp. 57-8.

158 Halcombe, *The Church and her Curates*, p. 8.

159 *Report Church Congress, Shrewsbury*, 1896, pp. 478-9; cf. *Report of the Church Congress, Wolverhampton*, 1867, p.90, and Hart, *Curate's Lot*, pp. 178-9.

160 *Report of the Llandaff Diocesan Conference*, 1910, pp. 67-8.

161 *The Position and Prospects of Stipendiary Curates*, in passim; "Position and Prospects of Curates", *Church Quarterly Review*, XIV (1882), 199-219, in passim; *Guardian*, 28 February 1866, p. 217; 21 March 1866, p. 301; 11 July 1866, pp. 734-5; 4 February 1874, pp. 138-9; Halcombe, *The Church and her Curates*, p. 99; *Reports of the Church Congresses, Nottingham*, 1897, p. 101, and *London*, 1899, p. 249; *Church Quarterly Review*, 14 (1882), 212; an advertisement for the Society in *The Illustrated Guide to the Church Congress and Ecclesiastical Art Exhibition* (Swansea, 1909), p. 214; Haig, *Victorian Clergy*, pp. 218-33; Hart, *Curate's Lot*, p. 174.

162 Richard Davies, *Sermons &c* (Brecon, 1815), I-I, 272-4. Edward Edwards' sermon, *Pity upon the Poor* (Brecon, 1801), was preached before the subscribers of the Clerical Fund in the Archdeaconry of Brecknock, which was probably the same society.

163 Hinton, *The Anglican Parochial Clergy*, p. 89; Brown, *Evangelicals in the Church in Wales*, pp. 104-5.

164 Quoted in *Bye-Gones*, 9 May 1906, pp. 231-2.

165 *Llandaff Diocesan Magazine*, October 1913, pp. 71-2, and July 1914, p. 161.

166 Heeney, *A Different Kind of Gentleman*, p. 113.

167 *Guardian*, 21 March 1866, p. 301.

168 *Guardian*, 28 February 1866, p. 217.

CHAPTER SEVEN: THE ASSISTANT CURATE: THEIR DUTIES, CONCERNS AND DIFFICULTIES

1 In 1908 it was argued that stated terms of service were required for assistant clergy as to duties, holidays, the Whitsun offering and other matters: *Report of the Church Congress, Manchester*, 1908, pp. 489, 505-6.

2 As at Aberdare: Edwards, *Archbishop Green*, pp. 40-1.

3 Brown, "The Curate of Welshpool", pp. 38-46.

4 *Memoir of John Melbourne Perry* (Chelmsford, 1920), pp. 28-37, 64-72, 74-5. Letters testified to his sanctified life.

5 J.T.D., *In Memoriam: Rev. David Edmondes Owen* (1922), p. 8.

6 Davies, *Life and Opinions of Robert Roberts*, pp. 397-8, 402-7. A curate on the Welsh/English borders in 1906 was required to work six days a week, for what else would he do with himself, and when he asked if there was much work after dinner, he was told people in his position had supper: T.F. Royds, *Haughton Rectory or Four Country Parsons* (Shrewsbury, 1953), p. 26.

7 Davies, *Life and Opinions of Robert Roberts*, pp. 268-9.

8 John S. Peart-Binns, "Martinet and Shepherd: John Morgan (1886-1957), Archbishop of Wales", *JWRH*, NS4 (2004), 45.

9 Leech, *Rural Rides*, p. 288.

10 W.W. How, *Lectures on Pastoral Work* (London, 1883), pp. 43-4.

11 Brown, *Clergy and People of Welshpool*, p. 100.

12 *Garth Domain*, 28 (2005), 30-5.

13 Glendowor, *"Welsh Notes"* (Bangor, 1913), p. 49.

14 SA/DR/52, fol. 750.

15 David Lockwood, *Francis Kilvert* (Bridgend, 1990), pp. 49, 96-7; Rosalind Bolton, "Kilvert and Venables ... A Reassessment Reassessed", *Journal of the Kilvert Society,* 12 (September 2003), 8-10.

16 Davies, *Life and Opinions of Robert Roberts*, pp. 382-3, 388-90; Phillips, *Robert Roberts*, pp. 64-6. There was much concern that curates were required to preach two different sermons a week: A.G. Edwards in his 1890 Charge suggested they prepared one new sermon a week, and

then made use of the framework of a published one, though putting it into their own words, with the advice of their incumbent: *Charge (St Asaph)*, 1890, pp. 18-19. Nevertheless, many used commercially produced sermons, sent to them weekly: *Bye-Gones*, 15 April 1936, p. 31.

17 Davies, *Life and Opinions of Robert Roberts,* pp.326-7.
18 *Haul*, 1906, p. 426. John Griffith of Merthyr seems to have done the same, as his involvement in diocesan and national controversies hardly left him time to undertake any pastoral visitation: Brown, *John Griffith*, p. 125.
19 "The Position and Prospects of Curates", pp. 215. From the 1880s a pension was available, given in part from central funds but also made up of one third of the value of the living, thus diminishing it for a successor. The incumbent would have to find his own accommodation, whereas if he retained the living, and appointed an assistant for the work of the parish, he would probably have a better income plus the use of the parsonage house.
20 Brown, *Parochial Lives*, p. 128; SD/MISC B/79, notes some curates willing to accept a smaller stipend because the incumbents could not afford a full salary, as in Pembroke 1869 where the incumbent was blind or Meline where he was incapacitated and poor.
21 SA/DR/50, fol. 212. Edward Lewis, vicar of Glascwm, became a non resident for health reasons in 1851 and retired to Maderia, his place beng supplied by a curate, David Vaughan: F.W.D. Fenn and J.B. Sinclair, "Continuity and Change: A Welsh Border Parish and its Clergy 1750-1900", *T.Radns.S.,* 57 (1987), 68.
22 Evan Jones, *Atgofion am Ddeugain Mlynedd o'm Gweinidogaeth* (Carmarthen, 1894), p. 69.
23 *Chronicles of Convocation, Upper House*, 17 May 1881, pp. 211-2, and *Report on the Joint Committee on Pluralities*, no. 139, of 1882; Ollivant, *Charge* (Llandaff), 1872, p. 18; *Proceedings of the St Asaph Diocesan Conference*, 1895, pp. 7-9; *Report of the Llandaff Diocesan Conference*, 1898, p. 12. The 1898 Benefices Act allowed the bishop to inhibit the incumbent from interfering in the sequestrated parish, and allowed the bishop to appoint a curate immediately, instead of after three months if the incumbent had failed to do so by that time.
24 Brown, *The Cilybebyll Commission.* A similar incident took place at Beaumaris where a sequestrated incumbent tried to prevent the episcopally appointed curate from taking a service by padlocking the doors of the church: *Guardian*, 9 March 1881, p. 348.
25 Brown, *Ten Clerical Lives*, p. 164.
26 David Parry to John Griffith, 10 January 1870: South Glamorgan Libraries, Cardiff Ms. 3, 510; cf. Knight, *The Nineteenth-Century Church*, pp. 124-5.
27 SA/DR/46, fols. 240-1.
28 Brown, *David Howell*, p. 119.
29 Lambeth Palace Library, Benson Papers, 170/30, 44-5, 236; Brown, *Evangelicals in the Church in Wales*, pp. 166-8. John Griffith asserted in the mid 1840s that these men brought Welsh Methodism into the Church, using such practices as private meetings, extempore prayer and fencing the altar: Brown, *John Griffith*, pp. 22-4.
30 C. Tilney, *A History of the Parish of Penarth and Lavernock* (revision of 1988), pp. 53-4.
31 Lambeth Palace Library, Temple Papers, 33, fols. 293-4.
32 *CMG*, 20 November 1860, p. 5, and 1 December 1860, p. 8.
33 P.W. Jackson (ed.), *The Letter Books of W. Gilbertson and Co. Ltd, Pontardawe* (South Wales Record Society, Cardiff, 2001), pp. 375-6. Another case involved the curate of Fochriw, in the Rhymney Valley, J.A. Rees, who had lost a libel action against a licensed club, having refused a simple apology: *WM*, 4 February 1905, p. 5.
34 SD/Ch/Misc/133.
35 *CDH*, 3 October 1846, p. 3.
36 Lambeth Palace Library, Benson Papers, 3, fols. 110-125. The *Clergy List* of 1911 states he was curate of Barnard-town, Monmouthshire, 1882-90, perhaps suggesting he managed to hold onto his post.
37 Lambeth Palace Library, Benson Papers, 37, fols. 111-144.
38 Brown, *Ten Clerical Lives*, pp. 115-18.

39 Brown, *Ten Clerical Lives*, pp. 222-3: SA/DR/51, fol. 123 contains further statements on this controversy.
40 *CMG*, 31 October 1868, p. 8.
41 R.C. Wright, *The First Hundred Years: St John the Baptist Parish Church, Newport* (2000), p. 4. Cf. Frederick Wienholt, *Certain Correspondence between a Vicar and a Churchwarden* (Carmarthen, 1878), which criticised a curate of Laugharne's ritualistic and doctrinal position, whose father was the vicar of the parish.
42 *WM*, 16 April 1890, p. 3. The following year he had his own parish in Exeter.
43 Hart, *Curate's Lot*, pp. 137-9. This probably led to the section devoted to the assistant clergy at the Wolverhampton Church Congress of 1867. See Haig for the agitation these matters caused: *Victorian Clergy*, p. 226.
44 *The Unbeneficed Clergy and the Curate Question*, pp. 14-15. Suggestions for reform were set out on pp. 33-5.
45 "The Church and her Curates", pp. 224-5.
46 *Corbett's Legacy to Parsons*, pp. 107-8. Even a footman was not so dependent.
47 G. Hartwell Jones, *A Celt looks at the World*, p. 48.
48 Quoted by Lloyd, *The Church of England*, p. 152. It was stated that the policy of bishops was that disharmony in a parish was to be prevented at all costs, and as an incumbent could not be removed, the curate had to go: *Report of the Church Congress, Shrewsbury*, 1896, p. 482. C.A.H. Green claimed in 1905 that even the unbeneficed clergy had security of tenure and income as the bishop's licence could not be ended without episcopal consent, though this hardly offered much comfort to curates: *Report of the Llandaff Diocesan Conference*, 1905, p. 86.
49 *St Asaph Diocesan Directory and Clergy List*, 1911, p. 117; cf. Michael Stone (ed.), *The Diary of John Longe* (Suffolk Record Society, LI, Woodbridge, 2008), p. xxviii. In 1886 the new incumbent of Yarmouth dismissed 10 of his 11 curates and appointed 13 in their place: Noel Henderson (ed.), *The Goulburn Norwich Diaries* (Norwich, 1996), p. 369. C.A.H. Green, then vicar of Aberdare, argued that bishops were reluctant to exercise their power of agreeing to a curate's dismissal, but this "equitable principle" broke down when an incumbent vacated his living: *Report of the Llandaff Diocesan Conference*, 1905, p. 86.
50 *The Unbeneficed Clergy and the Curate Question*, p. 23.
51 Concern about this was expressed at several Church Congresses: *Reports of the Church Congresses*, Wolverhampton, 1867, pp. 93-4; Birmingham, 1893, pp. 214-5; Manchester, 1908, p. 491, when the bishop of Worcester said it rarely answered for the staff of a parish to continue with a new man and his new measures.
52 NLW, Bute Papers, L89/13 and 15. In the subsequent letter he requested that if the parish was sub-divided he might be considered for one of the appointments. Cf. Jacob, *Clerical Profession*, p. 71.
53 Brown, *The Letters of Edward Copleston*, p. 261.
54 *CMG*, 25 November 1848, p. 4.
55 SA/DR/54, fol. 369.
56 Brown, *Llandaff Figures and Places*, pp. 47-50. As Clarke was in arrears with his stipend he could not be dismissed until these had been paid.
57 Brush, *Thesis*, pp. 56, 89. She notes other examples from the 1920s but adds that many moved to parishes in the same area as they were aware of what posts were available.
58 Knight, *The Nineteenth-Century Church*, pp. 123-4. A curates' manifesto signed by 200 curates in 1885 alleged that many curates who had succeeded in filling churches had often been dismissed by the man their bishop would call "my dear rector", often because of jealousy at their success. As a result this manifesto petitioned for disestablishment: Howes, *The Church in Danger*, p. 17.
59 Llandaff Diocesan Memoranda Book, vol. 1, for 15 June 1853; *News of the Week*, 5 August 1893, p. 7.
60 Morgan Watcyn-Williams, *From Khaki to Cloth* (Caernarfon, 1949), p. 76.

61 Thomas Williams, *A Charge to the Archdeaconry of Llandaff*, 1852, p. 14. Ollivant in one instance allowed a curate to be placed on a trial and if approved to licence him: Llandaff Diocesan Memoranda Book, vol. II, for 14 March 1871. See also Hart, *The Curate's Lot*, p. 139.
62 As stated by the Rev. S.W. Thackeray at Shrewsbury Church Congress, *Report*, 1896, pp. 482-3.
63 *Report of the Church Congress, Wolverhampton*, 1867, pp. 96-8; Hart, *Curate's Lot*, p. 139. While a curate could make an appeal to the archbishop, the writer of *The Unbeneficed Clergy and the Curate Question*, pointed out this was a ludicrous privilege: p. 23.
64 Halcombe, *The Church and her Curates*, pp. 17-18, 26-7. He argued it was far better to urge the laity to give better support to the assistant clergy than to lower the standards for ordination, and he suggested more sub-divisions of parishes to create more livings.
65 "Position and Prospects of Curates", p. 210; *Reports of Church Congresses,* Wolverhampton, 1867, p. 100; Leicester, 1880, p. 480; Shrewsbury, 1896, p. 486; *Report of the Llandaff Diocesan Conference*, 1910, pp. 71, 74 (noting a proposal that clergy with two years in orders should be allowed to vote for proctors in Convocation); *The Church in Wales* (a periodical), no. 1 (January, 1873), p. xv. Concern was also expressed about the representation of curates provided by the new constitution of the Church in Wales, then being prepared prior to its disestablishment: *Official Report of the Proceedings of the Convention of the Church in Wales held at Cardiff, 1917*, pp. 226-7.
66 *Proceedings of the St Asaph Diocesan Conference*, 1890, p. 11; cf. *Report of the Llandaff Diocesan Conference*, 1901, p. 106; 1908, p. 23. The bishop responded to the query why so few unbeneficed clergy were appointed to the committees of the diocese by saying that it was open to the conference to elect them.
67 *WM*, 29 April 1885, p. 4. A talk was given on mission services.
68 *Report of the Llandaff Diocesan Conference*, 1908, p. 23.
69 *Report of the Llandaff Diocesan Conference*, 1903, p. 13. Many of the younger clergy died young, such as William Evans who died in 1837 aged 25, soon after his ordination by the bishop of Llandaff; J. Davies of Aberaeron who died in 1840 aged 29; Thomas Parry, curate of Henfrnyw who died at the same age in 1842; or David Edward Hughes, curate of Llanfairfechan, who died aged 24 in 1905: *Yr Haul,* 1837, p. 227; 1840, p. 131; 1832, p. 291; 1905, pp. 30-2.
70 *The Position and Prospects of Stipendiary Curates*, p. 11; *The Church and her Curates*, pp. 224-5; Haig, *Victorian Clergy*, p. 225.
71 *Reports of Church Congresses*: Birmingham, 1893, pp. 214-5; Shrewsbury, 1896, p. 486; Manchester, 1908, p. 491; "Position and Prospects of Curates", p. 203; Haig, *Victorian Clergy*, p. 225. Other suggestions were that bishops should appoint curates, possibly after a Parochial Church Council had drawn up a shortlist, and that once appointed a curate should be immovable on a change of incumbent.
72 *Report of the Church Congress, Leicester*, 1880, pp. 474-5.
73 *Report of the Church Congress, Wolverhampton*, 1867, pp. 89-91.
74 *CT*, 21 January 1898, p. 63. The requirement that a new incumbent should not be appointed until he had served a fixed term as a curate was a popular one, though the length of years suggested varied: *Report of the Church Congress, Wolverhampton*, 1867, p. 89; "Position and Prospects of Curates", p. 210; Halcombe, *The Church and her Curates*, pp. 94-5.
75 *Llandaff Diocesan Magazine*, October 1913, pp. 71-2.
76 *Reports of Church Congresses*, Leicester, 1880, p. 471; Derby, 1882, p. 185.
77 Halcombe, *The Church and her Curates*, pp. 30-2, 102-3; "The Church and her Curates", pp. 225. The position of the two northern dioceses in Wales was different as both bishops had substantial patronage, though more work needs to be done in this area.
78 As did Howell Jenkins who accepted the living of Glyncorrwg in 1901 with an income of £110: Brown, *Tribulations of a Mountain Parish*, pp. 28-9;cf. Halcombe, *The Church and her Curates*, p. 116.
79 *Guardian*, 28 February 1866, p. 217.
80 "The Church and her Curates", pp. 116, 225.

81 T.J. Jones, *How to Improve the Condition of the Welsh Church*, p. 15. It was natural, he added, that men wanted a permanent home and an independent sphere of work, and these could only be achieved by obtaining their own living: *ibid.*, pp. 16-17.
82 Halcombe, *The Church and her Curates*, pp. 66-7, 74-5, 81-2, 101-2. He held that it took on average 16 years to obtain a poor living and 28 years for a decent one. Guy Warman of St Aidan's Theological College said in the 1900s that if the patronage system worked with fairness these grievances would disappear: Lloyd, *The Church of England*, p. 153.
83 Virgin, *The Church in an Age of Negligence*, p. 202; *Report of the Church Congress, Shrewsbury*, 1896, pp. 484-5.
84 *Report of the Church Congress, London*, 1899, p. 184.
85 T.J. Jones, *How to Improve the Condition of the Welsh Church*, p. 17.
86 *The Position and Prospects of Stipendiary Curates*, p. 16 (the figures were 7,010 parishes between 21,000 clergy); Halcombe, *The Church and her Curates*, p. 83; *Guardian*, 11 July 1866, pp. 734-5.
87 Heeney, *A different Kind of Gentleman*, p. 111-2. An estimate of the same period suggested that over 10,000 candidates were chasing these 7,000 livings, though half of them were incumbents seeking to better themselves: *Report of the Church Congress, Wolverhampton*, 1867, p. 88.
88 Morgan, *Curates and Colliers*, p. 9; cf. Brush, *Thesis*, pp. 54-7, where she notes of the clergy in the deaneries of Edeyrnion and Penllyn between 1920-95 that three had served five curacies, one ten, another fourteen. Halcombe wrote that on average a man had to wait 12 years for a living: *The Church and her Curates*, p. 75. Haig, however, while he accepts the general accuracy of the picture, notes the position was much more complex on a diocesan scale: *Victorian Clergy*, pp. 235-7. The diocese of Llandaff, for example, had more curates than many other dioceses. In 1903 it had 199 curates and 226 livings: *Crockford*, 1903.
89 *Report of the Special Meeting of the St David's Diocesan Conference*, 1894, p. 19.
90 *Report of the Llandaff Diocesan Conference*, 1902, p. 11. A speaker at the Manchester Church Conference said much the same in 1908: *Report*, p. 496.
91 *The Position and Prospects of Stipendiary Curates*, pp. 4-5; Halcombe, *The Church and her Curates*, pp. 76-7.
92 *Guardian*, 11 July 1866, p. 734.
93 *Report of the Church Congress, Derby*, 1882, p. 187.
94 Williams, "A Neglected Radnorshire Cleric: the Revd. Joseph Bowen Evans, pp. 81-106.
95 Hart, *The Curate's Lot*, pp. 143-5.
96 Brown, "The Curate of Welshpool", pp. 33-4. Another example is John Pritchard Hughes, a St Bees man ordained in 1875 but not priested for 7 years, who served eight curacies in Bangor and St Asaph dioceses before being instituted to the parish of Gwaenysgor, Flintshire, in 1901: Pryce, *History of the Parish of Llandysilio*, p. 71.
97 Brown, *Llandaff Figures and Places*, p. 41.
98 Brown, *Church and Clergy at Castle Caereinion*, p. 40.
99 Brush, *Thesis*, pp. 56-7.
100 *Llandaff Diocesan Magazine*, January 1913, p. 249.
101 *CMG*, 5 June 1852, p. 4.
102 *CMG*, 15 December 1854, p. 4, and other similar references in ibid., 24 September 1853, p. 3; 15 December 1855, p. 6; 22 December 1855, p. 8; 31 January 1857, p. 8; 27 April 1861, p. 7; 29 March 1862, p. 5; 19 July 1862, p. 5; *Yr Haul* (1858), 28-9. A pocket communion set was still standard in 1907 when David Hughes left the parish of St Mark's, Swansea: *Swansea Parish Magazine*, April 1907, p. 63.
103 *CMG*, 24 February 1855, p. 3; 10 March 1855, p. 3.
104 *CMG*, 14 April 1860, p. 5.
105 NLW, Powysland Club Papers, Box 29. Other reports from the same period are in SA/DR/52, fol. 750 (a bicycle was the presentation), and SA/DR/54, fols. 298, 352, 458, 498.
106 SA/DR/50, fol. 202.

107 *Guardian*, 2 March 1881, pp. 323-4.
108 *Report of the Church Congress, Swansea*, 1879, p. 368; This was also asserted by Howes, *The Church in Danger*, p. 17.
109 *WM*, 7 September 1883, p. 4.
110 *WM*, 2 June 1875, p. 6.
111 *Report of the Llandaff Diocesan Conference*, 1902, p. 11.
112 *Report of the Church Congress, Wolverhampton*, 1867, pp. 90, 102. One such curate wrote that an older man probably knew "too much, and is continually treading on his incumbent's toes without intending it": *ibid.*, p. 102.
113 According to Halcombe the cost of curates by the mid-1870s had become such a burden to many incumbents that they were forced to discontinue their services or to obtain one at a lower stipend: *The Church and her Curates*, pp. 60, 94.
114 *Guardian*, 9 March 1881, p. 364. Another curate writing in the same paper alleged he was in the same position and must either turn schoolmaster or starve, and that his was not an unexceptional case: *Guardian*, 13 April 1881, p. 519.
115 *Report of the Llandaff Diocesan Conference*, 1910, pp. 68-9.
116 "Position and Prospects of Curates", pp. 216-8. The Llandaff Diocesan Conference of 1910 asked the Ecclesiastical Commission to consider the need for pensions for curates: *Report*, p. 74.
117 Conybeare denied this, suggesting that few men were in this position, and those who were did so from choice or because of demerit. But after he wrote, in the 1850s, the position changed dramatically: *Essays Ecclesiastical and Social*, p. 195. For example, a writer of 1843 wrote of the "heart sickening decay of hope [that] was a constant companion throughout life": quoted by McClatchey, *Oxfordshire Clergy*, p. 75.
118 *Y Cylchgrawn*, 19 (1880), 232.
119 Baker-Jones, *The Glaspant Diary 1896*, p. 170 [he is not recorded in the 1925 Church in Wales Directory). Some died before they could obtain incumbencies, as did Thomas Jones, who died in 1891 aged 49 as curate of Llansanffraid, his fourth curacy: *Bye-Gones*, 30 December 1891, p. 231; or William Kirkham, who died as curate of Merthyr Tydfil in 1899, his fifth curacy: *Llandaff Diocesan Magazine*, 1899, p. 61.
120 Brown, *Church and People at Welshpool*, p.58. He had been curate there 1885-8.
121 T.J. Jones, *How to Improve the Condition of the Welsh Church*, p. 17.
122 *Guardian*, 4 February 1874, p. 138; *Report of the Church Congress, Derby*, 1882, p. 188.
123 Quoted by Hart, *The Curate's Lot*, p. 131.
124 Barrow, *The Flesh is Weak*, pp. 176.
125 *WM*, 2 February 1897, p. 6; *Record*, 5 February 1897, p. 107.
126 Virgin, *The Church in an Age of Negligence*, pp. 141, 220.
127 *Report of the Church Congress, Derby*, 1882, p. 187.
128 *Report of the Church Congress, Shrewsbury*, 1896, p. 481. While some of them would have been retired or lived on independent means, Thackeray's claim that the number was 6,000 (*ibid.*, pp. 481, 486), was proven to be greatly exaggerated: Haig, *Victorian Clergy*, p. 226. His assertion that many had been drawn into the ranks of unemployment or lived in dread of it was nevertheless justified.
129 Virgin notes that of every 100 men ordained in the late Georgian Church 20% never had a benefice, 25% died young, emigrated or went into teaching, 20% had a benefice within five years, 20% between 6-15 years, and 15% over 15 years: *The Church in an Age of Negligence*, p. 141. Figures taken from some selected ordination lists printed in the church periodicals indicate that of 49 men made deacon between 1830-37, 25% were not found in a Clergy List of 1849; of 24 between 1857-8, 32% were not found in a Clergy List of 1878, while of 24 between 1868-71, 12% were not recorded in the 1893 edition of *Crockford*. Some may have died, and others found other employment: *Y Gwyliedydd*, 8 (1830), 326, 358; *Yr Haul*, 1835, p. 161; 1836, p. 512; 1837, p. 323; 1859, pp. 319-20; 1858, pp. 46, 317; 1868, pp. 124-5; 1874, p.351; 1871, p. 399.
130 Haig, *Victorian Clergy*, pp. 226-7; *Report of the Church Congress, Derby*, 1882, p. 186.

131 Brown, *Evangelicals in the Church in Wales*, p. 167.
132 A.O. Evans, *A Survey of the Clerical Staffing of Bangor Diocese*, p. 5.

www.ingramcontent.com/pod-product-compliance
Lightning Source LLC
Chambersburg PA
CBHW080026080526
44586CB00017B/2137